OVERREACH

OWEN MATTHEWS

OVERREACH

THE INSIDE STORY OF
PUTIN'S WAR AGAINST UKRAINE

MUDLARK

Mudlark
HarperCollins*Publishers*
1 London Bridge Street
London SE1 9GF

www.harpercollins.co.uk

HarperCollins*Publishers*
Macken House, 39/40 Mayor Street Upper
Dublin 1, D01 C9W8, Ireland

First published by Mudlark 2022

1 3 5 7 9 10 8 6 4 2

A catalogue record of this book is
available from the British Library

HB ISBN 978-0-00-856274-8
TPB ISBN 978-0-00-856277-9

FSC www.fsc.org FSC™ C007454

This book is produced from independently certified FSC™ paper
to ensure responsible forest management.

For more information visit: www.harpercollins.co.uk/green

For Ksenia, Nikita and Teddy

For with pomp to meet him came,
Clothed in arms like blood and flame,
The hired murderers, who did sing
'Thou art God, and Law, and King.
We have waited, weak and lone
For thy coming, Mighty One!
Our purses are empty, our swords are cold,
Give us glory, blood, and gold.'

Percy Bysshe Shelley,
The Mask of Anarchy, 1819

What this country needs is a short, victorious war.

Prime Minister Vyacheslav von Plehve
to Tsar Nicholas II, 1904

CONTENTS

INTRODUCTION

Everyone must understand: mobilisation is ahead and a global war for survival, for the destruction of all our enemies. War is our national ideology. And our only task, our leaders' only task, is to explain to and convince all the Russian people that this our heroic future.

Russian writer and volunteer Donbas fighter
Zakhar Prilepin, April 2014[1]

'You'd be happy to meet.' My old friend Zhenia's tone on the phone was flat and wary. It was 28 March 2022. The war in Ukraine had been under way for a month. 'You want to meet just for the sake of happiness – or are you going to try to tell me why I'm wrong?'

'Maybe you can tell me why I'm wrong? We can do that too. I'm in Moscow.'

There was a silence on the line.

'Maybe some other time,' he eventually replied. 'It's not a good idea for me to be seen with you right now.'

Once, Zhenia had been a rebel. At various stages of his career he'd worked as a labourer and a security guard, and served as an officer in the paramilitary OMON police and fought in Chechnya. He had edited the Nizhny Novgorod edition of the opposition *Novaya Gazeta* and had been a leading member of the revolutionary National Bolshevik Party. But by the time I met him at a literary festival in Saint-Malo, France, Zhenia had adopted a new pen-name – Zakhar Prilepin – and had become one of Russia's greatest and most controversial novelists. Zhenia was shaven-headed, physically strong and had a generally threatening mien that had got him into a spot of bother with Saint-Malo's CRS riot police. I helped him out of it. It was a bonding experience.

Zhenia – Zakhar – Prilepin was smart, well-read, unafraid. He was also passionate about his beliefs – which included a radical faith in the greatness of his country and a withering contempt for the venality of its current leadership. At a writers' forum in the Kremlin in 2007 he'd sat across from Vladimir Putin and fearlessly taken the president to task for corruption and thievery. After the February 2014 annexation of Crimea, the Kremlin's ideology had turned on its axis, and Putin and Zakhar found themselves in unexpected agreement: it was time for Russia to take up arms against her enemies. Soon after, Zakhar travelled to the rebel republics of Donbas in eastern Ukraine and became the deputy commander of a rebel battalion. In 2020, like his hero the radical writer and National Bolshevik Party founder Eduard Limonov, Zakhar founded a political party of his own. Its vision was of a manly, belligerent Russia whose destiny it was to purge the world of decadence through war.

Zakhar's views may have been poisonous and insane and were undoubtedly dangerous. But they were sincerely held. And unlike many armchair patriots in the Russian elite who spent most of their time plundering the country they professed to love, Prilepin actually risked his skin for his beliefs. He was once my friend. Now, I suppose, he has become a kind of honest enemy.

I start this story with Zakhar for two reasons. One is that I am interested in what he will do next. Currently, the Kremlin is riding the tiger of Orthodox-fuelled ultra-nationalism that until relatively recently had lurked on the lunatic fringes of Russian politics. What will happen if Putin falters, either through military failure in the field or by losing his grip on the Russian elite or security services? If that were to occur, Zakhar's vision of his country as a kind of new Sparta, implacable, militant and fired with holy righteousness, could be a terrifying glimpse into one of Russia's possible futures.

The second reason I mention Zakhar is his refusal of my invitation to meet. I never found out his reasons. Perhaps he was nervous of being caught talking to someone who could be presented as a Western spy. Perhaps he thought I *had* become a Western spy. Perhaps he assumed that I was being tailed by the Federal Security Service, or FSB. Perhaps he thought he was. Perhaps he was afraid of hearing a different version of events from me that would shake his faith in his belief that Russian Orthodox warriors were battling Ukrainian Nazis (admittedly unlikely).

Whatever his reasons, Zakhar had clearly caught a dose of the pervasive paranoia of the times. It was a paranoia shared by the majority of my Moscow friends, colleagues and contacts. In the days following the beginning of the war it covered the city as quickly and obtrusively as the peat-fire smog that blankets Russia's capital every summer. And like smoke, paranoia's lingering smell was pervasive and impossible to avoid.

I have spent, on and off, 27 years reporting in Russia – first as a metro and features reporter for *The Moscow Times* and then as a correspondent and Moscow Bureau Chief for *Newsweek* magazine. In over a quarter of a century a total of perhaps half a dozen people refused to speak to me because I was a foreigner, or because they feared repercussions from the authorities.

That changed dramatically after the beginning of Russia's invasion of Ukraine – or, more specifically, after the State Duma passed a law in early March making the 'dissemination of false news about the Russian Military' punishable with up to 15 years in prison. Soon afterwards the Duma also redefined an existing law on 'foreign agents' to include not just Russian individuals and organisations who actually received funding from abroad but also those who had come 'under foreign influence'. Weekly lists of new 'foreign agents' were published and soon came to include almost every non-Kremlin-aligned journalist, broadcaster, blogger and analyst.

To my shock, when I began reporting this book in the first days of the war, friends and contacts whom I had known for years and decades told me that they could not risk meeting in public or speaking on the record. Even pro-Kremlin officials, both current and retired, as well as prominent patriotic media and political figures, grew cautious to the point of absurdity. Many sources refused to meet me in public places where they would be recognised speaking to a foreign reporter. And many of the most revealing conversations took place at the dinner tables, dachas or – in classic Soviet style – the kitchens of mutual friends who were kind enough to arrange private gatherings, not always telling my fellow guests in advance that I, a dangerous foreigner, would be there.

Many of the sources cited in this book are, therefore, necessarily anonymous – in some cases to protect their identity, and in others because the remarks quoted were made in off-the-record social situations or in confidence. It's frustrating, as a reader, to have to take anything on trust – and equally frustrating for a reporter to have to ask. But such was the atmosphere in which this book was reported, in Moscow and Kyiv, between March and September 2022. What surprised – and chilled – me most was how quickly Russian society shut down. Before Putin's 2022 invasion there was a space in Russia's political ecosystem for political opposition and for free speech. The space was narrow, but it was defined by a series of unspoken rules that were observed by the authorities more often than they were broken. Private anti-Kremlin opinions, even when spoken in public places or on social media, were never proscribed. Before 24 February 2022 stories of covering the telephone at home with a cushion were a quaint tale from Soviet days. After, many of my sources insisted that we sit metres away from our smartphones, or leave them behind when coming to a meeting.

Fear is infectious. Fear breeds especially fast in a world where long-recognised rules have collapsed and new ones not yet formed. Opposition activists and journalists once jokingly described the Putin regime as 'vegetarian' rather than carnivorous. With a few notable exceptions, it tended to intimidate rather than destroy. The Kremlin's chief ideologue Vladislav Surkov – incidentally, a friend of Zakhar Prilepin's and a relative of his by marriage – presided over a system based on an essentially post-modern, consumerist and ultimately cynical attitude to ideology. Some Orthodoxy here, a dash of Soviet nostalgia there – Surkov played chords of ideas like the keyboard of the organ of scents in J. K. Huysmans' decadent literary classic *À rebours*. That relatively tolerant, vegetarian ecosystem collapsed after Surkov's departure from the Kremlin in February 2020. It was replaced, as we will see, by the exclusive rule of paranoid ex-KGB men convinced that the West was on a mission to undermine and destroy Russia.

Anti-Putin people had always tended to be cavalier, even fatalistic, about their security. A few continued to be outspoken after the invasion of Ukraine on 24 February 2022 – but by that time insouciance had become an act of great bravery. What was more striking to me was how the pro-Putin people suddenly discovered fear. The *ponyatiye* – the set of unspoken 'understandings' that had ruled their world – was suddenly superseded by a new and unfamiliar gravitational field of patriotism and war. What was permitted in wartime Russia, what newly forbidden? Nobody knew. One former KGB major-general, a close personal friend and former university classmate of one of Putin's most senior ministers, took me outside in midwinter to talk by a dacha's woodshed where he could be sure we would not be overheard or seen. The daughter of a major oil magnate close to Putin asked twice to move tables at the White Rabbit restaurant because she didn't like the look of people sitting nearby who might overhear us. And so on.

I mention these things not to give the impression that reporting in Moscow has become a cloak-and-dagger, le Carré affair, but to make the point that the political and media landscape of Russia changed very quickly and very profoundly in the aftermath of Putin's invasion. Some old friends became aggressive, even obnoxious, patriots. Others realised that a Russia where one could pretend to live an open, prosperous European life no longer existed – or perhaps had only existed in their imaginations. Thousands of Russia's best-educated people escaped into exile. But the vast majority remained and conformed – some actively, most silently. If the paranoia of war was like peat smoke, then the conformity was like snow, blanketing a whole society in a numbing blanket that deadened sound and feeling and sent people huddling for shelter. Some Russians found that shelter in the comforting tropes of their Soviet childhoods. Some found it in actively ignoring and blocking out reality. Until 21 September, six months into the war, life in Moscow continued as an almost aggressive simulacrum of total normality into which the war was not allowed to intrude. On that date Putin took the country – and his own elite – by surprise when he announced a partial mobilisation. Suddenly a war that had been all but invisible became, to tens of millions of Russians with male family members of military age, suddenly very up close and personal. From that moment on, no Russian was immune to the bitter political winter that had descended on their country.

The definition of a great conflict is that it results in the breaking of nations and a reordering of the world. By that measure, the Russo-Ukrainian War is the most serious geopolitical crisis in

Europe since the Second World War, and one which will result in far greater global consequences than 9/11. The world's security architecture, food and energy supply, balance of military power and alliances will be altered by it forever.

At best, Putin's botched invasion of Ukraine could prove to be the last convulsion of expansive imperialism in European history and mark the final death of the age of empires in the West. It may also give China pause in its ambitions to use conventional military power against its neighbours. In the first weeks of the war Ukraine surprised both its enemies and its allies by demonstrating that overwhelming armoured and airborne force could be defeated by modern infantry-carried weapons, upending traditional Cold War era calculations of attack and defence. The world's sanctions response to Russia's invasion also showed that true economic power – including the power to devastate whole economies overnight – has shifted from nation-states to corporations, whose ethical and political decisions can carry more clout than those of governments. And Russia's attempts to strike back by cutting gas supplies to Europe showed, surprisingly, that energy was in fact less potent a weapon than the West had once feared.

At the same time the Ukraine war made the world a far more dangerous place as Putin and his propagandists brought the idea of battlefield or even strategic use of nuclear weapons from the realm of the theoretical firmly into the realm of the possible. It also posed a fatal – and as yet unanswered – question about how much economic pain Western societies are willing to take in the name of defending the principles upon which their societies are founded.

The Ukraine war is the bloody final act of the collapse of the Soviet Union. Hostilities continue as I write, so the story is, therefore, necessarily incomplete. But though we have no idea of exactly how the conflict will end, we already know how it will not end. There will be no complete victory for either Russia or Ukraine. NATO is too invested to allow Kyiv to fall to the Russian army;

Putin's regime and his life are at stake if he allows Crimea, or for that matter the rebel republics of Donbas, to fall to the Ukrainians. He has said repeatedly that he is willing to defend that territory with nuclear strikes if necessary. Therefore this war will eventually end – as all wars that do not result in total victory end – with a negotiated peace.

Putin is likely to declare any final outcome a victory, and his control over Russia's media is so complete that there is a good chance he will succeed in convincing many of his people to believe him.

But it's also clear that however much formerly Ukrainian territory Putin manages to hang on to after the guns go silent, his attempt to reverse Ukraine's westward drift and assert Russia's new power and greatness has proved a catastrophic failure. Decades of careful economic planning have been destroyed, sympathetic allies all over the world alienated, hundreds of thousands of Russia's brightest and best exiled, the country's strategic independence profoundly compromised by a forced economic and political dependence on China. Putin has poisoned Russia's future in the root. His self-declared victory will be one of the uneducated over the educated, of the provinces over the metropolis, of the old over the young, of the past over the future.

Putin's invasion also precisely created the very things it was intended to avert. It united Ukraine and gave the country a true sense of nationhood. The war also reinvigorated NATO with new purpose, money and members, and also reminded the European Union of the post-war anti-totalitarian values on which European integration was first founded. On a more profound level, Putin reminded the democracies of the world that freedom does not just happen – the determinist conclusion that many in the West came to after the collapse of communism – but has to be fought for and defended.

This book was mostly written in Moscow and Kyiv during the course of the first six months of the war. It's not, therefore, the story of the war but a first draft of the history of how the war began – and how the conflict moved from Russia's blitzkrieg through stalemate to Ukrainian counter-offensive. My focus is on the most compelling mystery at the heart of Putin's invasion of Ukraine: how did the idea of violently carving out a Greater Russia, backed up by mystical Orthodox nationalism, travel from the marginal fringes of Russian politics to become official Kremlin policy? How and why did Putin decide to throw decades of carefully constructed macroeconomics and diplomacy out of the window and launch a war so reckless and risky that the full details were kept even from the majority of his most senior ministers right up until the very moment of the invasion? Who were the dogs fighting under the carpet – as Churchill memorably once described Kremlin infighting – who battled for and won Putin's ear, heart and mind? And most importantly, what was the true reason that Putin decided to go to war?

Moscow, 30 September 2022

PROLOGUE

THE BRINK

Moscow

Presidential residence of Novo-Ogarevo, Moscow region, 23 February 2022

Shortly after 11 a.m. Vladimir Putin boarded one of the three Mi-8 helicopters of the Presidential Flight at the helipad of his official residence at Novo-Ogarevo, 30 kilometres northwest of central Moscow. For security reasons two identical Soviet-designed Mi-8s took off with him, turned in formation and accelerated eastwards towards the Kremlin.

The air crews, like all other staff at Novo-Ogarevo, had been living in strict Covid isolation before coming into close physical proximity to Russia's *Pervoe Litso* – literally 'First Person', as the president is referred to inside his administration. For nearly two years since the beginning of the pandemic all visitors to Novo-Ogarevo and to the presidential residences near Lake Valdai and Sochi where Putin had spent most of lockdown had been required to spend a week of quarantine and daily tests in specially converted hotel blocks on the grounds of each residence. Always intensely private, Putin's personal contact had for years been limited to a small group of no more than three dozen insiders. During Covid that bubble had shrunk far tighter still.

Fifteen minutes after take-off, Putin's chopper landed at the helipad by the Beklemishevskaya Tower in the Kremlin's southeast corner. He stepped into his ZiL limousine for the short ride to the Great Palace of the Moscow Kremlin. During the pandemic, Putin had barely visited Moscow, much less been seen in public. But this was his third visit to central Moscow in as many days.

The first visit, in the early afternoon of 21 February, had been for an extraordinary – in more ways than one – session of Russia's Security Council. The venue was the soaring Hall of the Order of St Catherine in the Great Kremlin Palace, a vast colonnaded space usually used for official receptions, rather than the usual, much smaller room in the Senate Palace where the Council usually convened. There had been no time for the 12 permanent members of the Council to quarantine for the required week. The enormous space allowed for Putin, seated alone behind a large desk, to keep six metres' social distance from Russia's most highly placed – though not necessarily most powerful – men (and one woman). The choice of venue was also highly symbolic for a made-for-television event intended to signal a new phase of Russian assertiveness.

The ostensible reason for the Security Council meeting was a discussion of plans tabled in the Duma and its upper house, the Federation Council, to recognise the statehood of two breakaway republics in Ukraine's Donbas. According to a source close to Putin's spokesman Dmitry Peskov, all the participants in the Security Council meeting had been told that the proceedings were being televised live. That was not true. The evidence of the watches of the participants showed that it was in fact aired some five hours later. Peskov told the same source that only three people in the room apart from Putin himself knew the full extent of Putin's military plans to launch a full-scale invasion of Ukraine some 72 hours later. One was Defence Minister Sergei Shoigu, another was Nikolai Patrushev, chairman of the Security Council and Putin's KGB colleague since 1975, and the third was Putin's old St Petersburg University classmate and FSB head Aleksandr Bortnikov.

One by one, the Security Council's members stood to agree with the Duma's proposal to recognise the Donetsk and Luhansk People's Republics – collectively known as the LDNR – as independent nations. One – Sergei Naryshkin, head of the Foreign Intelligence Service – fluffed his lines and was publicly humiliated by Putin.[1]

The following day, 22 February, the Duma duly formalised the recognition. Putin travelled once more to the Kremlin for a rare press conference with a group of hand-picked journalists from the Kremlin press pool. According to one of the people in the room Putin looked 'pale and puffy but energised ... unusually emphatic and aggressive'.[2] Asked by veteran Kremlin correspondent Andrei Kolesnikov of the *Kommersant* daily whether he thought that 'anything in this modern world can be resolved by force', Putin reacted sharply. 'Why do you think that good should never be backed by force?' He also denied that Russian forces would 'deploy right away' to Donbas.[3]

Putin was lying. Russian forces were already mobilised. The first units – the vehicles of the army group based in the Southern Military District marked with a distinctive 'Z' to distinguish them from identical Ukrainian armoured vehicles – crossed the effectively non-existent border between Russia and the LDNR hours after the press conference. By mid-morning on 23 February Russian forces had deployed all along the line of control that rebel fighters had established with Kyiv's forces in 2015 after two brutal summers' fighting that had left 14,000 dead.

23 February – Defenders of the Fatherland Day – is an important Soviet-era holiday. It's a day for drinking with buddies, congratulating men for being men (the counterpart to the 8 March Women's Day) and watching patriotic war films on TV. More formally, it's a day to celebrate Russian armed forces past and present. Victory Day – celebrated on 9 May and traditionally marked by a major military parade on Red Square – is a more triumphalist celebration of the USSR's defeat of Nazi Germany in

the Great Patriotic War. But over the last decade of Putin's rule both 23 February and 9 May have become key parts of a Kremlin-fostered cult that has co-opted the memory of the Second World War to serve the glory and legitimacy of the current regime. The high point of both celebrations is a laying of a wreath by the president at the Eternal Flame that burns in front of the Kremlin.

Putin's motorcade emerged from the Kremlin's Spassky Tower gate, drove across Red Square and up to the elaborate wrought iron gates of the Aleksandr Gardens. Putin walked past an honour guard – all keeping their distance – and laid a wreath at the Eternal Flame. It was the first recorded occasion since the same day in 2021 that Putin had walked on a Moscow pavement.

A pre-recorded message from Putin celebrating the Defenders of the Fatherland holiday was broadcast nationwide. 'Respected comrades!' Putin began, a deliberate throwback to communist-era usage. He made only one oblique reference to Russia's occupation of the LDNR that had taken place that morning. 'Our country is always open to honest and direct dialogue ... but I will repeat: the interests of Russia and the security of our people are, for us, non-negotiable.'[4]

Back at Novo-Ogarevo by 5 p.m, Putin took a scheduled telephone call from Turkish President Recep Tayyip Erdogan. According to the official readout of the conversation, Putin 'expressed disappointment that the USA and NATO have ignored Russia's legal and reasonable concerns and demands'.[5] Though Putin and Erdogan had known each other for over two decades and described each other as 'friends', there was no mention in the conversation of any imminent full-scale invasion of Ukraine. According to a senior source in Turkey's Foreign Ministry who has worked with Erdogan since 2003, 'there was no indication or warning whatsoever of what Putin was planning'.[6]

At some point on the evening of 23 February, Putin sat down in the television studio at Novo-Ogarevo to record another message to his people, the second in as many days. This one announced that he had given orders to begin a 'limited military special operation' against Ukraine. It was broadcast at 6 a.m. the following morning. All along the 2,000-kilometre-long border between Russia, Belarus and Ukraine a force of at least 71 battalion battle groups totalling some 160,000–190,000 men – the biggest deployment of Russian troops on European soil since 1945 – rolled to war.[7]

Kyiv

Presidential Palace, Kyiv, 23 February 2022

Since November 2021, US intelligence had been warning Volodymyr Zelensky with increasing urgency and in remarkable detail that Putin was planning a full-scale, multi-front invasion of Ukraine that would involve a direct assault on Kyiv. Zelensky and his national security team had been 'not exactly dismissive, but sceptical' of the warnings, said one adviser to Zelensky's chief of staff Andriy Yermak. 'We were in no doubt that Putin would be capable of an invasion, that was not the question. We have been at war [with Russia] for eight years.'[8] But since the previous spring Russian military build-ups on Ukraine's borders – and warnings of a possible invasion – had become something of a regular occurrence. Putin had boosted troop numbers threateningly in March–April 2021, and again in September–October, only to stand them down again. The first build-up had been explained away as a test of the incoming US President Joe Biden's resolve, the second as a protest against Ukraine's participation in NATO land and sea exercises over the summer. With even very highly placed security sources and top government officials in Moscow confidently predicting that there would be no war, it was by no means clear that this, third, build-up would be the big one.

'There was always a question of whether this was just another Putin psychological operation ... to disrupt Ukraine,' said the adviser. 'On the one hand, there was concern, of course, each time that this would lead to war. On the other, there was the idea that we cannot let Putin send us into a panic every time he sends his troops on manoeuvres near our borders.' When the US and British Embassies pulled out of Kyiv on 12 February, Zelensky had said that 'right now, the people's biggest enemy is panic.' If Western powers had 'any firm evidence of an impending invasion', he had 'yet to see it'. So deep was the scepticism about a possible coming war that senior members of Ukraine's parliament and SBU intelligence service had taken to retweeting humorous memes of Mr Bean standing by a roadside, dubbed 'Waiting for the Russian invasion'.[9]

By 23 February, however, it was clear that this time it really was different. The previous night Russian troops had crossed into the breakaway republics of Donetsk and Luhansk. Russian troops had been operating more or less covertly inside the LDNR in force for years. But now that the Russian Duma had voted to recognise their independence, the occupation was now official. Yet the question remained: would Putin stop at the LDNR, or go further?

At midday on 23 February Zelensky convened a session of Ukraine's National Security and Defence Council (NSDC). Around the table sat the country's most senior military and intelligence chiefs, as well as civilian ministers. Some were lifetime soldiers and intelligence officers. Others were old friends whom Zelensky had known from childhood and worked with in show business for years.

Ivan Bakanov, a youthful 47-year-old who habitually wore blue glasses and fashionably tight suits, had grown up with Zelensky in the tough industrial town of Kryvyi Rih and had later headed the television production company they named Kvartal 95 Studio after their old neighbourhood. Zelensky had appointed his old friend, colleague and former campaign manager to head Ukraine's SBU security service in August 2019. Bakanov

– by training a lawyer who had spent his career as an entertainment executive – had no background in intelligence or secret police work, but was totally loyal to Zelensky. That was the point. Bakanov's job was to reform and to tame a secret service that had several times in recent history tried to undermine the government – and which was believed still to harbour thousands of pro-Russian sympathisers.

In manner and background Lieutenant-General Valerii Zaluzhny, 49, came from an utterly different world from Bakanov. Yet the career officer was also a Zelensky-appointed new broom. Too young to have served in the Soviet army, Zaluzhny was one of the first generation of Ukrainian officers to train with Ukraine's NATO partners, including a stint in the UK. Stocky, round faced and tough, Zaluzhny had distinguished himself in action as a divisional commander during the heavy fighting in Debaltseve in Donbas in 2015. Zelensky appointed Zaluzhny chief of the Ukrainian General Staff in 2021 with a brief to bring the army up to NATO standards and put an end to the thievery, bullying and stifling top-down command structures that had plagued the Soviet and Russian armies.

The third key attendee was Ukraine's foreign intelligence chief, Oleksandr Lytvynenko. A graduate of both the FSB's Institute of Cryptography, Telecommunications and Computer Science in Moscow and the Royal College of Defence Studies in London, Lytvynenko's appointment as head of Ukraine's spy service the previous July had been controversial. In 2015 Lytvynenko had been one of thousands of officials who had been suspended from serving in the government because of their previous work in the administration of disgraced, pro-Moscow president Viktor Yanukovych. Nonetheless, Zelensky judged that he needed a lifelong intelligence officer like Lytvynenko in charge of answering the single most pressing security question facing their country: was Putin serious about an invasion or not?

At the Security Council meeting, 'three basic points of view emerged,' recalled Serhiy Leshchenko, a prominent journalist and lawmaker who is a senior adviser to Zelensky's chief of staff. 'One was that Putin would stay in the [breakaway republics of] Donbas. Another was that he would try to create a corridor linking Crimea to Donbas and expand [the LDNRs' territory]. The third was that he would go ahead and launch a full invasion of Ukraine, including from Belarus,' which would mean an attack on Kyiv. All three versions were based on various conflicting pieces of intelligence and analysis. The NSDC's meeting was 'inconclusive', said Leshchenko.

Zelensky spent the rest of the day speaking to ambassadors and reading intelligence reports from his own services as well as those of NATO allies. He also penned a speech aimed directly at the Russian people. In the early evening, still convinced that Putin was undecided about moving further than the borders of the LDNR, Zelensky recorded his speech in a single take.

'I want to appeal today to all the citizens of Russia,' Zelensky said in Russian – his native language, but rarely used for public addresses, which he usually made in Ukrainian. 'Not as president. I am appealing to Russian citizens as a citizen of Ukraine ... Today, your forces stand along that border, almost 200,000 soldiers and thousands of military vehicles. [This] could become the beginning of a major war on the European continent. Any spark could set it off ... You are told that we are Nazis. But how can a people who gave more than eight million lives for the victory over Nazism support Nazism? How could I be a Nazi? Tell that to my grandfather, who went through the entire war in the infantry of the Soviet Army and died as a colonel in independent Ukraine.'

Zelensky did not mention his own Jewish roots. But he did speak of visiting his best friend in Donetsk before the war, cheering on the Ukrainian national football team in a match there and drinking beer in a park with a crowd of locals, united as fellow

Ukrainians. He concluded with an emotional appeal to Russians to 'remember that Ukrainians and Russians are different. But that is not a reason that we should be enemies ... Many of you have been to Ukraine. Many of you have relatives in Ukraine. Some of you studied in Ukrainian universities, befriended Ukrainian people. You know our character. You know our people. You know our principles. You are aware of what we cherish. So please listen to yourselves. To the voice of reason. To common sense. Hear us. The people of Ukraine want peace.'

Many of Zelensky's aides 'were almost moved to tears' as Zelensky recorded his speech. 'It came straight from the heart,' remembered one adviser. 'He wrote every word himself ... it was the best speech he had ever made.'[10]

In the evening Zelensky joined his wife Olena and children Oleksandra, 17, and Kirilo, 9, at the presidential residence in the suburb of Koncha-Zaspa, on the right bank of the Dniepr 15 kilometres south of central Kyiv. Ukraine's president had 'no forewarning' of the coming Russian attack, confirmed Leshchenko. Zelensky went to bed in the hope that the 'common sense' of which he had spoken earlier that evening would prevail. Within hours that hope would be spectacularly disappointed.

Belgorod

Belgorod Province, Russia, 23 February 2022

For the officers and men of the Kantemirovskaya Tank Division, Defenders of the Fatherland Day would usually be an important and much-anticipated holiday. Based in Naro-Fominsk, 70 kilometres outside Moscow, the division – formally known as the Yuri Andropov 4th Guards Kantemirovskaya Order of Lenin Red Banner Tank Division – had been one of the Russian army's elite units since its original formation during the Battle of

Stalingrad. But on 23 February 2022 nobody had time for celebrations. Orders had just come down for the division to mobilise for action.

A month before, the Kantemirovskaya had been deployed to Belgorod province, close to the northeastern border of Ukraine. Officially, they were on exercises. But it was clear enough to most of the men that they were there to invade Ukraine.

'Mom, my phone won't work for a week. I'm handing it over,' 21-year-old Sergeant Vadim Shishimarin had told his mother Lyubov on 22 February. 'Someone might tell you that I have left for Ukraine. Don't believe it.' Comrades of her son would later tell her that the unit's commanders had assured them that 'they would go in and out [of Ukraine] and that's it'.[11]

Shishimarin did not look like much of a military man. He was skinny and short, with an almost childish face. 'He doesn't give the impression of a professional soldier, let alone a member of an elite tank division,' Shishimarin's lawyer Viktor Ovsyannikov would later tell the press. He was born on 17 October 2000 in Ust-Ilimsk, an industrial town of 86,000 people about 700 kilometres up the Angara river from Irkutsk in eastern Siberia. Vadim was the eldest of five children – he had two brothers and two sisters, the youngest four years old – and was brought up by his mother and stepfather.

Like many of the troops deployed to Ukraine, Shishimarin was from one of Russia's most remote and impoverished provinces. Ust-Ilimsk was known for its hydro-electric dam, a timber mill and the remains of a notorious 1930s-era Gulag. A quarter of the population had moved away since the fall of the USSR. Vadim graduated from school aged 17, then trained as a mechanic in a vocational school. When later interviewed by journalists, neither of Shishimarin's parents could name any of their son's interests or hobbies. 'What would he be fond of?' said his father, Evgeny Shishimarin, who left his family when Vadim was small. 'He lived. He's a hard worker.'[12]

According to his mother, Shishimarin decided to travel to Moscow after leaving technical college because 'there are more opportunities there for work and education'. He worked in a tyre repair shop in the Moscow region and found a girlfriend. Then, like hundreds of thousands of young Russian men not in full-time education, Shishimarin was summoned for compulsory military service in 2019's annual spring call-up. His local Moscow region *voyenkomat*, or conscription office, assigned him to the nearby Kantemirovskaya Division. 'He was fit. The time had come to join the army,' said his mother. 'What of it? Everyone serves.'

In January 2020, nine months into Shishimarin's year-long term of conscription, his stepfather – a crane operator – was killed in Ust-Ilimsk. He was 'in the wrong place at the wrong time', explained Shishimarin's mother Lyubov. 'He was accidentally shot and killed. We don't know the full name of the person who did it.' Lyubov and her children were left without any reliable source of income. Shishimarin decided to join the Russian army as a full-time *kontraktnik*, or professional soldier, because there was 'no need to worry about housing' and that he wanted to 'help my mother and younger brothers and sisters'. To a 20-year-old man from Ust-Ilimsk, the army salary of 40,000 rubles – then around £400 a month – sounded like a good career proposition. 'He decided that there was nothing for him to do here [in Ust-Ilimsk],' said his mother. 'There really *is* nothing to do here.'[13]

By February 2022 Vadim Shishimarin was a sergeant – which unlike its apparent equivalent in the British or US militaries is a very junior rank in the Russian army. The equivalent role of Western non-commissioned officers is fulfilled in the Russian military by *praporshiki*, or warrant officers. Nonetheless, Shishimarin led a ten-man section in a platoon commanded by a Senior Lieutenant Kalinin.

On the evening of 23 February, Kalinin collected all the phones from the privates and non-commissioned officers in his unit as a security precaution. The men were also issued three days' *sukhoi paiok* – dry rations – which the commanders considered sufficient for what they expected to be a short mission. The Kantemirovskaya Division's estimated two hundred T-80U and T-80BV main battle tanks and approximately three hundred BTR-2 infantry fighting vehicles were armed and fuelled.

At dawn the following day the squad commanded by Shishimarin – Military Unit No. 32010 of the 13th Guards Tank Regiment of the Kantemirovskaya Division – moved forward from their positions outside Belgorod and joined a vast column of armoured vehicles heading westward towards the Ukrainian border, some 20 kilometres distant. At around 9 a.m. Shishimarin's unit crossed the border between Sumy and Ukraine's second city, Kharkiv.

Moscow

RIA Novosti Building, Novinsky Boulevard, Moscow, 23 February 2022

Anna Bondarenko, 40, a senior producer at a major state-run Russian news channel, had had a nightmare day. Just a couple of days before, the station's editorial line – agreed by her boss during detailed weekly planning sessions with the Kremlin's top communications team – had been that Russia had no intention of attacking Ukraine and that Putin's diplomatic efforts were proceeding well.[14] Foreign Minister Sergei Lavrov was the great peacemaker, and despite NATO's implacable aggression Russia was committed to peace. A lot of work had gone into planning news coverage, assigning news teams, and booking satellite link-ups to Washington and London. Bondarenko's channel had for years been signalling that the Ukrainian government was full of fascists, who were aggressively targeting the peaceful Russian-speaking people of Donbas. But there had been no specific propaganda preparation for a coming occupation of the LDNR, let alone a full-scale invasion of Ukraine.

Then, on 21 February, the official line had changed abruptly. Peace was suddenly off. Instead the new top line on the rolling news service, handed down from on high, was that the Donbas republics were under active attack from Ukrainian fascists. Civilians were being evacuated. Russian wire services were suddenly full of video feeds of the evacuation – as well as of supposed Ukrainian car-bomb attacks on border crossings featuring dead soldiers in Ukrainian uniform. The alleged upsurge of violence from the Ukrainian side was to be presented as an unfolding 'genocidal' aggression by Kyiv against the people of the LDNR.

Bondarenko, whose family were ancestrally Ukrainian, was personally 'furious when I saw those images', she recalled. 'How could the Ukrainians allow themselves to be taken over by ultra-nationalists?' What was their problem with Russian-speaking people like herself? Bondarenko had spent 20 years working in Russian TV news. She was not naive about the workings of the Kremlin's propaganda machine. But she saw no reason whatever to doubt the evidence of her own eyes as she watched the raw video coming in. NATO was on the march. Her people – Russian people – were being attacked, and the Kremlin had mobilised the army to save them. 'Where were you the last eight years?' was the new slogan for the operation to relieve the LDNR – along with 'We don't abandon our own.' Russia's troops had embarked not on a war of imperial aggression but on an urgent humanitarian mission to save their close kin from genocide.

As she handed over the news desk for the night shift on the evening of 23 February, Bondarenko had a ten-minute briefing with the incoming producer. They went through a list of expected newsfeeds from various RIA Novosti, TASS and other Russian state TV agency correspondents in Donbas, and the assignments and reports for their own correspondents on the ground in south Russia, Crimea and Donbas, as well as stringers in Kyiv and Kharkov. The news-line was all about how Russian troops were protecting the LNR and DNR from the Nazi Ukrainian attacks.

There was nothing on the news roster, no hint from her bosses and no rumours on the Moscow journalists' gossip mill of a strike against Kyiv or anything like it.

Kherson, Ukraine

Nova Kakhovka, Kherson Province, Ukraine, 23 February 2022

Larisa Nagorskaya, 44, heard the news that Russia had sent its troops into the LDNR on the television as she ate breakfast with her 11-year-old daughter Masha. Her first thought was whether her husband Serhii, 42, would be called up. 'It's begun again,' Larisa recalled thinking. 'Eight years we have been fighting, and now it's begun all over again.'[15]

Nova Kakhovka was a model Soviet town constructed in the mid-1950s for the workers constructing the Kakhovskaya GES, one of a series of giant hydro-electric dams built to harness the power of the Dniepr river. Larisa had lived there all her life. The furthest from home her younger daughter Masha had ever been was the regional centre of Kherson, 50 kilometres to the west. Her older daughter Ksenia, 19, was studying to be a kindergarten teacher in Odesa. Though Nova Kakhovka was just 70 kilometres north of the narrow isthmus that connected Ukraine to the Crimean peninsula that Russia had occupied in 2014, it did not occur to Larisa that her town – the nearest point on the Dniepr from Crimea and the linking point of a key canal that before 2014 provided most of Crimea's water – could become a target. 'We had heard on the television for months that Putin was planning to invade,' she said. 'But we assumed that was all about Donbas, not about us in Kherson [province].'

The population of Nova Kakhovka, like that of new melting-pot Soviet towns all over the region, had been drawn from all over the USSR two generations ago. Larisa spoke to her family in the local *surzhik* dialect – a mixture of Russian and Ukrainian that in the specific dialect of Kherson province contained a predominant admixture of Russian. Her daughters had been taught in pure Ukrainian at school, but Larisa herself was more at home speaking *surzhik* or Russian. At home the family watched Russian-language TV when together, while her daughters switched to Ukrainian-speaking channels when alone.

In common with swathes of Ukraine's east and south, before 2014 Nova Kakhovka had strongly supported the Party of the Regions and its leader Viktor Yanukovych – a Donetsk-based ex-convict turned businessman who had built a political career on championing the rights of Ukraine's Russian-speaking minority and advocating closer ties with Moscow. When Yanukovych was toppled from power in February 2014 by pro-European protests in Kyiv, many of Larisa's neighbours had mixed feelings. 'On the one hand, we learned that [Yanukovych] was a thief and wanted to sell out Ukraine to Putin,' said Larisa. 'On the other, people agreed with him that the government should not discriminate against Russian speakers. Many were scared that Russian would be banned altogether.'

Personally, Larisa was not much interested in politics. But she was angry when Russia annexed Crimea and Russian-backed 'bandits' took over parts of Donetsk and Luhansk, sparking two years of war. 'Putin should leave us to sort out our own problems,' she said. 'What business is it of his?'

Over the last few months before the outbreak of war, some strange things had been happening in Nova Kakhovka. In December, a local administrator had ordered the felling of a picturesque pine wood that stood on a ridge overlooking the Dniepr and the dam. Local people were angry, and the authorities promised that they would plant a new wood. But there was no convincing explanation given for why the trees had been cut down. Two months before that, a prominent deputy to the Kherson Provincial Council – a former supporter of Yanukovych and the Party of the Regions – had disappeared. People said that he had gone to Sochi, Russia, but nobody knew why.

Larisa worked as an administrator in the local water utility. In the office on the morning of 23 February most of her colleagues were 'indignant and fearful' about the news of Russia's occupation of the LDNR. The parents of young men worried, like Larisa, if their menfolk would once again be sent to fight. Like most of her neighbours and colleagues, Larisa just 'prayed for there to be no more war. That's all we really cared about. Anything but war.'

Oxfordshire, UK

Wantage, Oxfordshire, 23 February 2022

One thoughtless mistake would change Jimmy S.'s life forever. Just out of school in his home town of Reading, Jimmy and his mates decided to get some tattoos for a laugh. He chose a crown, like the crown on a playing card, on his right hand and a rose on the other. He didn't especially like or think about his new tats. But when Jimmy tried to join the British Army a few months later, he was told that there was a strict rule – no tattoos on the hands or neck. 'It's in case you ever have to meet the Queen,' the Army recruiting sergeant had told him. Jimmy tried again a year later, but still no dice. As a boy Jimmy had been really into war films and 'loved military stuff – guns, camping, good mates'. But the tattoos had scuppered his childhood dream of being a British soldier – 'at least till I save up enough money to have them removed'.[16]

Jimmy is of medium height, strong-built, decently good looking and fashionably bearded, on the taciturn side. He doesn't go out of his way to be liked, but is cheerful and polite when he's not nose-down in TikTok. Not much into news and politics, more interested in football and drinking with mates and chatting up girls. The kind of normal bloke who you'd meet in any local pub anywhere in England. After failing to get into the army, Jimmy had moved 40 miles from Reading to Wantage in Oxfordshire, worked a series of 'rubbish jobs' packing and heat-sealing ready meals and butchered meat. He moved in with a girlfriend and got her pregnant. But the relationship didn't work out, so Jimmy had left to live at a friend's place. The child – a boy named Isaac – was born in January 2022. Though the couple were no longer together, Harry's ex still wanted him to change nappies and help her look after the baby.

'Lambie', a mate of Jimmy's, got talking about a war that was brewing with Russia. Lambie said he was thinking of joining up as a volunteer with the Ukrainian army. He knew people who'd done it and loved it. Decent money, tons of lovely Ukrainian girls, beautiful and keen to go to bed with war heroes. No military experience required. 'I'd never heard of Ukraine before, to be honest with you,' Jimmy told me as we shared a compartment for a day-long train journey from Lviv to Kyiv in July 2022. 'Couldn't find it on a map.' He was surprised when I told him that Ukraine had once been part of Russia.

On 23 February, Lambie shared video clips of Russian tanks rolling into the LDNR with Jimmy and other friends on social media. 'It's kicking off,' Lambie wrote. 'I'm in. Anyone else?'

Mariupol, Ukraine

Mariupol, Donetsk Province, 23 February 2022

As a teenager growing up in the Ukrainian city of Kharkiv, just 30 kilometres from the Russian border, Mstyslav Chernov had learned how to handle a gun as part of the school curriculum. It seemed pointless. Ukraine, he reasoned, was surrounded by friends.

Chernov became an award-winning reporter and photographer for Ukrainian news agencies and later for the Associated Press. He covered wars in Iraq, Afghanistan and Nagorno Karabakh as well as Donbas. But when the Americans and then the Europeans evacuated their embassy staffs from the city of Kyiv in December, Chernov began to pore over maps of the Russian troop build-up just across from his hometown. His only thought was 'my poor country'.

When the news broke that Russian troops had occupied the LDNR, Chernov had a hunch that Russian forces would try to take the eastern port city of Mariupol, a strategic prize because of its location on the Sea of Azov, and a key to the creation of a land bridge between Donbas and Russian-occupied Crimea. So he spent 23 February hurriedly gathering supplies and equipment from his apartment and office in Kyiv. In the evening he set off on the six-hour drive to Mariupol with his long-time colleague photographer Evgeniy Maloletka in a white Volkswagen van. On the way, Chernov started worrying about spare tyres. As Maloletka drove, he found a man online from his mobile phone who was on their route and willing to sell them a set of tyres in the middle of the night. Chernov explained to the tyres' owner and a cashier at an all-night grocery store that they were heading south to cover the coming war. 'They looked at us like we were crazy.'

Chernov and Maloletka pulled into Mariupol at 3.30 a.m. on the morning of 24 February. Ninety minutes later, Russian rockets began falling on Independence Square in Chernov's hometown of Kharkiv.

Bucha, Ukraine

Bucha, Kyiv Province, Ukraine, 23 February 2022

Some things hadn't worked out in Irina Filkina's life. She was 52 years old, divorced, overweight and had a low-paid job in the boiler room of a shopping mall at the Epitsentr K shopping centre in central Bucha. But she had two pretty daughters and was well liked by friends and colleagues. She was cheerful and determined to turn her life around. Irina had recently begun taking beauty courses from a professional make-up artist in Bucha. To her delight, her fellow students had bought her some cosmetics with which to practise her new skills.[17]

On the morning of 23 February Irina 'was jumping for joy because for the first time in her life she had her own cosmetics which we had bought her,' recalled Anastasia Subacheva, Irina's make-up instructor. 'Every time she went to the office she sat and practised her [beauty] lessons more determinedly than anybody else in the class.' Irina would 'come to class and say how much her make-up was appreciated by new male admirers and how great she feels today!'

Bucha, like its neighbour Irpin, is a solidly upper-middle-class suburb of Kyiv a half-hour's ride on a commuter train from the city centre. The two suburbs are favoured by young professionals with families seeking more living space and fresh air. A set of new-built apartment buildings – many of them still under construction – rises around the town centre, which is dotted with hipsterish cafes, high-end bicycle stores, steak and pizza restaurants. The Epitsentr mall is – or rather was – a block-long shopping centre that housed a large garden centre, cafes, a home and building supplies depot and cash-and-carry style supermarket. Apart from the Ukrainian and EU flags flying in the large car park in front of it, Epitsentr could be in any well-heeled European suburb from Warsaw to Dusseldorf.

Irina Filkina lived in a poorer, older part of town, in a 1950s apartment building on Yablonskaya Street. Her neighbours were pensioners and lower-paid workers who cleaned offices or occupied minor clerical positions in the town. Irina had set off for work, as usual, by bicycle. She was happy. Subacheva had just given her a professional manicure and painted her fingernails a striking, deep red. Looking beautiful had cheered Irina up and given her a new sense of self-worth. 'She held my hand and told me, "In my old age I have at last understood the main thing – that you need to live yourself and life for yourself!"' recalled Subacheva. 'And at last I will live as I wish to! I realise that you can live as you please, as your soul wishes, not for men but for yourself!'[18]

PART I

BLOOD AND EMPIRE

CHAPTER 1
POISONED ROOTS

The history of Little Russia is like a tributary entering the main river of Russian history. Little Russians were always a tribe and never a people and still less – a state.

Russian literary critic Vissarion Belinsky, 1847[1]

Putin the Historian

In the later years of his rule, Vladimir Putin came to see himself as something of a historian. Locked down in strict Covid isolation from the spring of 2020 onwards, Putin spent months working on a 7,000-word historical essay where he laid out the historical thesis that would became the ideological blueprint for war. For Putin, Russia, Belarus and Ukraine are 'parts of what is essentially the same historical and spiritual space ... a single large nation, a triune nation'. Underlying all the practical and tactical factors that led to war, it would be a vision of history and historical destiny Putin largely borrowed from Russia's nineteenth-century imperial historians that he used repeatedly to justify his invasion. Putin's vision was based not on imperialism but on ethno-nationalism. Putin would claim that the war against Ukraine would be fought not to bring a foreign people under Moscow's rule but to protect the rights of people he regarded as essentially Russian.

Ukraine and Russia's 'spiritual, human and civilisational ties formed over centuries and have their origins in the same sources', wrote Putin in an essay published in July 2021. 'They have been hardened by common trials, achievements and victories. Our kinship has been transmitted from generation to generation. It is in the hearts and the memory of people living in modern Russia and Ukraine, in the blood ties that unite millions of our families. Together we have always been and will be many times stronger and more successful. For we are one people.'[2]

Europe's bloodiest war since 1945 was, by Putin's own account, being fought over history. Or, more specifically, over Putin's self-appointed historic mission to reunite a single people sundered by meddling foreign powers.

For many modern Ukrainians, as well as some Western commentators, the answer to Putin's 'one people' thesis is simple. 'The most important thing to know is that Ukrainians are not Russians, and that Ukraine is an ancient independent nation,' argued Israeli historian Noal Yuval Harari. 'Ukraine has a history of more than 1,000 years; Kyiv was a major metropolis and cultural centre when Moscow was not even a village.'

Both views were flawed. The Ukrainian nationalists were correct that theirs was indeed an ancient nation – but one which had rarely in its history been independent, and never in the borders it inherited from the Soviet Union in 1991. And Putin was correct that Russians, Belarusians and Ukrainians were all descended from the historical polity of Kyivan Rus' – but in the same way that the French and German states were jointly inheritors of the near-contemporary empire of Charlemagne, which hardly proved a recipe for subsequent historical unity.

Ukraine had always been a marcher country, a frontier. It was where the Eastern Slavic, Orthodox world met the Western, Catholic one. It was also where the Russian Empire met the Muslim world of the Ottoman Turks and the slave-raiding Tatars of Crimea.

Despite the two neighbouring people's shared history, Putin's fundamental error was to imagine that Russian-speaking Ukrainians naturally considered themselves ethnically and politically Russian. His invasion not only proved that to be largely untrue but forced many to make a choice in favour of their Ukrainian political identity over their Russian ethnic one. Millions of Russian-speaking Ukrainians fled from Moscow's forces, and tens of thousands volunteered to fight against their would-be 'liberators'. To historian Slava Shvets, an ethnic Russian born in Vinnitsa in central Ukraine, Putin's talk of 'one people' was the political equivalent of a wife beater who sends concerned neighbours away from the door with the angry insistence that his noisy abuse is just a 'domestic matter ... we sort out our problems in our own house.'[3]

Nonetheless, Putin was correct in another important aspect. To almost every modern Russian and Ukrainian, relations between the two nations are not an abstract matter of politics, much less history, but of blood and family.

We all like to believe that we think with our rational minds. But a little bit of us, a deep bit, thinks with our blood.

My mother Lyudmila Bibikova was born in 1934 in Kharkiv – Kharkov in Russian – a Russian-speaking industrial city in northern Ukraine. Her father Boris was born in 1903 in Simferopol, Crimea and her mother Martha Shcherbak in Poltava in western Ukraine in 1904. Yet the Bibikov family did not consider themselves Ukrainian. Quite the contrary. For two centuries the Bibikovs played a significant role in Russia's imperial rule over Ukraine, first as servants of the tsars and later as loyal lieutenants of Soviet power. The connection is not a comfortable one. Whether I like it or not, my family story – my blood – is intimately linked not only to Ukraine and Russia but to the history of the Russian Empire.

The Borderland

Ukraine literally means 'by the edge', derived from the Old Russian word *okraina*, or periphery. In modern Russian a speaker's political affiliation is instantly readable from how they parse the word. To say *na ukraine* – literally, 'on the periphery' – uses the word as an adverb. *V Ukraine*, or 'in Ukraine' elevates it to a place name. Most Russians, including, pointedly, Putin, use the former, dismissive usage that implicitly defines Ukraine as a borderland of Russia.

The term *okraina* first crops up in written sources from the twelfth century. But in fact the territory of modern Ukraine had been a borderland between civilisations for centuries before. The northern shores of the Black Sea were where ancient Greek civilisation first encountered the wild peoples of the steppe, who they named *barabaroi*, or barbarians, after their babbling language. 'It was the first frontier of a political and cultural sphere that would come to be known as the Western world,' wrote historian Serhii Plokhy. 'That is where the West began to define itself and its other.'[4] In the first century BC the Greek geographer Strabo drew the easternmost boundary of 'Europe' – the term he used to describe the expanse of the Greek presence in the outer world – at the Don River that today runs just east of Ukraine's border with Russia. Beyond lay Asia.

The state of Kyivan Rus' – held up not just by Putin but by Muscovite historians from the seventeenth century onwards as the origin of the greater Slavic state – was in fact a Viking principality founded to defend trading posts that stretched from the Baltic to the Black Sea. Its great founder, Prince Vladimir of Kyiv (c. 958–1015), would not have recognised the modern version of his own name. Like his uncle, King Haakon Sigurdsson of Norway, he spoke Old Norse and called himself Waldemar. His grandparents, known to Russian history as Prince Igor and his wife Olga, would have been known to their contemporaries as Ingvar and Helga.

One of Putin's obsessions in his 2021 essay was foreign meddling in Russian history. But Grand Prince (and to the Orthodox, Saint) Vladimir the Great of Kyiv – to whom Putin erected a 17-metre-tall statue outside the Kremlin in 2016 – was himself a foreigner. Not only was he a Scandinavian Viking by blood, culture and language, but he spent most of his reign as a pagan, took eight hundred concubines and erected numerous pagan statues and shrines. In 988 Vladimir, having carved out a kingdom that stretched from his native Novgorod near the Baltic to Chersoneses (modern Kherson) on the lower Dniepr, ordered his Slavic subjects to adopt Christianity as the price of his marriage to the sister of Byzantine Emperor Basil II.[5] His son Yaroslav the Wise – grandson of a Byzantine emperor and husband to the daughter of King Olof Skötkonung of Sweden – introduced a Slavic liturgy and translations of the gospels written in an alphabet devised in the previous century by two Greek monks, Cyril and Methodius, neither of whom ever visited Rus'. Old Slavonic, the language of the Russian Orthodox Church ever since, came to Rus' from Bulgaria, whose rulers had accepted Christianity earlier than the Kyivan princes.[6]

The Christianisation of Kyivan Rus' was cited by Putin as the founding moment of the Russian world. But it began with foreign princes imposing a foreign religion, language and script on their Slavic subjects in order to bring them into the European world of Christendom. Just like England, France, Italy, Spain and Germany, Russia's history and identity would be formed not by a single people's inexorable march towards their historical destiny but by successive waves of conquest and rule by outsiders.

It would be nearly nine hundred years before the lands ruled by Prince Vladimir would once again be reunited under a single state by another foreigner with no Russian blood – Sophie Friederike von Anhalt-Zerbst, better known as the Empress

Catherine the Great. For much of the intervening period the territory of modern Ukraine had been fought over and occupied by Mongols, Tatars and by the Polish–Lithuanian Commonwealth. To the north various warring Russian principalities had come to be dominated by Muscovy, which had by the end of the fifteenth century decisively thrown off the Mongol yoke. It was during this period that the first member of my mother's family known to history – born Bibik Beg, a Tatar warlord of the Golden Horde – joined the winning side by swearing fealty to Muscovite Prince Ivan III in 1486. The newly minted Russian nobleman Russified his name to Bibikov. Contra to Putin's ethno-nationalist narrative of the inexorable rise of the Russian people, by the end of the sixteenth century close to a third of the Russian aristocracy were in fact of Tatar origin.

With the power of the Mongols broken, Muscovy's most powerful rivals for the lands of Ukraine became the Grand Duchy of Lithuania and its successor, the Polish–Lithuanian Commonwealth to the west, and the Ottoman Empire and its Tatar allies to the south. The steppes of central Ukraine, with no easily defensible natural borders, became a disputed no-man's land. Slave raids by Crimean Tatars – the Turkic descendants of Central Asian invaders – made the steppes an exceedingly dangerous place to live. In the course of the sixteenth and seventeenth centuries an estimated 1.5 million to 3 million Ukrainians and Russians were sold at the slave markets of the Crimean peninsula, an Ottoman fiefdom. One Ukrainian slave-girl, Roxelana (1504–58), became the concubine and then the official wife of Sultan Suleiman the Magnificent.

The danger of slave-hunters and the lack of any central government meant that only the hardiest and most desperate men dared risk settling the lands of the lower Dniepr basin. The first Cossacks – the word originating from the Turkic term for a freeman or freebooter – were nomadic gangs of escaped serfs who lived from fishing, trapping and banditry. 'Some are hiding from paternal authority, or from slavery, or from service, or from [punishment for] crimes, or from debts,' wrote the early sixteenth-century chronicler Michalon Lituanus. 'Others are attracted ... by richer game and more plentiful places.'[7] Cossacks would become best known to popular history as the Russian tsars' most loyal and reactionary cavalry shock troops. But the original Cossacks were largely Ukrainian-speakers who fled servitude on the huge manorial estates, or *latifundia*, of the Polish–Lithuanian magnates and nobility for a free, if precarious, life in the dangerous steppes of what is now central Ukraine.

Most of what is now modern Ukraine was part of the Polish state for longer than it was inside the Russian Empire. By the seventeenth century the Cossacks of central Ukraine, who had come into existence on the margins of society and in opposition to an established polity, had become a political and military force in their own right. In their subsequent attempts to establish an independent state of their own they both found common cause with and rebelled against their neighbours the Poles, the Muscovites and the Ottomans. In 1610 and again in 1618 Cossack troops seized Moscow itself as part of a Polish army. But in 1654 Bohdan Khmelnytsky, the Hetman or leader of the Zaporozhian Cossacks, defied his Polish masters and swore allegiance to Tsar Aleksei Romanov of Muscovy. Three centuries later, the event would be lavishly celebrated by the Ukrainian-born Soviet leader Nikita Khrushchev as the 'reunification' of the 'fraternal peoples' of Ukraine and Russia. But the two sides needed interpreters to understand each other, and the Cossacks clearly saw the oath in terms of an alliance rather than an act of submission.[8]

Khmelnytsky's oath to Romanov would set the pattern for centuries of Ukrainian–Russian relations even into the twenty-first century – transactional, and dictated by expediency under pressure from outside powers. Indeed the first printed textbook of Russian history, published at the Cave Monastery in Kyiv in

1674 and hailing the city as the 'first capital' of the Muscovite tsars and the birthplace of Muscovite Orthodoxy, was published when Kyiv was preparing for an Ottoman attack and the Poles were demanding it back from Muscovy. The *Chronicles of the Origin of the Slavo-Rossian Nation and the First Princes of the Divinely Protected City of Kyiv* were written as a desperate appeal for military support from Moscow against Kyiv's enemies. The book that founded the myth still accepted by most Russians today about the Kyivan origins of their nation was, in fact, an early attempt by Malorossiya – Little Russia, as the book's authors described Ukraine – to bend history to serve the political exigencies of the day. In that sense the *Chronicles* were a direct antecedent of Putin's 2021 essay.

By the time of the last great Cossack revolt, led by Ivan Mazepa in 1708 against the Russian Tsar Peter the Great, the Hetmans of Ukraine would have a very different attitude to their supposedly shared history. 'Moscow, that is, the Great Russian nation, has always been hateful to our Little Russian nation,' wrote Mazepa in December 1708. 'In its malicious intentions it has long resolved to drive our nation to perdition.' Mazepa's revolt – which had been backed by Russia's arch-enemy, the Ottoman Empire – was brutally crushed. With Mazepa died the last serious attempt of Ukrainians to carve out a separate state until the Russian Empire itself collapsed two centuries later.

Blood and Empire

It was the Empress Catherine the Great, whose imperial vision of Russia entailed subduing all her immediate neighbours and rivals including Poles, Cossacks and Ottomans, who brought most of what is now Ukraine under Moscow's rule. The full incorporation of the semi-independent remnants of Mazepa's Cossack state as well as other self-ruling principalities into the Russian Empire became one of the empress's first priorities after she deposed her husband Tsar Peter III in 1762. 'Little Russia [Ukraine], Livonia [Lithuania and northern Belarus] and Finland are provinces governed by confirmed privileges,' wrote Catherine in 1764. 'These provinces, as well as Smolensk, should be Russified in the easiest way possible so that they cease looking like wolves to the forest ... When the Hetmans are gone from Little Russia, every effort should be made to eradicate from memory the period and the Hetmans, let alone promote anyone to that office.'

Catherine appointed her greatest general and administrator – also her lover and secret husband – Prince Grigory Potemkin to conquer the lands beyond Malorossiya from the Ottomans. The swathe of territory that stretched along the Black Sea coast from the lands of the Don in the east to modern Moldova in the west, as well as Crimea itself, would become known as Novo-Rossiya, or New Russia.

It was under the Empress Catherine that the Bibikov family's connection with Ukraine began. Aleksandr Aleksandrovich Bibikov was the son of the commander-in-chief of the Imperial Russian army. In 1767, at the tender age of two, he was enrolled into the Guards Izmailovsky Regiment with the rank of sergeant. In the summer of 1783 the young Captain Bibikov was one of the Russian officers who accompanied the empress on her first imperial progress through the newly conquered lands of south and west Ukraine. In Crimea, Catherine boldly (but intelligently) entrusted her security to an honour guard composed of her new Crimean Tatar subjects.[9]

Sweating in his heavy serge Guards uniform in the infernal heat and dust of a Crimean summer, Aleksandr Bibikov would likely have seen the great lands of New Russia – now made safe from Tatar slave raiders – as a fertile, empty prairie ripe for settlement by his countrymen. The valley of the Don River, later to be known as Donbass (Donbas in Ukrainian), would soon become the Russian Empire's Wild West, with thousands of

Russian-speaking settlers encouraged to move there to farm the rich fields. Greeks, Bulgarians and Moldovans from the Ottoman Empire as well as Mennonites from Prussia were also encouraged to settle, with land, tax breaks and benefits. Like English and Scottish Protestant farmers settled in Ireland by Oliver Cromwell or American 'sooners' flooding into the Great Plains, the separate non-Ukrainian identity of these settlers would in time become one of the roots of future conflict.

New Russia was very different from the old one. Like the Poles and Moldovans also subjugated to the Russian empire by Catherine, Ukrainians did not speak the same language as their new fellow countrymen. Ukrainian is as different from Russian as English is from Dutch – which both have a 35 per cent linguistic divergence (or 65 per cent similarity, depending on your point of view) – making the two languages similar, but not mutually comprehensible.

Just as importantly, the Russia of the tsars was a society of slaves and slave-owners, whereas Ukraine under the Hetmans had been one of free-holding yeomen-farmers where serfdom was rare. The Black Sea port of Odesa – one of the many great cities founded by Potemkin – was a cosmopolitan entrepôt where Russia met the Levant and the Mediterranean. The valley of the Don would, in the nineteenth century, become a land of industry and immigrant workers as enterprising Welsh mining engineers dug out coal to power Russia's tardy industrial revolution. Novorossiya was not an extension of the old Russia. It was old Russia's window onto southern Europe, and onto modernity.

The Bibikovs became a leading family of Russian ascendancy in Ukraine – and as such the enforcers of Catherine the Great's vision of Russifying the newest corner of the empire. A decree issued by Catherine in May 1783 prohibited close to 300,000 peasants living on gentry estates from leaving their home villages and obliged them to perform free labour for the landowners, effectively imposing serfdom on swathes of Ukrainian peasantry.

Through inheritance and gifts from a grateful empress, General Aleksandr Bibikov came to own 10,000 'souls' (defined as adult male serfs), meaning that over 25,000 human beings were his personal property.

But Russia's dominion was not, as later Ukrainian nationalist historians would have it, a straightforward colonial occupation. Many members of the Ukrainian elite would be incorporated into that of the empire and would, in time, come to rule it. Oleksandr Bezborodko, born into the family of the general chancellor of the Hetmanate and a graduate of the Kyivan Academy, became one of Catherine's most senior diplomats. There were twice as many Ukrainian as Russian doctors in the empire, and in the last two decades of the eighteenth century more than one-third of the students at the St Petersburg teachers' college came from the lands of the old Hetmanate – in other words from central Ukraine.[10] Henceforth Ukraine would provide a large proportion of the Russian and Soviet empire's elite – including Soviet leaders Nikita Khrushchev, Leonid Brezhnev, both born in Ukraine into Russian peasant families, and the half-Ukrainian Mikhail Gorbachev. Like the 1707 Act of Union that united England and Scotland under the British crown and Westminster parliament, the incorporation of Ukraine into the Russian Empire brought together two nations sufficiently close in culture and language for their elites to be interchangeable – but distant enough for the junior partner to demand back its historical independence when the empire's gravitational pull faltered.

Putin's idea of erecting a statue of Prince Vladimir the Great to symbolise the union of the two Slavic peoples was not original. Tsar Nicholas I's governor of Kyiv – Dmitry Gavilovich Bibikov, a grandson of Aleksandr's – installed a massive monument to Vladimir on the banks of the Dniepr in 1853.[11] New neoclassical boulevards were laid out in Kyiv and Jews were banned from the city. Russian became the language of administration, education and the lingua franca of Ukraine's increasingly multi-ethnic urban population. By 1897, the year of the first and only imperial Russian census, some 85 per cent of the overall population of the provinces that today form most of modern Ukraine were ethnic Ukrainians – but in the cities Russians formed the majority.[12]

Reaction to Russification focused, as was fashionable at the dawn of the age of romantic nationalism, on reclaiming Ukrainian language, folklore and history. In St Petersburg in 1840 Taras Shevchenko, the orphaned son of serfs, published a collection of poems in Ukrainian titled *Kobzar* ('the Minstrel'). His main theme was to link the notion of 'Ukrainianness' to the peasants' struggle against oppression.[13] 'Do not pay attention to the Russians. Let them write as they like, and let us write as we like,' wrote Shevchenko. 'They are a people with a language, and so are we. Let the people judge which is better.'

In Kyiv, Governor-General Bibikov was disinclined to take Shevchenko's advice. In neighbouring Poland, national cultural revival was going hand-in-hand with rebellion against Moscow's rule. Bibikov was determined to prevent the same happening in Malorossiya. He extended the network of Russian schools and devoted himself to the destruction of the Cyril and Methodius Brotherhood, a group of Ukrainian language and history enthusiasts. It was Shevchenko, however, who had the last laugh. The central boulevard of nineteenth-century Kyiv had been named in 1855 after General Bibikov. But the Bolsheviks changed it to Boulevard Tarasa Shevchenko to honour Ukraine's great national poet.

Another General Bibikov (there were to be 11 generals in the immediate family between 1760 and 1942) fought at the siege of the Crimean port of Sevastopol by the British and French in the Crimean War of 1853–56. The defeat in Crimea was painful evidence of the inability of feudal Russia to function in a modern world. Within five years the reforming Tsar Aleksandr II had abolished the institution of serfdom, liberating 23 million people from chattel slavery. By comparison, Abraham Lincoln's

Emancipation Proclamation freed four million souls. Jews, however – including angry young men like Lev Davidovich Bronshtein, later better known as Leon Trotsky – were still excluded by a strict quota system from education in major cities and their residence restricted to a Pale of Settlement that stretched from Western Ukraine through Poland up to Latvia. There, local Russian populations were periodically encouraged to rob and rape Jews in a series of pogroms that left thousands dead.

Soviet Empire

It is with my grandfather, Boris Lvovich Bibikov, that my family's involvement with Ukraine comes into sharp, personal focus. His father Lev had scandalised his anti-Semitic family by marrying Sofia Naumovna, a wealthy heiress to a Crimean flour-milling fortune whose parents had, like many Ukrainian Jews, converted to Orthodoxy to further their social ambitions. Their first son Boris was born in Crimea's capital Simferopol in 1903. When Boris was 14 the tsarist empire collapsed under the pressure of the First World War, and in October 1917 a Bolshevik coup toppled the provisional government. With its fall the former captive peoples of the Russian Empire, from Turkestan to Ukraine, decided that the moment had come for their break from imperial rule.

In January 1918 the Central Rada, the revolutionary Ukrainian parliament, dominated by socialist and leftist parties and led by Ukraine's most prominent historian, Mykhailo Hrushevsky, declared the creation of the Ukrainian People's Republic. It claimed – but in practice did not rule – most of today's Ukraine, including Donbas, but did not include the parts of western Ukraine still under Austro-Hungarian rule.[14] The Bolsheviks, in response, created their own Ukrainian Soviet Socialist Republic with its capital in Kharkiv. Moscow also invented a notionally independent socialist puppet state known as the Donetsk–Krivoy Rog Soviet Republic that held much of the Russian-speaking Donbas.

The Ukrainian People's Republic was the first time since the Hetmanate two centuries earlier that Ukraine had been a nation-state. And like the Hetmans, the fledgling state's leaders turned to outsiders to support them against Russia. Western and central Ukraine were occupied by German, then Polish armies. A warring patchwork of pro-Bolshevik, pro-tsarist and anarchist fiefdoms fought over Ukraine's territory. Between the collapse of the Russian army at the end of 1917 and the Bolsheviks' eventual victory in August 1920, Kyiv changed hands 16 times.

On 21 February 2022 in the speech in which he recognised the independence of the Donetsk and Luhansk People's Republics Vladimir Putin claimed that 'modern Ukraine was entirely created by Bolshevik Russia ... Lenin and his associates [created] it in a way that was extremely harsh on Russia – by separating, severing what is historically Russian land.' The modern state of Ukraine, Putin claimed, 'can rightfully be called "Vladimir Lenin's Ukraine". He was its creator and architect.'

In a technical sense, Putin was right – Lenin did indeed draw the first borders of the Soviet Republics of Ukraine, Belarus and the Russian Soviet Socialist Republic. It was the formal union of these three notionally independent states that created the Union of Soviet Socialist Republics in 1922 – and it was these republics' decision to dissolve that union at Belovezhskaya Pushcha in December 1991 that spelled the death of the USSR. But Putin ignored the most fundamental reason why Lenin created a separate Ukrainian republic in the first place. Ukrainian aspirations to independence were so strong in the wake of the civil war that granting a degree of autonomy and a status equal to Russia within the Soviet Union was essential if the Bolsheviks were to maintain their control over Ukraine.[15] Indeed for the first decade of Soviet power, Ukrainian became the official language of administration and education in the Ukrainian Soviet Socialist Republic. Hundreds of books – including history books – were published in Ukrainian, and the language was codified and given an official grammar for the first time.

Despite – or perhaps in deliberate defiance of – his birth into a prominent Russian noble family, Boris Bibikov became a passionate communist. Exactly why Boris Bibikov and his two younger brothers joined the Bolsheviks is not clear, though they were by no means the only members of their class and generation to do so. Felix Dzerzhinsky, founder of the Soviet secret police, was a Polish count and Lenin himself was a hereditary nobleman.

Bibikov joined the Communist Party in 1924, served as a commissar in the Red Army in 1926–28 and then as a Party organiser. As such, he was at the front line of the new Soviet government's most pressing and existential problem. Ukraine was at the same time the breadbasket of the empire and a hotbed of both active and passive anti-communist resistance. The USSR's fast-growing new cities needed Ukrainian grain, but the Ukrainian peasantry – far more independent-minded and wealthier than their Russian counterparts – resisted early attempts to give up their private property and force them into collective farms. Moreover, Joseph Stalin – the rising star of the Party – disagreed with Lenin's expedient accommodation of Ukrainian nationalism. For Stalin, an independent Ukrainian identity was an existential threat to the great Soviet project.

Stalin's solution was threefold. The rich and fertile farmland of Ukraine was to be turned into a 'grain factory', in Lenin's phrase, in order to feed the great cities and earn hard currency to buy foreign-made machinery. The peasants would have to be forcibly collectivised to cure them of their reactionary attachment to private property and capitalist enterprise. And the coal- and steel-producing areas of eastern Ukraine would be massively expanded, both with an influx of ethnic Russian workers and Ukrainian peasants freed up by the mechanisation of agriculture.

Work in the new factories would turn backward Ukrainian peasants into honest Russian proletarians.

In 1929 Stalin published his first five-year plan to bring Soviet agriculture and industry kicking and screaming into the twentieth century. One of the centrepieces was the building of a vast new tractor factory in Kharkiv, known as the KhTZ. Boris Bibikov was appointed the factory's Party boss.

Bibikov wore striped army shirts and played the bluff proletarian – though he lived in a luxurious four-room apartment with a live-in maid and was driven around town in a giant American Packard sedan. His wife, Martha Platonovna Shcherbak, was a peasant girl from Poltava. When Bibikov's first daughter – my aunt – was born in 1925 he loyally named her Lenina, after the Revolution's leader. As the KhTZ's party secretary he edited the factory's newspaper and organised 'storm nights' accompanied by a brass band to meet brutal deadlines imposed by the Kremlin's zealous planners. In 1931, on the factory's completion in record time, he was awarded the Order of Lenin for his work. He was 28 years old.

For Bibikov and the other builders of the KhTZ, the giant fields of Ukraine and the great new factory were anvils where a new kind of society would be hammered out. The tractors they built would free millions from the drudgery, ignorance, drink and viciousness of village life. Though he would have bridled at the comparison, Boris had become the latest in a long line of Bibikovs to impose Moscow's vision of progress and civilisation onto the lands of Ukraine.

But there was one problem. The new collective farms did not work, and the peasants fiercely resisted their new Soviet masters. Land, grain and livestock had to be forcibly confiscated at gunpoint. Soviet documents from 1930 record 13,794 'incidents of terror' and 13,754 'mass protests' – caused, in the opinion of the OGPU secret police, by resistance to collectivisation.[16] Peasants slaughtered and ate their livestock and horses rather than hand them over to the collective farms. The spring sowing of 1931 was hampered by an extreme shortage of grain, horses and tractors. And yet Stalin and the central planners in Moscow continued to insist that Ukraine produce its unrealistic quotas of wheat – much of it for export to buy machinery to fuel its crash industrialisation. In 1929 the USSR exported 170,000 tonnes of grain, in 1930 4.8 million tonnes and in 1931 5.2 million tonnes.[17]

The result was Stalin's most horrific crime – the Holodomor, or 'hunger-death', remembered in modern Ukraine as a genocide akin to the Holocaust. 'There was such inhuman, unimaginable misery, such a terrible disaster, that it began to seem almost abstract, it would not fit within the bounds of consciousness,' Boris Pasternak wrote after a trip to Ukraine in the wake of the man-made famine. The young Hungarian communist Arthur Koestler found the 'enormous land wrapped in silence'. Trucks roamed the streets of Kharkiv, Kyiv and Dnipropetrovsk collecting the dead bodies of starving peasants who had crawled into the cities in search of food. By the winter of 1933 between four and seven million Ukrainian peasants had starved to death.

Bibikov must have known of the daily patrols sent out to collect the emaciated bodies of peasants lying in the streets of Kharkiv, the ruthless Red Army units despatched to seize the last kernels of grain from starving people. He must have struggled to rationalise his place in that nightmare. Perhaps he believed his great tractor factory was going to help grow enough food to feed the gleaming cities Stalin promised – but maybe just a little too late to help the dying millions around him. Which is why Boris Bibikov, until then a loyal Party leader in service to the Soviet empire, made a fateful and ultimately fatal choice to push back against Stalin.

As the Holodomor unfolded, Boris Bibikov and many fellow senior members of the Ukrainian Communist Party chose to voice their opposition to Stalin's policies. Boris attended the 17th Party Congress – the so called 'Congress of Victors' – in Moscow in 1934. It would be the last time open opposition to Stalin was voiced in public. Like many of his Ukrainian colleagues, Boris backed Sergei Kirov, Stalin's main rival and an advocate for slowing the pace of collectivisation. Kirov was assassinated on Stalin's secret orders in December 1934. When Boris heard the news, his daughter Lenina recalled, he threw himself on the sofa and wept. 'We are lost,' my grandfather said. He was right. Between January 1937 and May 1938 a third of the Ukrainian Communist Party – 167,000 people – were arrested.[18] Of the 1,277 delegates to the Congress, over 800 who spoke against Stalin – many of them Ukrainians – would die in Stalin's Great Purge of the Party in 1937. Boris Bibikov was one of them.

My grandmother, Martha Platonovna Shcherbak, was arrested soon after her husband and sent to a Gulag in Kazakhstan for the crime of being the wife of an enemy of the people. She spent 15 years there and went insane. The Bibikovs' children, my mother Lyudmila and her elder sister Lenina, were sent first to a children's prison and then to an orphanage in Verhne-Dniprovsk, where Lyudmila nearly died of tuberculosis of the bones. 'Thank you, Comrade Stalin, for our happy childhood,' was one of the songs my mother learned at the orphanage.

From the point of view of the Soviet state, the Holodomor and the Terror were part of the same project. Class enemies, dissident Party members and Ukrainian nationalists were all 'waging a war against Soviet power', as Stalin wrote to the writer Mikhail Sholokhov in the spring of 1933.[19] Such people stood in the way of the great Soviet project and had to be eliminated from the path of history. 'Not one of them was guilty of anything,' wrote the Stalin-loyalist journalist Ilya Ehrenburg. 'But they belonged to a class that was guilty of everything.'[20] Even as hundreds of thousands of peasants starved in the countryside, the Soviet secret police systematically rounded up Ukraine's intellectual and political elites. Professors, writers, artists, priests, theologians, public officials and bureaucrats – anyone who had promoted the

Ukrainian language or Ukrainian history, or had been connected to the short-lived Ukrainian People's Republic of 1917, was targeted for arrest. Raphael Lemkin, the Polish-Jewish lawyer who coined the word 'genocide', spoke of Ukraine in this era as the 'classic example' of his concept: 'It is a case of genocide, of destruction, not of individuals only, but of a culture and a nation.'[21]

When Hitler's top lieutenants began to debate plans for an invasion of the Soviet Union in the autumn and winter of 1940, it was the seizure of the riches of Ukraine that interested his economic planners the most. The grain of central Ukraine and the coal, steel and factories of Donbas and Kharkiv would be essential to the Nazi war machine – and the fertile black-earth farmland would provide the *Lebensraum* for Aryan settlers. 'The war can only be won if the entire Wehrmacht is fed from Russia in the third year of the war,' concluded Herbert Backe, the Nazi official in charge of food and agriculture. But Backe also calculated that the Wehrmacht could only be fed if the Soviet population were completely deprived of food.[22] Like Stalin before him, Hitler planned to use mass starvation as a weapon against the Soviet people. The goal of Backe's 'Hunger Plan' – its official title – was for some 30 million people to 'die out'.

Operation Barbarossa was launched with a series of long-range bombing raids deep into Soviet territory. In the words of a popular Soviet wartime song penned by poet Boris Kovynev, 'At dawn on June twenty-second; At four a.m. exactly; Kyiv was bombed; And then we were told; That the war had begun.'[23] Eighty-two years later, on the morning of 24 February 2022, millions of Russians and Ukrainians would be surprised by almost the same shocking news that bombs were falling on Kyiv.

The build-up to Hitler's blitzkrieg had been widely signalled by at least 19 Soviet agents from Warsaw to Berlin and Tokyo. Stalin – like the Ukrainian leadership in February 2022 – refused to believe the intelligence reports. The Soviet air force was taken by surprise by massed air attacks that destroyed a large number of planes on the ground. Those that managed to take off – including a Polikarpov Po-2 biplane fighter piloted by Isaac Bibikov, Boris's younger brother – were quickly shot down by the more modern Luftwaffe. Within two weeks the German divisions has reached the gates of Kyiv. The retreating Soviets, determined not to leave anything for the invaders, mined Kreshchatik Boulevard, the capital's main street. Further east in Kharkiv, engineers prepared to dynamite the KhTZ.

After years of famine, mass deportations and political terror, some Ukrainians hoped that the new German occupation would be as benign as that of 1918. They would soon be proved wrong as Heinrich Himmler's SS began a sustained campaign of extermination against Jews, partisans and communist cadres. Nonetheless, some Ukrainians choose to fight alongside the Nazis against Soviet rule.

Stepan Bandera was the leader of the most radical wing of a paramilitary group called the Organisation of Ukrainian Nationalists (OUN). At the outbreak of war Bandera was in prison in Poland for terror attacks against ethnic Poles in western Ukraine, which between the wars was ruled from Warsaw. In February 1941 Bandera made a deal with the leaders of the Abwehr (German military intelligence) to form two battalions of 'special operations forces' from the ranks of OUN supporters. One battalion, *Nachtigall*, or Nightingale, was among the first German troops to enter the city of Lviv – part of the area of pre-war Poland that had been absorbed by the USSR under the Nazi–Soviet pact of 1939 – on 29 June 1941.[24]

German cooperation with Bandera quickly unravelled. One day after the Germans occupied Lviv, Bandera's faction of the OUN proclaimed Ukrainian independence. The Nazi high command, who had very different plans for their newly captured territories, arrested and shot hundreds of OUN members in Kyiv and other cities and towns of Ukraine. Bandera himself spent the rest of the war in the Sachsenhausen concentration camp outside

Berlin. By early 1942, both factions of the OUN were at war with the Germans.

Bandera himself never returned to Ukraine after his arrest by the Germans in the summer of 1941. But his name would always be associated in Soviet and Russian propaganda with the faction of the OUN that formed the core of the anti-Soviet Ukrainian Insurgent Army, or UPA. Though some of its most prominent commanders had previously fought in the *Nachtigall* battalion, the UPA regarded the Germans as their main enemies. In practice, however, they spent most of their time fighting the Soviets. At its height in the summer of 1944 the UPA's 100,000 soldiers were engaged as irregular units behind Soviet lines, disrupting Red Army communications and attacking Soviet military targets, Polish resistance fighters, and Polish and Jewish civilians. Units of UPA diehards would continue their guerrilla resistance to Soviet power in the forests of Belarus and Ukraine into the 1950s.

In addition to the few hundred Bandera followers who had served in the short-lived *Nachtigall*, close to 20,000 Ukrainians served in the 14th *Waffen*-SS Grenadier Division, known as the Division *Galizien*. An estimated quarter of the one million former Soviet citizens who joined German auxiliary units – known as *Hilfswillige*, 'willing helpers', or *Hiwis* – were Ukrainians. Many of them were recruited from German prisoner of war camps. Some worked as guards in Nazi death camps in Poland. After the war, more than 180,000 Ukrainians would be arrested and deported to Siberia for real or alleged collaboration with the Nazis or with the nationalist underground.[25] The last one brought to justice would be Sobibor guard John Demjanjuk, from Vinnitsa province, convicted in 2011 in a German court of 27,900 counts of being an accessory to murder.

Two generations later, as independent Ukraine turned westwards and away from Moscow's control, the memory of Ukraine's alleged collaboration with the Nazis would become an increasingly central part of Russian propaganda. In his 2021 historical essay, Putin wrote that after independence Ukraine's 'radicals and neo-Nazis became more open, more insolent in their ambitions ... they were indulged by both the official authorities and local oligarchs.' One of the stated aims of Russia's 2022 invasion was to 'de-nazify' Ukraine and liberate its people from a government that had been supposedly taken over by 'fascists'.[26]

But the historical truth was that the overwhelming majority of Ukrainian citizens had supported the Soviet side during the Great Patriotic War. Between 1941 and 1945 more than 7 million citizens of the Ukrainian Soviet Socialist Republic – from an overall pre-war population of 34 million – served in the ranks of the Soviet army. Among them was the Jewish grandfather of Volodymyr Zelensky, who marched all the way to Berlin. As will be discussed in more detail in the next chapter, the debate over the legacy of Stepan Bandera – a hero to Ukrainian nationalists, a collaborating traitor to many others – would become a flashpoint in the culture wars that followed Ukrainian independence. But to most modern Ukrainians, who like their Russian neighbours almost without exception lost relatives in the fight against Hitler, Putin's attempt to equate Ukrainian nationalism with fascism was profoundly offensive.

Between 1939 and 1945 Ukraine lost almost 7 million people – close to 1 million of them Jewish – or more than 16 per cent of its pre-war population. Between Nazi blitzkrieg and Soviet scorched-earth tactics, much of the country's industrial base was destroyed. But the USSR's comprehensive victory over Hitler also brought Stalin mastery of the entirety of Eastern Europe. Stalin incorporated three majority Ukrainian-speaking provinces – Galicia, Volhynia and Podolia, formerly under Polish and before that Austria-Hungarian control – into Soviet Ukraine. The inhabitants of these areas spoke a more Polish version of the Ukrainian language. They were also more likely to be Roman Catholics or Greek Catholics, a faith that used rites similar to the Orthodox Church yet respected the authority of the Pope. These areas even today remain not only strikingly un-Russian but even un-Soviet in their architecture and culture. And after Ukrainian independence in 1991 western Ukraine would become the most virulently anti-Russian in its politics.

Despite Stalin's bloody campaign against a separate Ukrainian identity in the 1930s, he nonetheless insisted that Ukraine and Belarus become, alongside the USSR, founder members of the United Nations. They joined the UN as if they were independent states at its founding conference in San Francisco in April 1945. In the post-war years Ukraine had more Communist Party members than any other part of the Soviet Union, and it was with the help of Ukrainian allies that the Donetsk-born Nikita Khrushchev emerged as Stalin's successor by 1954.

In January of that year Khrushchev organised lavish celebrations of the tercentenary of Khmelnytsky's oath of 1654 as the 'reunification of Ukraine with Russia'. More fatefully, the next month he would transfer the Crimean peninsula from the jurisdiction of the Russian Soviet Socialist Federation to that of Soviet Ukraine. In 1944 Stalin had deported the entire Crimean Tatar population for alleged collaboration with the Germans, leaving Crimea 71 per cent ethnic Russian. The peninsula is cut off from mainland Russia by the Kerch Strait but connected to Ukraine by a thin sliver of land. Khrushchev calculated that its incorporation into Ukraine would facilitate Crimea's post-war economic recovery. In the framework of the USSR, the transfer had little more than administrative significance. But it would, in time, become a time bomb under post-Soviet Ukraine's independence.[27]

Under Khrushchev and his Ukrainian-born successor Leonid Brezhnev, Ukraine would become one of the heartlands of the USSR's aviation, defence and nuclear industries. The largest missile-producing facility in all of Europe was built in Dnipropetrovsk. And it was Brezhnev's Dnipropetrovsk cronies who formed the core of Politburo power in the sixties and seventies. Huge construction projects, from hydro-electric dams on the

Dniepr to mines and factories in Donbas, brought hundreds of thousands of people from all over the USSR, who further erased the idea of a Ukrainian identity separate from a Soviet one.

But a growing underground dissident movement in Ukraine began to coalesce under the banner of democratic nationalism. Most of those involved were members of the country's intelligentsia, drawing their inspiration from fellow anti-communists in the Baltic republics and Poland who saw the USSR primarily in terms of a colonial oppressor. In that sense they were the direct spiritual heirs of the Ukrainophile intellectuals of the nineteenth century for whom language was the key to a non-Russian, post-imperial future. The explosion of the Chernobyl nuclear power plant on 26 April 1986 – and the subsequent cover-up by the Soviet government, which included a personal insistence by Mikhail Gorbachev that a May Day parade in nearby Kyiv go ahead, overruling the pleading of Ukrainian Party boss Volodimir Shcherbitsky – proved to be a major inflection point in Ukrainian–Russian relations. When Gorbachev allowed local elections as part of his liberalising campaign of *glasnost*, democratic nationalists, led by former dissidents and intellectuals, swept the board.

The stage was set for the coming collapse, and for Russia's humiliation. Whatever Putin's muddled theories on history, one thing is clear. If any historical event served as the root cause of the 2022 invasion it was not Kyivan Rus' nor the Hetmanate nor the Second World War, but Ukraine's role in precipitating the death of the USSR. That collapse scarred a whole generation of Russians, including Putin personally. As US ambassador in Moscow Robert Strauss put it at the time, 'The most revolutionary event of 1991 for Russia may not be the collapse of communism but the loss of something Russians of all political stripes think of as part of their own body politic and near to the heart at that: Ukraine.'[28] If history played any real role at all in Putin's decision to invade, it was first and foremost in the form of historical payback for Kyiv's betrayal of 1991.

CHAPTER 2
'AND MOSCOW IS SILENT'

Without Ukraine, Russia ceases to be an empire.

Zbigniew Brzezinski, US National Security Adviser 1977–81[1]

People Power

On the evening of 5 December 1989 a crowd several thousand strong gathered outside the headquarters of the Stasi secret police in Bautzner Straße, Dresden, East Germany. Weeks earlier the Berlin Wall had fallen, but the Communist East German regime was still clinging to power. 'We are the people!' chanted the crowd. Sensing a 'lynch mob atmosphere', the Stasi commander Horst Boehm opened the building and even the prison to the surging protesters, remembered democracy activist Herbert Wagner. Boehm 'was led across the inner courtyard. People were insulting him, spitting on him, kicking him. He fell to his knees. I stood in front of him to protect him,' said Wagner. 'If he'd gone down completely he would have been trampled to death.'[2] The crowd found that many secret papers had been hurriedly shredded – but eight kilometres of shelves filled with files had remained intact in a meticulously arranged archive that included informant, surveillance and interrogation reports detailing the lives of Dresden's citizens.

A small group of between 15 and 20 protesters headed to the nearby KGB headquarters, a two-storey art deco villa at Angelikastraße 4, to 'shut it down. The guard on the gate immediately rushed back into the house,' recalled one of the group, Siegfried Dannath. But shortly afterwards 'an officer emerged – quite small, agitated. He said to our group, "Don't try to force your way into this property. My comrades are armed, and they're authorised to use their weapons in an emergency."'[3] The officer was a 37-year-old KGB major named Vladimir Putin. The group quickly dispersed. But as Putin himself would later recall, he rang the headquarters of a Red Army tank unit to ask for protection. The answer he received was a devastating, life-changing shock.

'We cannot do anything without orders from Moscow,' the Soviet tank officer replied. 'And Moscow is silent.'

The confrontation at Angelikastraße was too minor to be reported in the local Dresden newspapers the next day. But the story would assume legendary proportions once Putin came to power 20 years later. 'A crowd of 5,000 people broke into the courtyard of the KGB headquarters, drunk, with beer bottles in their hands,' reported NTV news in 2002. 'Putin came out and had to face them down.' The 'Moscow is silent' moment is 'the key to understanding Putin', said Putin's German biographer Boris Reitschuster. 'We would have another Putin and another Russia without his time in East Germany.'[4] Putin's experience of the collapse of the German Democratic Republic would leave him with a deep anxiety about the frailty of political elites – and how easily they could be overthrown if central authority loses its nerve in the face of people power. Over the following two years Putin would watch as Soviet power collapsed after massive demonstrations in Vilnius, Kyiv, Moscow and his native St Petersburg. In 2004 and again in 2014 he would watch his ally, Ukrainian president Viktor Yanukovych, suffer the same fate.

In March 1990 Soviet Lithuania declared independence from the USSR. Alarmed, Soviet leader Mikhail Gorbachev began to negotiate a new Union treaty that he hoped would save the Soviet empire. But on the morning of 2 October 1990 dozens of students from Kyiv, Lviv and Dnipropetrovsk descended on October Revolution Square in downtown Kyiv – the future Maidan Nezalezhnosti or Independence Square – and began a hunger strike. Most were, by Soviet standards, members of a privileged middle class and had been inspired by the collapse of communism in East Germany, Poland, Czechoslovakia and Hungary under the pressure of people power the previous November. Among other things, they demanded the resignation of the prime minister and Ukraine's withdrawal from negotiations on the new union treaty.

Local authorities organised teams of loyalists to dislodge the protesters. But 50,000 Kyivans marched on the square to protect the students. Soon after, the city's universities came out on strike. The protesters marched on parliament, occupying the square in front of the parliament building. They were supported by Leonid Kravchuk, the newly elected chairman of the Ukrainian Supreme Soviet. Under pressure from the street, Kravchuk and the new parliament, the Soviet authorities decided to retreat. The so-called 'first Maidan' of October 1990 would be the first of three political revolutions against Moscow-backed power that would determine not only Ukraine's but Russia's politics over the next three decades.[5]

Putin would later claim that foreign meddling forced the USSR apart. In his 2021 essay he claimed that 'Ukraine was dragged into a dangerous geopolitical game aimed at turning Ukraine into a barrier between Europe and Russia, a springboard against Russia.'[6] But in truth in 1991 the United States indeed favoured setting the Baltic republics free – but strongly backed keeping Ukraine and the rest of the USSR together. US President George Bush visited Kyiv on 1 August 1991. In his address to the Ukrainian parliament Bush took Gorbachev's side, warning them to renounce 'suicidal nationalism' and avoid 'confusing freedom with independence'. For his cowardice in failing to endorse the independence aspirations of Ukraine's democratically elected deputies, American media dubbed it Bush's 'Chicken Kyiv speech'.[7]

Ignoring Bush's objections, in the aftermath of the hardliners' failed coup against Mikhail Gorbachev in Moscow on 19 August 1991 Ukraine overwhelmingly chose freedom from Russia over union. 'Continuing the thousand-year tradition of state-building in Ukraine,' read the declaration of independence drafted in late August by former political prisoner Levko Lukianenko, now a member of parliament, 'the Supreme Soviet of the Ukrainian Soviet Socialist Republic solemnly declares the independence of Ukraine.' The Soviet-era parliament, like that of the Russian Soviet Socialist Republic, had been set up as an obedient rubber stamp to approve Party decisions and had no constitutional authority for such a declaration. But they voted on it anyway. Three hundred and forty-six deputies voted in favour, five abstained, and only two voted against. The implications would be seismic. Not only would Ukraine soon vote to become a free country – but Russia, as a direct consequence, would cease to be an empire. 'Those participating in the referendum had changed not only their own fate but the course of world history,' wrote Serhii Plokhy. 'Ukraine freed the rest of the Soviet republics still dependent on Moscow.'[8]

By chance I arrived in the newly renamed St Petersburg on 18 August 1991, the eve of the attempted putsch against Gorbachev mounted by KGB hardliners. The next day I looked out of a window in the Winter Palace and saw Palace Square filled with people, a rolling sea of faces and placards. Near St Isaac's Square I helped students build barricades across the street out of benches and steel rods. Nevsky Prospekt was filled as far as the eye could see in both directions with half a million people protesting against the system that had shaped almost every aspect of their lives for three generations.[9] The same day in Moscow,

Boris Yeltsin emerged from the White House – the seat of the government of the Russian Soviet Federal Socialist Republic – and stood on a tank to address the crowds who had gathered to defend the building against the forces of reaction.

Boris Yeltsin had become a democratic hero to many. But his vision of the post-Soviet role of Russia in a reformed union remained clearly imperial. In the wake of Ukraine's declaration of independence, and his own victory against the putschists, Yeltsin sounded a sinister note. He declared that Russia would have 'the right to open the question of its borders with those republics' that unilaterally split from the USSR. 'Crimea and eastern parts of Ukraine, including the Donbas coal region [could be possible] areas of contention,' clarified Yeltsin's press secretary. The threat of partition if Ukraine insisted on independence would, in time, be picked up by his successor Vladimir Putin with fatal consequences.

Yeltsin's threat, just like George Bush's warning before it, fell on deaf ears. On 1 December 1991 Ukrainians went to the polls to decide whether to remain in a reformed USSR or leave it. With a turnout of 84 per cent, more than 90 per cent of voters supported independence. Even in Crimea, which by the last Soviet census in 1989 was 66 per cent Russian and 25 per cent Ukrainian, 54 per cent declared themselves in favour of independence (though importantly, in a separate referendum two months earlier, 94 per cent of Crimeans had voted to re-establish the Crimean Autonomous Soviet Socialist Republic, suggesting that what they really wanted was independence not only from the USSR but from Ukraine too). Ukraine's vote effectively spelled the end of the Soviet Union. On 25 December 1991 the Soviet flag on the Kremlin's Senate Palace came down and the new Russian tricolour went up.

Kravchuk, independent Ukraine's first president, refused Yeltsin's offer to sign a new union treaty. Instead the two men, along with Stanislaŭ Shushkevich of Belarus, created the

Commonwealth of Independent States, a new international body that the Central Asian republics joined on 21 December. The Soviet Union was no more. In his 2021 essay Putin would claim that 'in 1991, all those territories, and, which is more important, people, found themselves abroad overnight, taken away, this time indeed, from their historical motherland.'[10] He ignored the crucial fact that the 'territories' had not been taken away from their motherland but had overwhelmingly rejected it. The newly independent Baltic states, Belarus and Ukraine had no intention of continuing their subjugation to Moscow by another name.

Geopolitical Catastrophe

'The collapse of the USSR was the greatest geopolitical catastrophe of the 20th century,' Putin told the Russian parliament and the country's top political leaders in his 2005 state of the nation address. It is probably Putin's single best-known quote. But few remember its context. The 'genuine tragedy' Putin spoke of was for the Russian people: 'tens of millions of our fellow citizens and countrymen [who] found themselves beyond the fringes of Russian territory'.[11]

Putin's relationship with the legacy of the Soviet Union is actually more complex and ambivalent than one of simple nostalgia. In his 2021 essay Putin wrote that the 'collectivisation and famine of the early 1930s [was] a common tragedy' for both Russians and Ukrainians. He also criticised the Bolsheviks for their treatment of 'the Russian people as inexhaustible material for their social experiments'.[12] In 2007, as he laid flowers on a mass grave of KGB victims in Butovo near Moscow on the anniversary of Stalin's great purge, Putin remembered the 'hundreds of thousands, millions of people [who] were killed and sent to camps, shot and tortured. These were people with their own ideas which they were unafraid of speaking out about. They were the cream of the nation.' Such 'tragedies' happen, said Putin, because 'ostensibly attractive but empty ideas are put above fundamental values, values of human life, of rights and freedom.'[13]

Yet despite his later criticism, Putin had spent 20 years of his life not just as a loyal servant of the Soviet regime but of its most violent and fanatical wing – the KGB secret police. And he was undoubtedly one of the vast majority of Russians for whom life immediately after the fall was dramatically worse that it had been before it. On his return from his posting in Dresden in early 1990 Putin brought home a Volga car – once a sign of giddying privilege. But after he retired from the KGB with the honorary discharge rank of lieutenant-colonel the Putins had so little money that he had to moonlight as a taxi driver. 'We lived like everyone, but sometimes I had to earn extra money ... as a private driver,' Putin told a Russian Channel One documentary in December 2021. 'It's not pleasant to speak about, honestly, but unfortunately that is what happened.'[14]

Dozens of books have been devoted to explaining the innermost secrets of Putin's world view. However, I believe that there is less to Putin than meets the eye. Over his near quarter-century in power Putin has been described by Western commentators as a great tactician, manipulator and geopolitical mastermind. But most important for understanding the arc of his career, his uncanny tenacity in power and the path to the 2022 war is another, much more basic factor: that Putin is in many crucial ways the Russian everyman. Or more precisely, he is a smarter, fitter and more sober version of the Russian everyman – the kind of soft-spoken, effortlessly commanding man most Russians would like to be, or the kind of father, husband or son-in-law they would wish to have.

Putin's defining characteristic is his ordinariness, not his extraordinariness. Like most of his generation, Putin spent the first four decades of his life believing that he lived in the greatest and most powerful nation on earth. He grew up in conditions of ordinary provincial Soviet post-war deprivation, was educated by the state and joined one of its most prestigious institutions for what he thought would be a lifetime's career. Putin differed from most of his fellow citizens insofar as his posting in East Germany happened to give him a grandstand view of the collapse of the USSR's might. But again in common with the rest of his generation, he certainly felt the material and moral humiliation 'on his own hide', in the Russians phrase.

With a hypocrisy well-honed by a lifetime in the USSR, Putin both abhorred the corruption and thievery of the 1990s and partook of it when he could – just like all the rest of his generation. St Petersburg's newly elected mayor Anatoly Sobchak became Putin's new political mentor, hiring the 37-year-old ex-KGB man as his deputy in May 1990. A bribe here, a kickback there – Putin, in his new job as liaison between St Petersburg's deeply criminalised business world and the mayor's office, was simply doing on a high level what every Russian was doing, or would do if they had the chance.

Most importantly, even as he was ducking and diving, Putin held on to a characteristically Russian form of aggrieved patriotism that was formed of hurt and pride in equal measure. Whatever the humiliations Russia was forced to suffer by a vindictive and victorious West, she nonetheless remained a great country. 'A man may find himself drunk and broke, but at least he has the comfort of knowing that it is not his fault, but the work of enemies,' explained Yulia Mostovaya, editor-in-chief of Kyiv's *Zerkalo Nedeli* magazine. 'He may beat his wife. He may wallow drunk under a fence. But whatever his personal shortcomings he knows that whatever else fate may take from him it cannot take his Russianness, his membership of a mighty nation.'[15]

I lived in Moscow for much of the 1990s. The Russia I knew had caught a viral dose of the century's chaos. For Russians the shock of the implosion of the system that had sustained their every physical, spiritual and intellectual need was far more profound than anything the Soviet system had ever thrown at them – even the Purges, even the Second World War. Both those horrors, at least, had easy-to-understand narratives of enemies at the gate, enemies inside the house. But now Russians were hit by something entirely inexplicable – not an enemy, but an ideological vacuum and giddying economic collapse. During the first half of 1992, the average income of the population declined by an average of 70 per cent; the economy shrank by 40 per cent.

The first years of Yeltsin's rule were a constant – and at times bloody – battle with reactionary nationalists and communists, both of whom demanded the restoration of Soviet greatness. In parliamentary elections in 1993 the largest party – with 23 per cent – was led by ultra-nationalist Vladimir Zhirinovsky, who called for Russian soldiers 'to wash their boots in the Indian Ocean'. Diehard communists and nationalists in the Congress of People's Deputies repeatedly refused to ratify the Belavezh Accords on the termination of the existence of the USSR. Leaders of oil-rich republics such as Tatarstan and Bashkiria, as well as Chechnya, Ingushetia and diamond and gold-rich Yakutia, called for full independence from Russia. Russia's vice president, Aleksandr Rutskoy, denounced the Yeltsin programme of market reforms as 'economic genocide', and in October 1993 led an armed occupation of the White House where Yeltsin had made his famous speech from atop a tank two years earlier. Yeltsin shelled the rebels into submission.

The following year, with oil prices crashing, Yeltsin desperately filled the state's coffers by selling off swathes of state property – notably oil, steel, aluminium and nickel production, as well as TV and communications infrastructure – in rigged auctions to a tiny group of wealthy men who would become known as the oligarchs. He also sent Russian troops into Grozny, the capital of the rebel republic of Chechnya, to forcibly bring it back under Moscow's control. The assault failed spectacularly. In 1996

Yeltsin's re-election against the communists was won through wholesale (through voluntary) mobilisation of Russia's supposedly independent media to support the Kremlin. By 1998 Russia was so broke that it defaulted on its sovereign debt – and a $22 billion bailout from the International Monetary Fund was largely plundered by the oligarch owners of failing Russian banks. A year later NATO bombed Belgrade, capital of Russia's historic ally Serbia, to put an end to the genocide of Kosovo Albanians. To Yeltsin's profound anger – and also in a sign of how strategically insignificant NATO now considered Russia to be – Moscow was not consulted.

For an entire generation of Russians – including Putin – the 1990s were a decade of humiliation, failure and poverty. The deep scars that period left on both ordinary people and on the political class that lived through it are the key to understanding their later support for Putin's aggressive push to restore Russia's standing in the world. It was not Putin who invented that nationalist narrative. 'The belief that we Russians are a significant power – one that can push back against hostile powers and hostile influence from the outside world – is an important part of our collective identity,' said Lev Gudkov, director of Moscow's independent Levada-Center polling group. 'This belief in the Soviet Union and Russia's unique authority and in the fact that we are a special civilisation – this compensates for the feeling of dependence, poverty and humiliation that people have in their private lives.' In a poll conducted by Levada at the end of Boris Yeltsin's presidency in 1999, respondents had two main wishes of their new president: to end the economic crisis and to restore Russia to the status of superpower. Yeltsin had tried to drag the Russian people in the direction of democracy, capitalism and free speech – and by the outset of the final year of his first term his popularity had dropped to 10 per cent. Putin, by contrast, never tried to drag his people anywhere other than where they wanted to go – which was towards prosperity and national greatness.[16]

Vladimir Vladimirovich

In the final years of Yeltsin's presidency the members of his family – both in the literal sense and the mafia sense of the tight coterie of oligarchic cronies who controlled much of Russia's wealth – were looking for a man firm enough to take over the presidency but sufficiently loyal not to use his new powers to attack the people who had placed him on the throne. Vladimir Putin – modest and self-effacing, with a shy smile that hid inner toughness – seemed just the man for the job. Aleksandr Voloshin, the head of Yeltsin's presidential administration, had headhunted Putin from the St Petersburg mayor's office in 1997 and brought him to Moscow as his deputy. 'Part of [Putin's] head is KGB and Soviet, part of it is progressive,' Voloshin told me.[17] That seemed to make Putin a perfect compromise between the old world and the new – competent, level-headed, a safe pair of hands who knew the 'understandings' on which power in Yeltsin's Russia was based. With the support of leading oligarch and Yeltsin 'family' member Boris Berezovsky, Putin was promoted to head the KGB's successor, the Federal Security Service, and then to prime minister. 'I am a bad judge of people,' Berezovsky told me after he had been forced to flee to London. 'I was wrong about Putin. He would say anything to anyone. He looked modest and moderate. But in reality he was a street punk.'[18]

But as much as the support of the Yeltsin family, it was war that brought Putin to power as president. Putin's tough talk over Chechnya and the unrestrained brutality of the second war he unleashed against the rebel republic in September 1999 gave Russians their first military victory since the crushing of rebel Czechoslovakia in 1968. I spent six months with both Chechen rebels and pro-Moscow Chechen fighters during that war. In January 2000, standing on the roof of a nine-storey building in Grozny's northern suburbs, I watched the artillery of five Russian divisions pound the already-ruined remains of the city to drive out a final handful of rebels. I counted more than 60 detonations a minute – including massive half-tonne bombs dropped by low-flying Su-24 fighter-bombers. As the planes roared over our heads Beslan Gantemirov, head of a force of pro-Moscow Chechens, grinned like a delighted boy, pumping his hand in the air as the detonations came like titanic doors slamming under the earth.

The Ukraine campaign would be a re-run of that conflict. 'I have found it almost impossible to look away from the images of the carnage unleashed by Russian troops on occupied Ukrainian towns,' wrote Lana Estimirova, whose mother Natalia was one of Chechnya's most outspoken human rights campaigners before she was kidnapped and brutally murdered in 2009. 'All I can think is: "They have done this before. They are doing it again." The indiscriminate shelling, the looting, the evidence of rape, torture and executions, and, above all, the sense of enthusiasm with which these war crimes are being carried out are painfully familiar ... Before Bucha and Irpin there was Samashki, where on 7 April 1995, Russian troops carried out a *zachistka* – a "clean-up" operation. Soldiers shot civilians, raped women, and set homes on fire. At least 103 were murdered on that day.'[19]

Not only the military methods of the Chechen and Ukrainian wars but the propaganda narratives would be the same. In the run-up to the September 1999 invasion Kremlin TV spoke of a 'genocide of Russians' inside Chechnya. 'Russia's modus operandi in Chechnya served as something of a blueprint for the next two decades of the Kremlin's military and political strategy,' wrote Estemirova. 'A macabre methodology for breaking the will of restive populations in pursuit of its imperial interests. In the years since, we have seen – from Tskhinval [South Ossetia] to Aleppo [Syria], from Crimea to Central African Republic – a willingness to deploy violence with impunity across the world stage ... As a Chechen, I am tied to the Ukrainian people through a bloody bond. A victory for them would be a victory for every victim of Putin's regime.'

By February 2000 the Russian army, applying the same kind of overwhelming and indiscriminate firepower that they would later bring to bear on Mariupol and Severodonetsk, had crushed the Chechen rebel government that had defied Moscow since 1994. In presidential elections in March, Putin – already acting president – easily triumphed over his rivals with 53.4 per cent of the vote. It would be the first and only time Putin ever faced anything like real electoral opposition.

For Putin, the lesson of the second Chechen war was simple, according to a senior government minister who worked with him for eight years. 'Russia's might and empire could indeed be restored through military aggression – that was clear to all of us,' said the official. 'And it was also clear that Russian voters were sick of weakness and admired strength.'[20]

Chechnya had been bloodily and triumphantly subdued. But the rest of the old Soviet Empire fell into three distinct camps. The Baltic states, well on the road to membership of both the European Union and NATO, were far beyond recovery. The Central Asian states remained economically and politically tied to Russia by a physical network of Soviet-era gas pipelines on which they relied for their prosperity. Belarus had elected Aleksandr Lukashenko, a strongman Soviet nostalgist who favoured close ties to Moscow. But Ukraine, Azerbaijan, Armenia and Georgia remained on the fence, torn between the ambitions of their leaders and peoples for closer ties to the West and their economic dependence on Moscow.

Of these it was Ukraine that was by far the largest and most politically important. Ukraine had the biggest Russian-speaking population beyond the borders of Russia itself, and occupied a strategic position straddling the entire underbelly of southern Russia. More, the Crimean port of Sevastopol – home to the Russian Black Sea Fleet, including more than three hundred ships and 25,000 servicemen – was not a Russian sovereign base but leased from Kyiv on terms that varied depending on the political climate. It was a crucial military and strategic asset that the Kremlin was not prepared to forfeit to the Ukrainians, much less to NATO.

Tug of War

The first decade of Ukraine's independence was as chaotic as Russia's – and also encompassed economic collapse, the rise of an oligarch class that seized the country's assets with the connivance of a corrupt ruler and the rise of ultra-nationalism on the political fringes. And just as in Russia, many of Ukraine's best-educated and most motivated citizens emigrated. Among them were 78 per cent of its Jewish population, including the co-founders of PayPal (Max Levchin) and WhatsApp (Jan Koum). Between 1989 and 2001 Ukraine's population fell by nearly 5 per cent.[21]

After 1991 about half the USSR's strategic nuclear arsenal had been inherited by the Soviet Union's successor states. Formally, the weapons left in Ukraine, Belarus and Kazakhstan were controlled by the Commonwealth of Independent States, or CIS. But in practice, especially after Ukraine's parliament refused to ratify the CIS agreement, Ukraine found itself the world's third-largest nuclear power, with some 1,700 warheads. Washington, alarmed at politically unstable countries controlling strategic nukes, persuaded the three accidental post-Soviet nuclear powers to destroy the weapons and their installations. In exchange, in December 1994 the United States, Russia and Great Britain signed the Budapest Memorandum that offered security assurances to Kyiv and promised to 'respect the independence and sovereignty and the existing borders of Ukraine'.[22] Two decades later when Putin invaded Crimea, the supposed guarantors of Ukraine's security would utterly ignore their Budapest obligations.

But in the short term Ukraine's cooperation with disarmament and new status as a non-nuclear, Western-friendly power brought dividends. In 1994 Kyiv signed a cooperation agreement with the European Union, the first such agreement that the EU had offered a post-Soviet state. In the same year Ukraine signed up for NATO's Partnership for Peace agreement, which was upgraded in 1997 by a Charter on Distinctive Partnership, the second of many steps towards eventual full membership. Yeltsin objected strenuously, but according to declassified records he was assured by US President Bill Clinton at a personal meeting at the White House on 27 September 1994 that 'NATO expansion is not anti-Russian; it's not intended to be exclusive of Russia, and there is no imminent timetable ... the broader, higher goal [is] European security, unity and integration – a goal I know you share.'[23]

At a press conference in December 2021 Putin would claim that the West had repeatedly promised Russia that NATO would not expand, then broken their word. 'They cheated us vehemently, blatantly. NATO is expanding,' Putin said. He claimed that US Secretary of State James Baker had told Mikhail Gorbachev in 1990 that 'NATO will not move one inch further east.'[24] There is no trace of any such official assurance in a slew of US State Department records of multiple meetings between Russian and US officials that were declassified in 2018, though Baker has never explicitly denied that he said it privately. But the US was nonetheless clearly playing a double game. There was no formal, public promise that NATO would not expand – but apparently plenty of assurances were made that the expansion would not pose a threat to Russia.[25] In 1997 veteran US diplomat George Kennan denounced NATO expansion as 'the most fateful error of American policy in the entire post-Cold War era'.[26]

Clearly, if Putin were to stop Ukraine and Georgia joining NATO, it would have to be done in Kyiv and Tbilisi rather than through talks with Washington. Putin's first chance (of many) to install a more pro-Moscow government in Ukraine came in 2003 when the power of Leonid Kuchma, the second president of Ukraine, began to crumble under allegations of massive corruption and the murder of a high-profile journalist. The Kremlin's man inside the halls of power in Kyiv was Viktor Medvedchuk, a prominent Soviet-era lawyer turned energy tycoon who served as head of Kuchma's presidential administration. When Kuchma's Prime Minister Viktor Yushchenko turned against his boss and began to prepare his own presidential run, Medvedchuk led the efforts to undermine him in the coming political fight. Medvedchuk was assisted by a team of 'political technologists' sent from Moscow – all experts in winning elections who had cut their teeth in Yeltsin's 1996 campaign and Putin's in 2000.

'Our task was clear – to stop [Yushchenko] getting into power, and to promote a candidate who would be in favour of closer ties to Moscow and respect the rights of the Russian-speaking population,' remembered Kremlin spin doctor Gleb Pavlovsky. Their methods were 'the same as we used in Russian elections. Reputation management, controlling the narrative, publicity, persuading the local press to run the stories we needed to be run.'[27]

It was the political technologists sent by Putin who first came up with the idea that Ukrainian nationalists were 'fascists'. In October 2003 Viktor Yushchenko visited Donetsk – heartland of support for the man who would become his opponent in presidential elections the following year, Viktor Yanukovych. Yushchenko was met with billboards put up by Yanukovych's Party of the Regions that read 'Russian Movement of Ukraine: No to Fascism! No to Nationalism! Yes to Friendship and Agreement!'[28] Yanukovych held a rally for several thousand supporters at Donetsk's *Yunost* Palace of Youth. 'At some moment a taunt from the old children's game "Our Guys versus the Fascists" swam up,' recalled Donetsk photographer Sergei Vaganov. 'The crowd started to chant that Yushchenko was "fascist". The use of that word was so profoundly uncouth, so far beyond the border of decency, that I felt physically sick.'[29]

In the West the impact of the word 'fascist' has been eroded by overuse and irony. But in post-Soviet societies it remains one of the worst insults one can throw. Nonetheless, in televised debates the following year Yanukovych took to calling his opponent a 'Nazi'. For Yushchenko, whose father had been a Red Army soldier imprisoned at Auschwitz and whose mother risked her life by hiding Jewish refugees during the Second World War, the insult was particularly egregious.[30] Yet the slur stuck. Twenty years later, ridding Ukraine of its supposedly 'fascist' leadership would become one of the cornerstone justifications for Putin's invasion.[31]

In November 2003 the Kremlin suffered a serious setback in another corner of its former empire. In the aftermath of a rigged election in Georgia, 20 days of street protests in central Tbilisi culminated in an angry crowd storming parliament. They were led into the building by passionately pro-Western opposition leader Mikheil Saakashvili, who carried a bunch of roses that gave the protests their name – the Rose Revolution.[32] The pro-Moscow President Eduard Shevardnadze was ousted and Saakashvili elected. The new regime declared European and Euro-Atlantic integration as its main priority, putting Georgia on a collision course with Moscow.[33]

Putin could not allow the same to happen in Ukraine. In March 2004 four former Soviet satellites – Bulgaria, Romania, Slovakia and Slovenia – plus the former Soviet republics of Estonia, Latvia and Lithuania joined NATO. In November of the same year Poland, Hungary, the Czech Republic, Slovakia, Slovenia and the three Baltic nations also joined the European Union. The central plank of Ukrainian presidential hopeful Viktor Yushchenko's campaign was for Ukraine to follow suit.

As the battle between the pro-Western Yushchenko and the Kremlin-backed Yanukovych intensified, Medvedchuk became not only Putin's de facto emissary on the inside of Ukrainian politics but also a personal friend. In early 2004 Putin became godfather to Medvedchuk's daughter Daria. Medvedchuk would later insist that he never agreed with Putin's idea that Ukraine and Russia should be reunited. 'Putin said that we are not two peoples but one people,' Medvedchuk told the American film-maker Oliver Stone in 2019. 'I had a long discussion with him about this ... I am a supporter of the sovereignty of Ukraine and consider that the path that was chosen in 1991 was correct. Our opponents call us pro-Russian, but this is wrong. We speak for people who want to be friends with Russia and who are against the policy that buttresses government power with radical Russophobia and anti-Russian hysteria. They want normal relations with our neighbours.'[34] Nonetheless, for the next decade Medvedchuk would play a central role in Putin's plans to shift Ukraine's strategic direction away from the West and towards Moscow.

Pre-election polling showed a narrow plurality of Ukrainian voters preferring Yushchenko's pro-Western policies to Yanukovych's pro-Russian ones. As Yushchenko pulled ahead, his enemies turned to more radical methods to stop him becoming president. After a dinner in Kyiv on 5 September 2004 with senior officials – including Volodymyr Satsyuk, the deputy chief of Ukraine's security service – Yushchenko was taken seriously ill with symptoms of apparent poisoning. He was flown to Vienna's Rudolfinerhaus clinic, where doctors discovered one thousand times the usual concentration of TCDD dioxin in his body. The poison had been developed in KGB laboratories.[35] Yushchenko survived, but his face was horrifically scarred. Satsyuk, a dual Russian–Ukrainian citizen, and two other men present at the dinner fled to Russia.

In the first round the two candidates tied on 39 per cent, with Yushchenko fractionally ahead. As the country prepared for a run-off election on 21 November 2004, the outgoing Kuchma administration went into overdrive to ensure a win for

Yanukovych. On election day domestic and foreign election monitors reported widespread ballot-box stuffing, especially in Yanukovych's home turf of Donbas. Exit poll results suggested an 11 per cent lead for Yushchenko, but official results gave the election win to Yanukovych by a 3 per cent margin. As telephone intercepts of discussions between members of Yanukovych's campaign staff showed, they had tampered with the server of the state electoral commission to falsify election results submitted to Kyiv.[36] Later, Viktor Medvedchuk would be one of the top officials questioned by Ukraine's SBU Security Service on vote-rigging accusations, though no charges were brought.[37]

Thousands of Ukrainians refused to accept the result. Maidan Square in central Kyiv filled with angry protesters waving the orange banners of Yushchenko's party in scenes reminiscent of the 1991 protests that had caused Soviet power to crumble – and of the previous winter's Rose Revolution in Tbilisi. Local protests, general strikes and sit-ins erupted across the country.[38] Counter-demonstrations in favour of Yanukovych in Crimea, Donetsk, Luhansk and other cities of Donbas demanded semi-independence or even secession from Kyiv.

After two weeks of political turmoil Ukraine's Supreme Court annulled the results of the original run-off, and Yushchenko won the re-vote by 52 per cent to Yanukovych's 45 per cent. For Putin, the nightmare he had witnessed in Dresden in 1989 was repeating itself – first in Georgia and now in Kyiv. The Orange Revolution caused 'horror, indignation, anger' in the Kremlin, recalled one official who held a senior government post at the time. 'Putin himself was convinced that this was the direct result of meddling from the West ... they wished to turn Ukraine into an anti-Russia.' Yushchenko's pro-Western administration in Kyiv was an 'emergency of the highest order'.[39]

The prospect of Ukrainian entry into NATO was 'the brightest of all redlines for the Russian elite (not just Putin)', wrote William Burns, then the American ambassador to Moscow, to Secretary of State Condoleezza Rice in 2008. 'In more than two and a half years of conversations with key Russian players, from knuckle-draggers in the dark recesses of the Kremlin to Putin's sharpest liberal critics, I have yet to find anyone who views Ukraine in NATO as anything other than a direct challenge to Russian interests.'[40]

The Kremlin's first move was to cut off the possibility that Western interference could spark a Maidan-type protest inside Russia itself. Putin's chief spin doctor Vladislav Surkov – whose career we will examine in more detail later – was put in charge of creating a patriotic youth movement on the lines of the Soviet Communist Youth organisation. Surkov's 'Youth Democratic Anti-Fascist Movement' – known as '*Nashy*' (or 'Ours') for short – held summer indoctrination camps, and staged youth festivals and concerts attended by hundreds of thousands of Russian teenagers and young people. Its members also systematically harassed and heckled Andrew Wood, the British ambassador to Moscow, and leading opposition figures.[41] At a political education event in summer 2006 Kremlin adviser Gleb Pavlovsky chided *Nashy* members that they 'lacked brutality ... you must be prepared to break up fascist demonstrations and forcibly prevent with force any attempt to overthrow the constitution.'[42]

The Kremlin's parallel priority was to malign Yushchenko's pro-Western rhetoric and undermine his narrow majority by making Ukraine as economically dependent on Russia as possible. Gas would be both Putin's carrot and stick. Through a mixture of selective gas cut-offs and sweetheart deals with prominent Ukrainian politicians – notably Yushchenko's deputy and ally Yulia Tymoshenko, the golden-haired 'goddess' of the Orange Revolution – Russian state-owned gas corporation Gazprom and its Ukrainian subsidiaries systematically corrupted a swathe of Kyiv's political class. Ukraine's heavy dependence both on cheap Russian gas and on revenue from Russian gas transit via Soviet-era pipelines that traversed the country meant that Yushchenko had to tread carefully. 'The extreme lengths [Putin] was willing to go to in order to get what he wanted [were] clear,' recalled Yushchenko. '[But] I needed to try to keep a workable relationship with him as the leader of our neighbour in the east.'[43]

Under strong pressure from his nationalist political base in western Ukraine, Yushchenko declared Stepan Bandera a Hero of Ukraine, to Moscow's outrage. Leonid Kuchma had instituted an annual Holodomor Memorial Day in 1998, but Yushchenko upgraded it to a day of national mourning, with all entertainment programmes banned from the airwaves. But at the same time Yushchenko was careful to avoid blaming the Russian nation for the tragedy. 'We appeal to everyone, above all the Russian Federation, to be true, honest and pure before their brothers in denouncing the crimes of Stalinism and the totalitarian Soviet Union,' Yushchenko told a crowd in Kyiv who had brought flowers and symbolic gifts of bread to place beside the Holodomor monument in 2008. 'We were all together in the same hell. We reject the brazen lie that we are blaming any one people for our tragedy. This is untrue. There is one criminal: the imperial, communist Soviet regime.'[44]

Predatory Autocracy

Yushchenko had another reason to avoid antagonising Putin – the threat of a Russian invasion. In the wake of the supposedly Western-fomented Rose and Orange revolutions, Putin latched on to the idea that Russia's main role on the world stage was to create a 'multipolar' world and oppose the strategic hegemony of the US and its allies. The end of the Cold War, Putin told the Munich Security Conference in 2007, had left the world 'with live ammunition, figuratively speaking' in the form of 'ideological stereotypes, double standards, and other typical aspects of Cold

War bloc thinking'. Putin accused an unchallenged West of 'creating new divisions, new threats, and sowing chaos around the world ... it is a world in which there is one master, one sovereign.'

The Munich speech 'was the moment when there was no longer any doubt that Putin was a Russian imperialist', Poland's Foreign Minister Radosław Sikorski, who was in the room at the time, told me in 2022.[45] In fact, the speech was more nuanced. As well as attacking the US, Putin appealed to European leaders to step out of the US's shadow and make their own security arrangements with Russia.

But if Putin had hoped that his aggressive rhetoric would curb the desire of Russia's nervous neighbours to join NATO he was very wrong. At NATO's summit in Bucharest in April 2008, Georgia lobbied hard to be allowed to accelerate its path to membership with a formal Membership Action Plan, or MAP. The United States and Poland were in favour. Others, led by Germany and France, refused, fearing the decision would anger Russia, and a MAP for Georgia was rejected. But NATO did, fatefully, issue a special communiqué that assured the Georgians that they would eventually join the alliance once the requirements for membership were met.

Georgia's President Mikheil Saakashvili believed that NATO's woolly letter of intent would offer him the alliance's protection against Russian invasion. He was mistaken. In August of 2008, during the Beijing Olympics, Saakashvili launched an ill-judged attempt at a military takeover of South Ossetia, one of the tiny republics that had split from Georgia in the aftermath of the break-up of the USSR in 1992 and a de facto Russian protectorate ever since. Saakashvili had walked into a trap. In response to the Georgian mini-invasion, Russian forces rolled into South Ossetia and on, over the line of control, to within 40 kilometres of Tbilisi. NATO strongly condemned the invasion, but did nothing. Russian troops eventually retired to the pre-war border. But Moscow recognised both South Ossetia and its fellow breakaway

Republic of Abkhazia as independent states. It was a fatal blow to Georgia's NATO hopes, as the rules of the alliance precluded the membership of any states with unresolved border disputes.

Putin's next challenge was to stop Ukraine's drift towards NATO membership. His opportunity came at the end of Yushchenko's presidential term in 2010. Voters were angry and disappointed by the lack of any tangible benefits from the Orange Revolution. Orange candidate Yulia Tymoshenko had been tainted with allegations of corruption over her deals with Russia's Gazprom. Putin's hopes rested in Viktor Yanukovych, the pro-Moscow candidate whose attempt to rig the 2004 election had failed disastrously but who continued to enjoy wide support in Russian-speaking eastern and central Ukraine.

Yanukovych enjoyed a major advantage in the form of an election war chest of $150 million, which he used to hire American political consultants.[46] Chief among them was Paul Manafort, a veteran Republican Party campaign consultant, who would go on to be campaign manager for Donald Trump. Other Americans on the Yanukovych payroll included Manafort's long-time deputy Rick Gates (later Trump's deputy campaign manager), Tad Devine (who went on to manage the 2016 US presidential campaign of Senator Bernie Sanders) and Adam Strasberg (who had worked on Senator John Kerry's 2004 US presidential run). The high-powered American consultants proved more effective than the Russian spin doctors of 2004, winning Ukraine's 2010 presidential elections with 48.95 per cent of the vote compared with 45.47 per cent for Tymoshenko.[47]

In many ways, Yanukovych proved to be a president in Putin's own image. He rewrote the constitution by forcing parliament to yield more power to the presidency. In the summer of 2011 he jailed Tymoshenko for her gas deals with Russia. Yanukovych also engaged in massive corruption on the model of Putin's own entourage of bureaucrat-oligarchs. Yanukovych's son Aleksandr became one of the richest men in the country during his father's presidency, with his businesses winning nearly half of all state tenders in January 2014. And, according to financial records later painstakingly pieced together after an attempt by aides to destroy them, Yanukovych transferred up to $70 billion into foreign accounts held by members of his family and entourage. But Yanukovych differed from Putin in one crucial respect. His attachment to power and to the billions he was raking off from the Ukrainian economy would in time trump his loyalty to Moscow.

In autumn 2011 Putin was preparing to resume his presidency after a four-year hiatus, during which he had stepped aside in favour of Dmitry Medvedev after serving his constitutional maximum of two terms. Putin had ambitious plans for what opponents contemptuously referred to as his 'second Tsardom'. Among them was a Eurasian Union that Putin hoped would form a rival to the European Union. 'We are not talking of restoring in some way or another the USSR,' Putin wrote in a pre-election manifesto. 'We are proposing a model of powerful supra-national union which can become one of the poles of the modern world and with that play a role of an effective link between Europe and the dynamic Asia Pacific region.'[48]

The angry reaction to Putin's inevitable re-election in October 2011 took the Kremlin by surprise. A crowd 100,000 strong gathered on Moscow's Bolotnaya Square to protest against his return for power. Another, even larger demonstration in December filled Moscow's Academician Sakharov Prospekt, a venue named after the dissident physicist who had helped bring down the USSR. The mood of righteous indignation among the vast crowd reminded me strongly of Palace Square in St Petersburg in 1991. That comparison – as well as with the Rose and Orange revolutions – was not lost on Putin, who drew the line at a third protest at Bolotnaya Square, which was brutally dispersed by thousands of OMON paramilitary police. After the Bolotnaya protests 'everything changed' for Putin, said one of his former ministers.

He 'saw it as a Western plot to remove him from power ... a direct coup attempt'. It was a challenge that could only be answered by an 'aggressive – indeed armed – pushback' against democrats and Western agents both at home and in the near abroad.[49]

Tsar of Eurasia

Expanding Putin's Eurasian Union – intended to ultimately become a Russia-led economic, political and military anti-Western bloc – became an urgent Kremlin priority. But just like the Russian and Soviet empires before it, a Union that did not include Ukraine would be meaningless. Putin's close ally, Belarus's Aleksandr Lukashenko, signed up to a slightly rebranded version, now known as the Customs Union. So did Kazakhstan, whose gas pipeline dependence on Moscow gave its authoritarian president Nursultan Nazarbayev little choice but to agree.

But, as negotiations continued through 2012 and 2013, Yanukovych stubbornly refused to join. Though he had campaigned on closer ties to Russia and had been heavily backed by Moscow, the European Union had another, possibly better offer. Brussels suggested an association agreement that included a free economic zone between Ukraine and Europe, international investment, visa-free travel for Ukrainians to the EU and possible future membership. Crucially for Yanukovych, Europe's offer was incredibly popular among voters, and he opened formal negotiations.

In a conversation with Aleksei Venediktov, editor-in-chief of the Echo Moskvy radio station in 2000, Putin made a distinction between opponents and traitors. 'The enemy – you fight, look into his eyes, and shoot him,' Putin told Venediktov. 'Then you can sign a peace agreement and start to be friends. An enemy is someone noble. But a traitor will shoot you in the back with no mercy.'[50] Yanukovych, by talking to the EU, had by Putin's definition become a traitor.

On 27 June 2013 Putin visited Kyiv to celebrate the anniversary of the baptism of Rus' – the last time he would visit Ukraine. 'We are all spiritual heirs of what happened here 1,025 years ago,' Putin told a Kyivan audience. 'And in this sense we [Ukrainians and Russians] are, without a doubt, one people.'[51] It was an utterly tone-deaf statement, heard by millions of ethnic Ukrainians as a denial of their culture, history and language. Putin showed equal contempt for Ukraine's president, spending a total of 15 minutes with Yanukovych. He spent the rest of his two-day visit with his old friend Viktor Medvedchuk at his luxurious Crimean dacha in the Crimea – which just nine months later would be overrun by Putin's troops.[52]

Coming up with a Russian counter-offer that Yanukovych could not refuse was the job Putin handed to his economic adviser Sergei Glazyev. The carrot was a $15 billion loan to save the cash-strapped and corruption-ridden Ukrainian government from imminent default.[53] The stick was a ban on Ukrainian imports into Russia that would cripple the economy.[54] The plans were leaked to the Ukrainian press in August 2013, and caused a sensation.

Public support for signing the EU's Association Agreement skyrocketed after Glazyev's ham-handed attempt to force Ukraine into rejecting it. Yanukovych was under strong pressure to make a final choice. Just a week before a signing ceremony scheduled to coincide with the EU summit in Vilnius on 28 November 2013, Yanukovych announced that he'd asked the EU for a delay.

On the eve of the summit Yanukovych attended the birthday party of Ukrainian oligarch Igor Surkis, the owner of the soccer club Dynamo Kyiv and a business partner and friend of Medvedchuk's.[55] Other guests included many of Ukraine's top oligarchs, including Dmitry Firtash and Igor Kolomoisky, all members of a self-described 'Ukraine management committee' set up in the wake of the Orange Revolution. Yanukovych announced to the assembled oligarchs that he was cancelling the European integration project altogether. 'All Yanukovych's supporters were shocked' that Yanukovych had reversed himself so completely on the issue of EU integration, wrote Kyiv investigative journalist Sonia Koshkina. Members of his Party of the Regions who had publicly questioned the EU agreement had been excluded from the party and expelled from parliament. Some had even been prosecuted. Now Yanukovych himself had changed his mind.[56]

EU leaders, too, were shocked when Yanukovych not only refused to sign the EU agreement in Vilnius but also proposed that Russia join the talks. 'I'd like you to listen to me,' Yanukovych was overheard telling German Chancellor Angela Merkel and Lithuanian president Dalia Grybauskaite. 'For three and a half years I've been alone. I've been face-to-face with a very strong Russia on a very un-level playing field.'[57] In the end Yanukovych, caught in an impossible bind, would sign neither the EU Association Agreement nor join the Eurasian Economic Union.

Winter on Fire

A small group of protesters, mostly students, had camped out on Kyiv's Independence Square on the evening that Yanukovych first announced the delay to the signing. Over the next week the protesters were joined by others, mobilised by social media. Yanukovych, fearing a repeat of the Orange Revolution, ordered riot police to disperse the students on the Maidan on the night of 30 November. The brutal attack left dozens hospitalised – and had precisely the opposite effect to the one Yanukovych had intended. The next day more than half a million Kyivans, some of them parents and relatives of the students beaten by the police, showed up on the Maidan. They would not disperse for 96 days of escalating confrontation and violence.

What Ukrainians were later to call the Revolution of Dignity brought together diverse political forces, from liberals in mainstream parties to radicals and nationalists. What had begun as a demand to join Europe turned into another – the third in as many decades – of Ukraine's people power revolutions. In its wake Putin and his propagandists would call it a Western-sponsored 'coup'. The most symbolic moment of alleged US meddling, endlessly repeated by Kremlin TV, would be when US Assistant Secretary of State Victoria Nuland and Senator John McCain visited Kyiv on 16 December and Nuland distributed cookies to the Maidan protesters.

'We are here to support your just cause – the sovereign right of Ukraine to determine its own destiny freely and independently,' McCain told cheering crowds who waved EU and US flags. 'And the destiny you seek lies in Europe.'[58] The fact that McCain was then in opposition to the administration of Barack Obama was lost on both the crowd and on the Kremlin. What they heard was that the US was with the protesters in their struggle with Russia.

McCain's speech was denounced as a 'crude intervention in Ukraine's politics' by Russian Prime Minister Dmitry Medvedev. 'Yanukovych's mistakes were compounded by Washington's provocations,' Putin's spokesman Dmitry Peskov told Russian political writer Mikhail Zygar. Americans 'flew in with money, while day and night there were lights in all the windows. Everything played out according to plan. It was a direct challenge to Russia's security.'[59]

In response to the supposed US interference, the Kremlin was preparing an even cruder intervention of its own. Russian military advisers began to arrive in Kyiv, as well as snipers and paramilitary police officers experienced in crushing street protests. In mid-January 2014, after weeks of peaceful protest, bloody clashes began between government-hired thugs – *titushki* or provocateurs – on the one hand and protesters on the other. Activists occupied the Trade Unions Building on Independence Square and began building barricades that would reach three storeys tall. Instead of helping Yanukovych, the escalation marked what Peskov would later describe as 'an uncontrollable descent'.

More apparent evidence of American perfidy came on 15 February, when the US and Russia faced off in an ice-hockey match at the Winter Olympics in Sochi. Ice hockey had long been a personal obsession of Putin's and he regularly played matches with his closest advisers. Sochi, too, was the most expensive Winter Olympics ever staged by a factor of ten. The Sochi games were Putin's pride – as was Russia's Olympic ice hockey team. With the crucial US–Russia game tied at 2–2 in overtime, Russian forward Fyodor Tyutin scored a third goal. But American referee Bradley Mayer disallowed it because the net had become dislodged. To Putin's fury, Russia lost the penalty shootout, and the game.[60] 'It's a pity that the referee didn't notice the dislodged net earlier, because it always helps the defending team if the ref can't see it,' complained Putin to journalists with his characteristic blend of passive-aggressive understatement. 'But referees make mistakes, so I'm not going to pin the blame, but simply say that we were the better side.'[61] American hypocrisy and cheating had once again, to Putin's mind, been revealed.

The violence on the Maidan reached its peak on 18 February 2014, when a crowd 20,000 strong attempted to march on the parliament building. Protesters also stormed the headquarters of Yanukovych's Party of Regions headquarters on Lypska Street. Yanukovych and his Russian advisers decided that the time had come to crush the revolt by any means necessary. Medvedchuk and the Kremlin played a crucial role in Yanukovych's decision making. According to Ukrainian intelligence phone intercepts Medvedchuk and Yanukovych spoke 54 times between December 2013 and February 2014.[62]

Members of the Berkut paramilitary police force – modelled on Putin's OMON and its leadership dominated by supporters of Yanukovych – opened fire with rubber bullets and shotguns. Later, snipers opened fire with high-powered military rifles on crowds in the Maidan itself. Over the next three days, at least 77 people died – nine police officers and 68 protesters.[63] According to an investigation conducted later by the Ukrainian Security Service, the snipers who opened fire on the Maidan and killed dozens of people had come from Russia.

Throne of Bayonets

Europe, alarmed, sent the foreign ministers of Germany, France and Poland – Frank-Walter Steinmeier, Laurent Fabius and Radosław Sikorski – to attempt to defuse the crisis. Putin sent the recently retired Russian ombudsman for human rights, Vladimir Lukin, as his official representative, as well as Vladislav Surkov as his unofficial one.

The Kremlin had also begun to prepare for a total breakdown of Yanukovych's rule. On 18 February, as police in Kyiv moved to disperse the protesters on the Maidan, Moscow transferred Russian special forces from the southern port city of Novorossysk to reinforce the garrison at the Russian Black Sea Fleet's base in Sevastopol. Two days later, the 25,000 Russian troops in Crimea received an order from the Kremlin to stand by to blockade Ukrainian military installations across the peninsula in order to 'prevent bloodshed' between protesting pro-Russian and pro-Kyiv groups on the peninsula – though no such clashes had yet taken place. For the moment, Russian troops remained in their barracks as the Kremlin waited to see if talks between Yanukovych, opposition leaders and EU foreign ministers would succeed.

On the evening of 20 February an emergency session of the Rada, Ukraine's parliament – with a very narrow quorum after the Communist Party of Ukraine and some 80 per cent of the Party of Regions had boycotted the session – voted 236 to 2 to condemn the recent violence, ban the use of weapons against protesters, and withdraw troops and the police deployed against them. Commanders of the Interior Troops, the Armed Forces of Ukraine, the SBU and other government agencies were banned from carrying out any 'counter-terrorism operations'. Yanukovych's closest allies had little faith that the talks with the opposition could save their boss or their own backsides. On 20 February, the day the EU delegation arrived in Kyiv, 64 private planes bearing government officials and their families, cash and valuables departed from the city's Borispil International Airport.[64]

Over two days of tense negations between Yanukovych, the EU and representatives of the parliamentary opposition, a deal was brokered whereby Yanukovych would remain in power until new elections in December. Yanukovych had kept in constant touch with Putin throughout, telephoning the Kremlin just before signing the deal designed to keep him in power at least until the end of the year.

Vitali Klitschko, former world heavyweight champion boxer and prominent parliamentary opposition leader, took to the stage on the Maidan to try to sell the idea of delayed elections that he and other opposition figures had struck with Yanukovych to the tens of thousands of protesters still gathered there. But the crowd had different ideas. 'Our leaders shake hands with murderers!' shouted opposition activist Volodymyr Parasyuk, pointing accusingly at Klitschko. 'Shame on you! No more Yanukovych. If by 10 a.m. tomorrow our politicians do not call for Yanukovych's immediate resignation, I swear we will storm the government!' The Maidan crowd began chanting, 'Criminals out!' At that moment coffins containing the bodies of several protesters killed in the previous days' violence were brought out onto the square, and all the opposition leaders, including Klitschko, knelt down.[65]

The following morning all Berkut forces withdrew from central Kyiv, effectively leaving Yanukovych and his remaining supporters undefended. At least 70 top Berkut officers fled to Donbas, fearing reprisals. Yanukovych called Putin to confirm that he had signed an agreement – and intended to leave Kyiv for the relative safety of Russian-speaking Kharkiv.

'You're going *where*?' Putin shouted at Yanukovych, according to a senior Kremlin official interviewed by Zygar. 'Sit still! Your country is out of control. Kyiv is at the mercy of gangs and looters. Are you insane?'

'Everything is under control,' Yanukovych replied.

'I never imagined that he was such a cowardly piece of shit,' Putin told aides.[66]

With parliament against him, the riot police gone from downtown Kyiv and the centre of the city in the hands of the Maidan protesters, Yanukovych retreated with his mistress Lyubov Polezhay to his private suburban palace of Mezhyhirya outside the capital. Security camera footage showed that Yanukovych's staff had spent the previous three days removing valuables into a fleet of cars and minibuses.

At the same time pro-Yanukovych elements in Ukraine's military and SBU security service were preparing a major military counter-offensive to take back Kyiv, mobilising units from eastern Ukraine to the capital. Military officers in strongly pro-Yanukovych Crimea decided to ignore the Rada's ban on the use of force against protesters and despatched a major force – including Ukraine's 25th Airborne Brigade, the 1st Marine Brigade, the 831st Anti-sabotage Unit and the 2nd Marine Spetsnaz – from Kozachia Bay in Sevastopol, headquarters of the Ukrainian Black Sea Fleet, to Kyiv. The units' command was transferred to the SBU for an 'anti-terrorist' operation against the Maidan protesters.[67]

They were too late. Faced with a choice of fighting a shooting war against the protesters in Kyiv and escape to his electoral heartland of eastern Ukraine, Yanukovych chose escape. 'Yanukovych is a hated figure in Ukraine today,' said political consultant Olesya Yakhno. 'But he deserves credit for choosing not to start a civil war. He realised that the only way he could stay in power was on a throne of Russian bayonets. He decided there had already been too much blood.'[68]

On the evening of 21 February Yanukovych summoned the head of his administration, the speaker of the Verkhovna Rada and the remaining Party of Regions deputies to his suburban residence at Mezhyhirya for a farewell dinner. Rybak came to tender his resignation. The rest agreed that a separatist congress would be held in Kharkiv. Over dinner Yanukovych discussed the idea of breaking up Ukraine if Kyiv refused to grant the eastern provinces sufficient independence.

'What could we call this new country?' Yanukovych asked his closest political allies, according to an eyewitness interviewed by journalist Sonia Koshkina.

'China,' joked one of them.

'There already is a China,' replied another.

'Are you all making fun of me?' fumed Yanukovych. The idea of an independent eastern Ukraine still seemed, even to its most powerful political leaders, absurd.[69]

After dinner, Yanukovych and his remaining loyalists boarded a fleet of jeeps and drove to Kharkiv. Hours later, a vast crowd of protesters arrived at the gates of Mezhyhirya, intending to storm the palace that symbolised the corruption of the old regime.

CHAPTER 3
THE BLEEDING IDOLS

We respect the Ukrainian language and traditions.
We respect Ukrainians' desire to see their country free,
safe and prosperous.

Vladimir Putin, 'On the historical unity
of Russians and Ukrainians',
July 2021[1]

'This is what a revolution looks like'

Many of the protesters who arrived at Yanukovych's Mezhyhirya residence on the morning of 22 February 2014 had come straight from the barricades of the Maidan. They still wore their make-shift protesters' outfits of miners' hard hats, Soviet steel helmets on top of thick woollen watch caps, motley camouflage and work uniforms. They carried batons, steel riot shields, hunting rifles. They found the gates unlocked. The 650-strong garrison, drawn from the same Berkut paramilitary police who had tried and failed to clear the protesters from the Maidan by force, had, along with their master, fled into the night.

The protestors found a vast palace complex that officially never existed. On paper, Yanukovych's official presidential residence was a small nearby wooden dacha known, modestly enough, as the House on Stumps.

The property at Mezhyhirya was listed as an administrative office of the president's Dubai-based company, Tantalit. In reality, Yanukovych commissioned the complex soon after coming to power in 2010 as a lavish private estate. The main residence was a three-storey wooden building built in Germany and transported in pieces to Kyiv for assembly. Perhaps because of its oddly pre-fabricated appearance, the house earned the nickname 'Honka' after the Finnish maker of budget ready-made log cabins.

The interiors were anything but cut-price. Even the inside of the lift was covered in mosaics and mirrors. The ground floor was paved in Florentine-style *pietro duro* cut stonework. The ground-floor suite of rooms was decorated in neo-medieval style, including reproduction suits of armour, oak neo-Gothic panelling and mosaics of chivalric scenes on the walls. In the personal suite of the president's mistress the soft oak parquet of her dressing-room floor was a sea of small dents left by her stiletto heels. Lyubov Polezhay had abandoned a large pile of paperback romantic novels, including one entitled *Why Do We Need Men?* Many had been chewed, apparently by a small lapdog. She'd also left her pedigree cat, which had shat on the carpets and upholstery after it was locked in the room.

In President Yanukovych's bedroom suite lay a dozen handmade shoe trees, without shoes, all with identical wooden patches corresponding to the president's bunions. In the library was an extensive collections of world literary classics, from Machiavelli to Schopenhauer, apparently never opened, though a selection of paperbacks on Russian sport were well thumbed. I considered personally liberating an English translation of Yanukovych's book *The Road to Success*, but doubted that his advice would prove very useful. In the Gothic-panelled private film theatre were his and hers matching brown leather massage chairs and a large collection of DVDs and Blu-Ray discs, including *Run Fatboy Run*.

In the grounds was a private zoo containing ostriches and exotic birds, a golf course, a large collection of vintage motorcycles, cars and boats, and a dog-breeding centre with a veterinary surgical theatre and canine exercise machines. Most significantly, floating in the water by a lakeside dining room built in the shape of a pirate ship were thousands of documents. Later recovered by protesters and volunteer divers, the cache included receipts for cash bribes, files on opposition journalists and records of the president's private meetings, including with Vladimir Putin in Moscow.

Yulia Kapica, a financial analyst from Berdyansk, spent the first days after the Maidan fishing documents from the lake and drying them out on the palace's marble floors with hairdryers, then scanning them and sending the material to the Ministry of Finance and the police. 'For me the Maidan wasn't about the EU agreement but about getting our people to discover their Ukrainian identity,' said Kapica, a 30-something blonde who had become one of the self-appointed 'people's guardians' of the palace, which would later open officially as a Museum of Corruption. She wore her hair in a traditional Ukrainian braid held up with a hairband of blue and yellow plastic flowers. 'Before the Maidan people were ashamed to be Ukrainians. After they were proud. They had stood up for themselves.'

Petya, a 34-year-old grocery salesman from Lviv, scuttled down the long, echoing corridors of the palace with a prim, clockwork gait organising rosters of volunteers to look after the abandoned property. He wore a traditional embroidered Ukrainian peasant shirt and the red-and-black flag of Stepan Bandera's UPA draped over his shoulders. 'This is what a revolution looks like,' he said, peering out of the window at crowds of Kyivans who had come to gawk at the *ancien regime*'s excesses.[2]

By the morning of 22 February Yanukovych had reached Kharkiv. There he learned that his beloved Mezhyhirya had been seized by a crowd. He recorded a televised address in which he described the Maidan revolution as 'gangsterism, vandalism, and a coup d'état'.[3] Then he drove to the Kharkiv Palace of Sport for the planned congress. As he got out of his jeep and walked towards the doors he received a call on his mobile. Pro-Maidan soccer fans had broken through the cordon around the building and were about to storm the congress. Yanukovych turned around, got back into his car and drove four hours south to Donetsk Airport where his Falcon jet awaited. But Donetsk air-traffic controllers refused to clear his plane's flight plan to Rostov, in south Russia. He once again got in his car and headed to the coast of Crimea, where he was picked up by a Russian helicopter.[4]

While crowds wandered through the fallen president's bedroom at Mezhyhirya, an atmosphere of high tension prevailed at Putin's suburban residence of Novo-Ogarevo. The decisions taken by Putin over the 24 hours after Yanukovych's flight from Kyiv would lay the foundations not just for the annexation of Crimea but also for the invasion of 2022.

Putin 'invited the leaders of our special services and the defence ministry to the Kremlin' on the evening of 23 February, he told Andrei Kondrashov, a journalist with state-run channel Rossiya-1. In attendance were the closest members of Putin's inner circle – Defence Minister Sergei Shoigu, Security Council secretary Nikolai Patrushev, FSB head Aleksandr Bortnikov and his chief of staff Sergei Ivanov, according to a Kremlin press pool source.[5] The first item on the agenda was to 'set them the task of saving the life of the president of Ukraine, who would simply have been liquidated', Putin told Rossiya-1. The second item was a military takeover of Crimea – supposedly to protect the local population from 'anti-Russian' violence by pro-Maidan elements.

Nikolai Patrushev and Sergei Ivanov, backed by FSB head Aleksandr Bortnikov, told Putin that private polls conducted by the Federal Protective Service showed that the Crimean population overwhelmingly supported joining Russia. They also argued that the Ukrainian state was effectively leaderless, with the remaining elements of government split between pro- and anti-Yanukovych forces. There was no commander-in-chief to authorise Ukraine's military to defend Crimea. And in any case both the Ukrainian military and security services were themselves split between pro- and anti-Russian factions – thanks in part to major influence and bribery operations by Moscow's own secret services. Shoigu, however, was more cautious, listing arguments against that included the possibility of NATO involvement and international economic sanctions.[6] He also pointed out that there was no concrete military or political plan for the takeover or its political aftermath, meaning that major strategic decisions would have to be made on the fly.

After hours of discussion, the hawks – led by Patrushev and Putin himself – prevailed. 'We finished about seven in the morning,' Putin told Channel One in 2015. 'When we were parting, I told all my colleagues, "We are forced to begin the work of returning Crimea to Russia."' Putin was misremembering. In fact, it would be weeks before the Kremlin finally decided that Crimea would become a part of Russia rather than a notionally independent puppet state like South Ossetia and Abkhazia.

Despite his earlier objections it was Shoigu, as defence minister, who was handed responsibility for the operation to take over Crimea. He was told to proceed with 'extreme caution'.[7] Hours later, Shoigu despatched his old friend and long-serving deputy Vice-Admiral Oleg Belaventsev as his political envoy to Sevastopol. The operation to take Crimea was under way.

Empire, Defence or Opportunism?

Boris Yeltsin first threatened to take back Crimea from Ukraine in the aftermath of the Rada's declaration of independence from the USSR as early as August 1991. Ultra-nationalist firebrand

Vladimir Zhirinovsky had periodically raised the issue in the nineties, as did politically ambitious Moscow mayor Yury Luzhkov as he manoeuvred, unsuccessfully, to succeed Yeltsin in 1999. But retaking Crimea had never formed part of Putin's rhetoric. A deal to build a bridge across the Kerch Strait to connect southern Russia and Crimea had originally been signed by Yanukovych and Medvedev in 2010. But in the intervening four years Moscow had shown so little interest in the bridge project – or indeed in Crimea in general – that no feasibility study was undertaken. Nor had independence from Ukraine ever been a particularly popular or important issue in Crimea itself. Yanukovych's pro-Moscow Party of the Regions had enjoyed strong support, but overtly pro-independence parties polled less than 5 per cent of the vote.

Between his successful annexation of Crimea in 2014 and his full-scale invasion of Ukraine eight years later, Putin would indeed develop something of an obsession both with mystical nationalism and historical justifications for Russia's imperial greatness. But Moscow's policies and behaviour towards Crimea before the final crisis of 22–27 February 2014 strongly suggest that the Kremlin's priority was to retain Russian influence over the whole of Ukraine rather than carve off pieces of the country. It was only in midwinter 2013–14, as Yanukovych was visibly losing his grip on power, that the idea of actually taking over Crimea began to circulate in the Kremlin.

Vladimir Konstantinov, chairman of Crimea's regional parliament, laid the groundwork. As the Maidan crisis gathered strength in Kyiv, Konstantinov made several trips to Moscow. In December 2013 he attended a meeting of Russia's Security Council, chaired by Putin's closest ally Nikolai Patrushev, former head of the FSB and the Kremlin's top security official. Konstantinov told Patrushev that Crimea would be ready to 'go to Russia' if Yanukovych were overthrown. According to journalist Mikhail Zygar, Patrushev was 'pleasantly surprised' by the news. In late January a policy paper written by Orthodox billionaire Konstantin Malofeev – of whom we will hear more later – outlining the practicalities of a takeover of Crimea began to circulate among the Kremlin's top advisers. The document, obtained in February 2015 by *Novaya Gazeta*, provided the Russian government with a strategy in the event of Yanukovych's removal and the break-up of Ukraine – and also outlined plans for annexing Crimea and the eastern portions of the country that were closely matched by actual events. Malofeev and his co-authors also outlined plans for a public relations campaign to justify Russian actions.[8]

Putin would later explain the Crimean operation as a preemptive strike against the possibility that Ukraine's new government might join NATO, resulting in Russia's Black Sea Fleet losing its historic headquarters in Sevastopol. Putin had 'heard declarations from Kyiv about Ukraine soon joining NATO', he told Russian TV. But in fact such an outcome was, in 2014, highly unlikely. The UK, French and Germans' clear refusal to advance Kyiv or Tbilisi's applications for NATO membership in 2008 had been reinforced by Putin's subsequent invasion of Georgia. And the election of Yanukovych had put Ukraine's NATO ambitions not only on the back burner but made them actually illegal after a law barring Ukraine from participation in any military bloc was passed in 2010.

True, Ukraine under Yanukovych had indeed continued to participate in some NATO military exercises and contributed a ship to NATO anti-piracy operations. But if Putin was urgently concerned about NATO expansion, he failed to mention it to the Americans. Michael McFaul, who served as US President Barack Obama's special assistant on Russia from 2009 to 2012 and as the US ambassador in Moscow from 2012 to early 2014, was present for all but one of the meetings between Obama and Putin or Dmitry Medvedev and also listened in on all the phone conversations Obama had with the Kremlin. McFaul could not 'recall once that the issue of NATO expansion came up' during any of those exchanges.[9] The sudden overthrow of Yanukovych and the likelihood of a strongly pro-Western government succeeding him was indeed a strategic concern for the future. But there was no likelihood, much less a clear and present danger, of NATO's accepting Ukraine's membership on the eve of Putin's Crimea operation. Top Russian officials 'weren't afraid of Ukraine joining NATO', a senior military source told UCLA Professor Daniel Treisman at a meeting of the Kremlin-sponsored Valdai discussion club in 2015. 'But they were definitely worried that the Ukrainians would cancel [Russia's] lease on Sevastopol and kick out the Black Sea Fleet.'[10]

But the events of February and March 2014 suggest a third – and most convincing – explanation for Putin's decision. His takeover of Crimea was opportunistic, unplanned and based on a snap assessment of fast-moving events. As Putin told Treisman in October 2015, the operation to seize the peninsula was 'spontaneous' and was 'not at all' planned in advance.[11] The decision came first, the justification later.

The Chinese ideogram for 'crisis' is, as Winston Churchill most famously remarked, a combination of the characters meaning 'danger' and 'opportunity'. For the men assembled in the Kremlin that February night, the danger was the supposed threat to the future of Sevastopol. The opportunity was the chaos in Kyiv that meant that Russia had to strike immediately or not at all.

Betrayal

As well as calculated opportunism, powerful emotion was at work too in the form of anger at the West's supposed treachery. Yanukovych had, under pressure from the Kremlin, done everything the NATO foreign ministers had asked of him – and nonetheless been deposed. 'He signed an agreement, ordered the withdrawal of the police, and remained in the country,' an indignant Peskov told Zygar in 2015. 'The European mediators promised to guarantee the implementation of the agreement. What happened was simply appalling and absolutely unprecedented.'[12]

For Putin – unable, after a lifetime in the KGB, to imagine that an angry crowd might act spontaneously rather than on the orders of some higher puppet-masters – the Maidan's victory was a personal turning point. Putin had spent the first 14 years of his career playing on the West's terms. He had dutifully shown up at G8 summits, even proudly hosted one in his native St Petersburg. He had regularly spoken to Western leaders, constantly arguing Russia's demands for its security interests not to be ignored. And yet Russia – and Putin personally – had been repeatedly ignored and, to his mind, humiliated.

'Putin always behaved like an uncouth provincial invited to dinner by his aristocratic relatives,' said a source who has known Putin as a close family friend since childhood. 'He was delighted to be at the table, but angry that he thought people were looking down on him.'[13] Putin himself had confirmed his deep sense of personal grievance in a 2007 interview with *Time* magazine after the US publication had made him 'Person of the Year'. 'Sometimes one gets the impression that America does not need friends. Sometimes we get the impression that you need some kind of auxiliary subjects to take command of,' said Putin. To Americans, Russians 'are a little bit savage still or they just climbed down from the trees, you know, and probably need to have their hair brushed and their beards trimmed. And have the dirt washed out of their beards and hair.'[14] In the wake of the West's supposed perfidy over the Maidan, the time had finally come to show that Russians were not savages, but a country that was determined to command respect. When Echo Moskvy editor-in-chief Aleksei Venediktov suggested to Putin that the annexation of Crimea had violated international law, Putin's response was telling. 'Unfair, is it? But was it right?' Putin told Venediktov. 'Crimea is Russian by its nature. So it was the right thing to do.'[15]

Everything that would later precipitate Putin's 2022 invasion – the fear of foreign encroachment, the anger at Western hypocrisy, the imperial ambition – fell into place in the hours and days that followed Yanukovych's fall. For Putin, the real target of the Western powers who had supposedly orchestrated the Maidan's victory was not Yanukovych but Putin himself. The Maidan 'was a direct threat to Russia,' Peskov told Zygar. The West's 'goal was to get rid of Putin. They do not like him. Russia is too obstinate under Putin and unwilling to make concessions. They are ready to do anything to get rid of him. We sensed this even before Ukraine, but afterward it was a different matter. After Ukraine the diplomatic masks came off. Before that, the confrontation was wrapped up in diplomatic plastic wrap, but now the plastic wrap was removed.'[16] From 23 February 2014 on, Putin considered himself at war with the collective West.

Crimea Is Ours!

Vice-Admiral Oleg Belaventsev arrived at Simferopol airport in Crimea around midday on 23 February. A long-time aide to Russian Defence Minister Sergei Shoigu, Belaventsev was both a naval officer and – like Putin, Patrushev, Bortnikov and Ivanov – a former career KGB officer. He had served as a spy in the Soviet embassy in London and later managed various controversial businesses connected to Shoigu.[17] For all his skills as an intelligence officer, military commander, Kremlin insider and bureaucrat-businessman, Belaventsev had little experience of Crimea's political scene. After considering and rejecting two veteran Crimean politicians he eventually found the man he was looking for to lead Crimea out of Ukraine and into Russia.

Sergey Aksyonov, leader of the little-known Russian Unity party in Crimea, was not an old-school machine politician but a former boxer and pro-Russian businessman universally known by his underworld nickname 'Goblin'. 'The speaker of the Crimean parliament told me [that Aksyonov is] our Che Guevara,' Putin told Russian TV the following year. 'Just what we needed.' Aksyonov would be the first of a long series of underworld bosses hired by the Kremlin to secure its new territories in Ukraine.

To help install Aksyonov in power, 'advisers' were despatched to Simferopol from the FSB and the GRU, Russia's military intelligence service. Among them was Igor Girkin, a former FSB officer and enthusiastic military re-enactor, who under his new nom-de-guerre Igor Strelkov ('Igor the Shooter') would soon go rogue and begin his own private war in Donbas. An emergency meeting of Crimea's parliament was swiftly called for 26 February. Deputies who refused to attend were kidnapped from their homes by plainclothes FSB officers and frog-marched to the session by force. As rumours spread that Crimea's Supreme Council was going to ask Putin to accept the province into the Russian Federation, scuffles broke out outside the parliament building. Russians – reinforced by plainclothes FSB men – had come out in support, Crimean Tatars in protest. Two people were killed in the ensuing fight – one crushed, the other dying of a heart attack.

Shoigu now had his excuse to move in, ostensibly to prevent further unrest. Overnight ten Russian military aircraft landed in Simferopol carrying paratroopers from the 76th Guards Division based in Pskov.[18] By the following morning, servicemen in Russian uniforms without insignia had seized Crimea's regional parliament and other key government buildings. They occupied the peninsula's two airports and fanned out onto the streets of Simferopol and Sevastopol. Putin and Shoigu publicly and repeatedly denied that they were Moscow's troops. 'Anyone can buy

Russian uniforms in a shop,' Putin told Russian TV with his trademark smirk. The state-run Russian media, taking the cue, delightedly dubbed the mysterious troops 'little green men' and 'polite people'.

On 28 February another Russian Il-76 military transport aircraft landed at Simferopol bearing civilian volunteers. They would prove a far more dangerous cargo than the Russian elite troops who had preceded them. The first 170 Russian volunteers were mostly veterans of Afghanistan and Chechnya, as well as athletes, members of motorcycle gangs and 'patriotic clubs'. They had been mobilised by Duma member Franz Klintsevich, leader of the Veterans of Afghanistan Union and a long-time friend of Shoigu. Like the FSB/GRU teams flown in a few days earlier, their task was not fight but to play the part of ordinary Crimeans, protesting and demanding that Russia retake control of the peninsula.

In all, the takeover took just four days. It was quick, relatively bloodless (the exception being a handful of opposition activists who were kidnapped, beaten and murdered) and largely supported by the population. But even with Crimea under Russian military control, Putin hesitated. Despite what he later told Russian TV, Putin did not make the decision to 'return Crimea to Russia' on 23 February. Indeed when Crimea's parliament voted on 27 February to hold a referendum on 25 May the choice was to be between the current status quo or to make Crimea 'a self-sufficient state ... that is part of Ukraine on the basis of treaties and agreements'.

On the night of 1–2 March Putin spoke to Obama for an hour and a half. 'What cannot be done is for Russia, with impunity, to put its soldiers on the ground and violate basic principles that are recognized around the world,' Obama later told reporters. The US threatened to boycott a G8 summit in Sochi, scheduled for June, and also to take 'diplomatic steps' to 'isolate Russia'.[19] Not for the last time, Putin found himself trapped by the momentum of his own military operation. Independence for Crimea within Ukraine would mean the return of Kyiv's troops and withdrawal of Russian ones – a humiliating climb-down in the face of a scolding from the US president. That, Putin refused to countenance.

Putin – again not for the last time – also found himself a prisoner of the patriotic propaganda that exploded in Russia's media. 'The euphoria over Crimea was so intense,' recalled Katya Bondarenko, a senior editor of a Russian state-run TV network. 'Crimea was where we spent our childhood holidays. Every Russian citizen over a certain age knew and loved it. It was like our Russian paradise, regained.' Even longstanding critics of Putin found themselves agreeing that Crimea was indeed 'ours'. 'For 20 years we [Russians] had been ignored and mocked all over the world,' said Bondarenko. 'Now Russia was finally standing up. People in the newsroom were crying. It was incredibly emotional.' Putin's rating soared past 87 per cent. Cars full of people waving Russian flags drove around Moscow's Garden Ring, tooting their horns. The Russian people were ecstatic. Putin was their leader. He had to follow them.

At a press conference on 4 March Putin publicly denied that Russia was planning to annex Crimea, though in fact the decision to do exactly that had already been made. Putin prepared the ground by talking about Kosovo, the Yugoslav province that had gained independence after NATO's 1999 bombing of Belgrade. 'Nobody has ruled out nations' right to self-determination,' he told reporters. Decoded, what Putin meant was that while he indeed had no plans to annex Crimea, he would accept Crimea's request to join Russia if its people wished to do so. It was a classic piece of Putin doublespeak, correct in letter but a gross lie in spirit.

By 16 March a hastily organised referendum duly showed that 96.77 per cent of Crimea's population supported joining Russia.

Two days later a formal treaty admitting Crimea to the Russian Federation was signed by Putin, a formula that he would repeat precisely in September 2022 when snap referendums in the occupied Ukrainian provinces of Luhansk, Donetsk, Kherson and Zaporizhzhiya were followed by swift annexation. A day after that came Putin's apotheosis, the Kremlin equivalent of a Roman emperor's formal triumph. In a carefully choreographed ceremony, the gold doors of the Kremlin's St George's Hall swung open to admit Putin, who strode confidently up a staircase lined by troops of the Kremlin's honour guard dressed in Napoleonic-era uniforms. Waiting for him were over a thousand members of Russia's political, military and cultural elite – every member of Russia's upper and lower houses of parliament, all its governors and a constellation of film stars and directors, sports celebrities, loyal journalists and artists, every one of them cheering and applauding.

In his speech, Putin squarely blamed NATO for forcing Russia to act. 'They are constantly trying to drive us into a corner because we have an independent position, because we maintain it and because we tell it like it is and don't engage in hypocrisy,' Putin said to wild applause that interrupted his speech 27 times – the final two standing ovations. 'But there is a limit to everything. And with Ukraine, our Western partners have crossed the line, playing the bear and acting irresponsibly and unprofessionally. They act as they please: here and there, they use force against sovereign states, building coalitions based on the principle "If you are not with us, you are against us" … NATO remains a military alliance, and we are against having a military alliance making itself at home right in our own backyard; in our historic territory.' In addition to this familiar litany of grievances, Putin also sounded a sinister new note. 'Some Western politicians are already threatening us with not just sanctions, but also the prospect of increasingly serious problems on the domestic front.' He then asked, 'I would like to know what it is they have in mind exactly. Action by a fifth column, some bunch of national traitors?' But Putin did add one important caveat, explicitly ruling out seizing more territory. 'Don't believe those who try to frighten you with Russia and who scream that other regions will follow after Crimea ... We do not need this.' His own later actions would show him to be a liar. In the same hall on 30 September 2022 Putin would convene a similar gathering of Russia's elite to approve his annexation of four more Ukrainian provinces that he said would, like Crimea, be 'forever part of Russia'.

After Putin concluded, the entire Grand Kremlin Palace arose in unison and began chanting 'Russia! Russia!' and 'Putin! Putin!' On his way out, Chechen president Ramzan Kadyrov was seen singing the Russian national anthem in a full-throated baritone. 'Right, what's next?' he joked to an acquaintance. 'Alaska?'[20]

A week later the United Nations General Assembly voted 100 to 11 to declare the Crimean referendum and annexation invalid. Clearly, Putin didn't care. The West also protested – but not very hard. Radosław Sikorski, Poland's outspoken foreign minister, called the annexation of Crimea an attempt 'to redraw the map of Europe along ethnic lines ... Europe is based on the principle of overcoming borders rather than redrawing them.' Sikorsky compared Putin directly to Hitler: 'No one has the unilateral right to move borders in response to presumed ethnic grievances. We've seen what happened when a European leader tried to do that before: the peoples of the Soviet Union paid one of the biggest prices for this.'

And yet the only concrete action taken by the US and the EU was the announcement of personal sanctions against a handful of Putin's closest associates. Just as in the wake of Putin's Georgian invasion, there were no serious immediate penalties for the Russian state or companies. And as Putin had predicted, the Western reaction to the annexation of Crimea would amount to little more than a gentle slap on the wrist.

The Bleeding Idols

Ukraine's Russian-speaking minority was shaken and angered by the flight of Yanukovych, who had styled himself their champion and protector. Large protests broke out in the cities Russian speakers called Lugansk, Kharkov, Odessa and Dnipropetrovsk, as well as in Donetsk. The crowds carried posters that said 'Berkut – Yes!' and 'No to Fascism!'[21] 'You had your Maidan in Kyiv,' recalled Donetsk University history student Sergei Fedorenko. 'This was our Maidan.'[22]

By early April 2014 it was clear that local self-rule – if not outright separatism and war – had strong support across the east and south of Ukraine. After a few uneasy weeks of relative calm that followed the Crimea operation, a small but violent pro-independence movement flared in the eastern Ukrainian cities of Slovyansk, Luhansk (Slavyansk and Lugansk to Russians) and Donetsk, led by irregular troops carrying a motley variety of weapons. They were very different from the disciplined, uniformed men without insignia – in fact Russian regular troops – who had been deployed across the Crimea. 'These men looked like a bunch of bandits,' remembered Sofia Ivleva, owner of a women's clothing store in downtown Donetsk, two blocks away from the headquarters of the local government. 'They arrived at the local administration building and told the guards to get lost. They wore cloths over their faces and resembled bank robbers.'[23]

The most prominent rebel leaders were Russian citizens with strong ties to Moscow's security services. Many had arrived in Ukraine as 'volunteers' flown in by Belaventsev in late February. Igor Girkin (aka Strelkov), who led the rebel takeover of Slovyansk, was a former FSB officer.

By Girkin's own account, the decision to launch an armed uprising in Donbas was his, not the Kremlin's. 'At first, nobody wanted to fight,' Girkin told the ultra-nationalist newspaper

Zavtra. 'I'm the one who pulled the trigger of war. If our squad hadn't crossed the border, it all would have ended [in failure] like [the abortive uprisings] in Kharkiv or Odesa. There would have been a few dozen killed, burned and arrested. And that would have ended everything. Our squad set the flywheel of war in motion. We reshuffled all the cards on the table.'

Girkin was lying. There was direction from Moscow, though not necessarily directly from Putin. In August 2016 Ukraine's SBU security services published telephone intercepts going back as far as February 2014 between Russian presidential adviser Sergei Glazyev and Konstantin Zatulin, the first deputy chairman of the Russian Duma's committee for the CIS.

'We have financed Kharkiv, financed Odesa,' Zatulin was overheard telling Glazyev. 'Small sums of two, three thousand ... I have four requests signed by [self-declared mayor of Sevastopol Aleksei] Chaly for fifty thousand.'

'So, you paid,' Glazyev answered. 'You have to make a cost estimate, I will give it to those [in charge], let them work on the estimate.'

Zatulin confirmed in an interview with Business FM Radio that the calls had indeed taken place, but said that the recordings had been 'taken out of context'.[24] In other calls Glazyev was recorded instructing newly installed Crimean leader Sergey Aksyonov on how to formulate the wording of the referendum. And, most seriously, the tapes revealed that Glazyev gave organisers on the ground direct instructions on how to mount armed coups against local authorities.

'Specially trained people should knock the *Banderovtsy* [Ukrainian neo-Nazis] out from the [Regional] Council building,' Glazyev told an activist from Odesa. 'Then they should arrange a meeting of the regional state administration, gather the executive authorities ... as it was done in Kharkiv. In Kharkiv people threw all *Banderovtsy* out, found the local arms depot and distributed [the weapons]. They will summon the Regional State

Administration and then will also appeal to our President [Putin].'[25] Glazyev repeatedly emphasised that the organisers should take great pains to maintain the appearance of demonstrations being 'local' and 'spontaneous'.[26] He also promised the local activists backup from Russia, including 'sending in our guys'.[27]

Of Glazyev's 'guys', it was Girkin who quickly became the highest-profile separatist leader thanks to his discipline and military bearing. With his clipped moustache, pressed fatigues and careful charm, Girkin styled himself on a pre-Revolutionary tsarist officer. He banned his 1,000-strong self-styled 'local defence force' from swearing and ordered two of his own men to be summarily executed for looting. Aleksander Borodai, a local businessman who had headed the Donetsk branch of the MMM pyramid scheme in the early 1990s, also mustered forces drawn from among the local mafia.

In Russian-speaking cities across Ukraine, popular support for the rebels – and anger at the interim government that had taken over after the Maidan – grew in the run-up to new presidential elections at the end of May. In Odesa an anti-Maidan camp had been set up on 26 January on Kulykove Pole in the centre of the city. On 2 May the tent camp was to be dismantled by agreement with local authorities. But instead a radical group of anti-Maidan protesters – among them activists who had earlier been in touch with Glazyev – took over the nearby House of Trade Unions. Running street battles broke out between rival factions, which the police did little to stop. A fire deliberately started on the ground floor of the Trade Unions building trapped hundreds of protesters inside. The inferno left 46 dead from smoke inhalation and gunshots.

In Donbas a series of inconclusive military skirmishes between rebels and freelance Ukrainian nationalist militias made it increasingly obvious that the separatist areas of Donetsk and Luhansk would only be brought back under Kyiv's rule by a full-scale military intervention. The newly elected president Petro Poroshenko – a chocolate magnate – announced an 'anti-terrorist operation' and began mobilising the army.

Fighting alongside the Ukrainian army were a collection of hastily formed 'patriotic people's militia battalions' drawn from the nationalist fighters who had been bloodied on the Maidan. 'The Battalions', as they were known, did some of the earliest and the hardest fighting. Essentially, they were private armies. Some were funded by Ukrainian businessmen like the prominent Dnipropetrovsk oligarch (and Jewish activist) Igor Kolomoisky, who backed a battalion called Dnipro-1 and another known as the Azov Battalion (later the Azov Regiment). Others were one-man shows, like Oleh Lyashko's ultra-nationalist Ukraine Battalion. Lyashko became notorious for touring eastern towns in an armoured truck, kidnapping local mayors and driving them around until they agreed to sign a pledge of loyalty to the Kyiv government. A few of the militias, like the armed wing of Right Sector, were the self-declared military wing of political parties. For the first months of the war all were outside the direct control of the Ukrainian government and military.

Many of the freelance battalions – including the ones financed by Kolomoisky – had links to Ukraine's far right. Ukrainian ultra-nationalist parties like Right Sector never gained more than low single figures in national elections. But their prominence on the battlefield spawned a myth that Russia would quickly weaponise – that the Kyiv government was dominated by 'fascist' forces. Right Sector 'began as an organisation which encompassed everyone from ultra-radicals to liberals,' explained the party's deputy chief Boroslav Bereza in a Kyiv cafe decorated in the black and red of Stepan Bandera's UPA. 'At the beginning there were plenty of "ultras" like White Hammer, the Tribune of Bandera, Patriots of Ukraine and so on. They were all organisations who wanted independence for Ukraine, and Right Sector united them. Some changed their philosophy to mainstream.

Some didn't – like White Hammer. They are not disciplined; they are not part of the Right Sector anymore.' To increase the ideological confusion, Bereza put his hand inside his shirt and pulled out a Star of David on a gold chain. 'I am a Jew but I am a Ukrainian Jew,' he told me. 'This is my motherland. I love her and want my kids to live here. Ukrainian fascism is an invention of Russian political technologists.'[28]

By June 2014 the Ukrainian army began to win back cities across Donbas, including Mariupol, which had been briefly occupied by the rebels the month before. Girkin evacuated Slovyansk on 5 July and retreated to Donetsk as the full-scale conflict he had done so much to provoke unfolded around him. Rebel leaders – including Girkin – began to bitterly criticise Putin for abandoning their bid for independence. In response the Kremlin sent heavy weapons operated by Russian troops temporarily 'discharged' from the army – including at least one Buk surface-to-air missile system. On 17 July, one day after the Buk had successfully downed a Ukrainian transport plane, the operators mistook a Malaysian Boeing 777 for a military aircraft and shot it down, killing all 298 people on board.

The wreckage of the airliner – tray tables, wheelie bags, in-flight magazines, overhead luggage lockers and fasten-your-seat-belt signs, toilet doors, the galley drinks tray, blankets, headphones, coats, jumpers and shoes – lay scattered over three villages. Walking through the remains of the aircraft was one of the most horrifying experiences of my twenty-five-year career spent in war zones. The West was outraged; the Kremlin lied barefacedly that the plane had been shot down by a Ukrainian jet. Harsher sanctions excluding Russian state companies from raising international financing followed – but not harsh enough to discourage Putin from ramping up his covert support for the Donbas rebels but without ever officially engaging the Russian army.

In July 2014 Ukrainian troops and rebels from the newly proclaimed Donetsk People's Republic, or DNR, fought pitched battles around a giant Soviet war monument at Savur-Mohila, some 65 kilometres east of Donetsk. In 1943 this strategic height on the Donets Ridge – the site of a prehistoric burial ground, hence its name, the 'Barrow of Savur' – had been the scene of titanic battles between the Germans and the advancing Red Army. Over 150,000 Soviet troops were buried in a mass grave there. Their sacrifice was commemorated in 1963 by a 300-metre-high concrete obelisk decorated with a larger than life bronze statue of a Soviet warrior. The monument was blasted to pieces by Ukrainian warplanes and rebel howitzers, leaving a wide field of broken concrete and a tangle of twisted rebar as high as a house. A maze of churned mud dugouts twisted down the hill, punctuated by the occasional deadly dull shine of unexploded shells buried in the hard earth and new-dug rebel fighters' graves festooned with orange-and-black St George's ribbons.

Ukrainian forces pushed into the suburbs of Donetsk itself, wrecking a recently built state-of-the-art airport and football stadium. In August the Donetsk regional museum was hit by rocket fire in August, demolishing a wing and killing three people who were getting into a minibus nearby. In the museum courtyard stood a row of ancient Scythian fertility idols, at least three thousand years old – all big-hipped women with pendulous breasts and pointed hats or possibly hairdos. Shelling decapitated one of them and the others were spattered with shrapnel, which exposed the light sandstone under their weathered black exterior. It looked as though the statues were bleeding.

It was clear that the DNR irregulars and Russian volunteers could not hold back the Ukrainians on their own. The decisive defeat was delivered by incognito regular Russian troops and artillery, who smashed the Ukrainians at Ilovaisk on 24–26 August. European leaders pressed Poroshenko to negotiate a ceasefire with the rebels, even as Putin himself insisted that Russia was not a party to the war.

Meanwhile the Donbas republics began to assume a semblance of normality in the ruins of a post-war limbo, no longer part of Ukraine and not part of Russia either. Around two-thirds of the pre-war population of Donetsk and Luhansk fled, most of them to Ukraine. The new administration consisted of local mafia kingpins, former communist apparatchiks and a strange assembly of ultra-religious and ultra-nationalist locals and Russians.

The DNR's deputy defence minister was Fyodor Berezin, a carefully dressed man in his fifties with a neat white moustache, half-moon glasses and a benevolent smile. He wore natty American fatigues – the uniform of the well-to-do rebel – decorated with an extravagant St George's ribbon tied in a bow on his shoulder. He looked like a cross between Colonel Sanders and Colonel Kurtz. In his previous life Berezin had been an author, penning 22 volumes of futuristic military science fiction that featured epic battles between a resurgent Soviet Union and decadent America. Uncannily, the cover of Berezin's 2009 novel *War of 2010: Ukrainian Front* featured a civilian airliner being blown out of the air by surface-to-air missiles. The blurb of his *World War III: On the Threshold of a World in Flames* read: 'Armed conflict in Crimea threatens to spread throughout Europe! And Russia does not stand aside from these critical events. The crucial battleground of the War for the Future will be – the Ukrainian Front!'

Some of Berezin's views were eccentric – such as his belief that humanity lives in a matrix controlled by a complex computer program. Others were more or less in step with Putin's own. 'The Third World War began on 11 September 2001,' Berezin told me as we sat in Donetsk's Havana Banana nightclub – a Cuban-themed basement bar decorated, eccentrically, with enlargements of the owner's slightly off-brand holiday snaps of Machu Picchu. 'The imperialists did not investigate whether the attack was committed by the CIA or a real terrorist organisation. Instead, imperialism decided that the natural resources are finite on this planet and we don't care with whom we go to war to get hold of them. That war began in Iraq, then moved to Syria and Libya and now they have come to Ukraine ... Only Russia is a counterweight. Russia says – no! Maybe the West will eventually say, OK, we will concentrate on developing our own resources and not stealing other people's anymore.'[29]

At the other end of the ideological spectrum was Boris Litvinov, Chairman of the DNR's Supreme Soviet, as the rebel legislature called itself. Litvinov – at 60, a generation older than most of the rebel leadership – graduated from the Institute of Marxism and Leninism in Moscow as well as the Donetsk Conservatory, where he studied the double bass and played bass guitar in a jazz and rock band. He had also spent six months working as a coal miner. For him, the rebellion had given Donetsk the opportunity to bring back the Soviet Union in a new and improved form. 'Over the last 25 years Ukrainian propaganda painted a very negative image of the USSR,' he told me, still at his desk at the Donetsk Administration building at 11 p.m. 'They emphasised the purges, the starvation. But they forgot about the social justice of the USSR, the great victory in World War II, the conquest of space, the greatness of our scientists and academics. They forgot the way that we would always confidently look towards tomorrow. This is what we want for the DNR.'

Russia's great mission, as he saw it, was to save the world from petty nationalisms and fascism. 'Russian nationalism does not exist,' said Litvinov. 'Rather, we are talking of internationalism. That is the basic reason why we had our revolution. All the early presidents of Ukraine ... governed only for Ukrainians. The Russian language was discriminated against. History and memory were changed. But the Donbas and Kharkov are different. We are young regions, not like Kyiv. We were founded during the industrial revolution only 150 years ago. People came here from all over the world. The USSR was international. And we in the DNR are internationalists by tradition and by spirit.'

Litvinov believed that the new revolutionary republic should introduce 'war communism' – meaning the nationalisation of private industrial enterprises and land, and the creation of Soviet-style collective farms. I ventured that the last time this had been tried in Ukraine it had not ended well. 'Of course the Holodomor was regrettable,' said Litvinov. 'But we need to take all the best from the past with us into the future! We are beginning from zero. Less than zero!'[30]

CHAPTER 4

TOMORROW BELONGS TO ME

Sooner or later the endless spectacle will be over.
Then we will take revenge; mercilessly.

Aleksandr Dugin[1]

Apotheosis

The six years between the seizure of Crimea in 2014 and the Covid-19 pandemic of 2020 marked the apotheosis of Vladimir Putin's popularity and power. They also laid the foundations for a fatally inflated personal and national self-confidence that would lead directly to the 2022 invasion of Ukraine.

The return of Crimea to Russia sent Putin soaring in the polls and triggered a nationwide euphoria that swept up not just nationalists and conservatives but also surprisingly large numbers of Russia's liberal intelligentsia. Even veteran Putin opponent Aleksei Navalny agreed that the people of Crimea had the right to join Russia – even if he disagreed with Putin's methods in taking it.

True, the ultimate fate of Ukraine remained unfinished business. Russian-backed insurgents in Donbas had succeeded in carving out less than half of Donetsk province and some 35 per cent of Luhansk. But the two instances where Russian regular troops intervened directly and fought Ukrainian forces in the field – at the battle of Ilovaisk in August 2014 and the battle of Debaltseve the following summer – appeared to confirm Russia's overwhelming military superiority. That numerical and technical superiority grew over the inter-war years as Putin poured money into his military. And with it grew a conviction that next time Russia would win easily if they chose to commit a full-scale invasion force.

But crucially, the dream of Novorossiya – the project of bringing the ethnic Russian populations stranded by the collapse of the USSR in Ukraine back into a greater Russia – remained, for the time being, in the hearts and minds of a group of Russian-Orthodox nationalists who were close to the Kremlin but not yet central to Putin's plans and thinking. Between 2014 and 2020 the ideology of creating a Greater Russia by force travelled from the fringes into the political mainstream and eventually to the heart of official government policy. That transformation was primarily the work of three key ideologues – a philosopher, a billionaire and a monk – and a handful of their influential allies inside the Kremlin.

The Fascist Philosopher: Aleksandr Dugin

Since the 1980s, philosophy professor Aleksandr Dugin had believed that Russia's manifest destiny was as a Christian Orthodox and imperial power entirely distinct from, and in direct opposition to, Western liberalism. In person Dugin's craggy, bearded face and fiery self-belief made him seem a modern re-incarnation of a *starets*, or holy man, from a Tolstoy novel. But his passionate dogmatism – firing long quotes from Martin Heidegger and Karl Haushofer as he poked you in the chest – was also very characteristic of the late Soviet intelligentsia's habitual conflation of information with knowledge and facts with truth. Like many thinkers of his generation, Dugin disguised an implacable fanaticism and self-belief in the trappings of intellectual debate.

Dugin's career was a mirror of his country's ideological journey from the intellectual chaos of the dying days of the Soviet empire to the aggressive revanchism of the late Putin era. Dugin, an academic philosopher by training, became an anti-communist dissident in the 1980s. Unlike many dissidents, however, he rejected the idea that Russia should become a liberal Western-style democracy. Instead he advocated a vision of Russian ethnic nationalism twinned with a mystical religiosity that became the foundation of his own particular brand of Russian fascism. In 1988 Dugin founded an ultranationalist, anti-Semitic political group called *Pamyat* – 'Memory' – which posited that the holy, divinely ordained Russian Empire had been hijacked, undermined and ultimately destroyed by godless Bolshevik Jews. In the febrile ideological churn of post-Soviet politics Dugin's overt anti-Semitism did not stop him from helping to write the political programme for the newly re-formed Communist Party of the Russian Federation.

By 1993 Dugin had persuaded the radical writer Eduard Limonov to join a new, more actively revolutionary movement that they dubbed the National Bolshevik Front (NBF). The NBF's symbol was a black hammer and sickle inside a white circle on a red background – the new swastika of Russian fascism. Four years later Dugin published two key tracts. One was *Foundations of Geopolitics* (the title a nod to the Nazi Eurasianist thinker Klaus Haushofer), which was later adopted as a textbook in the Russian military's Academy of the General Staff.[2] The other was *Fascism – Borderless and Red*, which, less officially, would became the ideological blueprint for the final phase of Putinism. Dugin described Russia transitioning from a corrupt, Western form of liberal capitalism to a form of 'national capitalism' that would in turn transform into a 'genuine, true, radically revolutionary and consistent, fascist fascism' in Russia.[3]

In Dugin's vision, 'Russian fascism is a combination of natural national conservatism with a passionate desire for true changes.'

Freed of the corruption imposed by Western liberals, Russia would be free to pursue its true imperial destiny. 'We conservatives want a strong, solid state, want order and healthy family, positive values, the reinforcing of the importance of religion and the Church in society,' Dugin wrote in 2012, by which time he was already working with the Kremlin. 'We want patriotic radio, TV, patriotic experts, patriotic clubs. We want the media that expresses national interests.'[4] He also railed against the internet – 'a phenomenon is worth prohibiting because it gives nobody anything good' – and called on 'all Orthodox Russians ... to unite around the president of Russia in the last battle between good and evil, following the example of Iran and North Korea'.[5]

Dugin idealised Putin personally, even as he opposed the liberal economic policies of the Kremlin technocrats who surrounded him. 'Putin is everywhere, Putin is everything, Putin is absolute, and Putin is indispensable,' Dugin told me in 2007.[6] Nonetheless, before early 2012 Dugin, like the rest of the National Bolsheviks, had considered himself part of the radical nationalist opposition to the Kremlin. But as mass protests rocked Moscow and St Petersburg in the wake of Putin's return for a third presidential term, chief Kremlin ideologue Vladislav Surkov decided that Dugin's fiery rhetoric should become a useful part of Putin's new ideological chorus. Dugin was invited to address a Surkov-orchestrated 'anti-Orange' mass meeting to oppose the pro-Western protests in February 2012.

'The global American empire strives to bring all countries of the world together under its control,' Dugin told pro-Kremlin crowds in 2012, many of whom were old members of Surkov's *Nashy* movement.

> They come in through the fifth column, which they think will allow them to take over natural resources and rule over countries, people, and continents. They have invaded Afghanistan, Iraq, Libya. Syria and Iran are on the agenda. But their goal is

> Russia. We are the last obstacle on their way to building a global evil empire. Their agents at [Moscow's] Bolotnaya Square and within the government are doing everything to weaken Russia and allow them to bring us under total external control. To resist this most serious threat, we must be united and mobilized! We must remember that we are Russian! That for thousands of years we protected our freedom and independence. We have spilled seas of blood, our own and other people's, to make Russia great. And Russia will be great! Otherwise it will not exist at all. Russia is everything! Everything else is nothing![7]

Every one of the statements that in Dugin's mouth seemed so radical in 2012 would by 2021 be adopted – often word for word – by Putin himself.

By early 2014 Dugin was deeply involved in practical politics, for the most part still independently from Kremlin control. His major project was to push his radical policies in pro-Moscow circles in Ukraine. Oleg Bahtiyarov, one of the members of the 'Eurasia Youth Union of Russia' movement founded by Dugin, was arrested by the Security Service of Ukraine (SBU) in March 2014 for training a 200-strong anti-Maidan group that was plotting to seize the Rada and other government buildings in Kyiv. Skype calls intercepted by the SBU showed Dugin providing instructions to separatists of south and eastern Ukraine. Dugin was not yet in full ideological lockstep with the Kremlin. In July 2014 he joined with Igor Girkin in bitterly criticising Putin for failing to support the Donbas separatists as they fell back under attacks from the regular Ukrainian army. According to Dugin, the Kremlin had been held back from full-scale invasion of Donbas by a group he dubbed a 'sixth column' – officials around Putin who pretended to be loyal but were in fact 'the same American riffraff' as the openly treacherous, pro-American 'fifth column' of opposition activists.[8,9] Vladislav Surkov – the man who had brought Dugin into the political mainstream – would by

2020 effectively find himself accused of being one of these secret traitors.

In August 2022 Dugin would receive tragic payback for his role in bringing Russia to war when a car bomb killed his 30-year-old daughter and only child Daria Dugina. Dugin and Russian TV blamed the Ukrainian SBU, describing Daria as a 'martyr' who had 'died for Russia'.[10] The Ukrainians claimed the attack was a false-flag operation by the FSB. But nobody was in any doubt that Daria had paid the ultimate price for her father's ideas.

The Christian Oligarch: Konstantin Malofeev

From 2015 onwards Dugin would no longer have to rely on Kremlin approval for nationwide media and political exposure. A rising star of the ultranationalist Christian right, businessman Konstantin Malofeev, decided to found a new, private national television station he called Tsargrad TV. Dugin was hired as its first editor-in-chief and ideological mentor.

Malofeev, like many of the smartest members of a generation that came of age as the Soviet Empire collapsed, made his fortune as a capitalist. But instead of parlaying a fortune made in banking and private equity into yachts, mistresses and London property, Malofeev decided to use it to fund a crusade to save his country from moral and political turpitude.

If Dugin's path to extreme Russian nationalism was an intellectual one, Malofeev's was more spiritual. Unlike Dugin, Malofeev was a passionate believer in divine-right monarchism and in creationism. But what both men had in common is that they became adherents of Orthodox imperialism when the idea was still on the political fringes. Under their active promotion, many key members of Putin's inner circle moved towards them – and with them the Kremlin's ideology itself. Among the prominent members of the Kremlin's inner circle who became early adopters of Malofeev's ideas were Vladimir Yakunin, the head of Russian railways and a longtime Putin ally; Igor Shchegolev, a university classmate of Putin's who served as Russia's telecommunications minister; and most crucially Yury Kovalchuk, Putin's close business associate and personal friend from his St Petersburg days.

What was unusual about Malofeev is that, unlike many of the older generation of Putin's KGB-linked associates, he had extensive experience in dealing with the world beyond Russia's borders and spoke English fluently. During his private equity days, Malofeev worked closely with Western companies including French insurer Axa and US fund Paul Capital.[11] But rather than becoming a member of what Dugin disparagingly called 'the globalist elite', Malofeev was drawn to – and learned from – the extreme right wing of Western politics, from the US evangelical movement and far-right European politicians such as France's Marine Le Pen and Austria's Heinz-Christian Strache.

Malofeev's connections with the West's traditionalist Christian right were the basis of his first official interactions with the Kremlin. Putin's Eurasian Economic Union had been designed to restore Russia's leadership of the former Soviet Empire. But the Kremlin's spin doctors also sought to project Russia's soft power further afield by reinventing Putin as 'World Conservatism's New Leader', a term coined by the Centre for Strategic Communications, a Kremlin-connected think tank. The idea was to create a kind of Conservative International on the lines of the Communist International of the 1920s. And like the Comintern the new international movement was intended both to lever Moscow into the leadership of world ultra-conservatism and to use those forces to destabilise and undermine Russia's enemies in the West.

Moscow's propaganda machine and a network of newly created think tanks based in Paris and Washington supported

Scottish and Catalan nationalists, US anti-abortionists, Brexit activists, Polish, French and Italian anti-immigration movements, and indeed any anti-establishment conservative group anywhere in the West. In his annual state of the nation speech to Russia's parliament in December 2013, Vladimir Putin assured conservatives around the world that Russia was ready and willing to stand up for 'family values' against a tide of liberal, Western, pro-gay propaganda 'that asks us to accept without question the equality of good and evil'. Russia, he promised, will 'defend traditional values that have made up the spiritual and moral foundation of civilisation in every nation for thousands of years'.

Many across Europe, from rising Italian nationalist Matteo Salvini to French Front National leader Marine Le Pen, Britain's Nigel Farage and US commentator Pat Buchanan, spoke publicly in support of various elements of Putin's conservative message. Buchanan, one of the architects of the Reagan-era 'Moral Majority' movement that heralded the rise of the Christian right as a political force, voiced his approval. 'While much of American and western media dismiss him as an authoritarian and reactionary, a throwback, Putin may be seeing the future with more clarity than Americans,' wrote Buchanan in a 2014 blog post.[12] And when Malofeev created his own Fox-style Christian nationalist TV network the following year he hired former Fox News director Jack Hanick to run it.

Like Dugin, Malofeev also played a very direct role in the unrest in Russian-speaking areas of Ukraine that followed the annexation of Crimea. By his own account, his inspiration was divine. In late January 2014 Malofeev had been travelling with Patriarch Kirill, head of the Russian Orthodox Church, taking a collection of ancient Christian relics on tour through Russia, Ukraine and Belarus. The group's plane was unexpectedly grounded in Sevastopol by an ice storm. The stop was unscheduled, but 100,000 people – a third of Crimea's population – turned out to pray with the relics. 'It was one prayer from all the people:

for Sevastopol to once more be part of Russia,' recalled Malofeev.[13] 'God's will.'

Two key future Donbas rebel leaders were Malofeev's former employees. Aleksander Borodai, who would become the prime minister of the self-declared Donetsk People's Republic, worked as the businessman's public relations consultant before leaving to serve as political adviser to Crimea's new pro-Russia premier, Sergey Aksyonov. Igor Girkin had also worked for Malofeev – though Malofeev denied that he was still 'paying them a salary or that we're in the same business'. He did, however, admit to sending nearly a million dollars in what he insisted was 'humanitarian aid' to Donbas. Nonetheless in July 2014 Ukraine's interior ministry announced it had opened a criminal investigation against Malofeev for financing 'illegal armed groups', branding him a 'sponsor of terrorists'.[14]

The Crusading Monk: Metropolitan Tikhon

One of the key figures in Tsargrad TV – and another crucial link between the Kremlin and the orthodox nationalists – was Metropolitan Tikhon, born Georgiy Shevkunov. A screenwriter by profession before joining the priesthood, Tikhon was Superior of Moscow's Sretensky Monastery from 1995 to 2018, where he created the Russian Orthodox Church's largest publishing house as well as its most popular website, pravoslavie.ru. Kremlin-connected banker and senator Sergei Pugachev, by his own account, introduced Tikhon to Putin in the late 1990s.[15] Tikhon himself said that Putin 'appeared at the doors' of the Sretensky monastery. In any case it was the start of a close and very public association. The monk accompanied Putin on several international trips, leading to rumours that Tikhon had become the president's *dukhovik*, or spiritual father – which Tikhon neither confirmed nor denied, though he did emphasise that 'I am no

Cardinal Richelieu.'[16] But in 2009 Tikhon did publicly pray that 'he who loves Russia and wishes it well can only pray for Vladimir, placed at the head of Russia by God's will.'[17] Tikhon's double entendre deliberately conflated Vladimir the Great with Vladimir Putin. It was a comparison that Putin himself would take very seriously and led to his erecting a statue to his tenth-century namesake next to the Kremlin.

Whatever Putin's private spiritual motivations, association with Tikhon also made good public relations sense. The Russian Orthodox Church was one of the most trusted public institutions in Russia – after the president and the army – and Tikhon was one of its superstar communicators. He had produced, written and directed a popular documentary film called *The Fall of an Empire – the Lesson of Byzantium*, which updated the centuries-old claim that Moscow was the spiritual successor of the Roman Empire and the sole guardian of true Christian values. His 2012 autobiography, *Everyday Saints and Other Stories*, was Russia's top-selling book that year, beating even the translation of *Fifty Shades of Grey*. And after 2015, with Malofeev's Tsargrad TV as his mouthpiece, Tikhon became a figure of national prominence.

In 2017 Tikhon was appointed by Patriarch Kirill to lead a commission investigating the execution of Tsar Nicholas II and his family in Yekaterinburg in 1918. Tikhon's conclusion was that the killing 'was a ritual murder that held special significance for Bolshevik commander Yakov Yurovsky' – a thinly veiled reference to the Jewish birth of the commander of the execution squad.[18] In the run-up to the 2022 invasion, Tikhon was a vocal advocate of the idea that Ukraine was the spiritual home of Russian Orthodoxy – and that it was Russia's duty to cleanse it of what Patriarch Kirill would call 'forces of evil' that are 'hostile to the unity of the Russian people and Church'. By his own account, Tikhon discussed the matter with Putin on the eve of the invasion. 'On the basis of my discussions with [Putin], I can say that, if he had not considered that there were reasons of vital importance, an imminent danger for the Russian people, making this operation indispensable, he would not have undertaken it,' Tikhon told worshippers in his diocese in a sermon on 8 April 2022. 'If he had not done it now, but later, Russia would have been attacked, with the risk of having millions of victims.'[19]

The Nationalist Bureaucrat: Sergei Glazyev

Another key figure who linked the Orthodox ultranationalist right to the Kremlin was Sergei Glazyev, an economist and member of the Academy of Sciences who had served as minister of foreign economic relations under Boris Yeltsin. Like Dugin, Glazyev had been a member of the nationalist opposition in the early years of Putin's rule. In 2003 both men had been founding members of the *Rodina* (Motherland) party, led by Dmitry Rogozin, the hawkish chairman of the Duma's foreign affairs committee.[20] Glazyev even stood against Putin in the presidential elections of 2004 on a platform of Christian values, increasing Russia's influence in the near abroad and standing up to US hegemony.

By 2012, as we have seen, it was Glazyev, born in Soviet Ukraine, whom Putin tasked with the economics of diverting Yanukovych away from the EU association agreement and cajoling him to join the Eurasian Union instead. According to a political adviser who worked with him at the time, Glazyev also played a key role in circulating to top officials in the Kremlin Konstantin Malofeev's policy document advocating the annexation of Crimea and breaking up Ukraine. Glazyev 'was running in front of the [Kremlin's] locomotive,' says the adviser. 'He pushed the boundaries ... He wished to set the agenda.'[21]

In the chaos that followed the Maidan, as already mentioned, Glazyev was also heavily involved in directing pro-Russian demonstrations in Odesa, Kharkiv and other cities. By 2017 he was again anticipating the future hard Kremlin line when he said that 'today Ukraine is an occupied territory ... there is no legitimate power, there is no one to talk to, there are no people who can take responsibility for the implementation of political agreements.' To Glazyev, the Kyiv authorities 'are only servants of American aggressors who receive instructions from the American embassy, from which they receive funding [to] serve American interests in Ukraine'.[22] In 2019, in a further sign of Putin's rising esteem and ideological closeness to Glazyev, he was promoted to minister for the integration and macroeconomics of the Eurasian Economic Union.

The Grey Cardinal: Vladislav Surkov

Surkov was the most paradoxical and fascinating figure ever to have worked in Putin's Kremlin, exemplifying both the postmodern sophistication of the younger members of the Kremlin inner circle and their boundless cynicism. Surkov was born Aslambek Dudayev to a Chechen father and ethnic Russian mother in the North Caucasus in 1964. He adopted his mother's surname in 1969 after his father abandoned the family, and he and his mother moved to the Ryazan region of central Russia. In the 1990s Surkov, by now a professional theatre director, was hired by oligarch Mikhail Khodorkovsky to oversee his advertising and public relations department. His future wife was also a Khodorkovsky employee. Before Khodorkovsky's arrest and imprisonment for fraud in 2003 Surkov was headhunted by the presidential administration for his remarkable PR skills.

In the wake of the colour revolutions in Tbilisi and Kyiv in 2003–04, Surkov was instrumental in inventing the term 'sovereign democracy' – a grand-sounding concept that actually described its own opposite, the surrender of democracy into the hands of the state. Surkov's *Nashy* youth movement used the fashionable jargon of management and personal growth to disguise the fact that the organisation was devoted to brainwashing Russia's youth into hating the trends and values of their peers in the West. In place of the ideological vacuum of Yeltsin's Russia, Surkov brilliantly created a catch-all state ideology that was wide enough to contain the ambitions of all Russians' hopes and dreams. It was confected from the wide-eyed idealism of Great Patriotic War epics, Orthodox nationalism and Soviet nostalgia, and aimed to create a postmodern sense of national pride in Russia that everyone from gaming geeks to babushkas could get behind. As Surkov wrote in his novel *Almost Zero* (written under the pseudonym Natan Dubovitsky, a nod to Surkov's wife Natalia Dubovitskaya, whose hero is a poetry-loving and gun-toting PR guru thriving as a publishing bootlegger in ruthlessly capitalist post-Soviet Russia), the new ideology was 'at any moment ready to perform tragedy, or pastoral, or something ambiguous'.[23]

It was Surkov, who rose to the rank of deputy prime minister, who also helped shape the media culture of Putin's Russia, a relativistic world of wheeling conspiracy theories, where, in Peter Pomerantsev's memorable phrase, 'nothing is true and everything is possible.' He worked hand-in-hand with a new generation of TV executives who had come into the Kremlin's orbit, like Surkov himself, from the liberal media world of the 1990s. Under the leadership of Konstantin Ernst, another former liberal television producer and cult film director, Russia's Channel One copied Silvio Berlusconi's feel-good brand of TV nationalism and Fox News' aggressive partisanship. Surkov's heroes were American rapper Tupac Shakur and beat poet Allen Ginsberg, photos of whom adorned his Kremlin office. He wrote lyrics for the pop group Agata Christie and showed up for feisty debates at the London School of Economics in 2010 and 2013 – where he admitted that the Bolotnaya protesters were Russia's 'creative class' whose opinions should be heeded. But despite his fluent

English and admiration for heroes of US counter-culture, Surkov was very far from a Western-leaning liberal. Putin chose Surkov to work alongside Glazyev and spearhead the public relations wing of the Kremlin's campaign to derail Yanukovych's dangerous flirtation with the EU in 2013.

Surkov's job was to make sure that a future Ukraine would resemble loyal, Moscow-controlled Belarus rather than the rebellious, Western-orientated Baltics. 'There is no Ukraine, there is just Ukrainian-ness,' maintained Surkov. 'It's a specific kind of mental illness ... Oddly enough, I'm a "Ukroptimist". In other words, I think there's no Ukraine yet. But it will [form] over time.' What Surkov meant was that it was not yet too late to prevent Ukraine from coalescing into a coherent independent state that could become a Western-sponsored 'anti-Russia'.

The debacle of the Maidan marked a serious setback for Surkov's reputation as a political technologist and PR wizard. But Putin gave him a second chance, quickly reappointing him as the Kremlin's policy supremo on all things Ukrainian in April 2014. With a firmly anti-Moscow administration in place in Kyiv in the aftermath of the Crimea and Donbas operations, Surkov's challenge was to cripple Ukraine's westward path from the outside. Hence the Kremlin's chosen spoiling tactic – to use the rebel Donbas republics to bog Kyiv down in a low-level forever war, disrupting Ukraine's politics and statehood with a never-ending discussion of whether and how to bring the breakaway republics back under Kyiv's control. The underlying idea of the Minsk-1 and 2 accords, signed by Poroshenko in 2014 and 2015 with European support and Putin's behind-the-scenes blessing, was to keep Donbas inside Ukraine as a counterweight and drag anchor on any attempts to take the country into NATO and the EU.

Putin continued to refuse both to recognise the LDNR's sovereignty or formally annex them to Russia, like Crimea. But as Surkov himself admitted in 2015, Russia's supposed insistence that the Donbas republics should rejoin Ukraine was made in entirely bad faith. 'I don't have a strong enough imagination to envision' the LDNR returning to the Ukrainian government's control, Surkov said. 'Donbas doesn't deserve such humiliation. Ukraine doesn't deserve such an honour.'

The Kremlin's Gas Weapon

Though the ruble lost some 40 per cent of its value in the wake of the Crimea annexation, and personal sanctions were imposed on members of Putin's inner circle and on state-owned companies, Western solidarity crumbled on the one point where it could have had a real impact – energy. Neither Russian gas nor oil were included in any sanctions package. Nonetheless, in early January 2015 Gazprom cut supplies though pipelines to Europe in half, blaming EU sanctions for the go-slow. (In July 2022 Gazprom would begin a new and far more serious gas war against Europe by adopting precisely the same strategy of gas shutdowns, again based on spurious claims of technical problems.)

In 2015 it worked. Germany's then-Chancellor Angela Merkel defied US pressure and signed an agreement to build a second major pipeline linking Russia directly to Germany under the Baltic Sea – Gazprom's €9.7 billion Nord Stream 2. Despite Dutch anger at the previous summer's shooting down of Malaysian Airlines Flight MH-17, Royal Dutch Shell signed up to Nord Stream 2, as did Germany's Uniper and Wintershall, as well as France's Engie. Even as Europe condemned Putin for Crimea, it continued to ramp up its dependence on Russian gas. At the same time Merkel pressured Poroshenko to sign the two Minsk accords that effectively legitimised the rebel Donbas regions as self-governing entities – albeit formally still within Ukraine.

Nobody in 2015 could have predicted that a war in Ukraine would result in the destruction of both Nord Stream pipelines in

September 2022, almost certainly by Russia itself. But the conclusions drawn by the Kremlin at the time were obvious. One, that reducing gas supplies to Europe focused Western politicians' minds wonderfully fast. And two, that whatever their moral scruples over Russia's actions – up to and including the murder of hundreds of innocent European citizens – Europe's need for gas would always trump questions of moral principle. Logically enough, Putin's inner circle assumed that the West would remain equally divided and self-interested as they planned the 2022 invasion.

Syria

In 2015 Putin further boosted his military credentials, this time on the international stage. The Ba'ath regime in Syria, like its ideological cousin in Iraq, had been a client of the Soviet Union for decades. The political and economic collapse of the USSR had left Soviet allies across Africa, the Middle East, Central America and the Caribbean high and dry. But when the regime of Bashar al-Assad came under attack from a major rebellion in the wake of the pro-democracy Arab Spring in 2011, the cash-flushed Russian government saw an opportunity to return to the international stage as a Soviet-style power broker. Putin had begun to supply Assad with arms and advisers since the beginning of the Syrian civil war. In September 2015, after an official request by the Syrian government for air support against rebel groups, the Kremlin doubled down. Deploying a single squadron of 36 Russian Air Force warplanes to the airbase at Khmeimim near Latakia, supported by some 2,300 ground crew, immediately changed the course of the war in Assad's favour.

Russia began with airstrikes against Islamist groups that the US and its coalition partners had also been bombing – the Islamic State of Iraq and the Levant (ISIL), al-Nusra Front (al-Qaeda in

Syria) and the Army of Conquest. Two weeks after Russian airstrikes forced ISIL to abandon the desert city of Palmyra in June 2016, Kremlin spin-doctors arranged world-renowned Russian conductor Valery Gergiev to give a concert with the Mariinsky Orchestra in the city's Roman theatre. In front of a crowd of Russian soldiers, government ministers and journalists, Gergiev conducted pieces by Bach, Prokofiev and Shchedrin. The scene of Russia returning culture to a devastated part of the Middle East was a brilliant piece of political theatre.

Putin's planes began to attack groups supported by the US, such as the Syrian National Coalition and the Kurdish groups along the Turkish border. Russian air power devastated the remaining rebel strongholds of Aleppo and Idlib while Russian advisers and mercenaries from the Wagner Group – whose activities will be discussed in more detail later – fought on the ground alongside Assad's and Iranian Revolutionary Guard troops. Washington and Brussels criticised Putin fiercely for effectively winning the war for Assad but, apart from a few airstrikes on Wagner forces, did nothing to stop him from doing so. In December 2017 Russia announced that its airbase at Khmeimim and a small Soviet-era naval base at Tartus would become permanent overseas military bases.

Syria was Putin's fourth victorious war after Chechnya, Georgia and Crimea. More, for the first time in a generation Russia was once more a major international player, able to project power not only in its own backyard but across the world. And unlike America, Russia had shown that it could decisively win a Middle Eastern war. The West had predicted disaster and quagmire. Instead, Putin's reformed army and air force had apparently succeeded where the Americans' trillion-dollar war against terror had failed.

Russiagate

Small wonder that a newly confident Russia decided to continue its pushback against American domination by attempting its greatest coup yet – influencing the outcome of the 2016 US presidential election. The initial goal was to hurt Hillary Clinton, a bugbear of the Kremlin's after her strong support for the Arab Spring and later for the Maidan as Obama's secretary of state, rather than support the as-yet undeclared Donald Trump. Starting in 2015 two distinct groups of hackers, including programmers recruited from the criminal world by the FSB and GRU, began a series of 'phishing' attacks that bombarded the Democratic National Congress with fake emails containing malware that enabled the hackers to break into email records. These hacks resulted in a haul of embarrassing, though not particularly compromising, emails that would later be released on the eve of the 2016 vote. In the run-up to the November 2016 election itself the GRU's hackers also broke into some of the online systems that controlled electronic voting.

The other prong of the attack was a social media campaign mounted unofficially by Putin's close ally, billionaire caterer Yevgeny Prigozhin – who also helped found and finance the Wagner group of mercenaries. Prigozhin set up a troll farm in St Petersburg that employed hundreds of young hackers to create fake Twitter and Facebook accounts and fill social media with both sponsored and manufactured posts attacking Clinton.

The FBI began investigating Russian hacking as early as November 2015, although despite the furore that followed the revelations of the full extent of Russian election interference, there is no evidence that any of the Kremlin's meddling came close to changing the actual result. But it was the furore itself that constituted Putin's victory. In January 2017 the US Office of the

Director of National Intelligence delivered a declassified report representing the work of the FBI, the CIA and the NSA that concluded: 'President Vladimir Putin ordered an influence campaign ... aimed at the U.S. presidential election. Russia's goals were to undermine public faith in the U.S. democratic process, denigrate Secretary Clinton, and harm her electability and potential presidency. We further assess Putin and the Russian Government developed a clear preference for president-elect Trump. We have high confidence in these judgments.'[24] Thanks to Russiagate, Putin had gone, in the eyes of the US media above all, from the leader of a 'regional power' (as Obama had dismissively called him) to a dangerous global mastermind able to sow discord and hysteria in the very heart of his enemy's capital.

The Russiagate hacking cost the Russian state 'single-figure millions of dollars', says a senior Russian government official who saw Putin regularly during that period. 'But the effect was as powerful as any billions we could have spent on defence ... it was a triumphantly effective operation. A classic judo move ... You use the enemy's weakness against him.'[25] Putin's interference was not, in fact, decisive in getting Trump elected. But sections of the US media maintained that it had been – and that suited Putin just fine.

On 8 November 2016 a party was thrown in a Moscow bar to mark US election night. The celebration turned raucous as polls showed that Trump was heading towards victory. A crowd of young Russian women, some state TV employees, began chanting 'USA! USA!' in imitation of a Trump rally. Everyone got very drunk. Presiding over the festivities were a pair of heroic hand-painted portraits of Trump and the Russian nationalist right's other darling, Marine Le Pen – whose Front National had accepted funding from backers allegedly connected to the Kremlin. There were many Americans present, some in classic red 'Make America Great Again' baseball caps and others in specially made caps that said 'Make Russia Great Again'. Among the guests was former Fox News director Jack Hanick, now working for Malofeev's Tsargrad TV. A gaggle of Russian TV news cameras surrounded Hanick all evening. 'Even though Clinton professes to be a Christian, all of her policies are actually moving away from those positions,' Hanick told the cameras. The United States was 'losing its moral core and fiber ... Russia is moving toward Christianity; America is moving away from Christianity.' In 2022 the US Department of Justice would charge Hanick with violations of US sanctions and false statements in connection with his work for Malofeev.[26]

The euphoric mood at that election-night party marked another milestone in the Kremlin's sense of its own growing power – and a conviction that Russia's unity and ideological coherence would beat the weak and fatally divided West. 'The world is going our way, you cannot deny it!' said Ekaterina Tokareva, a producer on Rossiya-1's *60 Minut* current affairs talk show, who had invited me to the election-night party.[27] It was this sense of invincibility, and a certainty that Western criticism was hollow, that would underlie all Russia's future actions in and against the West – including the attempted poisoning of former GRU defector Sergei Skripal and his daughter Yulia in Salisbury, England, in March 2018.

Illusions of Grandeur

In truth, Russia's new might was largely illusory – or, at the very least, highly qualified. The first illusion was that Russia's defeats of the Ukrainian army in Ilovaisk and Debaltseve in 2014–15 had demonstrated Moscow's overwhelming military superiority. But Russia had in fact won both those engagements by covertly deploying devastating artillery force against a Ukrainian army that had hitherto been fighting and winning against lightly armed rebels. Moscow's intervention was a gun brought to a knife fight – which proved sudden and decisive, but not lasting proof that they could do the same in full-scale battle against the Ukrainians.

Russia's energy blackmail in 2015 may have been brutally effective in kick-starting the stalled Nord Stream 2 pipeline. But equally it kick-started a major strategic debate in the West about the dangers of Europe's reliance on cheap Russian gas. Former German chancellor Gerhard Schröder and his successor Angela Merkel believed that integrating Russia into Europe's economy would help moderate Putin's aggression, not exacerbate it. The US and UK, on the other hand, fiercely opposed it – and Washington threatened sanctions against any Western company participating in the project, forcing Gazprom to finance Nord Stream 2 on its own. The pipeline never received German government approval to open before the invasion, and even before it was mysteriously blown up on 26 September 2022, spilling 300 million cubic meters of gas into the atmosphere, Nord Stream 2 had already become a very expensive piece of scrap metal on the bottom of the Baltic Sea.

Syria, too, was a brilliant example of how tiny numbers of modern military planes could devastate an enemy with no aviation of its own – especially if that air power was used with no regard for civilian casualties. But Russia, unlike the US in Iraq, never engaged on the ground, and it intervened to support an existing regime, not topple one. Furthermore Russia's military were able to turn the tide of the war first and foremost because the US had chosen to stay out of the conflict. As Russia would find to its cost in Ukraine 2022, its air power didn't amount to much when opposed by a comparably equipped air force and modern anti-aircraft defence systems.

The true scale and impact of Russian interference in the US election, too, was blown out of all proportion by the culture wars that followed Trump's election. The fiendish power of Putin to manipulate US democracy became a touchstone of anti-Trump media – a belief fuelled, consciously or subconsciously, by a refusal to accept that the American electorate could be deluded enough to vote for Trump without malicious outside intervention. But in reality the Kremlin had played no decisive role either in Trump's victory, the Brexit vote, Catalonia's unilateral referendum on independence from Madrid, Marine Le Pen's resurgence or any other of the grand interference conspiracies in which Putin had been implicated.

The worldwide renaissance of Russian military and diplomatic power may have been an illusion – but it was a powerful one. Putin had, in the opinion of a large majority of Russians, finally helped their country stand up from its knees after decades of humiliation. The 'Crimea effect' had taught the Kremlin that military victory was the secret formula for boosting Putin's popularity. And, fatally, it led the hawks who had pushed through the Crimea operation to believe that the trick could be repeated again on a larger scale in the future.

Ukraine Betrayed

The Minsk accords had left Ukraine worse than dismembered – they'd left the country isolated and basically betrayed by the West. For all the fighting talk during the annexation of Crimea and the Donbas war that such behaviour was unacceptable and that Russia would be made to pay, it was clear that neither the EU nor the Obama administration were willing to actually help Ukraine push back the Russians. Germany's green-lighting of Nord Stream 2 showed where the West's real interests lay. 'Essentially [the Ukrainians] were screwed over by the West, whom they loved so much,' a senior state TV executive I will call Kirill Molody told me, gloatingly, in 2015. 'They waved their Euro flags on the Maidan, then Europe came and said, OK, give up now, we need Russian gas.'[28]

Petro Poroshenko had won the post-Maidan presidential election in May 2014 on a platform of strident Ukrainian nationalism, and a promise to continue to strive for NATO and EU membership and fight against corruption. In practice, he failed at all of his goals. In February 2015 Poroshenko hired Mikheil Saakashvili, the former president of Georgia whose enthusiastic embrace of NATO and rash attempt to seize South Ossetia had sparked the Russian invasion of 2008, to clean up Ukraine's corruption as governor of the Odesa province. Saakashvili resigned after a year. 'The region is being handed over not only to corrupt people, but also to enemies of Ukraine,' Saakashvili complained, accusing Poroshenko of personally supporting 'corruption clans in Odesa'.[29] Poroshenko's administration appeared to be mired in the same corrupt habits of his disgraced predecessor Yanukovych.

Ukraine's continued corruption suited the Kremlin just fine. A corrupt Ukraine was a weak Ukraine. 'I promise you, they [the Ukrainian elite] need no lessons from us,' joked Molody, whose TV channels covered the twists and turns of Ukrainian government corruption in detail. 'If you want a world-level masterclass in *razpil* [skimming] and *otkat* [bribery], ask a Ukrainian governor.'[30] Russia had systematically used corruption as a deliberate tool both to blackmail and split the country's elite and to link the oligarchs to Moscow through their extensive business interests both in Russia and the occupied territories of Donbas.

The Actor and the Oligarch

'Nowhere are there such lousy politicians as in Ukraine,' observed a Ukrainian actor and screenwriter of the corruption that surrounded Poroshenko. 'There is corruption in Russia too ... but their politicians there still possess some core values – the idea of statehood. This is what the Russian politicians believe in, it is their ideology. Ukrainian politicians have no values. They are ready to promise anything if that helps them stay in power.'[31] The pervading cynicism of Ukraine's ruling class was not only beggaring the country but actually preventing it from being a functional country at all.

The actor decided to write a television satire about a provincial teacher whose angry rant against political corruption goes viral and unexpectedly propels him into power as president of Ukraine. The series would be called *Servant of the People* – and its lead actor and writer decided to register a real-world political party with the same name for good measure. His name was Volodymyr Zelensky.

Zelensky was an only child, raised in a family of Russian-speaking Jewish intellectuals in Kryvyi Rih in central Ukraine. His father Oleksandr was a computer scientist and professor of technology at the local university, while his mother Rymma was an engineer. His grandfather Semyon was the only one of four brothers who returned alive from fighting the Nazis in the Second World War – he would rise to the rank of colonel and became Kryvyi Rih's chief of police. Both of Zelensky's great-grandparents had been massacred when the Germans destroyed their village. Compared with many other Ukrainian Jews, the Zelensky family had escaped relatively unscathed from the horrors of the twentieth century. But his background and family history made Putin's later accusation that Zelensky was a fascist all the more bizarre and offensive.

At school Zelensky showed a talent for humour and showmanship, and he and his friends formed a team to compete in the amateur student comedy tournaments known as KVN, or the Club of the Funny and Inventive. KVN was a well-loved Soviet tradition – and one that survived the break-up of the Soviet Union, with nationally televised finals in Moscow that included teams from all over the former empire. They named their stand-up team Kvartal 95, after the Kryvyi Rih neighbourhood where Zelensky grew up.

After graduating from the law faculty of the local university, Zelensky went into show business, producing and acting in a series of hit comedy shows and KVN tournaments that were also broadcast in Russia. In 2006 Zelensky and his partner won the Ukrainian version of *Strictly Come Dancing*. In 2010 Zelensky and his Kvartal 95 team were hired as the entertainment at President Viktor Yanukovych's 60th birthday party at the state dacha at Foros in Crimea.

Zelensky's humour was raunchy and, by Western standards, very un-PC. Among his most famous skits was one where he pretended to play the piano with his penis, and another where he played a gay cop flirting with drivers. His shows were also strongly political – and often aimed at Russia and at Putin himself. In spring 2014 he wore a shocking pink dress to impersonate Putin's alleged gymnast mistress Alina Kabaeva, furious at her lover's late return home. A flustered Putin explained that he was late because he had been discussing sending troops into Crimea with Sergei Shoigu. 'Don't lie!' Zelensky-Kabaeva replied. 'I watch Russian television. There are no Russian troops in Crimea!' The following year Kvartal 95 launched the first season of *Servant of the People*, which became Ukraine's most popular comedy show.

With his boyish grin, small stature and comic persona as a naive idealist, Zelensky was an easy man to underestimate. Russian propaganda and his Ukrainian political opponents would relentlessly mock Zelensky as a joker, a drug addict and an unserious amateur. Putin and his inner circle, too, would fatally confuse the role with the man playing it. 'An annoying little Jew playing at politics,' was how Molody, who heads a major Russian TV channel and has worked closely with the Kremlin for over 20 years, described Zelensky in 2021 (the phrase he used was the staggeringly racist *vyazky zhidenok*). 'He's a sock puppet for the usual oligarchic interests.'[32]

Zelensky quickly became not only one of Ukraine's most popular actors but head of the country's biggest and most profitable television production companies. Andriy Bohdan – who would later become Zelensky's first chief of staff – claimed that he was the first to spot Zelensky's political potential. Bohdan had once been close to the administration of Viktor Yanukovych – indeed he had been a member of a government delegation led by Prime Minister Mykola Azarov that flew to St Petersburg for negotiations with the Russians on joining the Eurasian Union in November 2013.[33] Bohdan was the personal lawyer and senior adviser to Igor Kolomoisky, one of Ukraine's wealthiest oligarchs. Kolomoisky's $3 billion business empire spanned Ukraine, Russia, Romania and Scandinavia, and included interests in ferroalloys, finance, oil products, airlines, metals and petroleum, newspapers and TV stations – including the 1+1 Media Group that broadcast Kvartal 95's shows.[34] Kolomoisky was also a skilled political survivor, first supporting Yanukovych's Party of the Regions before switching to backing the Maidan. At the end of February 2014 the interim post-Maidan government appointed Kolomoisky governor of his native Dnipropetrovsk province.

Spotting the potential to turn *Servant of the People* into a real political platform, in 2015 Bohdan suggested that Zelensky run as a regional mayor in Dnipropetrovsk, with Kolomoisky's support. Zelensky refused – indeed, according to a member of his Kvartal 95 team, he joked with colleagues that 'they want to make my show come true in real life.'[35] A recurring storyline in *Servant of the People* was a group of Bond-villain-like oligarchs who believe they can buy off the idealistic teacher turned accidental president Vasyl Holoborodko.

But as Poroshenko's presidency became increasingly mired in corruption and discontent, there was more and more talk in Zelensky's circle that they really could make life imitate art. According to Ukrainian political commentator Serhii Rudenko, Bohdan accompanied Zelensky on trips to Geneva and Tel Aviv – Kolomoisky's two residences outside Ukraine – for discussions with the oligarch. Bohdan also had a personal agenda in encouraging Zelensky to go into politics. Poroshenko had removed Bohdan as a candidate from his party's voting lists and filed criminal cases against him. Kolomoisky, too, had a personal grudge against Poroshenko, who had fired him as Governor of Dnipropetrovsk in March 2015. Poroshenko then removed Kolomoisky's protégé as a chief executive of the UkrTransNafta, the country's oil-pipeline authority, prompting Kolomoisky to despatch his private security guards to seize control of the company's headquarters and expel the new government-appointed management.[36]

Kolomoisky's Privat Bank was also coming under legal attack both from Poroshenko's administration and EU investigators. A Latvian subsidiary was shut down after the Bank of Italy found breaches of money-laundering regulations. Billions of dollars in soft loans had been handed out to firms owned by seven top managers and two subordinates of Kolomoisky. 'Large-scale, coordinated fraudulent actions of the bank shareholders and management caused a loss to the state of at least $5.5 billion,' said Valeria Hontareva, a former chairwoman of Ukraine's Central Bank. The sum represented some 33 per cent of all private bank deposits. In 2018 Privatbank was nationalised and bailed out with a $5.6 billion loan from the International Monetary Fund.

Facing ruin and possible criminal prosecution, Kolomoisky fled Ukraine and did not return till 2019. The disgraced oligarch 'was looking for a candidate who could overthrow his arch enemy [Poroshenko] and protect his interests', says the Kvartal 95 source. 'He thought he'd found one in [Zelensky] ... he thought we were for sale, just like all the politician-prostitutes in our country.'[37]

Servant of the People continued to air weekly and became a showcase for Zelensky's political ideas – mockery of the corruption of the political class and of the stranglehold Ukraine's oligarchs held over the country's politics and media. Zelensky formally announced he was running for president on New Year's Eve 2018. 'I'm not kidding,' was the slogan broadcast on the radio and on billboards across the country.[38]

Kolomoisky-controlled TV channels and newspapers rallied to support Zelensky's candidacy. But the key moment of Zelensky's campaign came when he invited Poroshenko to a live debate – not in a TV studio but at a Kyiv soccer stadium in front of a large audience. Zelensky's video challenge to Poroshenko to attend the debate was a classic piece of political theatre. Like a boxer preparing for a bout, Zelensky was filmed walking along the corridors of the stadium, entering the field and then dramatically calling on his opponent to face him there – if he had the guts. At the debate itself Zelensky was in his natural element: live on stage, with spotlights, TV cameras and an audience to play like a bell. Zelensky's gut-punch to Poroshenko was the kind of lapidary, emotive phrase that would later make him a darling of the world's media. 'I am not your opponent,' Zelensky belted out. 'I am your verdict.'

According to opposition politician Serhiy Haidai – later appointed by Zelensky as governor of Luhansk – Poroshenko believed 'that a voter is a shallow person who simply forgets what he is promised from one election to another. And he wants to hear certain lies during the campaign. The elections consist of a kind of competition between liars. And people vote for the most talented and boldest one.'[39]

Perhaps Poroshenko told the wrong lies, or failed to tell them convincingly enough. Or, more likely, Ukrainians were tired of years of war and confrontation with Moscow, and preferred Zelensky's promise to bring peace to Donbas and reverse discrimination against Ukraine's Russian speakers. In any case on 21 April 2019 Zelensky was elected in an unprecedented landslide, winning 73 per cent of the vote to Poroshenko's 25 per cent.

'He won by showing us that we belong in this twenty-first century. We exist. Here and now. Independent and strong,' said

Zelensky's press secretary Iuliia Mendel. 'Volodymyr Zelensky showed us that we can be different: confident, powerful, with a seat at the table.'[40] By Serhii Rudenko's account, Zelensky's victory was underpinned by something more prosaic – a profound revolt against the corruption of the old political class. Either way, in eight years Zelensky had gone from being President Yanukovych's birthday entertainment, to playing a fictional president on TV, to becoming president in real life.

Reality TV

There is a scene in the first season of *Servant of the People* where the neophyte fictional president Vasyl Holoborodko fantasises about charging into parliament, a machine gun in each hand, and gunning down the old guard who have frustrated his every initiative. The real-life Zelensky attempted something along the same lines – though without the *Scarface*-style machine guns. He demanded the immediate resignation of the head of the Security Service of Ukraine, or SBU, the defence minister, the prosecutor general and a swathe of other officials. Most of the members of Zelensky's first cabinet were under 40 years old and only one – veteran interior minister Arsen Avakov – had previously served as a minister. Oleksiy Honcharuk, Zelensky's first prime minister, arrived for his first day in office on an electric scooter and wearing a polo shirt, jeans and sneakers.

Zelensky's first problem was a parliament still dominated by members of the defeated Poroshenko's party. In April 2019 the Rada, knowing that its days were numbered, passed a controversial law mandating that all civil servants, soldiers, doctors and teachers use only Ukrainian at work. It was the latest in a long series of laws seeking to impose Ukrainian on the 40 per cent of the country's population that spoke Russian as their native language. One of them was Zelensky himself. The law immediately drew sharp criticism both within the Russian-speaking eastern regions of Ukraine as well as from abroad – not least because the latest legislation seemed to contravene the European Charter of Languages, drawn up to protect the rights of minority language speakers.

Among the most outspoken critics of the law was billionaire oligarch Viktor Medvedchuk. 'The biggest strategic mistake of the current government is trying to build a single national identity for a country where people speak different languages, profess different religions and have different views on history,' Medvedchuk told the filmmaker Oliver Stone in 2019. 'That [single] identity will never be established on the territory of all of Ukraine.'[41] The criticism was unfair. Zelensky would later make significant efforts to defuse the question of language as a hot-button political issue and made several significant political speeches in Russian. The law had been passed not by his government but by a lame-duck parliament – a parliament that Zelensky immediately moved to dissolve by calling snap elections for July 2019.

In those elections Zelensky had expected his Servant of the People party to win about 80 seats out of 450.[42] Instead they gained 254 – leaving some 154 parliamentary seats with no immediate candidates to fill them. Zelensky had to find like-minded people to implement his vision for a modern Ukraine, and fast. Zelensky had campaigned on the slogan of 'No to nepotism and friends in power!' In practice, he ended up hastily nominating childhood and university friends, a swathe of Kvartal 95 employees and associates as well as photographers, party planners, celebrity restaurateurs and television executives to positions in parliament and his administration. One childhood friend and business partner became head of the SBU. The former director of Kvartal-Concert went from organising Kvartal 95's live shows to becoming Rada deputy and adviser to Ukraine's National Security and Defence Council. Kvartal 95's lawyer Andriy Yermak would replace Bohdan as head of the

Office of the President, with the company's former creative producer and screenwriter as his deputy. And so on. 'The Poroshenko Family was replaced by the Zelensky Family,' said Rudenko. 'Or, more precisely, by Kvartal 95 Studio ... People who, without Zelensky, would never have found themselves involved in Ukrainian politics.'[43]

In the Kremlin, Zelensky's election was met with mixed feelings. On the one hand, Zelensky was considered a 'clown, a drug addict and a joke', recalled Russian TV producer Anna Bondarenko. 'The [bosses] said, go crazy on this guy's ass. We had a lot of fun replaying all his funniest clips ... in high heels, playing the piano with his dick, juxtaposed with him trying to look serious and presidential.'[44] Zelensky's apparent weakness could make him easy meat for a fresh round of Kremlin influence operations – and his stated willingness to work with Russia to find peace offered opportunities that had been impossible under the implacably anti-Moscow Petro Poroshenko. On the other hand, Zelensky's election was also seen as the latest stage in a US-orchestrated operation to take over Ukraine and use it as an instrument against Russia. 'The actor was hired to do his job,' Senator Oleg Morozov, then a member of the Federation Council's International Affairs Committee, told me at the time. 'Washington put its guy in to push their usual programme further ... the creation of an anti-Russia.'[45]

The Kremlin was not alone in probing the inexperienced Zelensky for weakness. In July 2019 Donald Trump phoned Zelensky and asked him to investigate the Ukrainian business activities of Hunter Biden, son of Trump's opponent in the upcoming presidential elections in November, as well as to assist Trump associate (and former New York Mayor) Rudy Giuliani in his enquires about alleged interference in the 2016 election sponsored by pro-Russian Ukrainian oligarchs. Though (controversially) a verbatim transcript was not kept, the readout of the call that the White House was later forced to publish suggests that Trump hinted strongly that further US military aid to Ukraine would be contingent on Zelensky's cooperation.

'The international media later claimed that Trump was trying to arrange a quid pro quo deal … Ukraine [was] unfortunately presented as a victim of its long-time ally,' recalled Zelensky's press secretary Iuliia Mendel. 'It was a hard thing for Ukraine, whose national image was one of self-reliance and strength, to have to plead for aid to support our military.' Zelensky himself was placed in a bind. 'Hunter's father, Joe, might soon become the next president, so it was certainly not in our interest to make an enemy of the United States,' continued Mendel. After Congress convened hearings to impeach Trump over his attempted extortion, Zelensky himself insisted that 'I never talked to the President from the position of a quid pro quo. That's not my thing … I don't want us to look like beggars.'[46] Nothing compromising was found on Hunter Biden and a package of $400 million in US military aid was released to Ukraine. But Zelensky's role as the victim of an attempt by Trump to bully allies diminished his international standing.

Zelensky's newly elected real-life servants of the people worked, by Iuliia Mendel's account, like a 'mad printer' that shot out new laws weekly. But Andriy Bohdan believed, according to Rudenko, that 'Zelensky's victory in the election was his own.'[47] Bohdan, appointed as head of Zelensky's presidential administration, began to remove officials who appeared a threat to Kolomoisky's interests, among them the prosecutor general and the governor of the National Bank of Ukraine. When Zelensky's first prime minister Oleksiy Honcharuk tried to loosen Kolomoisky's control of a state-owned electricity company, he too was fired.

By the end of Zelensky's first year in power it looked like his administration – despite its early idealism – was sliding into the familiar mire of corruption that Zelensky himself had once railed against so passionately. In October 2019 Ukraine's Anti-

Corruption Prosecutor's Office opened a criminal case involving 14 members of parliament, 11 of whom were members of the Servant of the People party, for allegedly receiving $30,000 each for voting against a bill to eliminate corruption schemes in real estate valuations. None of the suspects ended up in jail, and none resigned their post as a people's deputy. Alexander Trukhin, another Servant of the People MP, avoided jail for crashing his car while under the influence of alcohol.[48]

Ironically in the light of his later adamantine resistance to the Russian invasion, in the first part of his presidency Zelensky was frequently attacked for being too ready to deal with the Kremlin. It was true: Zelensky was determined to fulfil his central campaign promise to end the Russo-Ukrainian War and resolve the Russia-sponsored separatist movement there. In June 2019 he appointed former president Leonid Kuchma – a veteran of talks with Moscow who had longstanding contacts in Russia – as Ukraine's representative in the Tripartite Contact Group for a settlement of the conflict. In July he held his first telephone conversation with Putin and urged him to enter into a new round of talks mediated by European countries. He also asked Putin to consider an exchange of 35 Russian prisoners of war for the same number of Ukrainian soldiers and sailors in Russian captivity – including filmmaker Oleg Sentsov, sentenced to 20 years' imprisonment by a Russian court in August 2015 on charges of plotting terrorism.

The prisoner exchange eventually agreed in September 2019 could have been a vital step towards a lasting peace. On his way to meet the returning captives, Zelensky rashly tweeted news of the coming swap – which immediately triggered a last-minute Russian demand that one more prisoner be added to the list: Vladimir Tsemakh, a separatist fighter from eastern Ukraine and a key witness to the downing of Flight MH-17 by a Russian missile in July 2014. The Dutch, who were leading the investigation into the atrocity, asked Zelensky to refuse. But the Ukrainian leader was trapped – having already announced the swap, he had no way to back down.[49] The fragile rapprochement that Zelensky had tried to build with Moscow broke down almost as soon as it had begun.

Putin's last-minute bullying over the prisoner exchanges was 'the moment that [Zelensky] really understood at first hand what kind of people we were dealing with' in the Kremlin, recalled a senior Zelensky adviser who was directly involved in the prisoner-exchange negotiations.[50]

Nonetheless Zelensky pressed on, negotiating directly with the rebel leadership in Donbas. A key measure in the 2015 Minsk-2 agreement had been the holding of a referendum in the LDNR on whether the people of the rebel republics wished to remain part of Ukraine. But a major sticking point was that the Poroshenko government had refused to countenance such elections being organised by the rebel administrations rather than by the Kyiv authorities. But in October 2019 Zelensky announced that he had struck a preliminary deal with the separatists, under which the Ukrainian government would respect elections held in Donbas in exchange for Russia withdrawing its unmarked troops.[51] The formula for a referendum had been drawn up in 2016 by then German foreign minister Frank-Walter Steinmeier and included supervision of the vote by independent representatives of the Organization for Security and Co-operation in Europe, or OSCE. If the OSCE were to judge the balloting to be free and fair and the result were in favour of remaining within Ukraine, then Ukraine would be returned control of the regions under a special self-governing status.

Zelensky approved the Steinmeier Formula, as did the LDNR and Russia. Unhelpfully, separatist media in the occupied Donbas crowed that Zelensky's signing of the agreement was 'a victory for the DNR and the LNR over Ukraine'.[52] But the most passionate opposition to Zelensky's initiative came from hardline Ukrainian nationalists. Thousands of protesters gathered on

Kyiv's Maidan Square under the slogan 'No capitulation!'[53] More menacingly, several Ukrainian nationalist militias, including the Azov Battalion that was then fighting in the Luhansk region of Donbas, refused to accept the agreement. Andriy Biletsky, the leader of the far-right National Corps and first commander of the Azov Battalion, accused Zelensky of 'disrespecting' veterans and of acting on behalf of the Kremlin.[54] Zelensky met Biletsky and other militia leaders in an attempt to convince them to surrender their unregistered weapons and accept the peace accord. They refused, and the referendum plan collapsed – and with it any realistic chance of peace in Donbas.

Even three years later, the missed chance of a lasting peace in October 2019 remained an extremely touchy subject for senior members of the Zelensky administration. Zelensky's opponents 'said that he was the hostage of the ultra-nationalists – and frankly there was some truth to that', admitted one presidential adviser. '[Zelensky] had been elected to bring peace. But there were armed elements on both sides who were not ready to make the compromises necessary ... they preferred to fight than give one centimetre.'[55] The threat of a nationalist Maidan implacably opposed to any kind of compromise with the Kremlin had destroyed Zelensky's attempt to bring peace in 2019 – and would remain a major threat to any future negotiated peace in the endgame of the 2022 war.

But though the implementation of Minsk-1 and 2 was going nowhere, Zelensky pushed France and Germany to facilitate personal peace talks between him and Putin. The two leaders met for the first and only time in Paris on 9 December 2019. From the first moments of the meeting Zelensky was visibly nervous. During the protocol photoshoot before the talks Zelensky mistakenly took Putin's place, then turned to talk to journalists and inadvertently showed Ukraine's position papers for the talks to photographers. Putin, as usual, was late. The photoshoot over, Putin leaned over to Zelensky. 'Once everyone has left, we will start negotiations,' the Russian president said, stating the obvious in order to demonstrate that he was in charge.[56]

Publicly, Zelensky said he hoped to resume the dialogue for peace. But both he and Putin knew that October's 'No Capitulation' protests had shown how limited Zelensky's room for compromise was at home. Putin, for his part, intended to test how far the Ukrainian president's reopening of talks could be used to the Kremlin's advantage.

Zelensky and Putin's meeting made no political progress – nor could it, as Zelensky had already made significant concessions in October but been thwarted by his own nationalist opposition. Putin's hectoring style did not help. 'Putin knew how to give orders, but he didn't know how to negotiate,' recalled Mendel. 'For more than two decades, no one had contradicted him, nor had anyone been willing to bring him bad news. This made Putin a weak negotiator. Instead, he used only blackmail and various instruments of war to negotiate.'[57]

But the meeting did at least yield a ceasefire. Even before the Paris summit, the death tolls from the sporadic fighting along the line of control in Donbas were far smaller than they had been during the heavy fighting early in the war – in 2017 60 were killed and 308 wounded on both sides, in 2018 51 were killed and 304 injured, and in 2019 there were 36 dead and 129 wounded, according to the Ukrainian General Staff and the LDNR's own reports.[58] After the Paris deal casualty figures would sink to single figures – and the ceasefire held until February 2022.

But Zelensky's Ukraine was becoming a problem for Putin. The traditional methods that the Kremlin had hitherto used to control governments in Kyiv – gas wars, corrupting ministers and using oligarchic media influence – were no longer working as Zelensky moved to curb the power of the oligarchs, including his own one-time patron Kolomoisky. Most fatefully, Zelensky also began strengthening Ukraine's ties to NATO and accelerating its path to membership. To the Kremlin, it was further proof that

Zelensky was Washington's puppet. Zelensky's desire to move Ukraine from being a military and political ally of the West to becoming a fully integrated member of the Western alliance was the sum of all the Kremlin's fears.

PART II

WARPATH

CHAPTER 5
WARPATH

War is always a partial or full miscalculation. You miscalculate how strong you are and you miscalculate how weak the enemy is. You miscalculate how easy it's going to be, how low the costs are, how great the benefits.

Stephen Kotkin[1]

The Kremlin Has Many Towers

Separately, every contributing factor behind the Kremlin's decision to invade Ukraine in 2022 had been in place for years, even decades. Complaints over NATO expansion and resistance to a US-dominated 'uni-polar world' had been a staple of Russian political discourse since the 1990s. Kremlin threats to dismember Ukraine had been around since Boris Yeltsin tried to bully the Ukrainian Supreme Soviet by 're-considering' the status of Crimea as far back as August 1991. Fantasies about anti-Russian 'fascists' coming to power in Kyiv were, as we have seen, first entertained by pro-Russian propagandists in 2003. Frustration that millions of ethnic Russians had been abandoned beyond the borders of Russia after the collapse of the USSR was the 'geopolitical tragedy' that Putin spoke of in his 2005 address to parliament. Paranoia over Western attempts to subvert and undermine Russia through pro-democracy movements had formed the central pillar of the Kremlin's domestic policy ever since the colour revolutions in 2003–04. Putin's belligerent speech announcing war on the morning of 24 February 2022 contained nothing that he and his entourage hadn't been saying for years.

Some stories make more sense when you stand them on their head. So it's worth asking not why Putin launched his full-scale invasion of Ukraine in 2022, but why he did not do it sooner? What changed between 2014 – when Putin held back from an all-in military annexation of Donbas and other Russian-speaking areas of Ukraine – and his final decision to do so in 2022?

The answer can be divided into three sets of factors.

First and foremost in the minds of Putin's entourage was the conviction that by the end of 2021 the jeopardy from Western influence in Ukraine and Russia had become too threatening to ignore – and all attempts to control it by meddling in Ukraine's politics had failed.

Second, the perceived economic downsides of the invasion were deemed to be acceptable to a small coterie of KGB men who had little knowledge of how Russia's economy really worked. A war chest of $650 billion in strategic reserves and European dependence on Russian gas, both carefully built up over a decade, were judged sufficient to ride out and mute Western protests.

The final factor was opportunity. A confluence of Western weakness in the aftermath of the humiliating withdrawal from Afghanistan, the retirement of Angela Merkel as Europe's senior statesperson, the electoral weakness of Zelensky and a revamped Russian army seemed to present a once-in-a lifetime opportunity. Now was the moment to put a dramatic end to decades of creeping Western influence and put Russia firmly back in the first rank of world powers. Not to strike would be to abandon Ukraine to the West – and fatally expose Russia to the encroaching existential political and military threat.

Such were the strategic considerations behind the war. But the Kremlin's policy was not made solely on the basis of abstract strategic factors. It was made by people – and in a system with a firmly entrenched and closed leadership circle like Putin's Russia, the decision to go to war was made by a tiny group of men with direct personal access to Putin himself. Some members of this inner Politburo had been Putin's colleagues and personal friends since the 1970s. All had occupied a variety of senior posts in his administration since 2000.

Over those years Putin's governments had included dissenting voices, competing interests and visions. In the Russian phrase, 'the Kremlin has many towers.' Various fashionable ideas had come and gone – including transforming Russia into a technological superpower, resetting relations with the US and achieving ideological leadership of the world's conservatives, to actively creating and supporting a 'loyal' liberal opposition and media. But by the beginning of 2020 the last of the original thinkers behind all these initiatives – people who could have seen the coming disaster and turned Putin and his inner circle of *siloviki*, or men of power, away from the path of war – had gone. Only one tower remained, and it contained Putin's oldest, most trusted and – tragically for Russia and Ukraine – most hawkish and paranoid allies. There was nobody left in the room who was free of the fatal groupthink that war was both inevitable and desirable.

As Bob Woodward brilliantly demonstrated in *Plan of Attack*, his narrative of America's path to war in Iraq from 2001–03, no political system is immune to groupthink. Even in advanced democracies, government bureaucracies – especially the intelligence services – have an inbuilt tendency to seek out facts to fit the preconceptions of their leaders. But in 2020 Russia's political system, a gerontocracy headed by men formed in the Soviet-era KGB who did not even use the internet, was particularly vulnerable. 'Nobody wants to bring bad news to the tsar,' said a former official who worked in the presidential administration until 2016. 'The [official] course is clear ... the competition [among advisers and institutions] is who can be most zealous in achieving the tsar's plan.'[2]

The invasion of 2022 was, in the minds of the men who planned and pushed it, first and foremost a pre-emptive strike to save Russia from a looming strategic threat from the West. But it was also a battle for Russia's future – and the future of powerful clans who wished to ensure that their power would survive the end of Putin's tenure as president. Their task was to create a Russia in which no future Western-inspired Bolotnaya protests would be possible. By that token, the attempted murder of Aleksei Navalny in August 2020 and the invasion of Ukraine were all part of a single overarching strategic task – to protect Russia from foreign interference, and thereby protect their own power and assets.

Soon after his appointment as director of the FSB in 2000, Nikolai Patrushev described the security services as Russia's 'modern neo-aristocracy'. The word for 'nobility' in Russian is *dvoryantstvo*, literally members of the royal *dvor* or court, where the sole fount of patronage and power is the tsar himself. Twenty years later, Patrushev and all the other leading *siloviki* had fulfilled not just the executive functions of pre-modern courtiers but the dynastic ones too.

The children of the new nobility were appointed ministers and heads of major state corporations in their own right. Nikolai Patrushev's son Dmitry, for instance, was appointed Russia's minister of agriculture in 2018 after a career in banking. Aleksandr Bortnikov's son Denis was deputy director of VTB Bank, the second-largest financial institution in Russia. The son of former Prime Minister Mikhail Fradkov – a classmate in the FSB academy of Bortnikov's younger son Andrei – was a senior executive at Gazprom Neft, the gas giant's oil-trading arm. They made dynastic marriages to each other and in turn gave birth to a third rising generation of Putin-era aristocracy who would in time also expect to inherit Russia and all that was in it. At the beginning of his reign Putin had eliminated and despoiled the elements of the Yeltsin-era business oligarchy who dared to challenge him. But he had also created a new oligarchy of securocrats loyal solely to him.

The ideology of late Putinism was the ideology of the institution that formed the men who led it – the Brezhnev-era KGB. In the words of the poet and critic Dmitry Bykov, 'special services have always been in the service of the past. Their main task is to stop the passage of time. They are constantly on the hunt for signs of the new because the future is advancing upon them and against them ... They do everything in their power to prevent their own abolition.'[3] But the existential fear of all gerontocratic regimes is that a new generation will inevitably challenge them and their values. 'Conservation is not creative, you cannot eternally conserve memory or conserve fear of the future.'[4]

In the late nineteenth century Russia's tsars, faced with a similar existential challenge from the encroaching forces of modernity, united their society behind the abstractions of 'Orthodoxy, Autocracy and Nationality' – underpinned by the creation of the myth of a sinister 'other' inside society in the form of Jews. The Soviet Union, for all its social conservatism, was paradoxically founded on the embrace of the future. It was, ostensibly, a state that demanded sacrifices of its people in the name of a bright, collective, communist world to come. But the tsarist-era tropes revived to underpin Putin's kleptocratic autocracy had limited appeal to a new generation of atheistic, net-savvy, naturally capitalist and inter-connected young Russians. Unlike China or the USSR, Russia had no highly developed government and party structure, no powerful and long-established state ideology of collective prosperity, no towering achievements in space exploration or world-aweing urban and technological development to unite behind.

Though neither Putin's *siloviki* – nor even ultra-conservative philosophers like Aleksandr Dugin – would put it in these terms, a war of national salvation was the only force powerful enough to stop the encroachment of the modern world and radically cut the country off from the West. The leaders of both the US and Russia during their last critical confrontation during the Cuban Missile Crisis were veterans of the Second World War and shared a deep horror of war, born of personal experience. Putin's generation, by contrast, missed the Great Patriotic War but were raised on heroic cinematic myths of the unity, nobility and purification that came of fighting a just war against the forces of evil. War would create a new Russia grounded in patriotism and sacrifice, not the selfish pursuit of comfort and prosperity. Above all, it would create a Russia that needed men of power to lead it. 'In wartime you do not think about IKEA or buying a new car,' said the TV executive Molody. 'In wartime you think of victory, and of the leaders who are saving your country from its enemies … in peacetime, you think how life could be better. In war, you think of how everything could be so much worse.'[5]

There was no explicit, dastardly plot to deliberately use war to turn the clock back to the future and create an isolated, reactionary Russia where they could rule unchallenged forever. On the contrary, the men who led Russia to war in 2022 insisted that they had no choice but to react to the West's relentless encroachment on Russia's strategic space. More, both Putin and Patrushev would claim that they were not taking anything but merely claiming what was Russia's own by ancient right. But in practice the war represented the final triumph of an elderly Russia over a young one, of paranoid Soviet-minded conspiracy theorists over a generation of post-Soviet, postmodern practical capitalists.

The Men of Power

Four men – three of whom were former or current directors of the FSB – were to play a decisive role in leading Russia to war: Putin himself, Nikolai Patrushev, Aleksandr Bortnikov and Sergei Shoigu. Of the latter three it was Patrushev and Bortnikov who were the prime political movers, Shoigu the sometimes hesitant executor. A slightly wider group of personal intimates, all linked to Putin through service in the KGB or membership of the exclusive St Petersburg Ozero dacha collective where the city's business and government elite lived in the 1990s, formed a chorus of approval. But, according to a source close to Kremlin spokesman Dmitry Peskov, they were not privy to the full details and scale of the invasion. This second circle of Putin's personal intimates included billionaire Yury Kovalchuk; foreign intelligence chief Sergei Naryshkin; Putin's former bodyguard and head of the Russian National Guard Viktor Zolotov; ex-KGB officer turned state oil tsar Igor Sechin; former Kremlin chief of staff and ex-KGB man Sergei Ivanov; Putin's ex-KGB colleague from East German days and head of the state-owned technology concern Rostec Sergei Chemezov; Igor Sechin, the former KGB man who headed Russia's Rosneft oil giant; and billionaire oil trader Arkady Rotenburg.

Other senior officials played important executive roles, but had no say in the decision-making of the innermost circle of Putin intimates and were not his personal friends. This group of loyal executives included Foreign Minister Sergei Lavrov, Sergei Beseda, the FSB colonel-general in charge of relations with the near abroad, and Dmitry Kozak, the Kremlin's man on the ground in the rebel Donbas republics.

Patrushev

Over the two decades of Putin's rule the title of 'grey cardinal' of the Kremlin has been attached to several prominent figures – most famously to ideologue Vladislav Surkov and Rosneft head Igor Sechin. But the title properly belonged to Nikolai Patrushev, consistently the single most important and powerful figure in Putin's inner circle from the late 1990s onwards.

Like most members of the Kremlin's top elite, Patrushev was born in Leningrad, in 1951, a year before Putin himself. The son of a Soviet naval officer, Patrushev studied at the Leningrad Shipbuilding Institute and briefly worked as a naval engineer before being recruited by the KGB in 1975. Putin, by contrast, was never headhunted by the secret police but, by his own account, applied to the KGB on his own initiative several times before finally being accepted.[6] The two young officers met in the Leningrad KGB. But of the two it was Patrushev, not Putin, who was the high flyer. Patrushev attended the KGB school in Minsk and later the higher school of the KGB in Moscow before joining the prestigious anti-smuggling and anti-corruption unit of the Leningrad KGB. Putin's career trajectory was far more modest – the KGB office in Dresden where he was posted in 1988 was a provincial post in a friendly, socialist country. 'The high flyers were posted to capitalist countries, or had responsibilities for economic crimes,' recalled one former KGB major-general who served in the KGB *rezidentura* in London during the 1980s. 'Dresden was a backwater. [Putin] was a grey moth, a nobody. His career in the KGB was completely mediocre.' It was Patrushev, not Putin, who was 'one of the [KGB's] rising stars of the 1980s'.[7]

Putin was still just a 38-year-old major when the KGB let him go in 1990. His promotion to lieutenant colonel – and with it the important-sounding honorific of 'colonel' – was a pre-retirement formality that allowed him to claim a slightly higher pension. Patrushev, by contrast, remained in the secret police after the collapse of the USSR, serving as minister of security of the Republic of Karelia in northern Russia and, from 1994 onwards, as head of the Directorate of Internal Security of the newly rechristened Federal Counterintelligence Service in Moscow. After March 1997, when Putin was recruited from the St Petersburg mayor's office to the presidential administration in Moscow, he did not forget his old colleagues from Leningrad. The following May, Putin was promoted to first deputy chief of the presidential administration – and brought in his old colleague Patrushev to take his old job as head of the Kremlin's Main Supervisory Department.

By this time the two men's roles had been reversed, with the younger and lower-ranking Putin now the senior man. When Putin was once again promoted to head of the FSB in July 1998 he soon brought Patrushev in as his deputy and chief of the prestigious (and profitable) Directorate for Economic Security. Putin's meteoric rise – sponsored by both Kremlin Chief of Staff Voloshin and oligarch Boris Berezovsky – continued with a promotion to secretary of the Security Council, leaving his old post as FSB director to be occupied by Patrushev. Putin was chosen as Yeltsin's prime minister – and likely successor – in August 1999. On New Year's Eve in 1999, on the night that Yeltsin made his surprise announcement that Putin would replace him as acting president, Patrushev and Putin flew to Chechnya with their wives to bolster Russian troops' morale, drinking champagne as they flew in the helicopter above the combat zone.[8] In March 2000 Putin made his old friend Patrushev a Hero of Russia, the nation's highest order of valour.

As Putin joked to a group of KGB veterans after his election in 2000, 'the special operation to take over the highest echelons of power has been successful'.[9] In December of that year Patrushev made his remarks about the security services being Russia's 'neo-nobility'. Explaining the preponderance of former FSB officials in the Kremlin, Patrushev told *Komsomolskaya Pravda* that there was a 'vital need to revive the Russian administrative corps with "fresh blood" ... not limp idealists, but tough pragmatists who understand international and domestic political developments, emerging contradictions and threats'.[10] Patrushev lost no time in taking the fight to the enemy, playing a key role in the 2006 poisoning of ex-FSB whistleblower and defector Alexander Litvinenko in London 'The FSB operation to kill Mr Litvinenko was probably approved by Mr Patrushev and also by President Putin,' concluded a UK public inquiry into the murder.

In 2008 Putin appointed Patrushev to the post of secretary of the Security Council, the fifth time in a decade he'd taken over a post formerly held by Putin. Patrushev would play a key role in an increasingly assertive foreign policy and repressive internal security practice. In the aftermath of the Maidan revolution in Kyiv, Patrushev's belief that the United States 'would much prefer that Russia did not exist at all' manifested in ever more aggressive influence operations in Eastern Europe – including a failed FSB-backed coup d'état in Montenegro in October 2016.

Patrushev had been always been one of the most talkative and high-profile members of Putin's inner circle, authorised to explain and decipher official Kremlin policy to the Russian press and public. It was a clear sign of his seniority and the trust placed in him by Putin personally.

In his many interviews Patrushev revealed not only a remarkable degree of paranoia but a willingness to believe some extraordinary conspiracy theories. In 2015, for instance, Patrushev said that 'the Americans believe that we control [our natural resources] illegally and undeservedly because, in their view, we do not use them as they ought to be used.' In support of this claim he cited former US Secretary of State Madeleine Albright, whom Patrushev claimed had stated that 'neither the Far East nor Siberia belong to Russia.' In fact Albright had never said any such thing. The quote came from a psychic employed by the FSB who claimed to have read the thoughts in Albright's mind while in a state of trance.[11] In April 2022 Patrushev claimed that a 'criminal community who fled Ukraine' were 'engaged in the widespread business of the sale of orphans taken out of Ukraine'. The trade in orphans was deliberately abetted by Western governments, Patrushev claimed. These same governments had also covertly 'revived the shadow market for the purchase of human organs from the socially vulnerable segments of the Ukrainian population for clandestine transplant operations for European patients'.[12]

In June 2020 Patrushev gave a lengthy and chilling interview where he outlined the world view that would become the underpinning of the Ukraine invasion less than two years later. According to Patrushev, Western efforts to 'destabilize the socio-political situation in our country' were intensifying. 'An extensive network of foreign non-profit NGOs and domestic public structures dependent on them is being created on Russian territory to implement so-called democratic programs and projects that meet the interests of Western states,' explained Patrushev. 'The West unites and supports [Russia's] non-systemic opposition financially ... interferes in Russian elections at the federal and regional levels.' Citing 'data at our disposal', Patrushev announced that US-backed subversive elements inside Russia were

> expected to intensify their work ... to provoke nationalist and separatist sentiments. Steps are planned to intensify information pressure on Russia in order to erode the Russian spiritual, moral, cultural and historical values that form the foundation of our statehood, to reduce the feeling of an all-Russian identity among the citizens of our country. Their main tasks are to split Russian society, impose values and development models that are beneficial to them, and manipulate public consciousness.

He specifically named the US State Department, a variety of American civil society NGOs and George Soros's Open Society Institute as the agencies involved in Washington's ongoing attack on Russia's statehood. Patrushev also claimed that between 2015 and 2019 Russian entities and individuals had received over 4 billion rubles – some £40 million – to fund 'subversive activities against Russia'.

To Patrushev, the threat of a Western-backed coloured revolution in Russia was real, immediate and growing. Revealingly, he claimed that the US plot was reliant on a new generation of 'people who entered adulthood after the collapse of the USSR and therefore did not have personal experience or real knowledge about the Soviet Union'. By Patrushev's calculation, this generation would 'naturally' become Russia's senior managers by 2036 – though he noted that the experience of Georgia and Ukraine showed that 'the process of formation of elites ... hostile to Russia can be accelerated artificially'.[13] In other words, the creeping rise of a post-Soviet generation most vulnerable to US propaganda was a direct challenge to Russia's national security. And taking decisive action to 'neutralise the threat' and 'counteract the unfolding anti-state process' was not just a race against time but a question of Russia's very existence.

Even as Patrushev spoke to *Argumenty i Fakty* in June 2020, a team of FSB operatives under the orders of FSB chief Aleksandr Bortnikov was preparing to fight back against the man regarded by the *siloviki* as the US's most dangerous agent inside Russia – opposition leader Aleksei Navalny. Flight records showed that agents had been following Navalny all year in his travels around the country as he rallied supporters to back a new smart voting initiative that threatened to topple incumbents from the ruling United Russia party from their seats in local elections. On 19 August 2020 a team broke into his hotel room in Tomsk, Siberia, and by their own account smeared Novichok nerve agent on the seams of Navalny's underpants as they lay in a drawer. The next day Navalny went into a coma on board a flight back to Moscow and would have died if the pilots had not made an emergency landing in Omsk that saved his life.

Inconveniently for the FSB, Navalny survived the poisoning – but obligingly voluntarily returned to Russia in December 2020, he was immediately arrested and soon convicted on charges of fraud. With Russia's leading opposition figure safely in jail, Patrushev moved on to framing a permanent solution to the Ukraine problem. In an updated version of Russia's national security strategy published in May 2021 and coordinated by Patrushev, the Russian state was explicitly allowed to use 'forceful methods' to 'thwart or avert unfriendly actions that threaten the sovereignty and territorial integrity of the Russian Federation'. In other words, the use of military force outside Russia's borders was effectively pre-authorised. It was a legal blueprint for the coming invasion.

Bortnikov

Aleksandr Bortnikov, born in 1951 in the Urals city of Perm, studied at Leningrad's Institute of Railway Engineers before being recruited to the Leningrad KGB in 1975, where he first met Putin. Like Patrushev, he remained in the KGB and its later incarnations FSK and FSB, rising to head the Saint Petersburg and Leningrad province FSB in June 2003. A year later he was brought to Moscow to fill Patrushev's old job as chief of the Economic Security Service – known as 'Department K' – of the FSB, and became a deputy director of the agency. Despite its innocuous-sounding title, Department K was in fact one of the most powerful and feared departments of Russia's secret police. According to an investigation by the independent Moscow magazine *The New Times*, Bortnikov was tasked by then-FSB Director

Patrushev with overseeing the 2006 operation to poison Alexander Litvinenko in London.[14]

When Nikolai Patrushev was moved to the Security Council in May 2008, Bortnikov was right behind him, stepping into his old patron's job as head of the FSB – a post that he still holds. Under Patrushev, the FSB had become 'the biggest business structure in Russia', according to a Moscow-based financial consultant who worked with current and former members of the FSB on various international investment schemes. 'Power to put people in jail can make you money,' said the consultant as matter-of-factly as though he were explaining the basic laws of physics. 'And money helps you keep your power, if you kick it up to the right people and don't get greedy.'[15] Officers of every level became notorious for threatening businesspeople with investigation and imprisonment unless they handed over their businesses to the FSB and its associates – a practice known as *reiderstvo*, or corporate raiding, Russian style.

A series of scandals – including massive FSB-orchestrated hostile takeovers of the Tri Kita chain of furniture superstores and the Evroset mobile-phone retail network – made it onto the front pages of Russia's newspapers and embarrassed the Kremlin. Bortnikov wanted the FSB to 'become the sword and shield of the Russian state once more, just like [secret police founder Felix] Dzerzhinsky intended', said the consultant. Bortnikov personally 'hated the idea of [state security officers] as thieves and dirty businessmen' and made a point of rewarding and promoting zealous young officers who sought out subversive groups and weeded out 'foreign agents', journalists, human rights activists and historians who challenged the official Kremlin view of history. 'He did not like people who undermined the motherland,' said the source, who had several personal meetings with Bortnikov between 2008 and 2015.[16]

Bortnikov was a reliable and relentless attack dog who turned the FSB back into the aggressive political inquisition it had been under the USSR – and sought to rehabilitate the reputation of the agency. On the hundredth anniversary of the foundation of the first Soviet secret police in 2017 Bortnikov told *Rossiiskaya Gazeta* that the archives showed 'a significant part' of the criminal cases of Stalin's purges of the 1930s 'had an objective side to them'. But he was also deadly serious not just about political security but also about practical national security issues. In 2018 he travelled to Washington with Foreign Intelligence Service head Sergei Naryshkin and military intelligence chief Igor Korobov to discuss with CIA director Mike Pompeo the threat of Islamic State fighters returning from Syria to Russia and Central Asia. In return for his loyal service Putin in 2019 made Bortnikov a Hero of Russia and appointed him General of the Army, the highest military rank in Russia – making the country's secret police chief the service equal of its minister of defence, Sergei Shoigu.

Shoigu

In both background and temperament, Sergei Shoigu was the outlier in Putin's inner circle. Putin and most of his old friends came from modest backgrounds and owed their social and professional mobility entirely to their service in the KGB. Shoigu, on the other hand, was born into the provincial Party elite of the Republic of Tuva, on the Mongolian border. His ethnic Tuvan father was a newspaper editor who rose to be regional Party secretary, and his Russian mother was a deputy in Tuva's Regional Council of People's Deputies.

Thanks to his father's Party connections Shoigu – a civil engineer by training – was appointed deputy chairman of the Russian Soviet Socialist Federation's Architecture and Construction Committee in 1990, where he held equal rank with rising Party star Boris Yeltsin. The following year, as the USSR's institutions were collapsing, newly elected Russian Federation President

Yeltsin appointed Shoigu to head the Russian Rescue Corps, which had been formed to replace the old Civil Defence Troops of the Soviet Ministry of Defence. The Corps – later renamed the Ministry of Emergency Situations – was a quasi-military body that eventually became responsible for fire-fighting, disaster response and civil defence, and was Russia's third-largest paramilitary force. Shoigu, now a major-general, coordinated an unsuccessful attempt to evacuate Russian-backed Afghan President Mohammad Najibullah from Kabul in 1992. The following year he was placed in charge of distribution of weapons from civil defence stocks to supporters of Yeltsin during an attempted coup in Moscow in October 1993. In 1999 Yeltsin leveraged Shoigu's popularity and reputation as a saver of lives by making him one of the leaders of the pro-government Unity Party, which backed Prime Minister Vladimir Putin's rise to the presidency. Shoigu was made a Hero of Russia in recognition of his political services.

Shoigu had showed himself a competent, loyal, safe pair of hands both as a minister and as a politician – but who crucially did not appear to have any political ambitions of his own. Putin formed a close personal friendship with Shoigu based on a shared passion for riding, hunting and shooting in the Russian wilderness. To Putin – a diminutive, weedy urban kid who had spent his entire career in offices – Shoigu's deep personal connection to a wild, manly and untamed Siberian world had a deep appeal. The famous 2017 photoshoot of Putin riding a horse shirtless was taken during a fishing trip to Shoigu's native Tuva. Personally, too, Shoigu was also a different kind of man to the desk-bound office Machiavellis who had surrounded Putin on his long scramble up the greasy pole of bureaucratic power. 'Serezha [Sergei Shoigu] is a very straight, honest guy,' said a former senior Yeltsin-era official who shared a passion for hunting with Shoigu. 'He is not a schemer. With him, words and deeds don't diverge … He is not a guy who tries to tell [Putin] what he wants hear.'[17]

In November 2012 Putin fired Defence Minister Anatoly Serdyukov after a series of high-profile scandals involving schemes dating from Serdyukov's tenure as Russia's top tax official to defraud the state of taxes paid by private companies. One of those scams had ended with the 2007 arrest and death in prison of whistleblowing lawyer Sergei Magnitsky, which led to the first ever round of US and European sanctions against the officials allegedly involved. The core 'St Petersburg group' of *siloviki* around Putin lobbied for one of their own to succeed Serdyukov, thereby bringing Russia's army into the web of power ministries already controlled by the ex-KGB clan. Putin, however, chose Shoigu – partly because of his proven no-nonsense competence, partly because of his personal loyalty to Putin himself and partly to balance out the power of competing clans.

Shoigu lost no time in firing Serdyukov's old Tax Ministry cronies from top Defence Ministry jobs and appointing military officers in their stead. Like Bortnikov over at the FSB, Shoigu believed that Russia's power ministries existed first and foremost to protect the motherland, not to act as a cash cow for ministers and generals. He also speeded up reforms to increase the number of professional contract servicemen in the hitherto conscript-dominated army as well as the creation of more battalion tactical groups (BTGs), the new basic operational unit of motorised infantry. He also created a Special Operations Forces Command to facilitate rapid intervention in conflicts within Russia's 'near abroad'. Under Shoigu Russia's military – which by 2020 was absorbing an enormous 7 per cent of Russia's GDP, compared with under 2 per cent for most NATO countries – was being brought to a state of high organisational readiness in preparation for a major conflict.

2020: The Plates Shift

The moment when the attack on Ukraine went from possible to probable was bookended by two events – the Kremlin's realisation that all its efforts to change Ukraine's westward course had broken down in early 2020, and Zelensky's decision that Ukraine would join major NATO exercises, including in the Black Sea, in March 2021.

Putin's Paris talks with Zelensky in December 2019 had yielded a ceasefire – but also a realisation in the Kremlin that the Donbas pseudo-states had failed to achieve their desired goal. The political leadership in Donbas had proved spectacularly corrupt and impossible to control. Since 2014 dozens of local officials from the LDNR had been fired or died violently in a morass of corruption allegations.[18] On the military front years of low-intensity conflict had actually strengthened Ukraine's statehood and sense of self, instead of splintering it and wearing it down as the Kremlin had wishfully intended. Most importantly, in the wake of Zelensky's humiliation by the 'No Compromise' mini-Maidan of October 2019 it was clear that the rebel republics would also never rejoin Ukraine as semi-independent regions as the Kremlin had intended.

The failure was placed at the feet of Vladislav Surkov, the Kremlin's man on the ground in Ukraine since 2013. Surkov may have been at the heart of the Kremlin's ideological policies since 2003, but he had never become a true insider. He was younger, far smarter, more internationally minded and more cynical than the older generation of Kremlin *siloviki* who had Putin's ear. After years of successfully negotiating the factional struggles between the Kremlin, the presidential administration, the FSB and the military, Surkov finally fell from the tightrope in February 2020.[19]

The truly fatal miscalculation that cost Surkov his career was not over Ukraine but his decision to publicly discuss what a post-Putin Russia might look like. In an essay entitled 'The Long State of Putin' published in *Nezavisimaya Gazeta* in early February 2020 Surkov was careful to emphasise that 'for many years Russia will still be Putin's state' even after Putin stepped down – and claimed that Putinism was 'the ideology of the future'.[20] His message to Putin himself was that he need not fear a transition as the supposed stability he had created would survive the retirement of its founder. Surkov's message to the elites around Putin was that they too had no reason to repeat the disasters of the late communist period where ailing leaders were kept in office until they died. Rather, an orderly transition of power would mean business as usual, preserving the delicate balance of their rival power bases and interests. And Surkov assured the Russian people that the smooth facade of 'sovereign democracy' would continue seamlessly because the people's interests were, he claimed, the same as those of their rulers.

Surkov could have been right. If more pragmatic, more imaginative and less paranoid men had been in Putin's inner circle, a smooth transition to a successor who would preserve the status quo would have been possible. But the *siloviki* drew precisely the opposite conclusion to the one suggested by Surkov. Rather than stability, they saw a post-Putin Russia as nation fatally vulnerable to the relentless Western subversion that so obsessed men like Patrushev and Bortnikov. As Surkov had been tactless enough to point out, the end of Putin's reign was indeed approaching. Whether he was suffering from a serious illness or not will be discussed in more detail below. But the basic fact remained that Putin would turn 70 in October 2022 – young, perhaps, for a US leader but already three years past the life expectancy of the average Russian male. However healthy or otherwise Putin might be, he could not live forever. Leonid Brezhnev – admittedly a smoker and big eater – died a month short of his 76th birthday after 18 years in power. In five or so years Putin would be a lame duck. And to the men of power, that meant that time was running out to find a decisive solution to the West's aggression. And that meant dealing once and for all with the problem of Ukraine.

Surkov resigned in late February 2020, citing 'differences' over Ukraine policy. 'Let's say the context has changed,' he said.[21] He was replaced as Donbas proconsul-in-chief by the Ukrainian-born Dmitry Kozak, a tried-and-tested troubleshooter who had previously wrestled thorny administrative problems like judicial reform and the troublesome North Caucasus.

With Surkov's departure, the Kremlin's policy in Ukraine began a steady drift towards confrontation. But his resignation was also significant in a deeper sense, marking the moment when the top decision-makers left in the Kremlin were those who actually believed the myths generated by Surkov's dream machine. 'Sovereign democracy' had been based on an ultimately cynical and transactional relationship with reality and ideology. In Surkov's world, Orthodox obscurantism could be packed alongside Soviet patriotism and the rhetoric of victim culture, tied up in glossy production values and served up to the public. In annual *Nashy* summer camps, nationalism had been packaged as self-exploration, a journey of discovery to your inner patriot. During Surkov's long tenure as the Kremlin's chief ideologue he had orchestrated the bells and whistles that kept the voters happy. But, crucially, major decisions were in the hands of hard-headed technocratic pragmatists. Professional managers like long-serving Finance Minister Alexei Kudrin – a personal friend of Putin's – managed a sound macroeconomic policy. But by early 2020, the last of those technocrats – for instance Prime Minister Mikhail Mishustin – had been relegated to strictly managerial positions, far outside the decision-making circle.

In truth, none of the so-called 'liberals' inside the Kremlin who had jostled with the *siloviki* for two decades were in fact particularly liberal, much less pro-Western. But figures like Kudrin, Surkov, and former prime ministers Sergei Kiriyenko and Dmitry Medvedev were at least recognisably post-Soviet. Unlike the *siloviki*, these technocrats were members of what an aide to George H. W. Bush once ironically described as 'the reality-based community'. The so-called liberals' common trait was a recognition that Russia's prosperity since the fall of the USSR had been built on its participation in Western banking, investment, trade and economic systems – as well as Western technology and know-how. Even after three decades, Russia still had not learned to manufacture anything the rest of the world wanted to buy (other than arms, though even those were reliant on imported computer chips). Everything that made Russia work, from mobile-phone routers to web servers and the engines of its Siemens-built high-speed trains and its fleet of Boeing- and Airbus-produced planes – was invented and largely manufactured by the West and its Asian allies. Even after 2014 a national push to wean Russia off its import dependence had failed to produce a wholly Russian-made mobile phone, laptop or even computer processing chip, much less a passenger plane.

But by the beginning of 2020 the only men left in the inner circle were not technocrats but Soviet-era fantasists and paranoiacs – people whom Putin trusted for no better reason than that they had proved their personal loyalty to him over 45 years of working relations. The Kremlin's mind was closing. And it was at this crucial moment that a black-swan event occurred that would make that closure into a physical reality. On 31 January 2020 two Chinese citizens in Siberia tested positive for a dangerous new virus.

Bunker Mentality

Covid hit Russia hard. Officially, the pandemic has caused nearly 310,000 deaths in the country – the ninth-highest fatality rate in the world. But the true figure may have been much higher. Government demographic statistics showed that Russia's population had declined by 997,000 between October 2020 and September 2021, its biggest-ever annual drop in peacetime.

In early March 2020 Putin at first tried to downplay the danger, then disappeared from public view. It was left to local leaders like Moscow mayor Sergei Sobianin to introduce draconian quarantine measures that included allowing Muscovites to leave their homes only on certain days, block by block, starting on 30 March. Schools, theatres, museums and international borders were shut all over Russia.

As the pandemic gathered pace in April, Putin retreated from his usual residence of Novo-Ogarevo in the suburbs of Moscow to a more remote presidential residence near Lake Valdai, between Moscow and St Petersburg. According to a reporter who has worked for over a decade in the Kremlin press pool, a small group of official photographers and cameramen were asked to sequester themselves with domestic and secretarial staff in a service wing of Novo-Ogarevo, where they were tested daily.[22] 'Everyone assumed that [the President] would be back in a few days,' recalled the reporter, who still works in the Kremlin. 'No one from outside was allowed anywhere near the residence.' But Putin was not to return to Moscow until 9 May, and then only briefly and in conditions of extreme Covid security, to publicly lay a wreath at the Eternal Flame in the Alexander Gardens after public celebrations were cancelled.

At Novo-Ogarevo and Valdai some $85 million was spent on building quarantine accommodation for staff and visitors as well as buying state-of-the art testing equipment.[23] Anyone coming into contact with Putin was required to observe strict individual quarantine on-site for at least a week. Fresh from victories in Tokyo, Russian Olympic medallists were told they would have to spend a week in quarantine before meeting the president – and were banned from any interaction with each other. 'I still can't believe I'll have to sit in one room for seven days,' Angelina Melnikova, a gymnast, wrote on social media.[24]

Moscow officially emerged from lockdown on 9 June 2020. Restaurants re-opened on 23 June, and the next day the postponed Victory Day parade took place with full military pomp in Red Square. Russian media announced that the pandemic was under control and generally avoided the alarmist, round-the-clock coverage that characterised the Western media response at the time. Deaths from Covid were also massaged down, under official pressure, with strict criteria for reporting deaths from Covid rather than with Covid present. As a result, a Levada poll showed that some 50 per cent of Russians declared that they were 'unconcerned' about Covid (though, in a comment about Russian fatalism, 27 per cent also reported that they knew someone who had died of it). Fully 61 per cent of Russians also said they believed that Covid-19 was a biological weapon.

Putin, however, remained in lockdown. He would continue to be extremely cautious to the point of paranoia about the virus two years later. In February 2022 French President Emmanuel Macron refused a Kremlin request that he take a Russian Covid-19 test when he arrived to see Putin in Moscow. According to two sources in Macron's entourage, French security advisers had warned their president not to allow Russia to get hold of his DNA.[25] (Putin himself had been equally cautious about his DNA for years, taking a chemical toilet with him on all foreign trips.) As a result, at their Kremlin meeting Macron and Putin sat at opposite ends of a vast white table at least six metres long, prompting much satirical comment on social media.

Why was Putin so scared of Covid? An explanation suggested by an open-source investigative group was that Putin was suffering from a chronic illness. In April 2022 the investigative journalism site Proyekt.media published a detailed study based on flight movements of top Russian cancer doctors and Putin's disappearances from the public eye between 2016 and 2020. From 2019 onwards Putin was accompanied on all his trips by no fewer than nine staff doctors – and the head of his medical team was appointed a deputy head of the presidential administration. Among the doctors who spent time with Putin were a team of neurosurgeons from the Central Clinical Hospital and Dr Evgeny Silovanov, a renowned oncologist specialising in thyroid cancer in the elderly, who spent 166 days with Putin over 36 visits. The Proyekt team suggested that Putin may have undergone surgery for cancer in September 2020.[26] His puffy appearance since that time has also been attributed to steroids used to treat cancer. In May 2022 the US filmmaker Oliver Stone – who interviewed Putin many times between 2015 and 2019 – claimed that Vladimir Putin has 'had this cancer' but 'I think he's licked it.'[27]

However, none of the sources interviewed for this book were able to confirm that Putin was chronically ill during lockdown or afterwards. 'Putin is not ill,' said Molody, who coordinated Putin's TV appearances throughout the lockdown. 'I watched dozens of hours of raw footage. He was fitter than ever ... But he has always been very protective of his health.'[28] In July 2022 CIA Director William Burns also said that he had found no evidence of Putin's alleged illness – and quipped dryly that Putin was 'entirely too healthy'.[29]

The Kremlin's behaviour during lockdown also belies the speculation that Putin's days were numbered. On the contrary, a nationwide referendum on a package of constitutional reforms that would allow Putin to run again for two more six-year presidential terms (as well as constitutionally banning same-sex marriage and placing the constitution above international law) was held, after a Covid-related delay, on 1 July 2020. It was the exact opposite of the course suggested by Surkov in his essay in February. Instead of preparing for a transition of power, Putin's inner circle seemed to be laying the political ground for him to remain in office until his death.

Always intensely private, Putin's personal contact had for years been limited to a small group of no more than three dozen insiders. During Covid that bubble had shrunk far tighter still. For the greater part of 2020 and 2021, the majority of Russia's most senior officials saw their president solely via video link. Only the closest personal friends and allies were admitted to Putin's presence. Most could not spare a week from their schedules for the necessary quarantine every time they went to see the president.

In the 'seclusion and inaccessibility' of his Covid bunker, surrounded with 'ideologues and sycophants', Putin developed a 'deep belief that Russian domination over Ukraine must be restored', according to former *Kommersant* political editor Mikhail Zygar.[30] Or as the CIA's Burns would put it in April 2022, 'Putin's risk appetite has grown as his grip on Russia has tightened. His circle of advisers has narrowed and in that small circle it has never been career enhancing to question his judgment or his almost mystical belief that his destiny is to restore Russia's sphere of influence. Every day Putin demonstrates that declining powers can be at least as disruptive as rising ones.'[31]

Over two years in isolation, Putin developed a longstanding enthusiasm for historical theorising which would culminate in the essay on Russia and Ukraine, published in July 2021. The essay, according to TV executive Molody, was 'entirely [Putin's] own work ... he consulted advisers of course, but it was really the result of much research and deep thought.' His companion in that process of deep thought was an old and trusted friend who was willing to put his business on hold and spend time inside Putin's Covid world – Yury Kovalchuk.

Kovalchuk

If Nikolai Patrushev was Putin's most powerful *silovik* colleague and ally, Yury Kovalchuk was his most powerful friend from the world of business. For Putin, Patrushev was an older and much respected former boss – as well as his closest connection to the

KGB of their shared youth. Kovalchuk was a friend from a different stage of Putin's career – the tangled web of business, Communist Party and organised crime interests that Putin navigated with great skill as consigliere to St Petersburg's mayor Anatoly Sobchak. According to a Russian government official I will call Sergei Ryzhy, a longstanding friend and colleague of a former prime minister who remains at the top of the Kremlin's 'power vertical', Patrushev was for Putin 'an ideal of KGB rectitude' and implacable, 'vigilant patriotism'. His relationship with Kovalchuk was different, if no less close. Kovalchuk was 'a man of a less exalted world', said Ryzhy, someone whom Putin trusted with the 'more mundane matters' of his personal business interests and those of his immediate family.[32]

When the Soviet Union began to disintegrate, Kovalchuk was a physicist at Leningrad's Ioffe Institute. In 1990 the Leningrad Regional Committee of the Communist Party of the Soviet Union (KPSS) had established a new bank as a repository for Party funds. They called it Bank Rossiya – 'Russia Bank' – just one Cyrillic letter different from Bank Rossii, which was the Central Bank of Russia. When the Communist Party was banned by Boris Yeltsin after the coup of August 1991, Bank Rossiya was suspended too. A group of Party members from the Fursenko Institute (a commercial affiliate of the Ioffe Institute) that included Kovalchuk and Vladimir Yakunin, a seconded KGB officer who headed the Institute's foreign department, set out to gain control of the bank and put the KPSS's frozen funds to good use. By Yakunin's account, the motivation for taking over Bank Rossiya was not profit but the desire to 'do something positive'. The would be-bankers shared 'an ideological affinity and it consisted in the fact that a complete shitstorm is coming'.[33] Yakunin appealed to his old KGB colleague Vladimir Putin, who by that time had become vice-mayor of St Petersburg, and introduced him to his physicist colleague Kovalchuk. Together, they helped re-found the former KPSS slush fund as one of the new Russia's most successful banks. In his memoirs Yakunin described the group of Bank Rossiya founders as a 'kibbutz' – and though Putin himself was not a shareholder, he quickly became one of the kibbutz's key members. Thanks to Putin's political rise, the kibbutz's members would ascend to being Russia's wealthiest and most powerful men – along with Putin's childhood friends Arkady and Boris Rotenburg and cellist Sergei Roldugin, who introduced Putin to his future wife Ludmila.[34]

In the early 1990s Kovalchuk bought a large country house in Solovyovka in the Priozersky District of the Leningrad region, located on the eastern shore of Lake Komsomolskoye near St Petersburg. Soon other key members of the city's elite – including Putin, Vladimir Yakunin, Andrei Fursenko and his brother Sergei (founders of the eponymous institute), Viktor Myachin, Kovalchuk's brother Mikhail, Vladimir Smirnov and Nikolai Shamalov – would also buy properties nearby. In November 1996 they united their adjacent dachas into a private compound under a co-operative society they called *Ozero* (or the Lake).

By 1997, when Putin joined the presidential administration in Moscow, Bank Rossiya had become one of St Petersburg's most profitable banks. Yakunin was responsible for working with government agencies, and Kovalchuk was responsible for attracting shareholders. Kovalchuk had introduced Gennady Petrov, one of the bosses of the notorious Tambov-Malyshev organised crime group – of whom we will hear more below – as a shareholder.[35]

By 1999 Putin had been appointed prime minister and was under serious consideration from the family of Boris Yeltsin as a possible successor. In the winter of 2000, between Yeltsin's resignation on New Year's Eve and Putin's election as president in March, Yeltsin's daughter Tatyana Dyachenko and her husband Valentin Yumashev visited the Ozero compound for a meal with Putin's own closest associates – including Putin himself, the Kovalchuk and Fursenko brothers, and Yakunin, among others.

Yeltsin's entourage got to know Putin's closest associates over cutlets and wine. As Yumashev confirmed, the invitation was 'from Putin's family' – but more symbolically, the Ozero get-together marked a handover of power from one extended family clan to another.[36]

In 2008 Kovalchuk's sometime candidate as a Bank Rossiya shareholder Gennady Petrov and other key members of the Tambov gang were arrested and convicted in Spain for racketeering. A key witness for the Spanish prosecutors had been ex-FSB officer Alexander Litvinenko, but he was poisoned in London in November 2006 on the orders of Patrushev while the Tambov gang investigation was still underway.[37] According to a separate investigation by the Bulgarian prosecutor's office, more than €1 billion – part of the Tambov gang's proceeds from drug trafficking, prostitution and protection rackets – had been laundered through banks in Bulgaria and Estonia.[38,39]

But by that time Kovalchuk had moved on from the murky world of St Petersburg business. In May 2008 *Forbes Russia* listed him as Russia's 53rd richest man, with an estimated fortune of $1.9 billion and Bank Rossiya's largest shareholder, holding 30.4 per cent of its stock. Part of Bank Rossiya's handsome profits came from a government contract to collect utility bills from millions of customers in Moscow, St Petersburg and other regions. The state-controlled company in charge of collection – Inter RAO – was from 2009 headed by Kovalchuk's son Boris.[40]

A rising tide floats all boats. Several St Petersburg protégés of Kovalchuk rose to powerful state positions – including Sergei Kiriyenko, a future prime minister, Alexander Beglov, who became governor of St Petersburg, and Lyubov Sovershaeva, a former Bank Rossiya employee who became Beglov's deputy.[41] Kovalchuk acquired media holdings, including the *Izvestia* newspaper and STS Media. Sergei Mikhailov, a long-time friend of the Kovalchuk family and the founder of the Mikhailov and Partners PR agency used by Rossiya Bank, became director of the TASS news agency – which in 2014 received a 350 million ruble credit line from Kovalchuk's bank. Yury Kovalchuk's son Boris joined the Board of Trustees of the Innopraktika Foundation – a body set up to help facilitate meetings between businessmen and heads of state companies – that was headed by Putin's daughter Katerina Tikhonova. In 2013 Tikhonova made a dynastic marriage inside the Ozero cooperative to Kirill Shamalov, son of Putin's old neighbour Nikolai Shamalov – who also owned a 9.6 per cent share in Bank Rossiya. Kovalchuk hosted the wedding at his ski resort at Igora in the Leningrad region, at which Putin was naturally guest of honour.[42]

Kovalchuk was also able to make financial arrangements for less official members of Putin's family, including shares in Bank Rossiya given to Putin's alleged mistress (and mother of his third, illegitimate daughter) Svetlana Krivonogikh through a shell company called Relax.[43] In 2014 the US government personally sanctioned Kovalchuk, alleging that he was the 'personal banker' for many senior Russian government officials, including Putin. The 2016 Panama Papers leak revealed that Kovalchuk had transferred at least $1 billion to a specially created offshore entity called Sandalwood Continental. These funds had come, according to the leaked records of Mossack Fonseca financial services firm, from a series of enormous unsecured loans from the state-controlled Russian Commercial Bank (RCB) located in Cyprus and other state banks. Some of the cash obtained from RCB was also lent back onshore in Russia at extremely high interest rates, with the resulting profits siphoned off to secret Swiss accounts.[44] The Panama Papers also appeared to link Kovalchuk's offshore holdings to payments totalling hundreds of millions of dollars made to entities owned by Putin's old cellist friend Sergei Roldugin.[45]

But international finance was not Kovalchuk's only interest. According to business associates who spoke to Mikhail Zygar, Kovalchuk had long been fascinated by the mystical nationalist writings of Ivan Ilyin, a 1930s philosopher of Russian fascism. Kovalchuk also, by his own account, had another key skill – never to bring the boss bad news. 'Put yourself in my shoes,' a friend of Kovalchuk's told Zygar, as related in Zygar's book *All the Kremlin's Men*. 'If I annoy Putin like [Finance Minister Aleksei] Kudrin does, telling him what he doesn't want to hear, what will happen? I'll get less access to "the body" [of the President]. I'll end up punishing myself. Why would I do that?'[46]

As Putin sat in lockdown researching and penning his long historical essay on Russian destiny and its relationship with Ukraine, Kovalchuk spent much of the time by his side at the Valdai residence. As president and banker sat together the ideological manifesto of the coming war's philosophy was born.[47]

CHAPTER 6
TRUTH OR BLUFF?

The weight of this sad time we must obey

William Shakespeare, *King Lear*

Breaking Out of Orbit

The appointment of Dmitry Kozak to replace Vladislav Surkov as the Kremlin's Ukraine supremo in January 2020 marked a decisive shift in Moscow's policy towards Donbas. As we have seen, Surkov's policy of using the rebel republics of Donbas as a brake on Ukraine's westward momentum had failed. In Paris in December 2019 Putin believed that he'd got the measure of Zelensky. Putin was convinced that 'Zelensky was weak, a puppet' of the West, recalled a close colleague of Foreign Minister Lavrov's. At the same time Putin also came to see Zelensky as a man with whom he could no longer do business, an 'incorrigible servant for NATO interests ... there was no point talking to him, only to his masters in Washington.'[1] The only course left to the Kremlin was to prepare the ground either for the Donbas republics' independence, or their incorporation into Russia.

Between late 2019 and February 2022 Russia issued over 650,000 internal Russian passports to the population of the LDNR. Zelensky denounced the 'passportisation' of eastern Ukraine as 'a step towards annexation'.[2] In response, Zelensky began to accelerate Ukraine's campaign for NATO membership. Over the following two years, the more Russia increased its pressure on Zelensky to turn away from NATO, the more Zelensky pressed for NATO security guarantees to protect his country from Russian aggression. The dynamic of the fatal escalation that would lead directly to war had begun.

That Ukrainian NATO membership was dangerous and intensely provocative to the Kremlin had been well known in the West ever since the 2008 Bucharest summit.

Between 2008 and the annexation of Crimea in 2014 NATO – and the Yanukovych government – pursued a strange compromise solution. Yanukovych continued to cooperate with NATO in the framework of the Annual National Programme, including holding joint exercises. But his government insisted that the continuation of Ukraine–NATO cooperation 'did not exclude the development of a strategic partnership with Russia'.[3] In June 2010 Ukraine's parliament passed a law that excluded 'integration into Euro-Atlantic security and NATO membership' from the country's national security strategy. Effectively, the Rada had declared Ukraine a non-aligned country.[4]

In retrospect, the neutrality law of 2010 was the great missed opportunity to stabilise relations between Moscow and Kyiv once and for all. But it was the Kremlin's greed that ruined it. Rather than being content with Yanukovych's commitment not to join NATO, Russia pressed for more: a further commitment to refuse the EU's Association Agreement as well. It was a classic illustration of Winston Churchill's warning of the dangers of conceding to aggression: 'An appeaser is one who feeds a crocodile, hoping it will eat him last.'[5] Yanukovych had taken the dramatic step of declaring Ukraine neutral – yet the Kremlin was not appeased and continued to press for more. The lesson of 2010 was not lost on Zelensky when he faced the same pressure in 2020–22.

Even in the immediate aftermath of the Maidan and the annexation of Crimea, Ukraine's interim government stuck to disgraced former president Yanukovych's commitment not to join NATO.[6] But once again, the Kremlin overplayed its hand. By August 2014, with regular Russian troops operating inside Donbas, the new President Petro Poroshenko reversed course and confirmed that Ukraine was once again committed to membership.[7] On 23 December 2014 the Rada renounced Ukraine's non-aligned status. Days later, Poroshenko promised to hold a national referendum on joining NATO (which never took place). Russia had gained two tiny and unstable rebel republics in Donbas – but in the process killed Ukrainian neutrality forever and set Kyiv firmly back on course towards NATO membership.

Five years of increasing cooperation between Ukraine's military and NATO armies followed – including thousands of Ukrainian soldiers and officers training alongside their Western counterparts, officers studying in staff colleges in the US and UK, and regularly participating in various NATO exercises. As Poroshenko prepared to face his new challenger Zelensky in the 2019 elections, he doubled down on Ukraine's engagement with NATO. In February 2019 the Ukrainian parliament voted to formally enshrine Ukraine's commitment to join both NATO and the European Union in the country's constitution by a majority of 334 out of 385 votes.[8]

For his first year in office, Zelensky tried to hold back from provoking Russia, concentrating instead on his doomed attempt to implement Minsk-2 by organising a referendum in the LDNR. The Putin–Zelensky Normandy Format summit in Paris 'was the last chance to try to save something, to recover trust – or so some people hoped', said a senior Zelensky adviser who was present. 'It was a false hope.' The two men would not only never meet but would never trust each other again.

Zelensky began a concerted campaign to put Ukrainian membership back into active consideration by NATO. In June 2020 Ukraine took another step along the road by joining NATO's 'Enhanced Opportunity Partner Interoperability

Program' – jargon for replacing Ukraine's Soviet-era weapons, command and control and communications systems with newer ones compatible with NATO's universal standards. By September 2020 Zelensky approved a new National Security Strategy for Ukraine that explicitly provided for 'the development of the distinctive partnership with NATO with the aim of membership in NATO'.[9]

A month later, Zelensky met British Prime Minister Boris Johnson in London to press his case for the final stage in the membership process: a formal Membership Action Plan (or MAP).[10] According to a top Downing Street official who saw Johnson daily during that period, 'Boris was very keen on getting the Ukrainians in[to NATO] ... He thought it was time for the French and Germans to stop cowering in front of Putin.'[11] Johnson was also anxious to strike some kind of retaliatory blow against the Kremlin for the 2018 attempted murder of GRU defector Sergei Skripal and his daughter in Salisbury with nerve agent. The operation by a pair of undercover GRU officers had resulted in the death of an innocent Briton who had picked up the discarded poison that had been concealed in a perfume bottle. After Salisbury – and the Litvinenko poisoning in London in 2006 – Johnson was in no mood to continue appeasing the Kremlin by holding back on NATO expansion. As a 'direct result' of Johnson's lobbying both of European partners and of the Biden administration in Washington, said the aide, the question of returning to an 'open-door policy' – including MAPs for Ukraine and Georgia – was put on the agenda for an upcoming NATO summit in Brussels scheduled for June 2021.[12]

For the Kremlin, the writing was on the wall. Zelensky had made his final choice. NATO seemed to have forgotten the qualms that had led to key members refusing MAPs for Tbilisi and Kyiv at Bucharest in 2008. There was a very real danger that, this time, the alliance would take the last, fateful step towards admitting Ukraine.

To Putin's inner circle, the war was about protecting Russia from American attack. Ukraine was merely the battlefield where the two former superpowers' interests came into direct confrontation – the location for what Putin's closest circle imagined was a millennial battle between superpowers. 'Ukraine does not exist,' Viktor Zolotov, Putin's former bodyguard who now heads the powerful Russian National Guard, told Aleksei Venediktov. 'It is the border of America and Russia.'[13]

Stopping Ukraine joining NATO – or, more specifically, stopping NATO basing its forces and missiles on the territory of Ukraine – was a much more important motivation than the pursuit of an abstract vision of a revived Russian Empire. But that fact leads to a dangerous and controversial question. Does that mean that NATO provoked the Russian invasion – or that NATO could have stopped it by pursuing a different policy?

The easiest way to answer is to pose the counterfactual. What could NATO have done to avert a Russian invasion? Was the 2008 Budapest NATO summit – with its fateful post-summit memorandum and its vaguely worded commitment to Georgia and Ukraine's eventual membership sometime in the future – the turning point? Scuppering Georgia's route to NATO was certainly one of the major causes of Putin's invasion of Georgia and subsequent recognition of the independence of South Ossetia and Abkhazia. The invasion was Putin's signal that Russian interests would not be trifled with. But it was also the trigger for increasingly large numbers of Ukrainians to begin to fear Russian aggression – and for NATO's newest members to actively rally behind the membership of their fellow former Soviet vassals. Putin's tragedy – in the literal, Greek-drama sense where the hero is the author of his own downfall – was that his every move accelerated and precipitated the very thing he feared the most, which was a flight of his frightened neighbours into the arms of NATO. His every aggressive move, from the invasion of Georgia and annexation of Crimea and war in Syria, only served to strengthen both many NATO members' resolve to expand and those neighbours' urge to join.

Post-Georgia, NATO–Russia relations fell into a fatal escalation loop where any compromise by the alliance would have been seen as a fatal sign of weakness and a reward for aggression.

To continue the counterfactual, at what point could NATO have paused? As early as 2008, key NATO powers Germany and France had already decided that geopolitical considerations – specifically, not angering Russia – trumped the agency and hopes of aspiring NATO members Georgia and Ukraine. And as a point of legal fact, neither country could have joined then – and still, legally, cannot join today – because they both already had unresolved border disputes with Transnistria (in Ukraine's case) and Abkhazia and South Ossetia (for Georgia), which by NATO's own charter is an absolute barrier to membership.

That begs another question. Why, if Ukrainian and Georgian membership were a legal impossibility, did NATO continue its engagement with Tbilisi and – especially – with Kyiv, to the extent of deploying in-country military trainers and mounting major joint military exercises? The answer continues the tragic theme. NATO believed that shows of military solidarity would discourage Russian aggression. But to Moscow, it was precisely such symbolic shows of military engagement that were so provocative. Between 2008 and 2022 the two sides were locked in an escalating dialogue of the deaf that would bring NATO and Russia's relations to a crisis point.

Fall of the Dark Prince

There was one final straw that was to set Kyiv and Moscow irrevocably on the warpath. Zelensky finally decided to move decisively against Putin's old friend and 'dark prince' of Ukrainian politics, Viktor Medvedchuk.

Every one of Ukraine's major oligarchs was, by definition, a political survivor par excellence. Under the ironic portrait of the oligarchs as a group of scheming Bond villains portrayed in *Servant of the People* was a profound truth. Between elections, the magnates who controlled Ukraine's metals, gas, mining, telecoms, grain, fertiliser and shipping businesses manoeuvred and bargained furiously to promote their political protégés and destroy their political and commercial enemies. Television stations, internet portals and newspapers were their weapons. A portfolio of media holdings was as essential to the survival of every oligarch as armour and a sword to a medieval magnate – whose feudal control of regions the oligarchs' power bases closely resembled.

Medvedchuk, like many other oligarchs, had over two decades served in various governments – effortlessly crossing back and forth between parallel roles in the state and his own businesses. His political power base, like his protégé Viktor Yanukovych, was in the Russian-speaking south and east, and his platform was the championing of their rights. Thanks to his personal closeness to Putin, Medvedchuk had a monopoly on the import of coal and liquefied natural gas from the occupied territories of Donbas into Ukraine. Dozens of companies listed in the name of his wife, Oksana Marchenko, were registered in Crimea and the LNDR. He also sold coal to Russia and controlled over a thousand kilometres of oil pipelines that ran from Russian-occupied territory into Ukraine. Yet despite the apparent conflict of interest, Medvedchuk also held a lucrative monopoly contract to supply diesel fuel to the entire Ukrainian army.[14]

There was a period after Zelensky's election in 2019 that it looked like Medvedchuk could become an ally of the energetic young president. Zelensky – who was himself a Russian speaker and had grown up in a largely Russian-speaking town – was keen to bring an end to the familiar culture wars that had obsessed Ukrainian politicians for two decades. Zelensky's aim was 'to deprive Russia of its claim on the Russian language' and 'to stop making the speaking of Russian in Ukraine a political issue'.[15]

But Zelensky was equally keen to dismantle the power of what his press secretary Iuliia Mendel called the 'invasive species' of oligarchs.[16] Furthermore, from early 2020 onwards it became clear that Medvedchuk's media holdings had no actual interest in defusing the Russian–Ukrainian culture war. Reconciliation was dangerous to the Kremlin's narrative of an implacable, racist and even 'genocidal' Kyiv regime. As Putin told his annual press conference in December 2021, 'Russophobia is a first step towards genocide. You and I know what is happening in Donbas. It certainly looks very much like genocide.'[17]

During the pandemic, Zelensky had refused Putin's offer of millions of Russian-made Sputnik vaccine doses – as well as the offer of a free licence to produce the vaccine in Ukraine. That political decision undoubtedly cost many Ukrainian lives – and resentment, particularly in the Russian-speaking East, ran high. Anger was strongly encouraged by relentless attacks by Medvedchuk's media. By the end of 2021 Zelensky's popularity ratings had been knocked down to just 39 per cent. Though Russian state TV channels had been banned in Ukraine, Medvedchuk's network of pro-Russian bloggers, pro-Russian newspapers and the pro-Russian party 'Opposition Platform – For Life' (OPZZh) regularly retranslated the attack-line themes generated by Kremlin media in Russia. A large network of social media bots amplified the message that Russians in eastern Ukraine were subject to discrimination and the peaceful population of the rebel Donbas republics was under constant attack from the Ukrainian military.[18]

On 2 February 2021 three Medvedchuk-connected television channels – 112 Ukraine, NewsOne and ZIK – were shut down on the orders of the National Security and Defense Council of Ukraine on national security grounds. Shutting down opposition media without any legal due process was a frankly undemocratic and highly risky move for Zelensky. Seeking to reassure Ukraine's Russian speakers that the move was not aimed against them, Zelensky delivered a nationwide televised address in Russian. 'Endless streams of lies in the Russian language, especially lately, have been poured into people's ears,' said Zelensky. 'I will debunk these lies in the Russian language ... a language that, according to one party and one country, has been severely oppressed [in Ukraine]. The language spoken by many of our frontline military ... who defend us against the "defenders" of that same Russian language that has been so badly "oppressed".'[19]

Days later, the National Security and Defence Council blocked access by Medvedchuk, his wife and his associate Taras Kozak to their assets, financial operations and private airplanes pending possible charges. All three were holders of both Ukrainian and Russian passports – in itself a violation of Ukrainian law. Soon afterwards oil pipelines controlled by Medvedchuk were also sanctioned with the objective of restoring them to state ownership. When war broke out a year later, Medvedchuk would be placed under house arrest, escaped, was recaptured after weeks on the run and humiliatingly paraded before TV cameras wearing Ukrainian military uniform and handcuffs.

But by taking down Medvedchuk, Zelensky had thrown down the gauntlet not only to Ukraine's oligarchs, but to the Kremlin itself. Putin, on hearing the news, was 'furious, insulted, outraged at [Zelensky's] total disregard for private property and the free press', recalled Molody.[20] The Kremlin's media machine went into overdrive to denounce Zelensky. And so, for the first time, Russia's military also launched a dress rehearsal for a full-scale invasion.

Sabre Rattled, Sabre Drawn

Two weeks after the shutdown of Medvedchuk's TV channels, the Russian Defence Ministry announced the deployment of paratroopers to the Russian–Ukrainian border for 'large-scale exercises'. On 3 March 2021 forward military units in the DNR were authorised to use 'pre-emptive fire for destruction' on Ukrainian military positions – the first major escalation since the post-Paris summit ceasefire two years before.[21]

On 16 March NATO began a series of long-planned military exercises known as Defender Europe 2021. Involving near-simultaneous operations across over 30 training areas in 12 countries and 28,000 troops from 27 nations, it was one of the largest exercises NATO had held on the continent in decades.[22] Predictably, the Kremlin expressed outrage and mounted its own massive deployment. By the end of March, Colonel-General Ruslan Khomchak, Commander-in-Chief of the Armed Forces of Ukraine, estimated that Russia had mobilised at least 60,700 troops in Crimea and along the eastern portion of the Russo-Ukrainian border, with at least 2,000 military advisers and instructors inside eastern Ukraine.[23] More Russian forces were sent to Belarus. Military observers spotted heavy military equipment and units brought from all over Russia, including from Siberia and the Russian Far East. Ships from the Caspian Flotilla, including landing craft and artillery boats, were transferred through the Volga–Don canal to the Black Sea, ostensibly for joint exercises with the Black Sea Fleet.[24]

In what would later become a familiar pattern, Kremlin spokesman Dmitry Peskov publicly insisted that 'Russia is not a threat to Ukraine, the movement of Russia's army should not be a concern.' The military build-up was entirely a matter of Russia's own 'national security', he insisted.[25] And in an equally familiar instance of the continued dialogue of the deaf between Russia and the West, the massive sabre-rattling deployment of spring 2021 had precisely the opposite effect to the one the Kremlin had intended.

At the NATO summit in Brussels in June 2021 no Membership Action Plan was agreed for Ukraine – though momentum for one was unmistakably growing, with even Russia-friendly Turkey officially expressing support. But the alliance gave its strongest statement yet in favour of Ukraine's eventual membership – along with an explicit warning to Moscow not to interfere in the process. 'Each country chooses its own path,' said NATO Secretary-General Jens Stoltenberg. 'It is up to Ukraine and the 30 NATO members to decide whether it aspires to be a member of the Alliance. Russia has no say in whether Ukraine should be a member ... They cannot veto the decisions of their neighbours. We will not return to the era of spheres of interest, when large countries decide what to do with smaller ones.'[26] A week later, to ram the point home, NATO launched a joint naval exercise code-named Sea Breeze 2021 in the Black Sea.

The road to any war is punctuated by many points of no return – most of them visible only in retrospect. But two events in the summer of 2021 convinced the hawks around Putin that they had no choice but to move towards a military solution to the NATO encroachment problem. The first would be the failure of the massive Russian military build-up of spring 2021 – the largest in Europe since the end of the Second World War – to instil any doubt, fear or caution into the minds of NATO leaders.

The publication of Putin's historical essay in July 2021 was intended as a direct response to the NATO summit the previous month. It served as a clear signal not only to the Russian public but to the Kremlin elite that rescuing the Russians of Ukraine from oppression was the new party line. It was a call to arms. At the CIA's headquarters in Langley, Virginia, the essay was immediately flagged up as the start of a new and dangerous phase in the Kremlin's thinking.

Just weeks before, Biden and Putin had held a summit on 16 June in Geneva which both had declared was 'constructive'. There had been no sense at Geneva that the Russians were planning to plunge Europe into a major war just seven months later. But the Putin essay 'caught our attention in a big way', National Security Adviser Jake Sullivan later recalled. 'We began to look at what's going on here, what's his end game? How hard is he going to push?'[27]

Then came the second trigger – America's disastrous withdrawal from Afghanistan. Despite the billions spent on supporting a new Afghan government and creating a national Afghan security force, both collapsed within days of the hurried US withdrawal. In Moscow the scenes of chaos at Kabul airport were greeted with open delight – not least because Russia had suffered a similar, though much slower, collapse of its own Kabul puppet regime in the 1990s.

To the Kremlin, the debacle of Kabul meant one thing – that Joe Biden had been completely discredited as a military leader. According to the source Ryzhy, top Kremlin officials saw Afghanistan as 'a gift from the heavens, a thunderbolt ... Suddenly the Americans were humiliated in front of the whole world.' If NATO's Brussels summit and the Sea Breeze 2021 exercise had convinced the *siloviki* that only an invasion of Ukraine would halt the West's expansion, then the fall of Kabul to the Taliban in August 2021 marked a moment of American weakness that provided an unmissable opportunity to strike their blow.

By midsummer of 2021, a 'critical mass' of opinion among the innermost circle of Putin's friends and advisers had coalesced around the necessity of landing a 'decisive military blow', according to Ryzhy.[28] The timing was judged uniquely propitious, an opportunity unlikely to be repeated while Putin lived – a chastened Biden, a West still struggling with the coronavirus pandemic, the imminent departure of Europe's de facto leader Merkel, a French president facing a re-election battle against a resurgent right wing and a Britain struggling with a post-Brexit exclusion from decision-making. Decades of Russian energy diplomacy – sometimes careful, sometimes aggressive – had swelled Europe's dependence on Gazprom to nearly 40 per cent of its natural gas imports. Years of careful macroeconomic policy had built up a $650 billion war chest that would allow the Russian economy to survive any sanctions. 'The time had come,' recalled Ryzhy, describing a conversation with his old friend the former prime minister. 'That was clear.'[29]

Exactly what form that blow against Ukraine would take – the creation of a pair of Georgia-style mini-states in Donbas, a Crimea-style annexation, or a full-scale strike to decapitate the Zelensky government altogether and install a puppet, pro-Moscow regime – remained undecided. But by late summer of 2021 the 'decision in principle' that an invasion had become necessary had already, according to Ryzhy, been made by top *siloviki* Patrushev and Bortnikov. All that remained was to assemble the necessary forces and to persuade Russia's ultimate decision-maker – Putin himself – to launch the operation.[30]

In September planned Russian joint exercises with Belarus provided the flimsy cover for a renewed military build-up. Except this time the forces amassed from all over Russia on the borders of Ukraine and in the Black Sea would be even more powerful. This time, the sabre was not being rattled. It was being drawn.

The Espionage War

Through September and October of 2021, as Putin's military began building up troops along Ukraine's borders and the FSB laid plans for installing a puppet government in Kyiv, several people apparently very high up in the Russian army or security services were talking to the CIA. For obvious reasons, the source or sources have been kept well concealed. But a senior British security official confirmed that the 'multiple resources' were from 'the operational to the decision-making level' inside Russia's 'military and security' establishment.[31] Combined with signals intelligence gathered through hacking, communications intercepts and satellite imagery, a detailed intelligence picture was coming together of serious plans for a major Russian offensive.

By early October, US National Security Adviser Sullivan was sufficiently alarmed to ask President Biden to summon his top military and intelligence officials in the Oval Office for an urgent briefing. Biden and Vice President Kamala Harris sat in armchairs before the fireplace, while Secretary of State Antony Blinken, Defense Secretary Lloyd Austin, chairman of the Joint Chiefs of Staff General Mark A. Milley, the CIA's Bill Burns and Director of National Intelligence Avril Haines sat on sofas around the coffee table. Milley, pointing to large maps mounted on easels in front of the Resolute Desk, explained the disposition of Russian troop build-ups – as well as the forces' intended targets inside Ukraine.[32]

Milley expounded Putin's plans in 'extraordinary detail', Haines would later tell *The Washington Post*. The Russian strategy was to attack Kyiv from the north with battle groups on both sides of the Dniepr River, one striking through the Ukrainian city of Chernihiv to the east of the capital and the other advancing from Belarus past the abandoned Chernobyl nuclear plant. Kyiv itself was to be seized in three to four days by Spetsnaz special forces tasked with locating and, if necessary, killing Zelensky, then locking down the capital as the FSB installed a Kremlin-friendly puppet government. The attack was planned for winter, before the spring thaw made terrain impassable for tanks. 'We assess that they plan to conduct a significant strategic attack on Ukraine from multiple directions simultaneously,' said Milley, describing the blitzkrieg plan as the Kremlin's 'version of "shock and awe"'.[33] Above all, the US's top security brass were convinced that, unlike the spring deployments, this time Putin's military build-up was not merely an exercise in coercive diplomacy but a serious plan of attack. Crucially, it was a plan for a military-supported coup rather than a drawn-out war.

At the October briefing Biden made three decisions: to try to dissuade Putin by spelling out that the Western response to an attack would be devastating; to persuade NATO allies to take the warnings seriously; and to warn and help the Ukrainians to prepare for a full-scale invasion. But the fundamental conundrum of how to avoid getting involved in a direct military confrontation remained. According to the briefing notes from the White House meeting that Milley shared with *The Washington Post*, the fundamental problem was 'how do you underwrite and enforce the rules-based international order' against a country with extraordinary nuclear capability 'without going to World War III'? Milley offered four possible answers: 'No. 1: Don't have a kinetic conflict between the U.S. military and NATO with Russia. No. 2: Contain war inside the geographical boundaries of Ukraine. No. 3: Strengthen and maintain NATO unity. No. 4: Empower Ukraine and give them the means to fight.'[34]

CIA Director William Burns had served as US ambassador to Russia and had had the most direct interactions with Putin of anyone in the Biden administration. Burns knew and understood Russia and its leader extremely well – and during his time in Moscow had been a frequent guest at concerts at my wife's family dacha. Putin's chief character traits were 'a mixture of insecurity and grievance', Burns told me soon after the Georgian war. 'He holds grudges.'[35] In early November 2021 Biden delegated Burns to fly to Moscow and deliver his blunt message in person. Burns met Putin's foreign policy adviser (and former ambassador to the United States) Yuri Ushakov in the Kremlin. Putin himself joined the meeting by phone from a residence outside Sochi, where he remained in Covid isolation. Putin reiterated a familiar litany of complaints about NATO expansion, the threat to Russian security and the illegitimacy of the Kyiv government.

Putin 'was very dismissive of President Zelensky as a political leader', Burns recalled. When the CIA director countered with details of a coming invasion gathered by US intelligence, Putin 'was very matter-of-fact' and did not bother to deny the veracity of the intelligence. Burns left a letter from Biden listing in detail the huge price that Russia would pay for any Russian attack on Ukraine. He also met with Security Council secretary Patrushev, who echoed Putin's points almost word for word. Burns left Moscow with the impression that the top Putin circle had formed itself into an 'echo chamber' – though he also believed that a final decision on actually launching an invasion had not yet been made, leaving a small window for diplomacy to work. 'My level of concern has gone up, not down,' Burns reported back to Biden.[36]

Biden, Blinken and Haines had an equally hard time getting NATO partners to take their warning of an imminent invasion seriously. Biden first shared the intelligence with the leaders of Britain, France and Germany at a private meeting during the G20 conference in Rome in late October. Two weeks later, Director of National Intelligence Haines shared the warning with all 30 members of NATO's North Atlantic Council in Brussels. Though the British, the Poles and the Baltic states were convinced, the reaction from the rest of NATO's members was one of scepticism.

According to a Downing Street aide with direct knowledge of Haines's Brussels presentation, 'most [Europeans] believed that Putin had not deployed enough troops for an invasion ... they also asked why he would risk ruining his economy.' And there were deeper-rooted objections. The voices clamouring about a coming invasion were those NATO countries who had previously been parts of the Russian and Soviet empires and were 'known for crying wolf' about Russia's imperial ambitions. Then there was a longstanding mistrust of US intelligence assessments, both recent – botched forecasts on the Afghan security forces, for instance – and ancient, going back to 'those hand-to-God assurances' by the US in 2003 that Iraq had weapons of mass destruction, recalled the Downing Street official. During the North Atlantic Council meeting, one British official stood to support Haines, telling his fellow council members, 'She's right!' The intervention was met 'with a bit of eye-rolling ... as in, those Brits and Yanks are at it again'.[37] Another problem was that at this early stage the US was initially wary of sharing operational details in full, even with NATO allies, for fear of compromising its sources inside Russia.

Perhaps strangely, the hardest sell of all was to the Ukrainians themselves. Secretary of State Blinken first warned Zelensky in early November 2021 at a summit on climate change in Glasgow, Scotland. 'It was just the two of us, two feet from each other,' Blinken would later recall. It was a 'difficult conversation' because it felt surreal to be 'telling someone you believe their country is going to be invaded'. Zelensky was 'serious, deliberate, stoic', but ultimately sceptical, and would remain so until just hours before the actual invasion was launched.[38] Two weeks later Ukraine's Foreign Minister Dmytro Kuleba and Zelensky's Chief of Staff Andriy Yermak went to Washington for a more detailed briefing. 'Guys, dig the trenches!' was how a senior State Department official greeted the two Ukrainians, recalled Kuleba. 'I'm serious. Start digging trenches ... You will be attacked. A large-scale attack, and you have to prepare for it.' Kuleba told *The Washington Post* that he asked the official for more specific details about what the US knew about Putin's invasion plans but 'there were none.'[39]

US and Ukrainian narratives of why Kyiv remained unconvinced until the last moment by the reality of an invasion differ widely. Officials in Kyiv insist that the US failed to provide convincing evidence that Putin's build-up was not just another form of heavy metal diplomacy designed precisely to shake European NATO members into pressing Ukraine to compromise with Russia in order to preserve their gas supplies. 'We have seen this kind of Russian psychological operation many times,' said former MP and Yermak adviser Serhiy Leshchenko. 'We have been at war with Russia for eight years already.'[40] Above all, Zelensky feared that rumours of war would create a panic that would cripple the Ukrainian economy and trigger a mass exodus not only of capital but also young men who would be needed to fight the Russians. For Zelensky himself, the priority was cajoling NATO into giving him the kind of offensive heavy weapons that his military lacked. 'You can say a million times, "Listen, there may be an invasion." Okay, there may be an invasion – will you give us planes?' Zelensky recalled in July 2022. 'Will you give us air defences? "Well, you're not a member of NATO." Oh, okay, then what are we talking about?'[41]

The Americans, for their part, grew increasingly frustrated that Kyiv's own insistence on downplaying the threat was feeding into scepticism among European NATO members – especially in France and Germany. But in truth the problem was not so much that the Ukrainians did not believe the warnings as much as they feared the consequences of panic. On 3 December 2021 Ukrainian Minister of Defence Oleksii Reznikov told the Rada of the possibility of a 'large-scale escalation' by Russia by the end of January 2022.[42] But the prevailing opinion in Kyiv in the three months before the invasion was that the coming war would be limited to an operation in Donbas – or at most a land grab to link Donbas to Crimea. A direct assault on Ukraine's capital remained, to the decision makers on Kyiv's Bankova Street government complex, a fantastical proposition.

Macron and the new German chancellor Olaf Scholz – who had been dealing with the Kremlin for years – also found it hard to believe that Putin would be irrational enough to damage his own economic interests so disastrously. The Germans and French suggested a top-level EU–Russia summit, only to be shot down by more Russia-sceptical members of NATO, who saw it as a dangerous concession to Putin's aggressive posture.

In a bid to shift opinion in European capitals, in December an unusual political decision was taken in Washington to publicly share the substance, if not the fine detail, of new intelligence on Putin's plans almost as soon as it came in. The White House published lists of Ukrainian politicians identified by the Kremlin as possible successors to Zelensky, along with 'kill lists' of politicians, activists and journalists in all major Ukrainian cities marked for assassination or arrest after a Russian invasion. The decision to publicise the information was partly an attempt to pre-empt Putin's invasion plans – but also, according to the UK intelligence source, 'to show Putin that he has a leaky ship ... and leaky ships tend to sink'.[43]

Full Readiness

The two final military elements necessary for a full-scale invasion were formally set in train at a crucial meeting of the Russian General Staff held in Moscow around 1 December 2021, according to a source close to Foreign Minister Sergei Lavrov.[44] The first was the final mobilisation orders to extra military units – notably the temporary relocation of the headquarters of Russia's Eastern (formerly Far Eastern) Military District from Khabarovsk, near Chinese Manchuria, to Belarus in time for previously planned joint military exercises to be held in February. Key combat units from the Eastern District's 5th, 29th, 35th and 36th Combined Arms Army, 76th Guards Air Assault Division, 98th Guards Airborne Division and the Pacific Fleet's 155th Naval Infantry Brigade began the huge logistical feat of transporting over 15,000 men and their materiel by train across 6,000 kilometres of Siberia.[45] Another powerful Siberian unit, the 41st Combined Arms Army based in Novosibirsk, had already been redeployed to Russia's Belgorod province. The build-up of a major strike force to the north and northeast of Ukraine could only have two targets – Kyiv and Kharkiv.

Orders were also issued to the Pacific Fleet sub-chaser *Admiral Tributs* and the anti-ship rocket cruiser *Varyag* (ironically, originally christened *Red Ukraine* when she was launched in 1983) to steam from their home port of Vladivostok to the Mediterranean as soon as possible. It was, in reverse, a repeat of the deployment of Imperial Russia's Baltic Fleet to the Sea of Japan in 1904 that ended in military humiliation and revolution. To Echo Moskvy editor-in-chief Aleksei Venediktov, the road to war was 'a lengthy process, and involved a number of processes'. But the key turning points were the redeployment of the *Admiral Tributs* and the Siberian divisions in December. Such a major mobilisation is 'an extremely expensive activity', recalled Venediktov, who asked his most senior military sources whether this was just a show of force. 'No,' they assured him. 'This is a direct threat.'[46]

Active preparations for a covert war also swung into action at the same time. According to a source close to the Russian military intelligence-connected mercenary Wagner Group – whose role in the war we will examine in more detail later – members received urgent orders to return to bases in south Russia.[47] There they received orders to form into small groups and travel to Kyiv under civilian cover. Some were Ukrainian and Belarusian citizens. Russian members of the group were issued with fake Ukrainian passports. Their brief was to form assassination squads to murder a list of over 30 top Ukrainian government and security officials, including President Zelensky himself.

At the headquarters of the FSB on Lubyanka Square in central Moscow, the network of Ukrainian local officials, politicians and security officers carefully cultivated and corrupted by agents of Colonel-General Sergei Beseda's Ninth Directorate of the Department of Operational Information was also mobilised. The unit, whose specific job was extending Moscow's control over its near abroad, had grown from 30 officers to over 160 between

2019 and 2021, according to Ukrainian intelligence officials. To attract recruits from other branches, Beseda's new department offered bonuses and free housing in buildings adjacent to the FSB training academy on Michurinsky Prospekt in Moscow. Incoming officers were assigned territories in Ukraine and tasked with developing lists of collaborators to work with, as well as adversaries to neutralise.[48]

Senior Ukrainian officials received cold calls from Russian intelligence offering them money and prominent positions in a future pro-Moscow administration if they agreed to change sides. Oleksandr Vikul, a prominent member of the Party of the Regions from Krivy Roh who had served as a deputy prime minister under Yanukovych, was called by a former minister of the interior of the DNR. 'You are a smart person, you see that the situation is predetermined,' the separatist minister told Vikul. 'Send a letter signed in the name of [the city of] Krivy Roh, a declaration of love and friendship for Russia, and you will be a big man in the new Ukraine.'[49] Vikul, by his own account, 'told the guy where to go, very rudely'. Kharkiv mayor Ihor Terekhov – also known as a pro-Moscow politician – was also contacted, and also refused to collaborate. Other officials received text messages such as 'Do not allow a humanitarian catastrophe' and 'Do not allow the nationalists to use you as cover.'[50]

Some Ukrainian officials, like Terekhov, refused the FSB's blandishments and cash. But many succumbed, among them Vladimir Sivkovich, a former deputy head of Ukraine's security council who was placed under sanction by the US Treasury Department in January for working 'with a network of Russian intelligence actors to carry out influence operations'. According to a subsequent Ukrainian investigation, Sivkovich recruited Oleg Kulinich, a protege of SBU Director Ivan Bakanov (himself a childhood friend of Zelensky's). After Kulinich's arrest for treason in July, prosecutors alleged that Sivkovich tasked Kulinich as early as 2019 to steal secret internal SBU files that would be of 'operational interest' to the FSB. The indictments also claim that on the night before Russia's invasion, Kulinich 'deliberately' blocked the dissemination of intelligence warning that Russian forces in Crimea were hours from launching an attack. (After Kulinich's arrest, Bakanov, who had been installed precisely to cleanse the security service's ranks of traitors, was fired for his misjudgements by an exasperated Zelensky.) A third Russian spy, Andriy Naumov, had been in line to take control of the SBU's counterintelligence department. Naumov was arrested in Serbia in June carrying cash and gems worth more than $700,000, according to Serbian authorities. The administration of occupied Kherson would be taken over by Oleksandr Kobets, a former KGB officer who had also once worked for the SBU. Overall, Ukraine would detain more than 800 people suspected of aiding Russia by acts of reconnaissance or sabotage, according to Ukraine's Interior Ministry, and would also launch investigations into hundreds of other lawmakers, security officials and senior establishment figures over suspicious contacts with the FSB.[51]

The Last-Chance Saloon

Despite military preparations kicking into high gear, Lavrov was given a final chance to make diplomacy work. Russia's foreign minister was fully aware that the momentum inside Putin's inner circle was already firmly resolved on war – though Lavrov himself would not know until the very eve of the operation that these plans would include an attack on Kyiv. 'Putin is our last hope to avert war,' Lavrov confided to an old university friend in late December.[52] Lavrov still held out some hope that the boss himself – if none of his *siloviki* around him – might still be persuaded to step back from the brink. But the momentum was so great that Lavrov would have to secure some truly dramatic, and frankly unrealistic, concessions from the West. Through the first and second weeks of December a working group personally convened by Lavrov put together a set of demands that he knew would be the very last shot at peace.[53]

The ultimatum-like set of demands published on 17 December 2021 were a major overshot. Russia demanded that NATO effectively retreat to its pre-2007 borders by promising not to deploy missiles, heavy weapons or large troop concentrations to any of the former Soviet bloc member states. To puzzled officials at Britain's Foreign Office, the Russian demands 'simply did not make any sense' to 'anyone who had any experience of Russia–NATO diplomacy', according to a senior source who spoke to British Prime Minister Boris Johnson on a daily basis during that period. 'It didn't read anything like a policy document ... there was nothing in it that NATO could possibly agree to.' The document was 'fantastical'.[54]

Fatally, top British diplomats – in common with many governments around the world, including Ukraine's – drew precisely the wrong conclusion. Lavrov's extreme demands were, in truth, an indication of how far the hawks in the Kremlin had moved away from the idea of compromise. But the British interpreted the Kremlin's bizarrely hard-line position as a sign that Putin would be willing to settle for far less – an outrageous gambit that could be bargained down. Downing Street fully believed the warnings of the Ministry of Defence and the Pentagon that Putin was '*ready* for war and had a plan for that war in place', recalled the Downing Street source. 'It's just that we believed that there was more of a chance to talk him back [from war] than there really was.'[55]

Putin's detailed plans for an invasion may not have been a secret to the CIA, but they were kept from all but the most senior Russian military commanders and certainly from their troops. The testimonies of Russian prisoners of war and relatives of military personnel all concur on one detail: the true purpose of the build-up was not revealed to any junior officers or servicemen until just a few hours before the order to mobilise. The full extent of the invasion plan was also kept secret from all but the innermost circle of Putin's confidants. Perhaps the only truly impressive operational detail in an invasion that would go disastrously wrong was the ruthlessly effective security that was maintained around the heart of Putin's plan – to decapitate the Ukrainian government with a blitzkrieg strike backed up by mercenary assassins.

Small wonder, then, that both Western leaders and most of the best-connected members of Russia's elite continued to believe that Putin was attempting to pull off a bluff of historic proportions. One source was personally assured by oligarch Mikhail Fridman just days before the invasion that Fridman's 'most highly placed friends in the security services' had promised him that there was 'no danger' of a full-scale war.[56] In the run-up to the invasion there was, in fact, a direct inverse relationship between how well-connected a person was and their belief in the reality of war. Indeed, as Putin's spokesman Dmitry Peskov admitted during a private lunch on the fourth day of the war, the majority of Putin's Security Council were told of the coming strike at Kyiv and Kharkiv only after the fateful 21 February meeting.[57]

On 19 January 2022 US President Joe Biden said his 'guess' was that Russia 'will move in' to Ukraine but Putin would pay 'a serious and dear price' for an invasion and 'would regret it'. But Biden left a fateful gap in his otherwise forceful message, suggesting that a 'minor incursion' by Russian forces might not prompt the severe response that he and allies had threatened.[58] It was an ominous hint that NATO was not as united as Washington wished to suggest.

From early January non-essential staff were evacuated from the US embassy in Kyiv, followed soon after by the rest, who decamped to the western Ukrainian city of Lviv and neighbouring Poland. In a last-ditch effort to defuse the tensions, on 21 January Deputy Secretary of State Wendy Sherman led a diplomatic delegation to Geneva to meet with her Russian counterpart Sergei Ryabkov. Sherman rejected Lavrov's December demands, but instead offered trust-building measures such as agreements on the deployment of troops and missiles in the vicinity of the border with Russia. The subtext of the US offer was to test whether the Russians were in fact serious about reaching a non-military solution. The answer was no. 'It became pretty clear, pretty quickly that [the Russians] were performing diplomacy, not actually undertaking diplomacy,' recalled Emily Horne, then the spokesperson for the National Security Council. 'They weren't even doing it with much seriousness.'[59]

Soon after, Sherman's boss Antony Blinken met with Lavrov, also in Geneva. The atmosphere was as frosty as the weather. After a fruitless hour and a half the formal talks concluded. Blinken took Lavrov aside into a small, adjacent conference room for a private talk. 'Sergei, tell me what it is you're really trying to do?' Blinken asked. Was this all really about the security concerns of Russia – or was it about Putin's almost theological belief that Ukraine is and always has been an integral part of Mother Russia? Lavrov walked out without answering.[60]

The US, with a growing sense of the inevitability of war, mobilised troops to reinforce front-line NATO allies. Paratroops from the 173rd Airborne were deployed to the Baltic states, with other US units moved from Italy to Romania, Hungary and Bulgaria. By the middle of February the US military presence in Europe increased from 74,000 to 100,000 troops, four airborne fighter squadrons were boosted to 12, and the number of surface combatant ships in the region increased from five to 26. Washington also stepped up deliveries of military aid to Kyiv – mostly in the form of defensive man-portable anti-tank weapons to slow a Russian attack. 'Nobody actually thought that [the Ukrainians] would be able to successfully repel a Russian attack on that scale, if it happened,' admitted the Downing Street official.[61]

Nonetheless, the Europeans persisted in trying to talk the Russians down. On 11 February British Defence Minister Ben Wallace visited Sergei Shoigu in Moscow and was told that Russia and Ukraine were 'all part of our same country', Shoigu offering the fact that his mother was born in Ukraine as evidence. Shoigu shrugged off Wallace's threat of sanctions with the assurance that Russians 'can suffer like no one else'. But the Russian also bluntly denied that his country had any plans to invade, 'just lying barefacedly to Wallace's face', recalled the Downing Street official.[62]

On 16 February an evacuation of civilians – extensively covered by Russian state TV – began from the Donetsk and Luhansk republics, supposedly to protect them from an escalation of Ukrainian artillery fire. Kremlin-controlled TV began spreading rumours of a coming Ukrainian offensive against the DNR and LNR. Two days later Russia's Duma appealed to Putin to recognise the republics to 'protect' them from invasion by Kyiv's forces. Photographs began circulating on social media of Russian armoured vehicles being painted with large 'V', 'Z' and 'O' symbols visible from the air – each letter signifying a different battle-group. US intelligence shared reports of massive amounts of medical supplies and even mobile crematoria being moved up to Ukraine's borders. Even Ukrainian Foreign Minister Dmytro Kuleba was finally convinced of the reality of an imminent attack after the Americans gave him 'more specific information' on five Russian transport planes on full alert, ready to take paratroops to Hostomel airport near Kyiv.[63]

Even as Putin's war machine gunned into high gear, France's Emmanuel Macron attempted a last-ditch reconciliation, calling Putin on 20 February and suggesting a summit in Geneva with Biden to discuss the 'security architecture of Europe'. Putin was evasive. 'To be perfectly frank with you, I wanted to go [play] ice hockey, because right now I'm at the gym,' Putin told Macron, according to a video recording of the conversation aired by

France 2 television. 'But before starting my workout, let me assure you, I will first call my advisers.' Macron thanked Putin and, after hanging up, laughed in delight. Emmanuel Bonne, Macron's diplomatic adviser, danced a triumphant jig.[64]

The French leadership's celebrations would be short-lived. The morning after his conversation with Macron – and, presumably, his workout and ice-hockey game – Putin flew to Moscow for his extraordinary meeting of Russia's Security Council.

The Tsar and His Court

The Security Council meeting of 21 February was remarkable in many ways. The setting of the Kremlin's St Catherine Hall was unique in its formality and grandeur – a clear signal that something momentous and historic was afoot. The vast, garishly restored ceremonial halls of the Kremlin were familiar to Russian TV viewers from various spectacles of adulation by the collected members of Russia's political and cultural elite as they listened to and applauded Putin's annual state of the union addresses. This time, the Kremlin hall was not packed but empty save for the president himself, seated at a vast white table, and the members of the Council seated at a bizarre distance from him. And as the meeting progressed, the content of the broadcast, too, became more and more extraordinary. The spectacle of humble ministers dutifully reporting to Putin was a staple of Russian television. So was the occasional ritual humiliation by Putin of oligarchs and senior officials. But for the first time the Russian public saw the chilling spectacle of the entire security establishment of their country assembled for a ritual, public obeisance to – and abuse by – their supreme leader.

In the Soviet era, the only public display that could hint at the changing power relations inside the inner Politburo was the order in which the USSR's gerontocratic rulers would file onto the roof of Lenin's Mausoleum for the annual May Day parade. Putin's regime offered something far more interesting – an hour-long spectacle of Russia's new Politburo offering their 'opinion' of a possible recognition of the independence of the Donbas republics, followed by a personal response by Putin himself. The spectacle was certainly carefully orchestrated. But it was also very revealing – including in ways that the Kremlin spin doctors did not intend.

It began with a mind game. As Peskov confided to the source with whom he lunched on 28 February, all the members of the Security Council had been told – falsely – that the meeting would be broadcast live.[65] That was a lie. As sharp-eyed reporters noticed, the times on the watches of the participants showed that the meeting took place hours before it was actually shown on TV. It continued with a ritual that Professor Mark Galeotti described as 'King Lear meets James Bond's Ernst Stavro Blofeld'.[66] One by one, the members of the Council stood not to speak their mind on whether the republics of the Donbas should be recognised as independent states so much as to count the ways in which they agreed with Putin.

The ultra-hawks Nikolai Patrushev and Aleksandr Bortnikov were the most obviously assured in their delivery and extreme in their lies and eschatological fantasies. FSB Director Bortnikov ran through an extraordinary list of alleged Ukrainian provocations – including 'genocidal' attacks on the civilians of Donbas. Security Council Secretary Patrushev claimed that the conflict was being driven by the machinations of Western powers whose 'goal is the destruction of Russia'. Defence Minister Shoigu – who, as we have seen, was the most cautious on the invasion of Crimea at the equivalent (though non-public) meeting on 21 February 2014 – bizarrely focused on the left-field idea that Ukraine was planning nuclear rearmament.

Federation Council Speaker Valentina Matviyenko led a chorus of support with a variation of the 'genocide' line, citing outrages against Russian-speakers in Ukraine. Deputy Chair of the Security Council Dmitry Medvedev, the former liberal appointed by Putin as his stand-in as president between 2008 and 2011, had reinvented himself as a hawk in a desperate bid to remain in Putin's inner circle. He pleaded for everyone to think of the children of Donbas who – he claimed, in defiance of then-current opinion polls – the people of Russia were clamouring to protect by means of war. Interior Minister Vladimir Kolokoltsev went for an even more hawkish position by arguing that Russia should not only recognise the current borders of LDNR along the 2015 line of control but also push to extend their borders to the whole of the Donetsk and Luhansk provinces, including Mariupol.

But the particularly interesting responses came from the members of the Putin cabinet who were clearly the most uncomfortable with the unfolding events. This group included the men best informed about Russia's position in the world, its economy and on the real situation on the ground in Ukraine.

Sergei Lavrov – playing the consummate diplomat – simply waffled and avoided giving a straight answer on whether he approved of the recognition of the LDNR. Prime Minister Mikhail Mishustin failed to keep Lavrov's poker face and looked distinctly uncomfortable and disgruntled, especially when Putin cut him off as he attempted to warn the Council of the economic consequences of an invasion. Cowed, Mishustin quickly toed the party line – even though he must have clearly realised that a national political and economic revival project that he headed was crumbling before his eyes.

The two men in the hall who had the most detailed knowledge of actual events and conditions in Ukraine came in for the roughest ride. Dmitry Kozak, the Kremlin's on-the-ground point man for relations with the LDNR and Crimea, had grown up in Ukraine. After a wordy exposition where he admitted that Kyiv was not ready to re-incorporate the LDNR on the terms set out in Minsk-2, Kozak attempted a real discussion on the future of the Donbas republics. But Putin brusquely cut him off, twice.

The spectacle demanded a victim from among the Kremlin courtiers – and Putin chose Sergei Naryshkin, head of Russia's Foreign Intelligence Service. Of all the people present, Naryshkin was probably the best informed on the true success of Russia's influence operations in Ukrainian society and establishment. Unlike Kozak or Mishustin, Naryshkin made no attempt to actually debate, much less contradict, Putin's decision. But he did fluff his lines, expressing his support for the recognition of the LDNR in a future tense of Russian suggestive of ambiguity. 'You *will* support, or you *do* support?' barked Putin. 'Tell me plainly, Sergei Yevgenievich.' Naryshkin, trembling at the podium like a flustered schoolboy, responded that he supported 'bringing them into Russia'. Wrong again. 'That's not what we are discussing!' Putin snapped. 'Do you support recognising their *independence* or not?'

Putin had made his official message clear in the characteristically direct and universally comprehensible way he had communicated for two decades – the language of boss–subordinate relations. At its most superficial, he had signalled that recognition of the Donbas republics was right and proper, in the collective and unanimous opinion of Russia's top public statesmen. Subconsciously, but with equal clarity, he had also denoted who was in the inner circle, who was in the chorus, who was on the edges. And most of all, who was the ultimate boss.

But Putin had also signalled something far more profound, something that would ultimately be far more significant for the coming conflict. The most deluded and the most ideologically driven members of Putin's entourage were on the inside, while those with the most detailed and forensic real-world knowledge were on the outside. Like King Lear, indeed, Putin showed in his Security Council meeting that he was interested not in debate but in ritual public displays of approval. Dissent – such as Shoigu's misgivings about the wisdom of annexing Crimea in 2014 – was no longer conceivable. There could be no clearer indication that the nature and power dynamics of Putin's court had changed. As had Putin himself. He had become the leader of a nation about to launch a great patriotic war.

CHAPTER 7
CRY HAVOC

No military plan survives its first contact with the enemy.

Carl von Clausewitz, *On War*

Kyiv

Just before 6 a.m. Moscow time – five in the morning in Kyiv – a pre-recorded message from Vladimir Putin was broadcast on all Russian state TV channels. He announced the launch of a 'special military operation' in eastern Ukraine in order to achieve the 'demilitarisation and denazification' of the country. Putin assured viewers that Russia had 'no plans' to occupy Ukrainian territory and that he 'supported the right of the peoples of Ukraine to self-determination'.[1] Minutes later, the skies above Kyiv, Kharkiv and a dozen other major Ukrainian cities lit up with the tail-flames of Kalibr and Kinzhal cruise missiles and incoming artillery. The 'shock and awe' blitzkrieg that General Mark Milley had predicted the previous October had begun – and as he had also predicted, the spearhead of the assault was an armed coup against the government in Kyiv.

In his top-floor apartment in Kyiv's fashionable Podol district artist Ilya Chichkan heard the sirens and went out onto his balcony. From the direction of Hostomel airport to the west of the city, he saw 'the biggest fireworks display I have ever seen ...

it was like a Hollywood film,' he recalled. 'It was hard to believe that it was really happening in front of my eyes. I thought, God damn. That crazy bastard's gone and done it.'[2]

Fifteen kilometres south of Kyiv in the presidential residence in Koncha-Zaspa, Volodymyr Zelensky had been awoken with the news of Russian mobilisation at half past four. When the bombardment began he and his wife Olena went to wake their children Oleksandra, 17, and Kirilo, 9. 'It was loud,' recalled Zelensky. 'There were explosions' as Russian rockets poured into Hostomel, to the northeast of the residence.[3] Olena and the children hurriedly crossed the gravel drive in front of the nineteenth-century merchant's mansion and hustled into cars to be evacuated to a more secure location in western Ukraine. A week later, a piece of Russian rocket would land just outside the front door of the residence ('Missed!' tweeted press secretary Sergii Nykyforov with the defiant humour that would become the trademark of Zelensky's government communications). For the first weeks of the war, Zelensky would speak only by phone to his wife and children, according to adviser Serhiy Leshchenko.[4]

Zelensky, in his usual work clothes of a white shirt and blue suit, was driven in a heavily guarded convoy to the closed street of government buildings in the heart of Kyiv known as the Triangle or 'Bankova', after the street's pre-revolutionary name. Over the previous few days and weeks the Triangle had been haphazardly fortified with roadblocks of 'hedgehog' tank traps and hastily constructed concrete pillboxes protecting the approaches. Inside the gaudily decorated presidential administration itself, sandbags had been piled up inside and outside all the doors and windows and offices hastily converted into dormitories for staffers and guards. Heavy desks and filing cabinets were used to block internal doors – makeshift fortifications that would remain in place for months. Zelensky and his top military and civilian officials convened in a more secure, if also more claustrophobic, venue in a Soviet-era bunker deep underground, a vast complex that included tunnels linking it to the Kyiv metro system at Arsenalnaya Station. Ordinary Kyiv residents followed suit, descending into a network of over 500 large bomb shelters and 6,000 reinforced basements constructed during the Cold War and refurbished by the city authorities after the annexation of Crimea.[5]

One of the first official calls Zelensky took was from President Biden, who offered full support – while other US officials offered to evacuate him and his family from Kyiv. The next day the Associated Press quoted a senior US intelligence official as saying that Zelensky's response had been, 'The fight is here; I need ammunition, not a ride.'[6] Aides who were with him at the time are doubtful that he actually uttered this exact phrase, but it certainly reflected two vital things about the first, chaotic hours of the war – Zelensky's upbeat defiance, and a conviction among NATO allies that Kyiv would soon fall to the Russian onslaught. Germany's Finance Minister Christian Lindner even initially rebuffed Zelensky's urgent appeals for aid and weapons, telling him 'you only have a few hours' before Kyiv fell, according to Ukraine's ambassador to Berlin.[7]

Despite the apparent defeatism of Ukraine's closest allies, the Ukrainian president 'was calm, calmer than the rest of us', recalled an adviser. 'He was in no doubt that his place was with his people, in his capital.' The adviser had hurried on foot to the Triangle in the early morning of 24 February with just a satchel containing his personal laptop and chargers, but no change of clothes. He would remain at the office, sleeping in makeshift dormitories alongside bodyguards, for three weeks.[8]

After his call with Biden, Zelensky hurriedly recorded a video address to his people on his smartphone. 'Good morning, Ukrainians, this morning President Putin announced a special military operation in Donbas,' he said. 'We are working. The army is working. Don't panic. We are strong. We are ready for everything. We will defeat everyone. Because we are Ukraine.'

Switching from Ukrainian to Russian, Zelensky addressed the Russian people directly. 'The people of Ukraine and the government of Ukraine want peace,' he said. 'But if we come under attack ... you will see our faces, not our backs.'

By mid-morning, still clean-shaven and wearing a dark jacket and white shirt, Zelensky made a more formal address from an official lectern in the Presidential Palace – this time aimed at an international audience. 'Russia has attacked Ukraine in a cowardly and suicidal way, just as Nazi Germany did,' he said. 'What is being decided is not only our country's future, but also how Europe will live in the future.' Zelensky ordered a general mobilisation of all Ukrainian males between 18 and 60 years old, who were also banned from leaving the country.[9] Within two days Kyiv's Territorial Defence Forces had so many volunteers that they were turning people away.[10] Civil defence units began distributing weapons to all able-bodied men in the courtyards of apartment buildings all over Kyiv, eventually handing out 18,000 guns and hundreds of thousands of Molotov cocktails.[11] Two artist friends of Ilya Chichkan's wandered out of an all-night party at his studio – and returned with a Kalashnikov and a heavy-calibre pistol.[12]

From before dawn on the war's first day, according to a source on the Zelensky team with direct knowledge of the events, the presidential security team had been reinforced by several 'foreign' advisers that included at least three senior US intelligence officials.[13] Zelensky and his top advisers were given secure satellite-based mobile phones provided by the Americans to make their movements less trackable. Zelensky also changed out of his dark blue suit and put on an olive-green Ukrainian army fleece top without insignia, army fatigue trousers and boots. The trademark informal war-leader look that would characterise Zelensky's future addresses to the nation – as well as to the European and British parliaments, the US Congress, the Cannes Film Festival and dozens of other video appeals to the world – was born.

'People say the look was made up by stylists or PR people. It was not,' said the adviser. 'It was Volodymyr Oleksandrovych [Zelensky's] own personal decision, his alone. He wanted to show solidarity with the ordinary Ukrainians who were defending their country. Everyone had become a soldier overnight – including the president.'[14] By the time I met Zelensky in Kyiv in July he cut a profoundly impressive figure – hard-eyed, emphatic in his speech, his trademark boyish grin long gone.

On the evening of 25 February – the second day of the war – Zelensky appeared on television in his new military look, unshaven and grim-faced. 'What do we hear today? It's not just rocket explosions, combat and the roar of aircraft,' said Zelensky, his manner transformed into something strikingly harder and more commanding that his pre-war, nice-guy persona. 'This is the sound of a new iron curtain lowering and closing Russia off from the civilised world. Our task is for that new iron curtain not to fall on Ukraine.'

In truth, Zelensky's defiance in the first days of the invasion was based on little more than bravado. Ukrainian forces were for the most part being badly beaten on the ground as the Russian steamroller gathered pace. In the south – as we will look at later in more detail – Russian units poured from Crimea almost unopposed, reaching and taking the strategic dam on the Dniepr at Nova Kakhovka in a matter of hours. Kyiv and central Ukraine were now cut off from river access to the Black Sea. Other forces were pressing east towards Mariupol in a bid to link Crimea to the Donbas republics. Massive columns of Russian armour were moving from the Russian border to surround Kyiv from two sides – exactly as the CIA's Russian informants had predicted – and the Kremlin's forces were already in the suburbs of the northeastern border cities of Kharkiv and Sumy. To the east, satellites showed Russians setting up field hospitals, resupply bases for artillery and rocket launchers – as well as vast columns of trucks loading at all available railheads.[15] Only the Ukrainian forces directly opposite Donetsk, firmly dug in since 2014, held the line – though the Russians quickly broke over the line of control in northern Donbas around Luhansk.

Most ominously of all, a lightning airborne assault on Hostomel airport on the outskirts of Kyiv had succeeded in capturing the strategic airport. Russian special forces in airborne-landed armoured vehicles were moving through the western suburbs of the capital, with firefights breaking out on Victory Prospekt, within four kilometres of the Triangle government compound downtown. Ukrainian forces dynamited two key bridges into Kyiv, enabling them to focus on defending a smaller number of choke-points. Ukrainian sappers also destroyed all connections between the Russian and Ukrainian rail networks in Kharkiv and Sumy provinces to prevent the invading force from ramping up their supply lines.

Amid the unfolding disaster, there were a few small hopeful signs. Russian troops who believed they would be met with flowers and smiles by the liberated local population were quickly disabused. Ukrainian social media in the first days of the war was filled with clips of civilians – some apparently insanely brave, others drunk, almost all Russian-speaking – roundly abusing Russian soldiers and telling them in no uncertain terms to fuck off home. A unit of Ukrainian marines became early national heroes for their radio message from their tiny garrison on Snake Island near Odesa to the heavy missile cruiser *Moskva*, flagship of the Russian Black Sea Fleet, which had ordered them to surrender. 'Russian warship, go fuck yourself!' they signalled defiantly, before being shelled and then captured. Within days, destinations on motorway road signs around Ukraine had been replaced with the words – spelled out in official municipal-issue transfer-lettering – '*Na Khui*', or 'Fuck Yourselves'.

Meanwhile, with the Russian military relying nearly entirely on unsecured analogue radio communications, amateur radio enthusiasts and hacktivist organisations like Anonymous quickly managed to block and surveil enemy radio frequencies. Aviarazvetka, a group of amateur drone enthusiasts who had volunteered for the Ukrainian army, unleashed a deadly swarm of small commercial drones to track advancing Russian armour. And most importantly, three key weapons that would prove unexpectedly decisive made their battlefield debut: Ukraine's 142-strong fleet of missile-armed Turkish-made Bayraktar TB-2 drones, British–Swedish NLAW and US-made Javelin shoulder-launched anti-tank missiles.

On the third day of the invasion, as intense fighting raged in the western suburbs of Kyiv, Russian State Duma Speaker Vyacheslav Volodin claimed on his Telegram channel that 'Zelensky hastily fled Kiev. He was already not in the Ukrainian capital yesterday. He fled to Lvov with his entourage ... [and is] currently under protection of neo-Nazis.'[16]

That evening – Saturday 26 February – Zelensky filmed himself and his closest aides, all dressed in military fatigues, exiting the doors of the Presidential Administration on Bankova Street and walking down the road, accompanied by a handful of bodyguards in tactical gear. The location – just 50 metres above the Khreschatyk Boulevard in central Kyiv – was unmistakable. 'Good evening, everyone,' Zelensky said. 'I want everyone to know that we are still in the capital, in our home. The leader of the presidential party is here. The head of the presidential office is here. Prime Minister [Denys] Shmyhal is here. [Mykhailo] Podolyak [adviser to the head of the presidential office] is here. The president is here. We are all here. Our soldiers are here. Citizens are here. We are all here protecting our independence and our country, and it will stay like that. Glory to the heroes, glory to Ukraine.'[17]

The stroll through downtown Kyiv was a calculated risk. Earlier that afternoon, Kyiv authorities had declared a strict 36-hour curfew in order to sweep the city for Russian saboteurs, warning civilians that they would be seen as Kremlin agents and risked being 'liquidated' if they stepped outside. Zelensky's security team had received intelligence that no fewer than three teams of Russian assassins deployed to Kyiv were hunting him.

The 400 Wagner mercenaries – most of them Russian special forces veterans – who had been covertly deployed to Kyiv in January had been issued with a list of key assassination targets that included Zelensky, the prime minister, the cabinet, the Mayor of Kyiv Vitali Klitschko and his brother Wladimir, both former world heavyweight boxing champions. The Wagner teams, promised high bounties for every kill, had spent the previous six weeks tracking the movements of their targets via their mobile-phone signals, a source close to Wagner told the British journalist Manveen Rana, who had cultivated contacts among the group's members in North and Central Africa.[18]

The Wagner men's orders were to wait until uniformed Spetsnaz – Russian special forces – teams reached the city to secure a corridor out of Kyiv once their targets had been assassinated. The mercenaries had also been told that Putin wanted to hold off on the killings to show that he was negotiating with Zelensky. Indeed Zelensky agreed on Sunday 27 February to send a delegation to meet a Russian team at the Belarus border – but expressed scepticism about Moscow's seriousness.

Wagner commanders assured their men in Kyiv that no deal would be reached and that the effort would be simply 'smoke and mirrors', a source close to senior members of the Wagner Group told Rana. But as the planned assault on Kyiv ground to a halt in the northern and western suburbs, the mercenaries came under fierce pressure from Moscow to bring forward their operations to secure a visible victory. Ukrainian intelligence would later report that the Wagner teams attempted to assassinate Zelensky on at least two occasions, only to be ambushed and killed. According to Rana's source the Wagner men on the ground were 'alarmed' by how accurately the Ukrainians had anticipated their moves, calling the intelligence of Zelensky's security team 'eerie' in its accuracy.

In addition to the Wagner killers – and unbeknown to them – a separate group of Chechen assassins were also on the hunt for Zelensky. Hours after Zelensky's walkabout, Ukrainian special forces 'eliminated' a group of Chechens on the outskirts of Kyiv before they could reach the president. Oleksiy Danilov, the head of Ukraine's National Security and Defence Council, told Ukrainian TV channels that the tip-off on their whereabouts came from inside Russian intelligence. 'I can say that we have received information from the FSB, who do not want to take part in this bloody war,' Danilov said. 'And thanks to this, the elite [Chechen] group which came here to eliminate our president was destroyed.' According to the Ukrainian Interior Ministry the Chechen death squad had been riding around Kyiv in a hijacked ambulance and were 'partly shot, partly detained'.[19]

Hostomel Airport, Kyiv

In the opening hours of the war's first day the Russian army's priority was to cripple Ukraine's military infrastructure – focusing on destroying air bases in an effort to quickly gain air superiority. Eleven military airports across the country were hit by Russian airstrikes on day one of the fighting, destroying a number of Ukrainian helicopters and airplanes on the ground. Ammunition dumps, too, were targeted. Fortunately, the Ukrainian army had moved to disperse its stores of artillery, weapons and aircraft as widely as possible in the days leading up to the invasion, partly neutralising the devastation of the first Russian airstrikes.

Russia's single most important strategic target was Kyiv's Hostomel airport. Gaining control of the airport and establishing an air bridge would allow a quick airborne assault on the capital, decapitating the government and allowing Putin to declare victory within days or even hours. From dawn on the 24th,

Hostomel received a brutal pasting from Russian jets. At noon, a large force of Russian helicopters – including troop-carrying Mi-8 workhorses and Ka-52 attack choppers – made their first daring attempt to land at the airport.

The hundreds of paratroopers from Russia's 31st Guards Air Assault Brigade who boarded helicopters on a remote plain on the Belarusian–Ukrainian border had no idea that they were going into combat. They had been told that they were deploying on exercises in western Belarus. But once the units were airborne, senior officers turned to the men to tell them that they were actually at war with Ukraine. Instead of heading to Grodno, the flight of choppers veered south, entered Ukrainian airspace and sped fast and low across the 66 kilometres from the Belarusian border to Hostomel.

'The troops were fucking shocked,' said Nikita Ponomarev, a paratrooper later captured by the Ukrainians. 'People turned gray, especially considering we took fire in the air.'[20] Under heavy small arms fire from the defenders, Ponomarev and his comrades fast-roped from the choppers onto the tarmac in Hostomel and fanned out across runways, hangars and airport buildings. During the initial assault, the Ukrainians reported shooting down seven helicopters – including two Ka-52s, the newest gunships in the Russian Air Force – with shoulder-fired MANPAD surface-to-air missiles. Though the Russian paras had secured the runway, the fire was so intense that a force of 18 Il-76 transport planes carrying the main Russian assault force were forced to abort their approach and turn back to base. The surviving troops of the 31st Guards Air Assault Brigade had to dig in around the airport's perimeter, defended by a few armoured vehicles that had been choppered in under heavy fire.[21]

Hostomel was too significant a strategic objective to abandon, so in the late afternoon of 24 February the Russians regrouped and attempted once more to land planeloads of paratroops to reinforce the men stranded on the ground. This time the Russians lost two Il-76s – one, according to the Ukrainian Air Force, shot down by a Ukrainian Su-27 fighter – killing close to 300 elite airborne troops on board.[22]

A 'Thunder Run' is what US airborne forces call storming airports without having first achieving air superiority. It worked for the US 101st Airborne Division and 173rd Airborne Brigade during April 2003's Operation Iraqi Freedom. It didn't work for the Russians at Hostomel. Despite Russia's massive overall superiority in aircraft – 1,511 combat planes and 1,543 combat helicopters to Ukraine's 98 warplanes and 112 helicopters – the Russian Air Force's failure to knock out their opponents and establish air superiority was fatal to their assault on Hostomel – and would become a serious strategic weakness as the war progressed.[23]

As the dawn of 25 February broke there was an 'ominous feeling' in the air at Hostomel, Ponomarev recalled. Ukraine's 4th Rapid Reaction Brigade of elite motorised infantry had moved into position in the small hours of the morning, tasked with retaking the airport. At first light, rounds from the Ukrainian artillery brought up overnight began slamming into the buildings, killing dozens of Russian paratroopers and destroying large amounts of equipment during a two-hour close-range barrage. 'There was nothing left – not even a [tank] turret,' Ponomarev said. 'Almost nobody survived that day.'[24]

One of the first Russians killed at Hostomel was Sergeant Ilnur Sibgatullin, 31, from Nizhnekamsk, a small city in the republic of Tatarstan. Sibgatullin's funeral, held with full military honours in his hometown six days after the start of the invasion, would also be the first official military funeral of the war. Hundreds turned out. Sibgatullin had been a 'kind boy, who makes your soul rejoice', his former teacher said in comments posted on the VKontakte social media site. As casualties mounted, local authorities across Russia quickly realised that such displays of public mourning were bad for morale. Soon, full military funerals would be reserved only for senior officers.

Officers of the beleaguered Russian 31st Guards Air Assault Brigade told their men that extra equipment and reinforcements would arrive within 24 hours. None did. 'After three days, it was still only us,' Ponomarev said.[25] By the time the unit was ordered to attempt a withdrawal on 27 February, up to 50 paratroopers from the 31st Brigade had been killed and as many wounded in Hostomel, according to Ukrainian intelligence – a quarter of the assault force that included its commanders, Colonel Sergei Karasev and Major Alexei Osokin. Photos taken after the airfield was retaken showed the bodies of Russian soldiers strewn across pavements and trenches and lying on top of burning tanks. A giant Antonov Airlines An-225 – the largest plane in the world – was destroyed by Ukrainian shelling during the final assault to retake the aiport during which Ponomarev and dozens of others were captured.[26]

Further north, two vast Russian columns, one moving towards Kyiv through the Chernobyl exclusion zone on the Belarusian border and another advancing down the eastern bank of the Dniepr through Chernihiv province, were running into trouble. The advancing force formed a near-continuous 60-kilometre-long column from the border towards the capital. By the third day of the war the column had become almost stationary due to breakdowns, fuel shortages and unexpectedly fierce resistance in the prosperous northern commuter suburbs of Kyiv whose names would, in time, become bywords for Russian brutality – Bucha, Irpin and Motyzhin.

The columns soon became sitting ducks for attacks by small groups of Ukrainian troops with NLAWs and Javelins, as well as long-range, low-and-slow-flying Bayraktar drones. One such group was formed of an irregular group of Kyiv professionals – including lawyers, engineers, accountants and cafe owners – who had formed a 'fight club' and signed up to the Territorial Defence Forces over the previous few years. Dmytro 'Lysy' – a nickname and nom de guerre that meant 'Baldie' – was a 42-year-old banker-turned-cryptocurrency dealer and online gamer who signed up in 2020 partly because he wanted to 'run around in the woods with a gun, like paintball, and get a bit fit' and partly 'because I am having an extended midlife crisis'.[27] (Lysy – a solidly built man who wore a hoodie printed with a cartoon Cossack flexing an outsize bicep – asked for his full name not to be used because he had relatives in Voronezh, Russia.)

But when Lysy saw his first Russian tank on the second day of the invasion, the war games turned deadly serious. On 24 February the members of his unit had driven their own cars to a pre-arranged rendezvous at a car park popular with picnickers in the Zalissia National Park to the northwest of Kyiv. The members of the 'fight club' had been issued with uniforms, service Kalashnikovs and helmets but no body armour – those who could afford it had bought their own. At least half a dozen of the group had also brought their own small commercial camera drones that provided live video feeds to their mobile phones ('we are basically a bunch of wannabe-bourgeois tech nerds,' he joked). They mounted army trucks along with a couple of dozen Ukrainian army regulars – who had brought a supply of NLAW anti-tank missiles in bulky plastic cases, 'like something you'd carry a tuba in'.[28]

The platoon-sized group spent a night in a barn trying to keep a low profile for fear of local informants – but villagers soon got wind of them. 'Must have been the smell of quality tobacco,' laughed Lysy, who smoked Rothmans. The locals brought them food, homemade moonshine vodka, pickles and smoked pork fat. The regulars' lieutenant accepted the food but sent back the moonshine. By the middle of the next morning – 25 February – artillery fire could be heard nearby. The officer couldn't raise his headquarters by his antiquated radio, so called them on his mobile instead. A column of Russians was heading their way, he was told. '*Razyeboshit', tak mozh'te* – engage, and fuck them up as best you can,' was Lysy's recollection of the gist of the orders.[29]

A host of little drones went up and quickly spotted the enemy about two kilometres away and closing fast. The Russian column was led by a T-72 tank, followed by a column of at least twenty BMP-2 armoured personnel carriers, interspersed with more tanks. The semi-civilian members of the 'fight club' were deployed along a roadside patch of woodland with their Kalashnikovs to engage any dismounted infantry – but there were none. The armoured column advanced unprotected. 'It was like they were driving to a parade or something,' said Lysy in a Kyiv cafe months later as he recalled his first firefight. The first NLAW strike came like a 'thunderclap, but a very, very short one', the missile's downward-firing warhead hitting the third BMP squarely from above at the vehicle's most vulnerable point. The armoured personnel carrier's ammunition began to detonate 'like firecrackers going off'. The rear hatch popped swung open, 'but no one got out ... the BMP cooked up too fast.'[30]

Moments later another NLAW fired from a few hundred yards away struck a tank, creating a much bigger explosion. Unlike US main battle tanks, a T-72's ammunition is all stored around the inside of the turret to make it accessible to the automatic loading system. The NLAW's direct hit detonated the ammo, causing the turret to 'pop into the air, cartwheeling far into the air high above the trees, just like in a film', recalled Lysy. 'That was my first "lollipop"' – the Ukrainian army's contemptuous slang for the lollipop-like appearance of the main gun and attached turret after it has been blown off by an internal explosion. The surviving Russian vehicles began firing indiscriminately, raking the undergrowth around them with heavy-calibre machine-gun fire. That – and the sound of an approaching helicopter – sent Lysy and his comrades scuttling for cover in a nearby half-frozen stream-bed. 'I lay face-down in the water [and] nearly caught my death of cold ... That would not have been very heroic.'[31]

Over the following two weeks, living rough in village houses and sometimes sleeping in freezing pigsties and stables, the 'fight club' found itself hooking up with several different Ukrainian units. The most dangerous part, Lysy recalled, was dodging groups of marauding Russians who were also scrounging food from stores and homes just like the Ukrainian irregulars. Lysy claimed to have personally witnessed 11 successful hits on Russian armoured vehicles. His only regret was two comrades killed in a rocket strike from a Russian helicopter on 2 March – and the fact that 'they never let me fire an NLAW to get my revenge on the fuckers.'[32]

Sumy

On the afternoon of 24 February Vadim Shishimarin's unit of the 4th Guards Kantemirovskaya Tank Division crossed the Ukrainian border near the village of Kozinka in Belgorod province, 20 kilometres northwest of Kharkiv. It was the first time Shishimarin had been outside Russia. But the landscape and buildings on the two sides of the border were pretty much indistinguishable: wooden single-storey village houses, standard Soviet-era five-storey concrete panel buildings, the flat, fertile farmland of the black-earth belt that spans all of northern Ukraine and south-central Russia.

The enormous column moving into Ukraine's Sumy province soon ground to a halt. Shishimarin's unit spent much of 24 and 25 February stationary 'in the middle of the road [where we] stood to regroup and refuel the equipment', he later told a Kyiv court.[33] By the afternoon of 26 February Shishimarin's 13th Armoured Regiment had made it as far as the small town of Komyshy on the western edge of Sumy province, just short of Poltava province. It had taken two days to move 91 kilometres inside Ukraine – in peacetime, barely a two-hour drive. The regiment formed up in a right-angled formation by a forest outside Komyshy and dug in.

To avoid the risk of late-night infantry raids, Russian sappers placed tripwires attached to noise grenades along the camp's perimeter. The soldiers were warned not to move more than 30 to 35 metres outside the camp. The precaution proved deadly. On the second night at Komyshy one man – 'probably a conscript', according to Shishimarin's comrade Private Ivan Maltisov – stepped on a tripwire. Other Russian soldiers on guard opened up with a burst of automatic fire, wounding their comrade. After five days at war, having spent more time stationary than moving and without having seriously engaged the enemy, Shishimarin's platoon had suffered four wounded, including the platoon's commander.[34]

The regiment's commanding officer ordered the wounded men evacuated to a military hospital in Russia. On the morning of 28 February, a convoy of five vehicles – two BMP-2 infantry fighting vehicles, a KamAZ truck with the wounded and two fuel trucks – formed up and moved out of the Komyshy camp, heading back towards Russia. Sergeant Shishimarin was detailed as one of the convoy's escorts.

The column with the wounded passed through the villages of Komyshy and Chupakhivka. Shishimarin and the other soldiers had had their cell phones confiscated, so they could not photograph or film their surroundings. But the officers kept theirs. Twenty-four-year-old Lieutenant Mikhail Shalayev, a native of Murmansk, made a sporadic video diary of his journey into Ukraine in a BMP-2 similar to Shishimarin's. When Shalayev was captured by Ukrainian forces on 3 April his cell-phone footage was passed to filmmaker Mikhail Tkatch, who edited it into the closest thing to a real-time, front-line documentary of the invasion to emerge from the Russian side.[35]

Shalayev filmed his unit – part of the 70th Battalion of the 42nd Guards Motor Rifle Division – rumbling through shelled villages in the south of Luhansk province. The claustrophobia and tension inside the infantry fighting vehicle are palpable. The roar of the engine is so loud that the crew have to shout to make themselves heard. The machine-gun belt to the right of the commander's seat jingles as the vehicle lurches over rutted roads. The only view of the outside world is through a narrow set of slits made of bulletproof glass. The six men in the belly of the vehicle have no view outside at all. The experience, as I learned travelling in the back of a Russian army BMP up to Shatoi in Chechnya, is like sitting in a crowded, hot tin can that's being kicked down the road.[36]

In the video, a BMP-2 travelling behind Shalayev's is hit. His column comes under fire for three hours. The BMP's machine gun jams. 'This is fucked up. They're fucking us up,' he shouts. 'We have to get the fuck out of here.' The next time Shalayev switches on his video he's on foot, the wreckage of his armoured vehicle billowing black smoke in the distance. He turns the phone camera to film what looks like a bin-bag-size chunk of charred meat that lies on the village street in front of him. 'Someone's meat,' says Shalayev in a bewildered voice. 'Someone got blown up.'[37]

Back in Sumy province, Shishimarin's convoy had got about a quarter of the way through their 100-kilometre journey back to Russia when they met a similar fate. On the outskirts of the village of Grinchenkovo the lead vehicle – a BMP-2 – suffered a direct hit from a shoulder-fired anti-tank guided missile. A second missile struck the KamAZ truck carrying the wounded. Under heavy fire from soldiers of Ukraine's 93rd Mechanised Brigade, Shishimarin and around 15 survivors loaded several wounded men into the remaining BMP, which turned and headed back towards Komyshy. Shishimarin and the remaining able-bodied men followed on foot.

Traces of the battle could still be seen on the road to Grinchenkovo three months later. 'A nauseating smell comes from the rusty frame of the BMP. Under it lies a charred helmet and dried half-decayed pieces of something which one does not want to guess what it might be – the fragments of a human body,' wrote BBC Russian Service reporters Svyatoslav Khomenko and Nina Nazarova. 'In what was once the back of a KamAZ truck you can see burnt metal mugs and the burnt aluminium boxes with barely visible labels – "Beef sausages", "Pork buckwheat porridge". A torn bulletproof vest is lying in a ditch.' By the side of the road, a rough cross made of two rusty pieces of iron marks the place where local villagers later buried the 'nine or ten' Russian dead abandoned by their retreating comrades.[38]

About a kilometre down the road, Shishimarin and other soldiers who were also fleeing on foot saw a grey Volkswagen approaching. The Russians opened fire, blowing out one of the front tyres. The driver dived out of the vehicle and took cover in a ditch. Though the car was damaged it was still running, and it might get them back to the safety of their unit. Five of the fugitive Russians piled in – Warrant Officer Makeev at the wheel and a man in camouflage without insignia in the passenger seat next to him. Shishimarin had never seen the man before, but from his bearing took him to be an officer. When the man was killed a few hours later, bank cards in the name of Ivan Kufakov would be found in his pockets – but his rank or unit would never be established.[39]

Shishimarin himself sat in the back seat behind the driver with his comrade Ivan Maltisov, a 20-year-old private from the village of Parapino in Mordovia who had served just three months in the army and signed up as a *kontraktnik* just weeks before. Senior Lieutenant Kalinin rode in the open boot of the car. The party drove off, the burst tyre flapping loudly, in the direction of the village of Chupakhivka.

Katerina and Alexander Shelipov's single-storey white brick house on the main street of the village is surrounded by red metal fence with a blue gate. Tulips grow in the yard. They used to keep cows, geese and ducks, but found it too much trouble and by the time of the Russian invasion their menagerie was just a single duck. Katerina Shelipova is from the Gomel region of Belarus and worked for 30 years as a kindergarten teacher. She met her husband in the early 1980s at a wedding. Alexander joined the army, served in the KGB Border Troops in Crimea, and after his service worked as a tractor driver, first class. 'He could work on any equipment – on a bulldozer, on a crane, on a combine harvester,' Katerina recalled. 'He was very kind. His neighbours loved him very much. Whenever anyone asked for help, he would quit what he was doing and go.' The couple had two children, a son and a daughter who died of cancer at the age of eight.[40]

On the first day of the war the nearby town of Akhtyrka was bombed. Soon columns of Russian armour were moving through Chupakhivka, and the Shelipovs moved into the small cellar under their house to shelter. Their next-door neighbours, who had no cellar, joined them. Katerina slept in the cellar, but Alexander preferred to stay upstairs to guard his wife, house and neighbours. One evening he counted 800 Russian military vehicles passing his house.

On the night of 27–28 February, the fourth day of the war, Ukrainian forces knocked out a Russian tank on the edge of the village. Katerina came up from the cellar in the morning to make breakfast while her husband took a nap after what he called his 'night duty'. After breakfast, Alexander told his wife he'd head over 'to take a look at the shell-hole'. She didn't want to let him go. 'I didn't give him a jacket,' Katerina told a Kyiv court two months later. 'I said, "Why are you going there?" And he said: "I'll be there and back in no time." He took his bicycle and went.' He was wearing a windbreaker and a knitted hat.[41]

Alexander joined several villagers who were admiring the wreckage of the burnt-out tank, then pedalled back in the direction of his house. He was nearly home when a friend – another tractor driver from Chupakhivka – called him on his old push-button Samsung mobile. He stopped, dismounted and took the call. A grey Volkswagen, a blown-out tyre slapping noisily on the recently laid asphalt, approached from the direction of Grinchenkovo.

Warrant Officer Makeev, at the wheel, and Ivan Kufakov, the apparent officer without insignia, were the first to notice Shelipov standing on the sidewalk talking on his phone. Makeev turned to Sergeant Shishimarin and 'ordered Vadim to shoot, saying that the man could be giving away our position to the [Ukrainian] military', recalled Ivan Maltisov. Vadim did not obey the order. Then Kufanov – whom neither Maltisov nor Shisihimarin had met or seen before – 'began shouting in a commanding voice that he should comply with this order, because if he didn't we could be handed over to the military, and we would never reach our guys to call for help'.

The Volkswagen had drawn nearly level with Shelipov. Shishimarin raised his automatic rifle and fired three or four shots, one of which hit Shelipov in the head, killing him instantly. 'I didn't want to kill him,' Shishimarin would later explain. 'I fired so they [his commanders] would leave me alone.'[42]

Katerina Shelipova was on the way to the well in their yard with empty buckets in her hands when she heard the shots. She began to dial her husband's number as she ran out onto the street. She saw the passing Volkswagen – and the skinny, baby-faced Russian soldier in the back seat with the Kalashnikov in his hand. Slamming the gate in fear, she remained motionless for five minutes before venturing out again. Her husband Alexander lay in a pool of blood on the pavement. 'I started screaming,' she recalled. 'Screaming a lot.'[43]

In the Volkswagen the officer who had given the order to fire reassured Shishimarin, who had never before fired a shot in anger. 'Don't worry, don't think about it,' he said. 'The most important thing is to save ourselves.' A few minutes later they encountered a white Lada Samara, stopped it, ordered the driver out at gunpoint and stole it. This time Senior Lieutenant Kalinin was inside the car, with Makeev in the boot. Kufakov was driving. 'What just happened?' the officer demanded. 'Why did you decide to shoot a civilian?' Hearing out the explanations, the lieutenant ordered everyone to put the safety catches on their weapons and not shoot at any more civilians.[44]

The owner of the stolen Lada was a local paramedic. He called friends in Perelug, the next village seven kilometres away, to warn them that a car full of escaping Russians was heading their way. Three men, all keen hunters, got their rifles and scrambled to set up an amateur ambush at a nearby bridge. 'We let them get closer and saw that there were really people in uniform inside,' recalled hunter Alexander Ivakhnenko, whose soldier nephew had been killed during the Ukrainian withdrawal from Ilovaisk in 2014. Ivakhnenko took aim and fired two shots from 50 metres' range at the driver, hitting Ivan Kufakov fatally in the head. The car veered off the road and plunged into a pond. The passengers clambered out of the car, returned fire and began to run. The three hunters, armed only with bolt action rifles, let them go. On Kufakov's body they found bank cards and 'pockets full of condoms', Ivakhnenko recalled. 'Fucking liberator.'[45]

The four survivors stumbled on through swamps, reed-beds and fields, discarding grenades and spare magazines as they went. Lieutenant Kalinin injured his leg, but limped on. They found shelter in a watchman's hut by a pigsty on the outskirts of the village of Olenovskoye. Nikolai Yaryzko, 62, returned to the hut at dusk to find the four soldiers – one lying on a bench with an injured leg – pointing guns at him. They asked for food, but he had none. Kalinin kept calling a comrade he addressed as 'brother' on his mobile phone. This comrade – presumably another officer – repeatedly promised to send a tank or an armoured personnel carrier to rescue the four men. None appeared all the next day. The rescue column had been attacked, Kalinin's 'brother' reported, the regiment's executive officer had disappeared and the regimental commander was gone too.

As they waited for rescue the Russians chatted with their hostage Yaryzko – whom they addressed respectfully as 'Dad'. 'The lieutenant says to me, "What are these villages you have here? Brick houses, paved roads. You call this a village?"' recalled Yaryzko, whose elder son fought in Donbas in 2015 and whose younger son was on the front lines. 'I said, yes, it's a village – a neglected village by our standards. It was amazing for them that we live this well.'[46]

The exhausted Russians asked 'Dad' whether they should surrender – but when he told them that there were hunters in the village they decided against it, fearing that they'd be shot. They were too scared to leave the hut, so went to the toilet in the adjacent pigsty. At night they took turns to keep watch as they waited vainly for help. But on the second night at two in the morning Shishimarin fell asleep on watch. Yaryzko took his phone from the table, along with a torch, and quietly slipped out into the night.

The police did not answer Yaryzko's call, so he indeed summoned the local hunters. But when they returned in a posse to the shed the Russians had fled. They walked all night, finally reaching Komyshi at dawn. But rather than return to their unit, the four decided to surrender. 'I didn't want to fight. When we arrived where our troops were camped, I saw no reason to go back there,' Shishimarin explained. 'I considered it necessary to surrender and stay alive.'[47]

The Russians were afraid of being lynched by the locals, so stole along the bed of a stream until they reached the centre of the village. There they walked into the square, laid down their arms and put up their hands. Villagers berated them, but did not harm them. Shishimarin and his three comrades were taken prisoner by the Ukrainian 93rd Mechanised Brigade. In the five days Vadim Shishimarin had been in Ukraine he had lost 11 immediate comrades, seen two Russian vehicles destroyed, hijacked two cars, taken one hostage and killed one unarmed civilian.

Nova Kakhovka

Larisa Nagorskaya was woken before dawn on 24 February by the terrifying sound of rockets and cruise missiles tearing through the sky over their house. The fiery barrage, she guessed, came from Crimea. No ordnance landed on Nova Kakhovka but flew northwards to targets deep inside Ukraine.[48]

Seventy kilometres to the south, thousands of Russian troops were pouring up the E97 highway that crossed the Perekop isthmus that links Crimea to Russia. The narrow neck of land, just five kilometres wide, could have been a formidable defensive point against a land invasion. But the Ukrainian defenders at Perekop offered little resistance. A second highway linking Crimea to Ukraine at Chonar, a few kilometres to the east, crossed a narrow bridge that was meant to be blown up in the event of an invasion. Yet the bridge remained intact – either through treachery or cowardice.

By noon on the first day of the war, the Russian tricolour flag was already flying over the Kakhovka dam. Russian units had sped north so fast that local authorities and the police were taken totally by surprise. The first Russian tanks to arrive took up positions at the location of the small wood that had been felled on the orders of a local official back in December. 'They had it all planned,' said Larisa. 'We were betrayed. The [Chonar] bridge wasn't mined. The [Russians] had their people here, collaborators.'[49] Her suspicions would later be confirmed when the former head of the SBU's directorate in Kherson was indicted by Ukrainian authorities for ordering subordinates to abandon their posts as Russian forces flooded the region.[50]

Nova Kakhovka was taken without a shot being fired. But as civilians tried to flee northwards in the afternoon several cars were shot up by Russian troops – killing three generations of a family who lived in Larisa's neighbourhood. Her husband Serhii wanted to go out and buy food but Larisa stopped him – he was much more at risk than her of being arrested by the Russians. Larisa herself joined a large group of neighbours who were panic-buying groceries in a small local supermarket. A Russian armoured personal carrier stopped outside and some Russian soldiers, their faces covered, walked into the shop. 'Nobody could say anything,' remembered Larisa. 'They had guns. Everyone just froze.' The soldiers helped themselves to armfuls of food – mostly biscuits, chocolates and cup noodles – and left without a word.

The local Ukrainian police were all quickly arrested – along with all veterans of Ukraine's 'anti-terror operation' against the rebel Donbas provinces. 'They had lists of people and addresses,' said Larisa. The occupiers also cut the local television and mobile-phone transmitters, leaving the people of Nova Kakhovka without access to news and unable to communicate with the outside world. One local pharmacy still had working Wi-Fi, and people congregated outside to message their relatives. Towards evening loudspeaker trucks patrolled the streets, ordering people to go home and warning of a strict curfew.

'We sat at home with some neighbours,' remembered Larisa. 'Everyone had heard rumours that people who had tried to escape had been shot in their cars. We were all afraid.'[51]

The Russian military had most success in its northward thrust from Crimea into the steppeland of southern Ukraine. As the Wehrmacht found in the summer of 1941, the flat, open country with little woodland favours easy movement for armour, and little natural cover for defenders. The targets of the Russian forces were twofold: one, to thrust east along the coast of the Azov Sea through Melitopol and Mariupol to create a land corridor to the Donetsk People's Republic; two, to push west to occupy Kherson, Mykolaiv and Ukraine's main port of Odesa, thereby cutting the country off entirely from the Black Sea.

Russian troops surrounded the regional capital of Kherson on 28 February. After three days' negotiations with the local mayor, the lightly armed Ukrainian garrison withdrew and the following day the Russians moved in. Putin's military planners had predicted that Ukraine's Russian-speaking cities would fall without a fight and that the locals would welcome Russians as liberators. In the event, Kherson and Melitopol would be the only major Ukrainian towns to fall without a furious battle. But in neither town would the Russians be welcomed.

Beyond Kherson, Russian troops crossed the still-intact bridges over the wide Dniepr River. Motorised infantry units rushed northeast and captured the city of Enerhodar, the location of one of Ukraine's 15 nuclear power plants that collectively provided over half the country's energy. They also pushed west to Mykolaiv, the last major city before Odesa. As the advance gathered pace in the first days of March it seemed that in this theatre at least the Kremlin's plan of a blitzkrieg operation was coming true.

The small town of Voznesensk, 85 kilometres north of Mykolaiv, became a key Russian target. Capturing Voznesensk's bridge over the Southern Bug River would allow the invaders to envelop Mykolaiv, push north to the main highway linking Odesa to the rest of the country and attack another major nuclear power station at Yuzhnoukrainsk, some 28 kilometres to the north. 'If they had taken Voznesensk, they would have cut off the whole south of Ukraine,' said Vadym Dombrovsky, commander of a Ukrainian special-forces reconnaissance group in the area and one of Voznesensk's 35,000 mostly Russian-speaking residents.[52]

Defending Voznesensk was a small force of Ukrainian regulars, backed up by several hundred members of the Territorial Defence Forces, which had been recruiting, arming and training local volunteers across the country for months. They had no tanks but carried rocket-propelled grenades and US-supplied Javelin anti-tank missiles. Units of artillery were brought up on the western side of the river to provide fire support. As the Russians approached, military sappers blew a railroad bridge over the

Southern Bug and a smaller bridge over the Mertvovod, a tributary of the main river. That funnelled the Russian attack towards the one possible crossing place – the main road bridge over the Bug.

On the morning of 2 March, a day after the fall of Kherson, a Russian Grad multiple-rocket launcher and artillery began lobbing unguided missiles and shells into central Voznesensk. The municipal swimming pool was destroyed, and several apartment blocks were hit. Mi-8 helicopters dropped Russian air-assault troops behind a forested ridge to the southwest of the town as an armoured column moved up from the southeast. According to Voznesensk's 32-year-old mayor, Yevheni Velichko, a former real-estate developer, the Russian column was guided along back roads by a local collaborator, a woman who drove a Hyundai SUV.

Russian troops and tanks moved into the nearby village of Rakove. Soldiers told locals to leave, parked their armoured vehicles between village houses and created a sniper position on one of the roofs. 'Do you have anywhere to go?' one soldier asked Natalia Horchuk, a 25-year-old mother of three. 'This place will be hit.' She said her family could hide in the cellar. 'The cellar won't help you,' he told her. Horchuk and most of her neighbours hid their valuables and fled.[53]

The Russians ransacked barns looking for sacks to fill with soil for fortifications, burned hay to create a smoke screen and demanded food. Five tanks, supported by a BTR armoured personnel carrier, drove to a wheat field overlooking Voznesensk's strategic bridge and opened fire on a small group of Ukrainian Territorial Defence volunteers armed with Kalashnikovs who had been hiding in a building on the field's edge. Outgunned, they retreated after taking casualties from the BTR's 30mm machine gun. Other Russian troops in two Ural trucks drew up and began to unload 120mm mortar ammunition when Ukrainian shelling began, forcing the invaders to withdraw.

By the evening of 2 March the Russians were in position for an assault on the bridge the next day. But the civilians of Voznesensk were also ready to phone in the enemy's coordinates to Ukrainian artillery via a network set up on the Viber messaging app before the assault began. Mykola Rudenko, a gravel transportation company owner, crept forward under cover of pouring rain and darkness to the positions his Territorial Defence unit had been forced to abandon earlier that day. Using Viber, he and other volunteers corrected the Ukrainian artillery fire. 'Everyone helped,' said Rudenko. 'Everyone shared the information.' Three of the five Russian tanks in the wheat field suffered direct hits. The surviving tank crews abandoned their vehicles and scrambled into BTRs or fled on foot, leaving at least two intact main battle tanks and a large quantity of ammunition.

Elsewhere around Vosnesensk, small groups of Ukrainian troops armed with Javelin missiles were wreaking similar havoc on the Russian armour. Over the course of the next day – 3 March – the Russians learned that expected reinforcements from the 126th Naval Infantry Brigade based in Perevalnoye, Crimea, had come under heavy shelling along the way and would not be coming. The commanders gave orders to withdraw – but not before randomly shelling the closest target to hand, the village of Rakove itself. Artillery destroyed the new roof of the village clinic.

According to Ukrainian military, the Russian battalion tactical group that assaulted Voznesensk lost nearly 30 of its 43 tanks and armoured personnel carriers, as well as multiple-rocket launchers, trucks and a Mi-24 attack helicopter downed by an anti-aircraft missile. Around 15 of the Russian vehicles had been abandoned in working or salvageable condition. During the course of the war fleeing Russian soldiers would, ironically enough, make Russia by far the largest foreign supplier of armoured vehicles to the Ukrainian army.

The human toll was equally devastating. In all, Ukrainian officers estimated, some 100 Russian troops died in Voznesensk

– roughly a quarter of the attacking force. Some bodies were retrieved by retreating Russian troops or burned inside their vehicles. But most were left where they fell, to be buried by villagers or collected by a municipal van painted, with grim irony, with the logo 'Cargo 200' – the Soviet army's Afghanistan-era code-word for dead bodies. Some of the bodies had been booby-trapped, according to local funeral director Mykhailo Sokurenko, who was accompanied by a Ukrainian army sapper as he drove round the area collecting Russian corpses. 'Sometimes, I wish I could put these bodies on a plane and drop them all onto Moscow, so they realise what is happening here,' said Sokurenko.[54]

Returning after the two-day battle, the villagers of Rakove found their homes ransacked. Cupboards and closets were still flung open from looting, and floors were littered with Russian military rations and half-eaten jars of pickles and preserves looted from the locals' cellars. 'Blankets, cutlery, all gone. Lard, milk, cheese, also gone,' said Natalia Horchuk. 'They didn't take the potatoes because they didn't have time to cook.'[55]

The two-day battle of Vozensensk marked the furthest extent of the Russian advance towards Odesa – and the end of Russia's blitzkrieg on the southern front. Russian units were also pushed back from around Mykolaiv to a line of control approximately 120 kilometres long and 20 deep along the western bank of the lower Dniepr.

By the end of the war's first week, four of Putin's fundamental fallacies had been exposed. One, the Ukrainians had not welcomed the invaders as liberators. Two, the Ukrainian army was not only ready but able and willing to fight in unconventional and devastatingly deadly ways. Three, Ukraine's leader Volodymyr Zelensky was not a drug-addled clown but a serious and inspiring wartime leader. And four, Putin's much-vaunted military, on which he had spent so much money and in which he had invested so much pride, had turned out to be embarrassingly unfit for purpose. From its Second World War-era armoured tactics, rigid plan of attack and its top-heavy command structure, the Russian military was attempting to fight a twentieth-century war in the twenty-first century – and failed utterly to deliver the blitzkrieg victory that Putin's securocrats had confidently told him to expect.

PART III

PYROKINESIS

CHAPTER 8
THINGS FALL APART

Everything we thought we shared with the civilised world was borrowed.

Moscow literary editor Varvara Babitskaya, February 2022[1]

Resistance and Repression

Protests flared across Russia on the first days of the war – especially in St Petersburg, where several thousand people gathered outside Gostinny Dvor shopping centre on Nevsky Prospekt on the evening of 26 February. A smaller crowd walked down Moscow's Rozhdestvensky Boulevard. But all protests were met with an overwhelming police presence, usually several times more numerous than the demonstrators. In Pushkin Square, a few hundred yards from the Moscow Kremlin, barriers shut off the central part of the square. Trios of OMON paramilitary policemen in motorcycle-style helmets, military urban camouflage uniforms and body armour were positioned like chessmen every five yards along the pavements. A few dozen young people sheepishly gathered, chatting and smoking in groups of three or four. Whenever six or more gathered, uniformed police swooped to check documents and rifle through bags.

'Everyone who comes out here has a death wish,' said 20-year-old Aleksandr, a filmmaker. 'It's not bravery. It's insanity. We're all risking throwing our lives away.'[2]

The authorities' machine of repression had been honed over two decades to a high degree of sophistication. Rather than breaking heads and tear-gassing crowds, Russian police would get up close and personal, putting young protesters on a pseudo-legal conveyor that threatened to destroy their lives if they persisted. Those arrested for 'participation in an unsanctioned meeting' for the first time received a 20,000 ruble (£120) fine and a criminal record. The penalty was issued on the spot, upon the signature of a confession. Suspects who refused to sign were remanded in custody for weeks, waiting for a court hearing – with a 99.5 per cent likelihood of their being convicted anyway. For the second arrest, the penalty was 15 days in jail – unless police chose to charge suspects for organising a meeting, for which they could face three months.

'We've been taken in,' Asya, 20, a film student, messaged my 19-year-old son Nikita on the third day of the war. 'We're sitting in a police paddy wagon. Bad news: we're in here with guys who have two, three prior arrests. We're screwed, guys.'[3]

Every young activist in the WhatsApp group set up to connect friends at Moscow protests knew immediately why Asya was so alarmed. Police had been arresting so many protesters that they didn't bother writing up separate charge sheets – they simply wrote the same one for everyone in each police van. Usually the charges were framed to nail the most hardcore protesters of every bunch. 'They're saying we swore. Bad. They took our fingerprints and they're checking our phones,' Asya told the group hours later, warning them that she was about to delete her incriminating WhatsApp and Telegram apps before a representative of the FSB on duty at the police station got to them.

Asya and her friend Yasha were eventually released at 5 a.m. Sitting dazed and subdued in a friend's apartment the next day, both students had been deeply chastened by the experience. 'My father says he's going to send me out of the country if I go to another protest again,' said Yasha, 21, with a grim smile. 'But even if he wanted to send me I can't leave Russia until I have paid my fine. And that will take at least two months.'[4]

Our conversation was interrupted by more bad news. Another friend – with three previous convictions for protesting over the last five years – had been picked up by police near a public prayer meeting on Gogolevsky Boulevard. 'We've been taken to the police department in Ryazan,' wrote the arrested friend – meaning that the prisoners had been driven to a town three hours to the east of Moscow for processing. 'We're still in the truck without food or water. A lawyer has been waiting for three hours at the entrance to the station. The police are inside deciding what to charge us with.' That arbitrary decision on charging would determine whether the detainees would serve months or years behind bars. He signed off with the slang for his particular form of incommunicado detention. 'They've put us in the "fortress".'[5] The next day, news came in from the protester's lawyer that she'd got him off with mere 'organisation' rather than treason – but nonetheless he was facing three months behind bars.

By day five of the invasion, as the prospect of a short victorious war receded fast, the Russian Ministry of Defence was forced to concede that hundreds of Russian soldiers had died in Ukraine. At the same time, authorities stepped up the pressure on dissent. Radio Echo Moskvy, a bastion of free speech long tolerated by the Kremlin, was shut down, as was *Novaya Gazeta* – whose editor-in-chief Dmitry Muratov had received the 2020 Nobel Peace Prize. *Meduza*, a Riga-based news platform, had its online service restricted for most of its Russian users, and the internet-based Dozhd TV was also raided by police and shut down.

Facebook, Twitter and Instagram – the favoured platforms for anti-Putin commentary and organising protests – were blocked for spreading 'extremism'. Some of the most vocal online voices went silent for fear of criminal prosecution for posts. Others, including the children of some of Russia's richest and most powerful men who evidently felt protected from the consequences that 'little people' might suffer for their opinions, were more outspoken. Sofia Abramovich, daughter of then-owner of Chelsea football club Roman Abramovich, told her 50,000 Instagram followers that 'the biggest and most successful lie out of the Kremlin propaganda is that most Russians are with Putin.' Elizaveta Peskova, 24, daughter of Kremlin spokesman Dmitry Peskov, posted 'No to the war' on Instagram, while Boris Yeltsin's granddaughter Maria Yumasheva, 19, also posted in support of Ukraine. Ksenia Sobchak, daughter of Putin's political mentor former St Petersburg mayor Anatoly Sobchak and now a TV presenter and opposition politician, also urged peace. 'No one, including me, until the last, believed that there would be a real conflict with Ukraine,' Sobchak wrote on Instagram. 'What's next, how will at least today's endless day end? It's impossible to calculate. The only thing known for sure is that people are dying.' Days later, Sobchak left with her daughter for Turkey.

The authorities scrambled to create new legal instruments sufficiently draconian not only to punish dissent but to decisively deter it. At the end of the first week of the war the Russian Duma voted through a hastily drafted new law with the Kafkaesque title 'On dissemination on public forums of obviously false information on the military deployments of Russia in defence of its citizens and in support of international peace and security'. The new legislation carried a 15-year jail term for spreading 'misinformation' about the war – and clearly included social media as a 'public forum'. That immediately criminalised anyone who dared to post anything 'false' about the war, defined by the Duma as 'contrary to the public statements of the Ministry of Defence'. One of the punishable 'falsehoods' was to call the invasion a 'war' rather than its official designation as a 'special military operation'.

The law was specifically designed to shut down political activists, bloggers and journalists. Russia's Justice Ministry compiled a special guide for police and prosecutors defining 'discrediting' the state as 'a negative opinion' while 'a statement of fact' was to be considered 'spreading false information'. By the end of the first six months of the war the Russian human rights group OVD-Info registered 17,500 arrests and over 200 prosecutions under what became known as the 'Fakes Law'.[6] After Putin announced partial mobilisation on 21 September 2022, a fresh wave of protests in at least 32 cities, including in hitherto quiescent Dagestan and eastern Siberia, would add another 2,300 to the tally. Vladimir Kara-Murza, a prominent activist who was imprisoned under the new law, called 'Article 207.3 ... a direct analogue of the infamous Article 58 of the Stalinist Criminal Code and Articles 70 and 190 of the Brezhnev Criminal Code, under which dissidents were imprisoned'.[7]

Kremlin propagandists heartily agreed. The law marked a shift 'into pure Stalinism', said a well-known television presenter who worked for state-controlled media, with a cynical laugh. 'But we're at war now. Isn't some Stalinism what we need? Stalin led us to Berlin, remember?'[8]

The sad truth was that his vicious joke actually spoke for the belligerent mood of a significant majority of Russians. Understanding polling in an authoritarian regime has its special challenges, which will be discussed in more detail below. But on 28 February a poll by the state-run All-Russia Public Opinion Research Center (VTsIOM) showed that 68 per cent of Russians expressed strong or mild approval of the war, with just 26 per cent against. Six months later, in August 2022, VTsIOM reported that its official polls showed the level of the Russian public's confidence in Putin had – officially at least – risen to 81.2 per cent.[9]

That almost unqualified support would continue until Putin's mobilisation announcement in September, which made the war suddenly up close and personal for millions of Russians who had hitherto ignored it, and radically shifted public opinion. A 22–28 September poll by the independent Levada-Center showed that 47 per cent of Russians felt 'anxiety, fear or dread' over mobilisation, with 13 per cent feeling 'anger' and 23 per cent responding that they felt 'pride in Russia'.

Propaganda

Television news was the Kremlin's primary tool of control and influence – as important to Russia's victory, said TV executive Molody, as 'a whole army in the field'.[10] At the outset of the war some 86 per cent of Russians watched state-run TV stations – and some 70 per cent of Russians said that Kremlin-produced TV was their main source of news.[11] Six months later, those numbers would fall by a third, according to the independent Rosmir polling centre. Nonetheless, TV remained the umbilical link between the Russian state and the hearts and minds of its people.

As we have seen, the invasion was in no way signalled by the Kremlin media in the weeks and months before 24 February. But as if making up for lost time, during the first weeks of the war state-controlled Channel One, Rossiya-1 and NTV ran marathon political talk shows up to six hours long, filled with angry talking heads denouncing NATO, the West, Ukrainian 'fascists' and 'provocateurs'. Evgeny Popov, the co-anchor of Rossiya-1's *60 Minut*, Russia's top-rated TV politics talk show, was adamant that Russian media was no better or worse than the West's. 'We see that you [in the West] have closed off all access to every Russian TV channel,' Popov told me. 'You hate the Russian point of view because you refuse to accept it ... Instead you broadcast Ukrainian propaganda, which is just fakes on top of fakes.'[12]

On Novinsky Boulevard, TV news producer Anna Bondarenko had been working double editorial shifts since the morning of 24

February. Her channel's bosses had their instructions – to go into overdrive to rally Russians to support the invasion and whip up indignation at the West for fomenting the conflict.

At the same time the Kremlin's orders were to hold back on images of actual fighting. For the first five days of the invasion, Channel One's *Vesti* nightly news did not broadcast images of combat at all, preferring to quote politicians speaking about the progress of the 'limited military operation' in Ukraine and, in a surreal throwback to Soviet times, showing what seemed to be pre-recorded footage of Putin visiting a technology plant – a practice known in TV circles as using *konservy*, or 'canned goods'.

In time the Kremlin press pool began to put out more recent footage of Putin, which appeared at the top of the news almost nightly. He looked puffy, stiff and old, and made basic grammatical errors in his speech (though as the war went on Putin would, paradoxically, look fitter and more confident, though also angrier and less connected to reality). Bondarenko was frustrated. 'This product is shit,' she railed as the videos of orderly troop movements and smiling soldiers provided by the Russian Ministry of Defence rolled in. Her state-of-the-art studio naturally had feeds from AP, Reuters and AFP, including lots of gripping footage showing Russian tanks, planes and helicopters exploding into spectacular fireballs. But under the new law such images were not under any circumstances to be aired on Russian TV. 'The news packages were just a mess' in the early stages of the war, Bondarenko recalled. 'We had been caught as unaware as everyone.'[13]

Russian TV also relied heavily on the testimony of foreign front-line reporters, a motley group of British and American video bloggers who became Russian media stars. The assumption was that foreign voices supporting the Kremlin's narrative were somehow inherently more credible than Russian reporters. Graham Phillips was a British civil servant before moving to Ukraine and then Donetsk, where in 2022 he married a beautiful

17-year-old local girl. Phillips, the self-described 'most honest journalist in the world', had been a video blogger popular in pro-Kremlin alt-right circles before the war.[14] After the invasion he toured occupied Ukraine as a guest of the Russian and DNR army and interviewed prisoners of war, including captured Brits. As a result the UK government levied sanctions on Phillips for contravention of the Geneva Convention.[15] Another Donetsk resident-turned-video-blogger was Russell Bonner Bentley III, aka Comrade Texas, a former tree surgeon who volunteered for the DNR's Vostok Brigade in 2015.[16] One of Comrade Texas's videos showed him, wearing a leather jacket and Mao cap, standing in front of a line of Russian tanks in Donetsk. 'It's Texas on the front line with the de-Nazifiers and liberators of Ukraine,' he announced. 'These guys are going to save and liberate all the good people of Ukraine. And the bad people? Boom! Kick their ass.'[17] Scott Ritter, a former UN weapons inspector in Iraq, was signed up by the Kremlin-funded RT (formerly Russia Today) after being arrested for exposing himself to a police officer posing as a 15-year-old girl online in 2011. A prominent voice in the anti-war movement, Ritter appeared often on RT blaming 'Ukrainian Nazis' for starting the war.[18]

Despite its dubious veracity, the Kremlin's message that Russia was fighting a defensive war against Ukrainian 'genocide' of Russian speakers in eastern Ukraine was relentless, and increasingly well packaged, and successfully convinced many Russians. A few friends and in-laws surprised me with their cult-like devotion to their leader and his infallibility. 'We didn't want this war, NATO started all of this,' said Oleg, 55, a former military pilot turned architect. I asked him where he got his news from. 'Not from your Western propaganda, that's for sure. Even the BBC has shown that Ukrainian news clips are fake.' Of our mutual friends who were planning to leave, he said, 'God speed them. If you live in Russia, you believe in Russia. If not ... why does Russia need you?'[19] Oleg would be happy to do without Western brands or foreign holidays, he claimed. He'd not grown up with them, he'd not grow old with them.

'When you see someone beating up their wife, a real man doesn't pass by,' said Vladislav, a Moscow taxi driver, echoing one of TV's most well-used tropes. 'You have to go in and help. It's our duty to help our Ukrainian brothers get rid of these little fascists.'[20] To which a former Russian radio presenter friend who was riding in the car reposted, 'Yeah. So we go over to our neighbour's place, rape his wife ourselves, kill him and say that we owned his house all along.' Even some of the mothers whose sons were serving in the Russian army were passionately behind Putin's war. 'It's men's duty to defend the Motherland,' said Viktoria Torchak, 44, a Moscow sales assistant whose husband was a paratrooper who served in Chechnya and whose 19-year-old-son was currently doing his military service. 'And it's women's duty to give birth to men to defend us.'[21]

There was a widely accepted narrative among Western commentators that Russians supported the war only because they had been deceived by the Kremlin's propaganda, and that if they only had access to the truth it would make them free. This was true – but it is only part of a much more important truth. Indeed, foreign news sites like the BBC and CNN were blocked in Russia, as were most Western social media. But accessing them was a matter of a couple of clicks required to install a virtual private network, or VPN, on a laptop or mobile – a process so simple that even my technophobic 70-year-old mother-in-law in Moscow managed it.

The problem was not one of access to the truth. The truth doesn't make you free if you don't want to hear it. Indeed some Russians I knew who have lived in the West for decades refused to hear it too, burrowing deep into the backwaters of Twitter, YouTube and Telegram to find 'unbiased' – in other words pro-Russian – news they found comforting.

Large numbers of Russians were indeed deceived by the Kremlin's propaganda. But they believed it because they wanted to believe. Putin's propaganda relied on consent, on people's willingness to buy into a glorious narrative of which they actively wished to be a part. And the propaganda worked because it was both drawn from and fed most Russian people's deepest prejudices and fears – fear of foreign aggression, contempt for Westernised young people and their non-traditional fads, yearning for protection from a hostile world and from their own failures, a hope for payback for years of poverty and humiliation, a desire to finally break free of slavish admiration for all things Western by proving that Russians were stronger, more united, more decisive, more righteous and generally greater than their fallen idols.

Western news consumers were saturated by exhaustive, and often shocking, coverage of Russia's brutal campaign to subdue Ukraine, naturally feeling horror, hostility and hatred. Russian TV viewers and readers of Kremlin-sanctioned news, by contrast, were fed a steady diet of updates on their army's heroic progress against Ukrainian 'fascist bands' and equally horrific footage of 'genocidal' Ukrainian attacks on civilians in Donbas. Hearing – and believing – that Russian boys were fighting and dying in Ukraine in order to save 'our people' from the clutches of fascists was comforting, understandable, a source of pride. The counter-narrative – that their country was engaged in an unprovoked war that had killed tens of thousands of civilians in the name of 'liberating' people who would rather flee than live under Russian occupation – was not. Russians – like most humans – preferred to believe the story that validated them, not the one that humiliated them. The lack of an immediately accessible alternative narrative simply made that choice easier. If Kremlin news was your only news – and the only news anyone you knew received – then your country, and your own skin, became an easier place to inhabit.

Furthermore, there was a strong element of performative ritual to Russian state TV, with a set of rules mutually understood by both the propagandists and the propagandised. 'The Russian people have always been spectators of their country's politics,' observed the poet and critic Dmitry Bykov. 'It's like a theatre ... today's Russian does what is expected of him. Sometimes he applauds, sometimes he wolf-whistles. But he is not required to actually believe. Everyone knows that the man on the stage is not Prince Hamlet but Laurence Olivier. Nobody believes that what is happening on the stage is actually true. Do you think anyone believes what is being said on TV talk shows? But [after the invasion] the theatre is coming more like a circus. The people are not stupid. They watch and laugh nervously and see how low the actors will go.'[22]

The same complex issue of ritual and self-delusion applies to polling in a totalitarian state. Many polls have been and will be cited in this book. They are problematic not so much because Russians feared the consequences of speaking their minds but because their stated opinion was often what they believed was expected of them, or what they wished were true.

An excellent example was when in July 2018 over 80 per cent of Russians claimed to believe that Sergei and Yulia Skripal were poisoned in their Salisbury home not by Russian assassins but by the British secret service. Or polls in March 2022 that showed that over 70 per cent of Russians blamed NATO for provoking the war and a similar number apparently believed that the Kyiv government and its Jewish leader Zelensky were literal Nazis.

Do these polls show that Russians are uniquely gullible or stupid? I think not. When Russian respondents claimed to believe that the British poisoned the Skripals or that Zelensky was a disciple of Hitler, most, I suspect, were signalling that they accepted the official line – that the fellow on the stage really was Hamlet – rather than expressing their actual deepest beliefs. Or put another way, their answer was effectively that they agreed with whatever the official line happened to be. Because life that way was easier, more comforting, less lonely. And because the truth, in Russia, was often so damn depressing.

In that sense, the war had thrown two Russias into sharp opposition. One was urban, educated, internet savvy and relatively wealthy – the people who had most to lose from an economic crash and would miss imported goods, foreign holidays and their middle-class European lifestyle. But more importantly that small minority of Russians were people who were accustomed to think critically, to draw their own conclusions about the world and their own country. The other Russia, the much larger Russia, was one that valued patriotism over material goods, preferred to believe in a glorious feel-good version of the world based on television news, had no interest in seeking out alternative truths likely to upset or disturb them. Most of all, that majority of Russians trusted the wise man in the Kremlin to guide them, think for them and protect them from the enemies all around. It would take something drastic, such as an undeniable battlefield defeat or the real prospect of their sons, brothers, husbands and fathers being sent to fight in Ukraine against their will, to change that profound faith.

Sanctions

The Kremlin had been prepared for economic sanctions following its invasion – indeed surviving sanctions and energy price crashes had been the twin strategic goals behind the Finance Ministry and Central Bank's careful, decades-long build-up of its $650 billion strategic reserve war chest. It was thanks to these reserves – and particularly to the pusillanimous sanctions response of the West – that Russia had easily weathered the economic fallout of the 2014 Crimea annexation. Not unreasonably, Putin's inner circle assumed that the same would happen in 2022: lots of vocal protest, little actual economic impact.

Except this time it really was different. Over the first months of the war Western governments would cut off most Russian banks from the SWIFT payments system; freeze Russian state assets and those of Western subsidiaries of Russian companies; and seize and freeze the property, yachts and cash assets of tens of thousands of wealthy Russians in Europe. But the most surprising and devastating sanction of all was the collective decision of over 1,300 Western companies to pull out of Russia under the pressure of social media and systematic online shaming – by Zelensky and his team – of companies who continued to do business with the Putin regime. It was a move that bewildered and blindsided the Kremlin.

'They didn't expect so many sanctions,' said Echo Moskvy's Aleksei Venediktov. 'I know for sure they expected government sanctions – freezing accounts, cancelling travel, restricting state companies like airline Aeroflot. [Sanctions] against the big players. But not sanctions from private companies ... Ford left, Renault closed. "What happened?" [top Kremlin officials] asked. These are thousands of jobs.' Even Western politicians who had accepted cushy jobs at Russian companies – like former French prime minister François Fillon, who had been hired as a director of the Sibur oil company in December 2021 – 'packed and left, despite being a close acquaintance of Putin, who personally offered him this job'. The former French premier's colleagues were 'amazed', according to Venediktov. '"Why did you leave, Fillon?" they asked. And Fillon answered, "I just can't stay."'[23]

The cash went first, disappearing from Moscow ATMs and exchange booths within hours of the launch of the invasion as Russians lined up to withdraw their savings. The ruble's value initially tumbled by 40 per cent against its pre-war value (though it would soon recover and even exceed pre-war levels once the

Central Bank intervened to limit trading). In several ATMs the daily cash withdrawal limit shrank to under £3. For the first time since the last days of the Soviet Union, what was effectively a black market in hard-to-obtain cash hard currency sprang up, with one exchange office just off Moscow's New Arbat quoting 300 rubles to the euro, against an official exchange rate of 145. The black market for foreign currency was not the only throw-back to Soviet days. In Kazan in the Middle Volga the local prosecutor's office arrested 'sugar speculators' caught selling sugar at inflated prices. Shelves emptied of imported electronics as consumers rushed to buy before prices rose dramatically.

Then the bank cards stopped working. As the SWIFT inter-bank messaging system disconnected 80 per cent of Russian banks, people desperately trying to buy tickets from foreign air companies found their cards disabled, and Russians abroad were stranded. 'I laughed at my friends when they said I should open an account in Riga [Latvia] a few months ago,' said Svetlana Terekhova, 38, a manager at a Moscow furniture import business who found herself stranded in Milan, unable to pay for her hotel room with her Sberbank- or VTB-issued cards. 'I said they were paranoid, told them that we live in a connected world.' Svetlana's company was also unable to make payments to their Italian suppliers, making any future orders impossible. 'Our business is dead. I'm out of a job.'[24] Apple Pay shut down at the end of the war's first week, blocking payments on the metro and in taxi apps. Many Western banks blocked transfers to and from most Russian banks – and in any case the Kremlin restricted sending money abroad to avoid an uncontrolled exodus of hard currency.

But it was the power of private companies, not states, that really bit. Ikea, Obi and Leroy Merlin, Zara, McDonald's, Starbucks, H+M, Uniqlo and hundreds of other popular retail stores closed. Luxury brands followed. The shelves of Gucci, Chanel, LMVH, Prada and dozens of other stores that have marked Moscow's sophistication and wealth stood empty. Microsoft and Adobe software stopped updating. Netflix pulled the plug on all Russian accounts. IBM, Samsung, TikTok, Airbnb, Booking.com, Boeing, Ford, Volkswagen, General Motors, Coca-Cola and Pepsi all pulled out. Some left early on as a matter of principle. Others, in a telling demonstration of the power of social media on companies' decisions, pulled out only after serious online backlashes from their customers around the world.

The full economic and political impact of sanctions will be discussed in more detail in the final chapter. But by the end of the first six months of the war the withdrawal of international firms had affected some 40 per cent of Russian GDP and threatened some 5 million jobs. Sanctions on the import of foreign-made technology and parts – above all computer processing chips – crippled Russia's automotive, manufacturing, aviation, high-tech and defence industries.[25]

Yet the most striking thing about wartime Russia was how utterly normal everyday life remained, how relatively invisible the impact of sanctions. By September the McDonald's and Starbucks on Moscow's Arbat Street had been replaced by local lookalikes. The shuttered H+M and Zara had been replaced by shops selling stock made by Belarusian clothes manufacturers. A Moscow coffee importer friend had been forced in the first weeks of the war to expensively offload his goods at a warehouse on the Polish–Belarusian border and reload them onto Russian trucks. But soon his customs agents found a more streamlined solution: to simply exchange the trucks' licence plates and swap the drivers around. Indeed by June the Russian government would effectively legalise sanctions-busting 'parallel import' schemes, keeping the shelves of high-end Moscow supermarkets filled with Swiss Gruyere cheese and Italian Parmesan. For millions of Russians it was very easy to believe the assurances of Kremlin propagandists and Putin himself that Russia would survive on its own great resources. 'I know some of you are finding this tough,' said Russian TV host Vladimir Solovyov as he complained about sanctions against him that saw his villa on Lake Como sequestered by Italian authorities. 'We'll overcome it all, we'll endure it all. We'll rebuild our own economy from scratch, an independent banking system, manufacturing and industry. We'll rely on ourselves.'[26]

Culture and sports sanctions followed the financial ones – again shocking the Kremlin. World-famous Russian musicians were dropped from performances in the West. And Putin, a passionate sports fan, was particularly indignant about the exclusion of Russian sportspeople from international competitions – for instance, a blanket ban 'for the foreseeable future' imposed by World Athletics.

'Suddenly the athletes are banned,' said Venediktov, quoting a close Putin associate on his reaction. '"Biathlon! You're crazy, why biathlon? We know how hard the athletes train. It's a tragedy for them ... And all the [soccer] fans, sitting and waiting for the World Cup? Holy crap!"'

Valery Gergiev – Russia's greatest living conductor and a much-respected personal acquaintance of Putin's – was told by the Mayor of Munich to 'condemn Putin or you are fired from the Munich Philharmonic', recalled Venediktov. 'Gergiev didn't condemn him, he got fired along with [soprano Anna] Netrebko.' Putin was personally insulted, by Venediktov's account. 'Who is the Mayor of Munich [to] touch the great Valery Gergiev? How dare they? It's a disgrace! He was kicked out of the Philharmonic like a lousy puppy. Putin's friend!'[27]

In response to the firing of Gergiev and Netrebko and the cancellation of a Bolshoi Ballet tour to London, Russian state media began to claim that Russian culture as a whole was being attacked. Electronic posters in central Moscow proclaimed that 'Chekhov has been cancelled in Europe.' In reality, at that moment no fewer than four Chekhov plays were playing in

London, more than in Moscow itself. Nonetheless, it was clear that the world's reaction to the Kremlin's invasion was of a different order of magnitude to that of 2014. And the Kremlin's own attitude to those Russians who disagreed, too, was more aggressive than anything seen since the end of the USSR.

Exodus: The Russians

For millions of Russians who believed that they lived a stable, middle-class, European existence, a world collapsed in the wake of the invasion of Ukraine. For Varvara Babitskaya, an editor at a Moscow literary magazine, 'the hipster bars we went to, the holidays we took in Europe, the idea that we could live a normal life even in a messed-up country – that was all an illusion ... In just a few days we realised that everything we thought we shared with the civilised world was borrowed. It was never ours. Never Russian. And now it's been taken away.'[28]

On 5 March Putin made an aggressive speech condemning 'fifth column' Russians who did not support the war and denouncing them as 'traitors'. Opposition activists found their doorways daubed with white 'Z' signs – the battle insignia on Russian tanks that had become the symbol of the war. At the same time Russian social media filled with photos of cars displaying 'Z' signs that had had their windows smashed by anti-war neighbours.

There was an old joke that was once funny: 'All Moscow theme restaurants actually have the same theme – The theme is: you're not in Moscow.' But abruptly, as Russia's invasion unfolded and the trappings of civilised life fell away with every new sanction, the observation became sad. The exposed brick walls, graffiti decor and hipsterish artisanal lightbulbs of 15 Bar and Kitchen had once made my local bar on Pozharsky Lane feel like an outpost of Brooklyn. Now the place seemed like a mocking reference to a receding, Westernised world that was becoming more distant by the day.

As pieces of their once hyper-connected lives went dark, thousands of wealthier Muscovites began to scramble to leave the country. On the seventh day of the war I met an old friend at the Moloko Restaurant for dinner at two in the morning. Alexei sat hunched in a leather banquette, drunk. He was too absorbed in his phone to notice my arrival. Despite sharing a name with the hangout of the sinister Droogs in *A Clockwork Orange*, Moloko was actually a homage to the Balthazar brasseries in New York and Paris. Tasteful, warm lamplight gleamed on sleek black pillars and polished brass. Alexei looked up, smiled crookedly and brandished his phone. He'd been looking up real estate listings in Tbilisi, Georgia.

Georgia, an easy-going, visa-free and Russian-speaking former Soviet state, had been the destination of choice for self-exiled Moscow journalists, artists, writers, architects, film and theatre people for some years. Suddenly – in the first days of the war everything seemed to be happening suddenly, in swooping downward lurches – Tbilisi became no longer a lifestyle choice but a Noah's Ark against a dark tide of political repression. Yet Tbilisi was already overcrowded with fleeing Russians, and a backlash was growing. Maja Kononenko, a gallery-owner friend who had lived there for three years, warned that the locals were quickly becoming resentful – especially the Georgian intelligentsia. 'They say – we stood and fought for our country when Putin invaded [in 2008],' said Kononenko. 'Why are you fleeing instead of fighting your regime at home?'[29] Rents rose fast due to the influx of Russian refugees, jobs were scarce. Many Georgian landlords refused to rent to Russians.

Alexei's options were running out. Earlier that day, a TV drama project that he had been working on with Netflix had been abruptly cancelled, a week into shooting. SWIFT had cut off Alexei's bank from the rest of the world, snapping shut his ruble savings. Tbilisi, resentful or not, would be preferable to Moscow. 'My life here in Russia is over,' he said, in that matter-of-fact way that Russians have when speaking of the disasters that periodically engulf their lives. 'I don't fancy sticking around while this place becomes North Korea. And you know what? I'm good with being a citizen of the world. See you on the other side.'[30]

Millions of educated, international Russians like Alexei faced a stark choice: adapt to a dark, repressive world of contracting economic possibilities at home, or try to flee the country for an uncertain future abroad. The plight of millions of Ukrainians fleeing for their lives from bombardment was infinitely more acute. The stakes, for them, were life and death. But the estimated half million Russians who eventually fled Russia in the first months of the war were also refugees from the Putin regime.

'Partisans. Burning tanks. People crowding onto train platforms. Emigration. Tell me this isn't a film?' Anna Kachurkovskaya, 47, a museum curator, stretched painfully on the bar stool where she'd been slumped for hours, doom-scrolling the news. 'You know what I miss most? Not the past. Which was two weeks ago. I'm nostalgic for a future I don't have any more. That fucker in the Kremlin has stolen my future.'[31] But in some ways Anna envied her Kyiv friends. 'They have hope. The world is on their side. Europe is welcoming them,' she said, flicking through images of seas of protesters around the world waving yellow-and-blue Ukrainian flags. 'When the war is over, they'll go back to a free, European country. But Russians? Everyone hates Russians. Even most Russians hate people like us, who are against the regime.'[32]

The exodus gathered pace. But even as flights out of the country dwindled, so did the number of places that Russians could go without visas. Most middle-class Muscovites had been used to having a European Schengen visa in their passports as a matter of course. But for two years the EU had not issued any tourist visas because of Covid. The US embassy had not been issuing visas for even longer since the Kremlin forced them to fire their Russian staff in 2017. Moscow friends swapped information on Facebook – until access was shut down and they switched to the more secure Telegram app. Turkey was visa-free for Russians, so was Armenia, Georgia, Kazakhstan. Many prescient members of Moscow's intelligentsia had got themselves Israeli passports by ancestry or marriage – making Israel an option for some. A restaurant-owner friend who had recently received an Israeli passport through his wife cracked an old Soviet joke from the 1980s, when Jews fled the USSR in their tens of thousands. 'A Jewish wife is now a form of transport,' he said, smiling wryly.[33]

'Get your son out of Moscow – NOW!' My old friend Varvara Babitskaya, the literary editor, was usually one of the most laid-back people I knew. Now she was near hysteria. 'He's 19,' she shouted. 'He's here on a Russian passport. He's not at university. If he doesn't report to the draft office he's breaking the law. What part don't you understand?'[34]

My son Nikita had been having the time of his life, spending his gap year working with a brilliant young team of actors at a prominent Moscow theatre. He had just been hired to co-produce Russia's top theatre festival, the Golden Mask. Nikita and his mates had turned the dining room of his grandparents' apartment into a modern version of Lenin and Trotsky's operations centre in the Smolny Institute, the long table piled with hard drives, spilling ashtrays, MacBooks and wine bottles. 'We're Russians, disaster is what we do best,' joked 20-year-old Yasha, a student film director who sported a hipster pencil moustache. 'We'll work things out, somehow.'[35]

The next day, Yasha was arrested. He and a female friend had been standing near to a protest on Gogolevsky Boulevard. When the heavily armed paramilitary OMON moved in, the girl had run. Bad mistake, explained Nikita to me the next night. If you can, stand your ground and smile vacantly at the cops like you're just a passer-by. *Especially* if you actually are a passer-by. My son – dressed in jacket and tie, important urban camouflage against arbitrary arrest – spent five hours in the processing centre getting them out. 'The cops hate having to do this,' he reported. 'They're people too.' Hate it because they're fundamentally decent people, I asked, or hate it because they're lazy and corrupt and would rather be doing nothing? Nikita frowned.

It was time to go. Russian planes had been banned from European, Canadian and US airspace, so Turkey was one of the few destinations still accepting flights from Moscow. One-way tickets to Istanbul were running at €1,700. But miraculously, I discovered some forgotten air miles. Even more miraculously, Turkish Airlines were still issuing award tickets. We were booked. Word spread that Nikita and I were leaving. Friends called to press money on me to take abroad. An old colleague's nanny came round with a thick packet of euros. My younger son's school fees in Rome were paid two years in advance by a television producer friend desperate to get money out of her Sberbank account while she still could. My Moscow apartment became an impromptu bank as I handed out hard currency to the relatives and friends of Russians who live abroad – and collected cash from others desperate to get money out. It was illegal to take more than $10,000 in cash out of the country, so soon I had to turn people away.

Disney, Warner Brothers, Sony and other major Hollywood studios blocked the release of their films in Russia. In (perhaps) ironic response, our local cinema on Arbatskaya Square began to show the cult films *Brat* ['Brother'] and *Brat 2* – movies about the desperate, violent, poverty-stricken 1990s, and the Russians who fled post-Soviet chaos to New York. A fortnight earlier they had been period pieces. Suddenly they looked like documentaries from the near future.

* * *

Varvara Babitskaya couldn't make a last dinner. She'd been arrested at a protest a few days before, fined £120 and given a criminal record. Sensibly, she preferred to stay off the streets, which were full of cops. 'We can go for a walk in my courtyard,' she offered. Unlike Alexei – and in common with most members of Moscow's intelligentsia – Varvara had no envelopes full of euros to spare. A ticket to Istanbul would cost five months of her now-devalued ruble salary. She was resigned – and in any case, 'Who's waiting for me anywhere in the world?' Varvara was Jewish, but hadn't been organised – or paranoid enough – to apply for an Israeli passport. 'I'll just have to become Russian,' she joked grimly. 'You know – learn to suffer for the Motherland and all that heroic shit.'[36]

Vnukovo airport was deserted except for a single check-in stand where two hundred passengers lined up with children, huge piles of luggage and an enormous number of dogs. There was no panic, as nobody was aware that this would be one of the last flights out of Moscow. A man checking in ahead of us graciously suggested we go to the next counter as he 'might be a while'. He had three large boxes on his trolley – and 17 more in a huge pile off to the side. 'My office equipment,' he explained. 'Going to set up in Riga.'[37] Despite stories that opposition activists had been questioned for hours by the FSB and had their phones searched for incriminating messages, Nikita and I passed through passport control and customs smoothly.

As we waited in the departure lounge, news came from a friend's son that his Aeroflot flight from Moscow to Tel Aviv had had to land in Sochi, southern Russia. While the plane was in the air the leasing company cancelled the contract. That day Russia's Ministry of Transport suggested 'nationalising' – i.e. stealing – all planes leased by Russian air companies. United Russia – Putin's party – tabled a plan to nationalise the property of all Western companies pulling out of the country. Within hours all flights and ferries in and out of Russia had been cancelled, and would resume tentatively with a very limited service only a month later. For most of March and April 2022, only the trains were still running, like it was 1917.

The streets of Istanbul were full of Russians. Over dinner at a fish restaurant in Istanbul's Karakoy district, in the shadow of a Russian rooftop church and pilgrims' hostel that had once been the refuge of thousands of exiles who fled the final collapse of White Russian forces in 1920, we swapped news with Russian friends of who had got out and who was stuck. The flint-built, medieval wall of the restaurant had heard this all before. Many years ago I interviewed an elderly Russian man who lay dying beneath a tattered portrait of Nicholas II. He lived in a garret under an abandoned rooftop church, one of several in Karakoy built atop hostels for Russian pilgrims en route to Mount Athos. His father had been the caretaker at the Imperial Russian embassy, just up the hill, where he had been born in 1915. Aged five, he watched from the embassy garden as hundreds of French and British ships filled the Bosporus carrying refugees from General Baron Pyotr Wrangel's defeated White armies. Today's influx of exiles was smaller and less desperate. But the sense of being expelled from home into a cold, hostile world was the same.

I read the diaries of Teffi – the pseudonym of Nadezhda Lokhvitskaya, a witty St Petersburg writer who fled to Kyiv after the Bolshevik Revolution. The fortunes of war carried her, like a defunct banknote blown in the wind, to Constantinople and later Paris. She described her exigent life of nostalgia and poverty, where former colonels were reduced to driving taxicabs, ex-noblewomen dressed up as gypsies to serve tea in cafes and all the castaways of the ancient regime clung absurdly to the affectations of their old way of life. 'Their eyes are dull, limp hands drop and the soul wilts ... we believe in nothing, want nothing, await nothing, dead. Afraid of Bolshevik death, we chose a living death over here.' Exile, Teffi wrote, was like being 'a poor relative who finds herself at a birthday party in a rich house'.

While Russians fled their home country, those already in Europe faced a backlash. My younger son's 17-year-old girlfriend was slapped in the face by a stranger as she stood on a Rome street speaking Russian on the phone to her mother. An older Russian woman who had lived in London for years was verbally abused in St John's Wood. Even prominent anti-Putin activists and journalists like writer Mikhail Zygar (who had escaped to Berlin after being labelled a 'foreign agent') found local European banks blocking their bank accounts for no reason other than they were held by Russians.

By August Estonia, Lithuania, Latvia and Poland sought to ban the issuance of Schengen tourist visas to Russians altogether. Brussels balked at doing so on the grounds of unjust collective punishment – but they nonetheless cancelled a visa facilitation agreement with Moscow, making the visa application process much longer and more complex. One way or another, by late summer official figures showed that 998,085 Russian passport holders had left the country since the invasion of Ukraine. Half of them never returned. But that was nothing compared with the 7.7 million Ukrainian citizens that had entered the EU (though 4.7 million of them had returned to their homeland by the end of August), as well as over a million more who escaped into Russia.[38,39]

Exodus: The Ukrainians

During the first days of the invasion, the main roads heading south and west from Kyiv, Kharkiv and Odesa were filled with vast traffic jams. Many major highways, especially those heading north and northeast, were blocked off by the Ukrainian army, fearing artillery strikes and to leave a free field of fire in case of a Russian attack. All but two of the bridges over the Dniepr and Irpin rivers at Kyiv had been dynamited by Ukrainian sappers to cut off the Russian advance.

Curator and art critic Maria Khromchenko was one of the thousands who got in their cars and fled after two days spent in the cellar of their apartment building in eastern Kyiv. As she risked a trip to her ninth-floor apartment she saw a Russian rocket tearing across the sky right over her house. Khromchenko, her husband and two stepchildren piled their old Toyota Land Cruiser with pillows, duvets, canned food, a pile of electronics ('though we forgot all the remote controls,' she recalled) and albums of family photographs. She had to abandon a lovingly assembled collection of antique Ukrainian embroidered peasant clothes and the family's dog, which had just undergone an operation and was left with neighbours to look after. But they took their two cats and joined a slowly moving column of vehicles heading south on a roundabout route to Vinnitsa.[40] While Khromchenko's husband's Israeli citizenship enabled him to leave, many of her friends faced an agonising decision – to escape and leave their husbands behind, or to stay, as all men under 60 had been banned from leaving under Zelensky's general mobilisation order.

It took the family five days to get out. Nervous Ukrainian soldiers, wary of saboteurs and Russian agents, stopped and searched every car and checked documents. At a truck stop near Bela Tsirkva they found a family who had been robbed at gunpoint of their cash, jewellery and electronics as they passed through a remote village; they had, however, been left their car and the village men had given them directions. 'It was a nightmare – though most people we met were kind, we were taken in and fed many times,' said Khromchenko. On the Romanian border they waited 20 hours to cross. But once they were safely inside the EU, they were met with a warm and well-organised reception. Volunteers and aid organisations from all over Europe had already turned up, many on their own initiative, offering hot food, hostels and offers of accommodation across Europe.

The EU quickly stepped up, extending the usual 90-day visa-free stay inside the Schengen area allowed to Ukrainians to an automatic three years, with the right to work. In the UK an appeal by the *Daily Mail* newspaper for Ukrainian refugees raised £8 million in less than a month. Khromchenko decided to stay on the Romanian side of the border and rent a large house to accommodate incoming refugees – a project that was crowdfunded by friends and wellwishers within weeks.

By the time my wife and son travelled to Przemysl, Poland, in May to work as volunteers for Russians for Ukraine, an organisation of Russian émigrés from the Putin regime, the reception arrangements were impressive. World Central Kitchen, a US charity, had set up a large catering tent to feed new arrivals with fresh pizza, salads and soups. A disused Tesco superstore on the outskirts of the Polish border town had been converted into a massive, hangar-like dormitory that could sleep 1,500 people. The former supermarket retail area had become a kind of trade-fair-style space, with dozens of booths where governments and charities from all over the world offered free rail and air tickets and accommodation with 'foster' families in Portugal, Switzerland, Canada and a dozen other countries. A pair of *carabinieri* policemen from Naples had taken a long weekend to drive a minibus full of humanitarian aid funded by their colleagues to Poland – and return with eight refugees to Naples.

At Przemysl rail station a dozen trains a day brought in up to 3,000 refugees, mostly women and children, and a huge number of pets. Many were exhausted and confused after days on the road. In their desperation many insisted on pushing on to Warsaw and Berlin. Both those cities were actually overwhelmed with refugees, who were mostly accommodated in huge tent cities and conference centres. My son Nikita – wearing a 'Russians for Ukraine' tabard with a Russian flag with no red stripe, just white–blue–white – personally spoke to over a thousand refugees a day, trying to persuade them to break their journey and head to the Tesco refugee centre to find better deals for their future lives in exile. Most of the refugees were Russian speakers from eastern Ukraine, fleeing 'liberation' from their self-declared Russian protectors. A few were initially hostile to being helped by Russians, but were quickly relieved to hear that Russians for Ukraine was not a Kremlin PR stunt but an organisation of ordinary Russians who had also been exiled by Putin. Almost all the refugees declared that they would return to their homeland as soon as it was safe to do so.

The refugees who made it to Przemysl, Poland, and other crossing points to Hungary, Slovakia and Romania were the lucky ones. Hundreds of thousands of Ukrainians found themselves overtaken by the war, with little choice but to flee through humanitarian corridors established by the Russian army and take refuge in Russia.

In Mariupol, teacher Larisa Boiko and her 11-year-old daughter Daria fled artillery and rocket fire on the first day of the war and took refuge in the cellar of their building, which had been converted eight years before into a bomb shelter. As determined Ukrainian resistance turned the Russian assault into a savage artillery duel, Larisa and Daria cowered as their home town collapsed overhead. The 60 residents in the cellar were organised by an elderly military veteran, Uncle Borya, who assigned bunk beds and organised rosters to scavenge groceries from apartments and local shops – and later from municipal trucks that braved the shelling to deliver food around Mariupol's neighbourhoods. The electricity failed on the second day, forcing the people in the shelter to use smelly Soviet-era paraffin lamps. So did the local mobile internet, though a weak phone signal could still be found by anyone brave enough to ascend to the third floor. A week into the siege, the shelter's toilet broke and everyone had to wait till dark to run outside to answer the call of nature.

'We cooked over a makeshift hearth constructed of bricks in the courtyard,' recalled Boiko when she had reached the safety of

Rome, where she and her daughter stayed in my home. 'Two pensioners – a man and a woman – died of heart attacks ... We had to bury them in the courtyard during breaks in the shelling.' Several women whose relatives were defending the nearby Azovstal steel works heard that the shelters there were better and safer so abandoned the basement for the risky trip across town to Azovtsal. Boiko never heard from them again.

After three weeks in the cellar, filthy, cold and hungry, a Ukrainian civil defence volunteer in a Red Cross bib appeared and announced that the Mariupol city authorities had agreed with the Russians to open a humanitarian corridor to evacuate civilians. Some of the shelter's residents wanted to wait until they could get to unoccupied Ukraine, or for Ukrainian forces to liberate them. But Boiko was desperate to leave. The next morning the shelling had indeed died down, and she and two dozen other residents picked their way through rubble-strewn streets and courtyards to the appointed rendezvous. 'My home city looked like a war film,' she recalled. 'It smelled of death.' A small fleet of municipal minibuses waited – and waited. But a commander with a radio aborted the evacuation, explaining that 'the Russians were shelling again.' He handed out provisions and sent everyone back to the shelter to await instructions. 'The waiting was the worst part. It was unbearable to go back down [into the shelter],' she recalled.

On the third attempt, Boiko and her daughter finally left Mariupol and were driven to a former boarding school outside Donetsk where they were fed buckwheat porridge with tinned meat, and allowed to take a shower. The Russian staff 'treated us with suspicion, like we were infected with Nazism or something' – though Boiko, like most Mariupol residents, was herself a native Russian speaker. The next day the group was broken up and taken to different 'filtration camps', still inside the DNR. After a five-hour wait, Boiko's phone was examined and she was questioned by plain-clothed Russians she assumed were from the

FSB. 'They asked me who all the contacts in my phone were, what my [ex] husband did, did I know any Azov people or officials or politically active "fascists".'

Boiko was lucky. Her interrogation lasted just 20 minutes and she and Daria were put on another bus, this time for the long drive to Rostov-on-Don, where they got new clothes, pocket money and beds in a dormitory. Over the next ten days mother and daughter travelled on a series of trains and buses to Moscow, then St Petersburg, then to Kaliningrad and finally to Poland. There a refugee organisation contacted a school friend who lived near Venice, bought her plane tickets to Rome and arranged volunteers to help her on the last leg of her journey to the Veneto. 'I was very fortunate,' said Boiko, who had somehow remained gracious and calm despite her nightmarish escape. 'We got out. We didn't go to Azovstal. We are very happy.'[41]

CHAPTER 9
OVERREACH

We used to believe the Russians had the second-best army in the world. Now we know they have the second-best army in Ukraine.

Ukrainian soldiers' joke

Negotiations

From his desk in the military command centre under the Presidential Palace, Volodimir Zelensky launched an offensive as militarily significant as the battles his armies were fighting on the ground – a personal and highly emotive appeal to the governments of the world to help. 'This may be the last time you see me alive,' Zelensky said in one of his first video calls to European leaders, saying that Ukrainian mothers would be 'watching their children die in pursuit of European values'. Would they die alone, or in vain?[1] In the first weeks of the war Zelensky spoke to almost every world leader and gave addresses to parliaments all over the world. 'We ask for a response. For the response from the world. For the response to terror,' he told the US Congress. To the British parliament, he echoed Winston Churchill: 'We shall not give up and shall not lose.'[2] Zelensky turned out to be a skilled communicator, using inspiration and emotional blackmail in equal measure. 'Tear down this wall,' Zelensky told German Chancellor

Olaf Scholz, quoting President Ronald Reagan's challenge to the Soviets to demolish the Berlin Wall, in support of his argument that Putin was once again trying to divide Europe. And he told Berlin's parliamentarians that they must step up in order that they 'will not be ashamed of yourselves after this war' – a heavy nod towards previous wars for which Germany might feel historical shame.

Initially, just as the Kremlin had predicted, the West was long on rhetoric but short on concrete aid – especially on the heavy weapons, armour and NATO intervention to create a no-fly zone over Ukraine that Zelensky desperately called for. In the first days the conviction that the Russian steamroller would soon crush Ukrainian defences was strong even inside Kyiv's presidential bunker. Only a single Ukrainian mechanised brigade – the 72nd – was available to defend Kyiv, forcing commanders to scramble all available tanks from training centres around the capital to form makeshift battalions. It was clearly insufficient to face down the bulk of the advancing Russian tank force if they broke through Kyiv's suburbs into the city itself. 'People who understood military things went up to [Zelensky] and said, "We're not going to hold,"' Zelensky adviser Oleksey Arestovych told *The Washington Post*. 'The simple issue is that all of our partners are telling us it will be very hard for us, that we have almost zero chances to succeed,' Oleksiy Danilov, head of the National Security and Defence Council, told Zelensky on the invasion's first day. 'We will not receive much support in the first days, because they will look at how we are able to defend the country ... Maybe they don't want a large amount of weapons to get in the hands of the Russians.'[3]

But the Russians never broke through. Their initial setback at Hostomel airport, combined with far fiercer resistance than expected from NATO-trained Ukrainian units armed with NATO-supplied anti-tank weapons, wreaked havoc on the Russian advance from the north. A massive international public response to Zelensky's stirring appeals began to shift the political mood in European capitals. Germany had initially offered to send nothing more deadly than body armour and helmets to help Kyiv, prompting a major media backlash. By 3 March, in a major shift of policy, the German Federal Ministry for Economic Affairs authorised the supply of lethal weapons in the form of 2,700 surface-to-air missiles (SAMs).[4]

At the same time Zelensky quickly moved to attempt peace talks with Russia. His first offer, made on the second day of the war, was to declare that the Ukrainian government was not 'afraid to talk about neutral status'.[5] Putin, too, claimed to be ready to negotiate a quick peace deal, telling Chinese President Xi Jinping that 'Russia is willing to conduct high-level negotiations with Ukraine'.[6] On 27 February Russian and Ukrainian representatives met in Gomel, Belarus. Putin's conditions were delivered by former Culture Minister Vladimir Medinsky, a well-known nationalist hardliner but minor functionary, whose low status seemed a calculated insult to the Ukrainians. As a condition for ending the invasion, Putin demanded Ukraine's neutrality, 'denazification' and 'demilitarisation', and recognition of Crimea as Russian territory.[7] Another meeting, this time brokered by Turkish President Recep Tayyip Erdogan in Antalya, Turkey, between Ukrainian Foreign Minister Dmytro Kuleba and Sergei Lavrov, also ended with no meaningful breakthrough.[8] But at this early stage of the war, Zelensky nonetheless made it clear that at least one of the Kremlin's demands – Ukraine abandoning its path to NATO membership – was still negotiable, even if surrender of any land taken since 24 February was not.

Ukraine would not join NATO 'anytime soon', Zelensky admitted on 15 March. 'It's a truth and it must be recognised.' Instead he proposed a neutral, non-nuclear status for his country – subject to a national referendum.[9] Putin spokesman Dmitry Peskov agreed that talks were 'progressing' – but demanded a 'de-militarisation' model for Ukraine along the lines of Austria and Sweden, both non-aligned countries with small armies. Ukrainian negotiator Mykhailo Podolyak countered with another plan: Ukrainian neutrality guaranteed by a concert of European powers and the US; enshrining rights for Ukraine's Russian speakers; a return of Russian troops to pre-24 February borders; and effectively ignoring the issue of the disputed territories of Crimea and Donbas until a later date.[10]

In retrospect, that would have been an excellent deal for Putin – a deal that would have allowed him to announce a quick victory and triumphantly declare newly independent Donetsk and Luhansk safe from Ukrainian aggression in time for the much-anticipated 9 May Victory Day holiday. But Putin, as usual, over-estimated his own powers and still appeared confident of a military victory. In reality, the mid-March peace offer at Antalya would be the deepest concession that Zelensky would ever make. During those first weeks, Zelensky was negotiating with 'his back to the wall ... Russians were within half an hour of central Kyiv,' recalled one of his senior advisers. 'We were not sure what level of support we could expect from NATO.' Zelensky was effectively 'ready to let the [LDNR] and Crimea go, for the sake of saving the lives of thousands of innocent people'.[11] That weakness would never be repeated. During April Boris Johnson, then other European leaders, would visit Kyiv with assurances of military support – and most crucially the US also began to deliver its first supplies of heavy weapons. By August Zelensky, emboldened by success in the field and massive NATO military aid, not only reversed his idea of conceding the loss of Crimea but would be demanding Crimea's return to Ukraine. He was also regularly bombing the Russian-held peninsula. By September, after Putin had formally annexed the partially occupied provinces of Kherson, Zaporizhzhia, Luhansk and Donetsk, Zelensky not only formally applied for fast-track NATO membership but declared that he was ready for talks with Russia – as long as it had another president than Putin.

The reason both for NATO's early hesitancy to help and for Putin's strategic greed went deeper than doubts over Ukraine's ability to resist. On the third day of the war Putin shocked the world with an announcement that he was putting Russia's strategic nuclear forces on 'a special preventative regime' – and warned foreign countries not to interfere in his invasion of Ukraine, saying it could lead to 'consequences they have never seen'.

Nukes and MiGs

Was Putin truly planning to nuke the West if it intervened in Ukraine – or was it just a bluff? Nobody knew for sure. In London, Boris Johnson summoned top military commanders to the secure Cabinet Office Briefing Room A – acronym COBRA – in Whitehall to discuss how seriously to take the threat. While top generals discounted the threat of a strategic strike as 'obviously suicidal', the possibility that Putin could use a battlefield nuclear weapon was taken much more seriously, according to a Downing Street official with direct knowledge of the meeting.[12] In Paris, Emmanuel Macron's advisers reached much the same conclusion – and also confidentially agreed that if Putin were to use a tactical nuclear device France would press NATO for 'an overwhelming conventional response … but not a nuclear one', according to a senior adviser who regularly spoke to Macron during that period.[13]

At a summit in Beijing on 4 February 2022 Xi Jinping and Vladimir Putin announced a 'friendship without limits' with 'no forbidden areas' of cooperation. Both leaders declared the new level of Sino-Russian strategic partnership 'superior' to the alliances of the Cold War era.[14] Beijing was aware of Russia's plans for a military operation, according to a source with longstanding close ties to the top levels of China's political and military leadership. But the Russians presented the coming military operation as a 'limited operation to recover a lost Russian province [and] reunite Russia within historical boundaries'. That narrative fitted China's own over Taiwan – though it was made clear that the Russian operation must not interfere with the Beijing Winter Olympics, which ended on 20 February 2022.

Most importantly, in a confidential annexe to the 'friendship without limits' was a mutual security guarantee that Russia had sought from China for decades but hitherto been unable to obtain, said the source. Like NATO's Article 5, Beijing and Moscow pledged to come to each other's aid militarily in the case of a foreign invasion of their territory and if special conditions were satisfied concerning the cause of such an invasion. That extremely canny and prescient proviso, inserted at Chinese insistence, would effectively exclude territories recently annexed during wartime, thus releasing Beijing from any commitment to respond to attacks on annexed territories in Ukraine.[15]

The scale of Russia's military operation – in particular the closely held secret of the blitzkrieg attack on Kyiv, of which even Lavrov was unaware as late as 21 February – took Beijing by surprise. Though the Chinese officially supported Putin diplomatically, blaming NATO for provoking the conflict, there was deep (and entirely well-founded) concern that Putin had overreached and would provoke the West into a united front that a limited operation in Donbas would have avoided. Putin's threat of nuclear escalation on 27 February alarmed the world, including the Chinese. A key priority for Beijing was for the Russo-NATO confrontation to 'avoid any nuclear escalation and to help in reaching a ceasefire', said the source, who has regular personal contact with the leaders of the People's Liberation Army (PLA). Now Putin had – wholly recklessly and dangerously, in Chinese eyes – carelessly played his most dangerous card right at the beginning of the conflict.

So when, a few days later, a further escalation threatened in the form of an offer by the Polish government to supply Ukraine with its entire fleet of Soviet-era MiG-29 fighters, the Chinese grew concerned. In truth, there was little likelihood of the Polish MiGs making much of a difference on the battlefield. At the end of the first week of March 2022 Ukraine's Air Force was flying approximately five to ten missions per day using a pool of about 50 fighter jets and had lost, according to the open source intelligence site Oryx, no more than seven fighters destroyed since the start of the Russian invasion. The Russians, by contrast, were making some 200 sorties per day but keeping their planes primarily within Russian airspace to avoid ground-based air defence systems.[16]

Poland's 26 to 33 MiG-29s had been made in the early 1980s for the East German Air Force and had been sold to Warsaw for the symbolic sum of €1 each in 2003. Romania, which owned 20 similar MiG-29 jets, had decommissioned them many years ago.[17] Nonetheless, a NATO country providing fighter jets of any kind to Kyiv represented an important symbolic, if not necessarily operationally significant, step towards direct NATO involvement in the conflict. Initially, Washington was positive. But a day later, on 9 March, the Pentagon abruptly reversed its position, pronouncing Poland's proposal 'not tenable'.

What changed Washington's mind? In part, it was an urgent and confidential back-channel initiative led by the UK-based Institute for East West Strategic Studies involving former European leaders, and ultimately endorsed by the Chinese. Ever since Putin's 27 February declaration on nuclear readiness, the PLA had been reaching out through military-to-military (as opposed to diplomatic or political) channels to top Russian general officers with whom they had made personal contact over years of joint military exercises and military procurement talks. Beijing's aim was to ensure that even if there were a political decision to use nukes, the Russian army would insist on sticking to its long-standing nuclear military doctrine to use them solely if provoked by attacks on Russian soil.

When the Polish MiG deal was reported, a trusted back channel – unusually, given a deterioration in mutual contacts during the Trump presidency – was opened between Washington and the PLA. Beijing agreed that if the US stopped the MiG deal, they would do their best to defuse Putin's nuclear threat on an operational level. 'It worked,' said the Chinese source, without elaborating. 'The [US] decided that supplying aircraft was a step too far.'[18]

Though this private, back-channel initiative of early March has not been previously reported, the fact that the US retained a fundamentally cautious attitude to supplying heavy weapons to Ukraine throughout the war effectiveness confirms that Washington remained deeply aware of Chinese concerns – which were shared with many of the largest nations in the European Union. Despite a dramatic escalation in supplies of money and military hardware – including NATO-standard 155mm artillery capable of firing guided shells and the High Mobility Artillery Rocket System (HIMARS) – NATO held back on providing attack aircraft, helicopters, NATO-standard tanks, long-range battlefield missile and cruise missile systems.

At the same time Chinese backing for Moscow remained equally cautious. Beijing offered diplomatic and informational support – but excluded significant military cooperation, forcing the Russians to buy drones from Iran, cannibalise domestic appliances for computer chips and attempt to buy back helicopters, missile and missile defence systems from its military customers around the developing world. As UK Defence Minister Ben Wallace said in May, British military officials who had been shopping round the world to buy Soviet hardware to buy up as military aid to Ukraine repeatedly 'bumped into the Russians looking ... for some of their resupplies'.[19]

But what truly changed both the narrative of Ukrainian attempts to find a reconciliation with Moscow – and the West's attitude towards arming Kyiv with heavy weapons – was the changing reality on the battlefield. By the end of the war's first month, Russia's forces had taken three southern Ukrainian cities – Kherson, Melitopol and the Azov Sea port of Berdyansk – without a fight. They had surrounded Mariupol, and were busy bombarding the city to rubble as the Russian army had, in 2000, blasted the Chechen capital of Grozny. But around Kyiv and Kharkiv a month of fierce Ukrainian resistance had fought the Russian advance to a bloody standstill. The Russians, decimated and under heavy counterattack both from artillery and small mobile groups armed with deadly anti-tank weaponry, responded with a vicious cycle of reprisals against the civilian population.

Bucha

The towns of Bucha and Irpin, some 20 kilometres to the north-west of Kyiv, had in Russian imperial and Soviet times been prosperous dacha villages set among thick pinewoods and winding rivers. The Soviets had built sanatoriums and a writers' resort there. Boris Pasternak wrote in a 1930 poem, 'Irpin is the memory of people and summer, of freedom, of escape from oppression.'[20]

On 27 February, as a battle raged for Hostomel airport a few kilometres to the south, Russian troops entered Bucha. The column was ambushed by Ukrainian forces. Artillery fire and Molotov cocktails thrown by local irregulars destroyed close to a hundred Russian vehicles in Bucha's Vokzalna Street and in nearby villages. Months later, most roadsides in the area were still scattered with twisted piles of wrecked tanks, rusting ration tins and the spinal cords of Russian soldiers who had burned alive in their steel seats.

Four days later the Russians had retreated from Bucha in disarray. On 3 March a group of Ukrainian soldiers raised the yellow and blue flag of Ukraine over the town hall. Local

Ukrainian Territorial Defence Forces volunteers – mostly unarmed – emerged from the cellars of their houses and took over makeshift checkpoints around the small town. Irina Filkina and the other employees of the Epitsentr K shopping centre thought the war was over.[21] 'We were so relieved,' recalled Galina Smirnova, who worked in Epitsentr's building supplies department. 'The girls at work all said that we got off lightly, that our boys had pushed out the occupiers.'[22]

They were very wrong. By the evening of 3 March another unit of Russians from the 64th Separate Guards Motor Rifle Brigade reoccupied the town, which was still littered with the burned-out carcasses of dozens of Russian armoured vehicles and civilian cars riddled with bullets as they had tried to flee in the first days of the invasion. Columns of Russian tanks flanked by dismounted troops moved through Bucha street by street. The Ukrainian Territorial Defence volunteers, severely outgunned, took shelter wherever they could. The Russians, going house to house, rounded them up and hustled a group of them, along with a crowd of dozens of locals, into the car park of an office building on Yablunska Street. After some peremptory questioning, eight of the nine Territorial Defence men were summarily shot. The only one to survive had agreed to act as an informer for the Russians and identify other comrades.[23]

Irina Filkina lived on Yablunska Street. Just a few days before, on the eve of the invasion, she had got herself a new manicure from her beauty instructor, local make-up artist Anastasia Subacheva. She had chosen cherry red for her new manicure for Valentine's Day, drawing 'a heart on her finger because she started to love herself', Subacheva told CNN.[24] Filkina's two daughters, who lived in nearby Irpin, had taken buses to Poland at the outbreak of the war. But Filkina herself had chosen to stay behind, volunteering to cook for people who had taken refuge in the cavernous Epitsentr shopping centre, as well as for the Ukrainian soldiers who had briefly reoccupied Bucha.

By 5 March, two days into the second Russian occupation, Filkina realised it was time to leave – urgently. Russians had been shooting civilians indiscriminately in the streets. The eight corpses in the office car park on Yablunska Street had been left to rot, covered in the rubbish thrown from the windows by occupying Russian forces who had taken over the office building and a nearby glass factory as a base.[25] A steady convoy of local cars was ferrying people from Epitsentr on the perilous journey across the front lines to Ukrainian-held territory. But there was no room for Filkina. Her elder daughter, 26-year-old Olga Shchyruk, begged her mother by phone not to ride her black bike home that day and urged her to try getting out on the suburban commuter trains that were still running. 'I told her that it was unsafe there,' recalled Shchyruk, a child psychologist who was volunteering to help other Ukrainian refugees in Poland. 'Russia [had] occupied the whole village – they were killing people.' Filkina replied, 'Olga, don't you know your mom? I can move mountains!'[26]

Filkina never made it home that day. Footage from a Ukrainian army drone captured the apparent moment of her death. In the footage a woman can be seen pushing a black bicycle round the corner of Deputatskaya Street and turning into Yablunska Street. A Russian armoured personnel carrier fired four rounds from a heavy machine gun, dropping the cyclist. Later video taken on the street showed the body of a woman with a blue jacket and light-coloured trousers sprawled alongside a black bike by an uprooted electricity pole and the debris of burned-out cars. One leg was mangled. Her arm lay to one side. Filkina's colleagues got word to the Ukrainian military that she had been killed, and her daughter Olga received a phone call later that day informing her that her mother had been shot dead. The military said it would be impossible to retrieve her body as a Russian tank was positioned nearby. At first she refused to believe the news. 'I imagined that [my mother] was just hidden in a basement,' said Shchyruk. 'That she saw occupiers and stayed somewhere to wait.'[27]

On 29 March, as another round of talks got under way in Istanbul, Russia's Ministry of Defence announced a 'drastic reduction of military activity' on the Kyiv and Chernihiv fronts. Russian negotiator Medinsky insisted that this was 'not tantamount to a ceasefire'. The Pentagon also believed that the Russians were engaging in 'a repositioning, not a real withdrawal'.[28] They were mistaken. Russian troops withdrew from Bucha – and all over Kyiv and Chernihiv provinces – on 31 March and kept going to the Russian border. By 1 April the 30,000-strong Russian force that had been sent to take Kyiv had entirely withdrawn, leaving hundreds of their dead and hundreds of burned-out tanks and armoured vehicles on the battlefield. They also left the corpses of hundreds of murdered civilians that would make the names of Bucha, Irpin and nearby Motyzhin synonymous with Russian war crimes.

Reuters photographers were the first to take images of Filkina's body on 3 April – her curled left hand peeking out of the blue sleeve of her coat with its distinctive cherry red nail polish, and a heart motif on one finger. When she saw the photos, recalled Shchyruk, 'I knew my mother had been killed ... I had a feeling my spine was broken. I lay down, crying with helplessness.'[29]

At least 20 other bodies of civilians lay unburied on Yablonska Street. In all, some 458 bodies would be found on the streets and buried in mass graves in Bucha alone.[30] Over 400 of the bodies had been killed by execution-style gunfire, torture or bludgeoning. Russia accused Ukraine of orchestrating a false flag in Bucha, with state TV piling in with accusations that the photos and videos were staged. Biden called for Putin to be tried for war crimes committed by Russian soldiers in Bucha.[31] Zelensky, wearing body armour and surrounded by journalists, toured the carnage on 4 April. His face was ashen and he struggled to control his emotions. 'I think [Zelensky] aged twenty years in that day,' said a close aide. 'When he returned to Kyiv he broke down. He was beside himself ... he is a very emotional person. It was hard for him to keep control.'[32]

On the day Zelensky visited Bucha 'something in him changed,' said the aide. And the war changed too. For Zelensky personally, as well as his entourage, Western leaders and millions of people around the world, Russia's invasion had been revealed as an act of savagery against civilians unprecedented in Europe since Bosnia – and before that, the Second World War. From that moment on, there could be no more compromise.

Everyone Was Shocked

At the end of the third week of the war Putin – wearing a €9,800 Loro Piano puffa coat and €3,000 roll-neck sweater by Italian brand Kiton – appeared before a 200,000-strong flag-waving crowd at Moscow's Luzhniki Stadium to deliver a defiant speech. The invasion of Ukraine was about defending the 'universal values' of all Russians, Putin said – before the live transmission cut out after some 17 minutes. The feed was cut for 'technical reasons', Putin's spokesman later explained. In fact video footage shared on social media showed that sections of the crowd had begun wolf-whistling the president – a gesture of extreme displeasure in Russian performance culture. A few days earlier a video had emerged of the governor of Nizhny Tagil being passionately berated by soldiers' mothers whose conscript sons had been sent to Ukraine despite a public promise by Putin that only professional contract soldiers would be fighting.

Behind closed doors Putin sacked eight top generals and was 'raging' at the FSB after failed intelligence and poor strategy – or at least so claimed Oleksiy Danilov, head of Ukraine's security council. Rumours began to circulate that the FSB's Colonel-General Sergei Beseda and his deputy had been placed under house arrest on charges of embezzling funds intended to bribe

Ukrainian army commanders and politicians.[33] Beseda later re-appeared in official circles apparently unscathed by his experience – as if it had never happened.

Elvira Nabiullina, the influential head of Russia's Central Bank, attempted to resign in protest at the damage the invasion was doing to the economy – but her resignation was not accepted, according to a source close to her.[34] In addition, it was made clear to Nabiullina that her family members' businesses would suffer as a result, so she stayed – but pointedly wore nothing but black clothing to future cabinet meetings.

There were also reported instances of insubordination and revolt in the military. In Crimea 12 members of the National Guard – including a captain – were dismissed for refusing to go to war in Ukraine on the grounds that their orders were 'illegal'. The 12 sued the government to overturn their discharge and get reinstated, a move that just a couple of months later would appear an unthinkable act of defiance.[35]

Even passionate self-styled patriots like Igor Girkin became sharp critics of the Kremlin's failing campaign. 'After 29 days of the special operation not one strategic goal has been achieved,' Girkin told the OSN website. 'My worst fear is that we are being pulled into a lengthy and bloody tug-of-war which will be extremely dangerous for the Russian Federation.'[36]

On 13 April the 11,000-ton guided-missile cruiser *Moskva*, flagship of the Black Sea Fleet, was hit by two Ukrainian Neptune anti-ship cruise missiles and set on fire. Mobile-phone footage shot from one of the rescue vessels showed the crippled vessel listing and belching thick smoke. Russian navy tugs attempted to take the *Moskva* under tow, but she sank at 3 a.m. the following morning. Just as after the loss of the submarine *Kursk* in 2000, the Russian navy's initial reaction was to deny and obfuscate. Black Sea Fleet headquarters in Sevastopol acknowledged that a fire had broken out on board, allegedly caused by a carelessly discarded cigarette – a go-to explanation that would later become the official cause of so many Russian munitions dump explosions, warehouse fires and attacks on airports that it became a popular, mocking, Ukrainian internet meme. Later that day the Russian Admiralty conceded that the ship was in difficulties, and eventually admitted that it had sunk in a storm with one sailor killed, 27 missing and 396 crew members rescued. It had been the cruiser *Moskva* to which the Ukrainian defenders of Snake Island had sent their defiant message, 'Russian warship, go fuck yourself!' The sinking of the *Moskva* – a veteran of conflicts in Georgia, Syria and Crimea, and by far the most powerful warship in the Black Sea – was Russia's most serious naval loss at war since 1944. The sinking triggered jubilation in Kyiv and across Ukraine, providing a vital morale boost in the aftermath of the horrific revelations of Bucha. The loss of the *Moskva* also became the subject of a set of commemorative Ukrainian postage stamps emblazoned with the famous (though asterisked) Snake Island message.

Despite Putin's public bravado, much of the Russian business and government elite were in a state of shock in the immediate aftermath of the invasion – a shock that seemed to deepen with every piece of bad news. The SWIFT shutdown, the closure of Western stores, the blocking of European airspace to Russian planes, the Russian Central Bank's ban on transferring money out of the country, five rounds of swingeing sanctions on exports to Russia, the retreat from Kyiv, the Bucha massacre, the sinking of the *Moskva* ... 'every morning I would put off looking at my phone till I had had a coffee and looked out the window for a while to gather my nerves,' said a senior colleague of Sergei Lavrov's, whom I will call Angelina Melnikova. 'Every day some crazy new shit.' For Melnikova, the moment when she realised that 'we were truly screwed' was when UPDK – officially Russia's diplomatic service arm, unofficially the business and property-management arm of the Foreign Ministry – ran out of paper on which to print documents, forcing the office to load old paper face-down in the office printers.[37]

'*Vse prosto okhuyeli*' was a phrase I heard in very many conversations with Moscow businesspeople, journalists and government contacts when I returned to Moscow in early May – a highly obscene and barely translatable expression that means, literally, 'everyone ate cock [from shock]'. One telecoms billionaire with close ties to state contracts and a business partner of one of Russia's most senior *siloviki* held a party for his closest friends on his private estate near Moscow in the first week of the war. 'We toast the past, the good times,' the businessman told his friends, raising a glass of his best claret. 'Those days are gone now ... we must all find our new happiness.' Talk around the dinner table, according to someone who was present, was about liquidating assets, selling pictures, getting rid of private planes that were no longer allowed to fly to Europe or the US with any Russian passport holders aboard.[38]

In the Foreign Ministry, 'everyone understood everything,' said Melnikova, who had had a highly successful business career and spent time in the US before becoming an executive at the Ministry. 'But nobody spoke about it. [The war] was like someone in the family had been arrested for something awful ... a painful subject that it would be tactless to bring up.' At the same time much of Melnikova's private anger was directed not at Putin but at the 'collective West who provoked this situation'. Like many Russians of her class and generation, Melnikova was a living exemplar of George Orwell's doublethink – defined as an ability to hold two mutually contradictory beliefs at the same time. Putin and his entourage were, to her, 'a bunch of crooks and old KGB apparatchiks' – yet to her the West's response was primarily motivated by 'fear of Russia ... and pure Russophobia'. Like many Moscow professionals, the prospect of emigration was a practical impossibility. There was no way that she could ever match her lifestyle of a mansion in a prestigious Moscow suburb, a team of nannies, two expensive cars and a stay-at-home husband in the West.

After shock came paranoia. An intense reticence overcame all my old contacts in government and the military. Of 60-odd text messages I sent over my first few days back in Moscow perhaps 20 were answered – most of those explaining that they could not be in contact with a foreign journalist. I asked one former senior official what his read was on the mood among his former colleagues in the Kremlin. 'What *mood*? You're on a train,' he replied. 'You're not the driver of the train. You know it's going somewhere you maybe don't want to go. But are you going to jump off the train and get left behind?'[39] Some old acquaintances were resigned, others had become aggressively nationalistic. One former editor at the liberal Echo Moskvy radio station – formerly a bastion of democratic values – drunkenly called to announce that he and some mutual friends were sitting at the dacha, drinking. 'Guess what we are drinking to?' he asked. 'The success of Russian arms!! Glory to Russia!'

State TV editor Anna Bondarenko seemed to blame me personally for sanctions and for provoking the war. 'What were you doing, with your NATO exercises?' she demanded. 'What did you expect us to do? You were just looking for an excuse to screw Russia.' What about her relatives in Ukraine, I asked? 'Oh, they've all become fascists,' she replied. 'They believed all your fakes about Bucha. Even though I sent them all the evidence – bodies standing up after the cameras had passed, corpses rolling over, all that. But they are too brainwashed. Told me to fuck off and not call them anymore.' Bondarenko seemed very sure that soon the shops of Moscow would once again be full – and even if they weren't she would buy all the designer clothes she needed in Dubai. 'No more shopping trips to Milan? Too bad for Milan. They'll go bankrupt without [Russian] clients,' she said. 'That's the price you will pay for your hatred!'

At the same time the 'Z' posters, scaffolding awnings and car stickers that had proliferated across Moscow in the early days of the war had, by May, completely disappeared. The city authorities seemed to prefer to pretend – in common with most of the capital's citizens – that the war was not happening. The city's cafes, bars, clubs, restaurants and theatres were all packed. But straining my ears to tune in to strangers' conversations, I never overheard a single person talking about Ukraine or the war in public before Putin's mobilisation order in September. Moscow, the capital of a power fighting a major war, was apparently the only place in Europe where one could very easily pretend that the invasion had never happened.

Kharkiv

For the first few weeks of the conflict Jimmy S and his mates in Wantage, Oxfordshire, had been following the Russian invasion on YouTube, TikTok – and video messages from their mate Lambie. Lambie's early videos were barely distinguishable from a fun stag weekend in Eastern Europe: Lambie with a bunch of 'great lads' holding up pints in a pub in Rzesow, Poland; Lambie embracing a pair of pretty Ukrainian girls at a bar in Lviv; Lambie pointing goofily with double thumbs-up to a Ukrainian Armed Forces baseball cap one of the girls had jammed on his head. Then there were videos of Lambie in Ukrainian pixellated uniform, a horizontal selfie of Lambie collapsed on the ground in exhaustion – but still grinning – after a training march. Then Lambie was on the front lines, filming explosions. He filmed tank rounds slamming into village houses, a Russian jet screaming low followed by a distant fireball. Most hauntingly, Lambie filmed a ghostly shower of what seemed to be bright, luminous snow falling slowly over a night-time winter landscape. 'White phosphorus,' explained Jimmy. 'Nasty stuff. Burns right through everything.'

Then Lambie was dead, killed by a shell in a trench somewhere near Kharkiv. Jimmy took the news as a sign that it was his turn. He booked a Ryanair ticket to Rzesow, then went to get a memorial tattoo for his friend on his right forearm: the word 'Lambie' inside a cartoon sheep. 'I went to fight because if we don't fight this war here we're gonna be fighting it at home,' Jimmy told me as we shared an eight-hour train journey from Kyiv to Lviv in June. 'I want my son to grow up in a world that's safe and free, y'know?' Apparently sensing a silent scepticism from me, he looked from side to side and lowered his voice. 'Also, my ex-girlfriend wanted me to change nappies all the time. Not havin' that.'

At the border crossing at Przemysl Jimmy walked up to a tent directly opposite the exit from Ukrainian customs that was marked with a large banner bearing the cross of the Armed Forces of Ukraine and the words 'FOREIGN VOLUNTEERS' in English, German and Polish. A couple of Ukrainian military clerks entered his details in a laptop and told him a contract would be ready to sign in a couple of days after security vetting. A minibus was waiting to ferry him and half a dozen of the day's volunteers to a nearby hostel, then once the clearance came through to a training centre. For three weeks, Jimmy learned basic small arms and infantry techniques with 'some fantastic lads from all over ... couple of Brits, ex-army. Some Poles, Germans.' A couple of British men of Pakistani origin from Leeds had joined up too – but Jimmy and his mates shunned them as 'a pair of nutters ... you don't want any nutters next to you in a trench, promise ya.' The officers and trainers of the International Legion were all Ukrainian and for the most part spoke no English. But they made themselves understood by 'shouting loud and swearing a lot', recalled Jimmy.

The new foreign recruits were given 'the worst equipment, terrible body armour' and were assigned to a quiet part of the front line near Kharkiv. Their job was mostly to hold trenches but never to attack – 'they didn't want us getting taken prisoner'. Some of the lads had brought their own expensive drones, but those were soon pinched from locked kitbags by their Ukrainian comrades. Jimmy had to order himself a fancy flak jacket from a US website for $800 and a high-quality Kevlar helmet that cost even more – heavy kit that he was lugging with him on leave to Lviv for fear of it getting stolen. The Ukrainians 'need us for PR, they don't let us do much fighting,' said Jimmy. Nonetheless, two members of his unit had been killed by artillery and mortar fire in heavy fighting south of Kharkiv. Their nicknames – accompanied with little Polish and German flags – formed part of another tattoo on Jimmy's forearm. 'Til Valhal' – the Viking battle cry – formed the legend across the top of the tattoo, with blank space left for three more names before it became symmetrical. I asked if that wasn't a bit morbid. 'Dunno,' he grinned. 'Could be optimistic.' Jimmy's plan was to spend his fortnight's leave partying in Lviv before heading back to fight. 'I'll go back home [to England] when the war's won, not before.'[40]

The industrial city of Kharkiv, just 30 kilometres from the Russian border and a Russian-speaking town with a notably pro-Russian mayor, should have been the Kremlin's easiest target. In 2014 the city saw some of the largest anti-Maidan demonstrations, and was a major target for Sergei Glazyev's influence operations to attempt to foment a pro-Moscow coup. In the first week of the 2022 invasion, massive Russian shelling and rocket attacks destroyed part of the main administration building on Kharkiv's main Freedom Square. But instead of capitulating, Mayor Ihor Terekhov came out fighting, posting images of himself on social media holding a pistol and vowing to resist the invaders. 'The Russian aggressors are trying to turn Kharkiv into a pitiful city, like the ones they have in Russia,' Terekhov told journalists – in Russian. 'But they won't succeed. And, as you see, the people of Kharkiv are defending their city, weapons in hand.'[41]

Just days before the invasion, Russian private Ivan Kudryavtsev had been told that his unit was about to embark on a training exercise. Kudryavtsev called his mother on 20 February and asked for money to 'buy food' before 'exercises'. He told her that his motorised rifle unit was on the border with Belarus. The next day he told his brother that they were 'moving out', without specifying where. It would be Kudryavtsev's last direct contact with his family.

Kudryavtsev was born in August 2001 in Omsk region, central Siberia. Like many of the soldiers who fought in Ukraine, he was a child of the Putin era – and had grown up in poverty in the deep provinces. When Ivan was seven his father left his mother, who, in turn, abandoned her three children – two sons, and a daughter who suffered from cerebral palsy. Ivan's brother, aged nine, called their uncle's wife Nina and begged to be taken in. 'It would have been a pity for them to be taken to an orphanage,' said Nina. 'Their mother refused them, their father didn't need them either, so we took them.' But Nina could not care for the boys' sick sister, who disappeared without trace into the Russian care system.

Kudryavtsev and his brother went to school in the small town of Nazyvaevsk, built to service the Trans-Siberian Railway, which runs through its centre. He loved football, Soviet war films, video games, and gathering mushrooms and berries in the forest with his grandfather. Ivan appeared twice in the local newspaper, *Nasha Iskra* – once as the local football team's newbie goalkeeper and again in the summer of 2020 when he and other 18-year-old locals voted for the first time. 'The guys say that they could not stay away from such an important event for our country,' wrote the paper. In 2021 he graduated from a course at Omsk's Technical Railway School – and he and his elder brother were both called up in October. Two months later Ivan called to tell his aunt that he'd signed up as a contract soldier, a month earlier than the earliest supposed date that conscripts could go professional. 'I don't know at all how he signed the contract,' Nina said. 'He said that they underwent accelerated training. Looks like they were preparing them [for something]. Nobody told us anything.'

On 21 March one of the mothers of the young men in Kudryavtsev's unit received a call from her son. He had been taken prisoner. 'He said: "We are sitting in the basement with no food, no drink,"' the woman told Ivan's aunt Nadezhda. '"We are being fed by elderly people, Ukrainians."'[42]

Five days later, on 26 March, Ukrainian Telegram channels reported that 30 Russians had been taken prisoner after heavy fighting in the small commuter town of Vil'khivka, 19 kilometres east of the centre of Kharkiv and some 50 kilometres from the nearest border crossing into Russia's Belgorod province. The prisoners were taken to the nearby village of Malaya Rohan' – six kilometres away from the Kharkiv Tractor Factory – for a brutal interrogation.[43] According to a series of short videos posted by pro-Ukrainian military bloggers on Reddit the next morning, at least a dozen men in Russian uniform, all of them apparently wounded and several of them with sacks on their heads, were lined up on the ground in a car park with their hands tied behind their backs.[44] All wore the white armbands used by Russians to distinguish themselves from the yellow or blue armband-wearing Ukrainians. A soldier in Ukrainian uniform – his face invisible in the video – calmly walks down the line shooting each prisoner in the legs with a Kalashnikov. 'Who are the officers?' he says in Russian as the shot men groan and scream. 'Who are the fucking officers? Talk ... What the fuck are you doing lobbing bombs into Kharkiv?'

Another Ukrainian soldier, checking one of the prone bodies, says, 'This one's a goner. He's fucked.'

'Where are the recon[naissance] units? The recon units, fuck?' continues the first interrogator, moving down the line. The prisoner, a bloodied bag over his head, answers in a whisper.

'They came through on the other side of the village ...' His voice dies away.

'Talk! Come on, talk!' says his interrogator. The soldier does not answer. The Ukrainian pokes him in the chest with his gun barrel. No response. He pulls off the hood, revealing a bloodied young face. 'This one's passed out.'

The wounded Russian was Ivan Kudryavtsev.

'His voice. Even before they removed the sack, I immediately said it was him,' said Kudryavtsev's foster mother Nina, who was alerted to the video on 10 April by an acquaintance of Ivan's. 'Ivan's voice is not broken yet, it's childlike, even though he's 20 years old,' confirmed his aunt Nadezhda. 'And his lips. Although they are bloodied and swollen, it is clear that they are his.'

Lyudmila Denisova, Ukraine's Commissioner for Human Rights, claimed that the video was 'a movie that the Russians themselves made ... a fake'. Commander-in-Chief of the Armed Forces of Ukraine Valeriy Zaluzhny also announced on Facebook that Russians were distributing 'staged videos supposedly showing the inhuman attitude of allegedly "Ukrainian soldiers" towards "Russian prisoners"'. But Oleksey Arestovich, a senior adviser to the Ukrainian president, admitted that the videos 'might show a war crime' and promised that the incident would be investigated. Arestovich also reminded Ukrainian troops of 'the importance of following the laws of war' and respecting the Geneva Convention.

For Ivan Kudryavtsev's relatives in Omsk, the debate over alleged Ukrainian brutality towards prisoners was cold comfort. On 4 May his foster mother Nina received an official notice from the Russian Ministry of Defence stating that 'Kudryavtsev Ivan Ivanovich, an ordinary conscript, has gone missing' – with no mention that he had signed up as a professional *kontraktnik*. Kudryavtsev's commanding officer back at the unit's base in Yelnya, Smolensk province, told her he had 'no information'. It was only through an informal Telegram group set up by relatives and friends of the soldiers shown in the 26 March video that Nina found out that three of Kudryavtsev's comrades had been reported dead. In early June, Russia's security services began to contact and question members of the Telegram chat, warning them not to talk to the press. Kudryavtsev's aunt and foster mother ignored them. 'We can't keep silent about this,' Nadezhda told journalists from *Meduza* in June. 'We are ready for anything. Alive or dead, so that our souls can be at peace. At least give him a decent burial. So that he does not rot there.'[45]

Kherson

The city of Kherson fell to the Russians on 5 March after the local mayor arranged a ceasefire and peaceful surrender, allowing the heavily outnumbered Ukrainian troops in the city to withdraw unmolested. The following day thousands of locals turned out to block advancing Russian columns with their bodies and shout 'Go fuck yourselves' to frightened and surprised Russian soldiers. Such a display of mass civil disobedience – even when the troops began firing into the air to disperse the demonstrators – was an entirely unknown thing in their young Russian lives in Putin's Russia. But the demonstrations did not stop the new Russian authorities from setting up a puppet government recruited from local pro-Russian activists and an ex-mayor who styled themselves the leaders of a new 'Kherson People's Republic'.

In Nova Kakhovka, 100 kilometres northeast of Kherson, Larisa Nagorskaya joined a group of friends and hundreds of residents in a pro-Kyiv demonstration on the town's main square. Some young men climbed up to the roofs of surrounding buildings and draped them with huge Ukrainian flags. Others tied rows of helium balloons to a giant yellow and blue flag and released it into the air, to cheers. Russian troops, all with their faces covered, stood by armoured personnel carriers around the edges of the square but did not intervene.

That night security cameras recorded a group of 15 armed men showing up at the home of one local activist woman who had helped organise the demonstration. The activist had gone to stay with her daughter; the next day she escaped from Nova Kakhovka across the front lines to Ukrainian-held Zaporizhzhia. Russians seemed to have lists of people who participated in the meeting – as well as lists of veterans who had fought with Ukrainian forces. 'Someone had betrayed them,' said Nagorskaya. 'They went door to door, arrested all men who were veterans and took them to a cellar somewhere.' The phrase *zabrali v podval* – literally, 'they took to a cellar' – became a commonplace shorthand for the systematic kidnap and torture by the Russians. The verb *prilitelo* – literally, 'flew in' – came to mean incoming artillery or missile strikes. The father of a friend of Nagorskaya's 11-year-old daughter Masha, a deputy in the regional assembly and a Ukrainian army veteran, received an urgent call on his mobile from a friend asking him to meet. Around the corner from his house, Russians were waiting and bundled him into a jeep. They kept the man blindfolded for a month in a freezing cellar, brutally interrogating and beating him regularly before eventually releasing him with his teeth, ribs and nose broken, according to Nagorskaya.

The local authorities began firing local officials who had not fled or been arrested. At Nagorskaya's place of work at the local water utility all workers were summoned for a meeting with the new director – a well-known local politician who had been a regional deputy from Yanukovych's Party of the Regions and had mysteriously disappeared six months before to Sochi, Russia. Now he was back with a simple message. 'This is Russia now,' the new boss told the water company employees, recalled Nagorskaya. 'You will be paid in rubles. Kakhovka will stay Russian forever. Anyone who doesn't like it is free to leave.'

Nagorskaya's husband Igor decided to take his advice. A seat in a taxi across the front lines to Zaporizhzhia cost the equivalent of $200 – and the Nagorskys were afraid that Igor could be questioned and drafted into the Ukrainian army. They were afraid, too, that he'd be drafted into the Russian army if he stayed. So Igor took a minibus to Russian-occupied Crimea, then on to Rostov and eventually made it to Wrocław, Poland, where he found work as a handyman to make some cash as he waited for the war to end.

All the Ukrainian police disappeared on the first day, to be replaced by patrols of marauding Russian soldiers. 'The Russians stole everything,' said Nagorskaya. 'Some local farmers had rented a warehouse to store 60 tonnes of sunflower seeds. Everything was stolen. We used to have the largest solar-electric station in Ukraine – but the Russians took all the panels away. Russians soldiers came into shops and helped themselves. Nobody could do anything.'

By the end of March, around 60 per cent of Nagorskaya's neighbours had left – a few to Ukrainian-held territory, but most choosing (like her husband) the longer but safer route through Crimea. Several families from Buryatia, in eastern Siberia – relatives of soldiers posted to Nova Kakhovka – had broken into the empty houses and began living in them. 'To us, these are modest houses of ordinary people. To the Buryats it was like they were living in a palace.' One new family broke down a garage and used the sheet metal to build themselves a high makeshift fence around the two-storey village house they had occupied. 'They must have been afraid that the locals hated them and would burn the house down.'

By Nagorskaya's count, about half the people left in Nova Kakhovka were actively pro-Russian – especially the families of old communist apparatchiks and people who were relatively recent arrivals from Russia. She claimed that around '90 per cent' of the local officials refused to work with the Russians. Those who did agree to collaborate received amazing promotions, such as one archivist who was appointed deputy director of the local tax inspectorate. Nagorskaya's neighbour, who had been fired from her job at a hospital for stealing and was 'angry at the Ukrainian authorities', offered to return and was reinstated by the new authorities. The director of Masha's school refused to teach the new Russian programme and was fired, to be replaced by one of junior teachers who agreed to do the job. Soon it became clear that working for the Russians was a high-risk career choice. In occupied Kherson and Zaporizhzhia provinces some 35 Moscow-installed officials would be shot, car-bombed and poisoned. In August, as his city came under sustained Ukrainian attack, the new head of Kherson's regional administration Kirill Stremousov recorded a defiant video message promising that the city would never be retaken – though it was clear from the domes of a cathedral visible over his shoulder that he was in Voronezh, Russia, rather than in Kherson.[46]

In Nova Kakhovka, Ukrainian channels disappeared from the TV, to be replaced by Russian-controlled channels from Luhansk, Crimea, Donbas 24 and central Moscow channels. Nagorskaya and her neighbours watched the destruction of Mariupol with horror – but their conclusion was that they were ready to do anything to avoid Nova Kakhovka meeting the same fate. 'The attitude of most people was, just let there be no war,' said Nagorskaya. 'They are ready to accept anything, even Russians, as long as they don't start shooting.'

By May a semblance of normality had returned. The Russian troops had stopped looting and were under orders to be polite. Local authorities began handing out Russian passports to pensioners, making it a condition of collecting their new ruble pensions. Russian products appeared in the shops – more expensive and much worse quality than the previous Ukrainian ones. But day and night up to 50 rockets and cruise missiles a day fired from Crimea screamed overhead on their way to targets all over

Ukraine. Then, in early June, the Ukrainians began firing back, hitting a major arms dump in Nova Kakhovka, which blew up spectacularly and burned for two days. Many neighbours' windows were blown out. Some were angry, others said it was a small price to pay for liberation. But a friend was told by some Russian soldiers that 'if they have to leave this place they won't leave one brick standing on another'.

Nagorskaya decided that the time had come to take Masha to safety. 'This war will roll back over Kakhovka before it ends,' she said as we shared a Polish train carriage from Przemysl to Krakow. 'And I don't want to be there when that happens.' She scraped together the $500 fare for a *provodnik*, or guide, to drive them across the front lines to Zaporizhzhia. Most of the money was needed to bribe Russian soldiers at the 20 checkpoints they would have to cross, their driver explained. Leaving their cats and dogs with relatives, Nagorskaya and her daughter set off for a new life in Wroclaw. At one of the checkpoints Russian soldiers asked her why she was leaving. 'It's so lovely here, such a rich land – and it's Russia now.'[47]

CHAPTER 10
STANDOFF

Everything fell apart, everything turned out to be rotten, and everyone around turned out to be traitors.

Soviet historian Yevgeny Tarle (1874–1955) on Nicholas I's defeat in Crimea[1]

The Rival Armies

'If I want I'll take Kiev in two weeks,' Putin told José Manuel Barroso, the outgoing president of the European commission, in the aftermath of his 2014 annexation of Crimea.[2] Both the Ukrainians and Western military experts believed him. The memory of the disastrous battles of Ilovaisk and Debaltseve – where Ukrainian armoured units had been surrounded and destroyed by the Russians – meant that NATO military aid had focused on training and supplying the Ukrainian military with light weapons best suited to a guerrilla-style resistance. 'The idea that the Russian army could be defeated in the field didn't enter into our considerations,' says one senior British army commander closely involved in NATO aid to Kyiv during that period. 'To be honest, we underestimated the Ukrainians and seriously overestimated the Russians.' When the 2022 invasion came, 'We were expecting a powerful [Russian] competent combined arms force that had some good coordination between infantry, tanks and artillery,' said the officer. 'Instead we saw tanks unsupported by infantry being picked off by raiders ... They had too much metal and not enough men.'[3]

In 2020 – the last official Russian statistics available – the total number of Russia's professional soldiers, as opposed to conscripts, numbered 405,000 across the air force, navy and army. Of those, Russia's total land forces strength at the beginning of the war stood at 280,000, according to NATO estimates. By adding units from the naval infantry, Rosgvardia paramilitary police, irregular units from Chechnya and mercenaries from the Wagner Group, Russia would deploy close to 200,000 men in their assault on Ukraine – to which they would add conscripted forces from the LDNR after the invasion.

At the outset of the war the Ukrainian army had about 90,000 combat-ready deployed troops, mostly stationed along the line of control in Donbas. But the overall strength of all Ukraine's armed forces officially stood at 195,626 active-duty personnel. And over eight years of war in Donbas, a staggering 900,000 more men and women had fought on the front lines, making a vast reserve force with recent combat experience. In the first days of the war Ukraine announced general mobilisation, forbidding any men aged 18–60 from leaving the country and requiring them to register at their local draft offices. By April 2022, some 6,970,035 Ukrainian men aged 16 to 49 had been judged fit for military service, although unlike Russia there was no forcible conscription, as even in late September Kyiv reported sufficient willing volunteers. 'For a successful attack, by all the canons of the Infantry Staff regulations, you need a superiority 1 to 3,' according to Russian military analyst Yury Fedorov.'[4] Russia's invasion force of under 200,000 was nothing like enough men.

Foreign volunteers, too, would form a small but symbolically important part of the Ukrainian army. Even before the war, several dozen mostly military veterans from the UK, US, France and even Morocco served as regular soldiers. With the outbreak of war several hundred more – including, according to Zelensky's adviser Arestovich, a 250-strong force of dissident Russians – would travel to Ukraine to sign up.[5] Among those Russians was Igor Volobuyev, 50, a former vice president of Russia's Gazprombank, who fled a comfortable life as an executive in Moscow to fight for Ukraine. 'The moment war broke out, I knew right away I wanted to go and defend Ukraine,' said Volobuyev, dressed in Ukrainian military fatigues with the badge of the 'Freedom for Russia' legion, a special military unit that was part of the Ukrainian armed forces and made up entirely of Russian nationals. The unit's logo was a white–blue–white tricolour – the flag of Russia with the red band changed to white to remove the association with 'blood and violence', said Volobuyev, whose defection in late February caused shockwaves in the Russian business community. 'I made compromises with myself for a long time ... But on 24 February, any talk of compromise became impossible. I could not be part of this crime. Defeating Russia now is the only way to create a democratic, civilised country.'[6]

With Ukraine's forces concentrated along the 2015 line of control in Donbas, Russia's attacks on the relatively undefended northern border towards Kyiv, Sumy and Kharkiv seemed a sensible knock-out strategy. When it failed, the Russian army found itself – paradoxically – outnumbered by a defending force raised from a population a quarter of its size.

The most fundamental reason for the Russian army's initial failure was Putin's refusal to actually declare war on Ukraine. The Russian military, like its Soviet predecessor, is still primarily designed to fight an all-out land war against NATO. The effectiveness of its fighting capacity depended on conscripts who could be quickly trained to perform basic tasks – most crucially, as infantry support for armoured units. But on 8 March – International Women's Day – Putin publicly promised the 'mothers, wives, sisters, brides and girlfriends of our soldiers and officers' that conscripts 'do not and will not participate' in hostilities.[7] A day later, the Russian Ministry of Defence admitted that 'the presence of conscripts in some units of the Russian armed forces on the territory of Ukraine has come to light' – but added that 'almost all' these accidental soldiers had already returned home.[8] Even as the Russian advance stalled, Putin continued to refuse to declare the 'special military operation' a war, or to introduce general conscription.

The Russian army was essentially sent into war in Ukraine in its peacetime configuration. Almost without exception the Russian army's units were deliberately kept manned at only 70 per cent of their full official capacity in the expectation that the shortfall would be made up by conscripts in time of war. Russian conscripts were also not trained centrally but distributed to individual units for basic training by professional contract soldiers. So when the call to deploy for the Ukrainian campaign came, every unit of the Russian army not only had to make do without an influx of newly mobilised conscripts but also had to leave their currently serving conscripts behind. A Russian brigade had a hypothetical wartime strength of 3,500. At 70 per cent peacetime readiness that actually made only 2,450 men. Without conscripts, every unit was down to only around 1,715 contract soldiers.

The backbone all-arms unit of the Russian army was the Battalion Tactical Group, or BTG, five of which would form a brigade. Every BTG was meant to have 600 to 800 men – including motorised infantry riding in armoured vehicles, as well as tanks, artillery, support weapons and air defences. Of all the elements of the BTG, infantry was the most important. Their job was to protect tanks and take terrain. Without infantry, armoured vehicles and tanks would be blind and almost defenceless against modern anti-tank missiles like the Javelin and NLAW.

In the build-up to the war Putin's army massively increased its number of BTGs – but was failing to recruit the professional soldiers needed to man them. Hardware was not in short supply, soldiers were. But rather than admit failure to fulfil the Kremlin's orders to expand the military, army generals solved the problem by simply reducing the strength of units. Motorised rifle battalions shrank from between 461 and 539 personnel to around 345 on the eve of the war, according to the British defence source. Russia had indeed boosted the number of its BTGs – but only on paper.

The estimated 120 BTGs that attacked Ukraine all went in with their full complement of armour and support arms, but far from their full combat strength of men. And that shortfall – in wooded country like that outside Kyiv and urban areas such as the city's suburbs – made all the difference. A typical motor rifle platoon in the Russian army was designed to field three squads of seven men, each operating out of an infantry fighting vehicle. Each vehicle needed a commander, a driver and a gunner, leaving four men to dismount and act as actual boots – and, more importantly eyes, ears and rifles – on the ground. But without conscripts each platoon was left with perhaps two fighting infantrymen per vehicle. Some Ukrainian forces reported attacking Russian armoured vehicles manned by their three-man crew alone. 'With no dismountable men you've got a motorised infantry unit that doesn't have infantry,' said the British source. 'Everyone's stuck in their vehicles. You're not going to have situational awareness. You don't have the numbers to do common infantry tasks like stacking up [advancing to contact in single file], clearing buildings or providing security for an element.'[9]

The Russian army's personnel problem was only made worse by heavy losses of its most highly trained troops in the first days of the war. The blitzkrieg strategy of Putin's generals meant sending in elite airborne forces and naval infantry to accomplish high-risk shock operations like taking Hostomel airport. In the first weeks of the war over 150 BMD light infantry fighting vehicles – used exclusively by Russian airborne forces – were verifiably destroyed, a massively disproportional loss to that suffered by regular army units. Officer obituaries reported in the local Russian press also show an enormous casualty rate among airborne forces – Russia's best troops.

By April Moscow's generals had begun to deploy training battalions to replace their battlefield losses. Every Russian army brigade had a 'third battalion' made up of experienced trainers and their reserve vehicles stationed at their home base, devoted to training conscripts. According to Ukrainian radio intercepts and human intelligence, more and more such training units were spotted in Donbas. In theory the Russian army could muster an extra 30 or 40 BTGs manned exclusively by relatively experienced and capable trainers. But such a deployment would come at the cost of crippling Russia's long-term ability to replenish and train new men.

The supposed efficiency and modernity of the army into which Putin had poured so much money was also exposed as a sham. In August Pavel Filatyev, a Russian professional soldier published detailed testimony of his time with the 56th Guards Air Assault Regiment on VKontakte, Russia's Facebook. On joining the supposedly elite airborne unit, Filatyev found no beds in his barracks, and often no power or water. A pack of wild dogs roamed through the buildings. Nor was there enough food, just stale bread and 'soup' that was raw potatoes in water. On paper his unit had 500 soldiers, but it was really just 300. He had to buy his own winter uniform after being given summer clothes and boots in the wrong size. His rifle was rusty and jammed after a few shots, and he was deployed to Ukraine without a flak jacket, which he assumed had been stolen and sold off by his officers. He was driven to the front in a truck that was carrying mortar bombs but had no brakes. 'All this [equipment] is 100 years old, a lot is not working properly, but in [the officers'] reports everything was probably fine,' wrote Filatyev, who deserted from his unit and fled to France. 'The Russian army is a madhouse and everything is for show.'[10]

With the Kremlin standing firm against full mobilisation, the army pushed hard to maximise the regular peacetime conscription campaign, which traditionally took place in spring and autumn. A law hastily passed by the Duma in the first week of the war made it compulsory for every man of call-up age – 18 to 26 – to register with their local draft office without waiting for a summons, on pain of imprisonment. The result was a string of arson attacks across recruitment offices across Russia, at least 16 of which were torched in an apparent attempt to destroy paper records of local potential draftees.

The army also went on a campaign of what was dubbed 'shadow mobilisation'. Existing conscripts who had served at least three months came under violent pressure from their officers to sign up as contract soldiers. Reservists – men who had completed their year-long conscription in the military – were also summoned for compulsory training, during which they were offered large bounties to rejoin the army.

Sign-up bounties of $3,000 to $5,000 were offered – close to a year's average salary in Russia's poorest regions, which include ethnic minority republics. Such non-Russian regions were also, by no coincidence, massively over-represented in terms of disclosed Russian casualties. Dagestan, a Muslim area of the North Caucasus, led the number of officially reported deaths with 207 in the first four months of the war, with the Siberian republics of Buryatia (164) and Tuva (127) second and third – though the true numbers were far higher. By contrast a search of social media posts, local newspapers and official announcements by the independent Russian website Mediazona found that in the same period only eight soldiers came from Moscow and 26 from the second-largest city, St Petersburg.[11]

By September, after the Russian military had lost over 6,000 square kilometres of territory near Kharkiv to Ukrainian counter-attacks, it was clear that attempting to fight the war with an army of expendables, including mercenaries, colonial troops and even (as we will see) prisoners, had failed. On 21 September Putin announced a 'partial' mobilisation of 300,000 reservists with military experience, although undisclosed parts of the order leaked to *Nezavisimaya Gazeta* showed that the government actually planned to mobilise up to 1.2 million men.

The scenes of chaos and mass flight of March were repeated with increased urgency. In a week a quarter of a million Russian men – considerably more than the Kremlin assembled for its original invasion force – fled the country. People waited three days to cross the border into Georgia, before non-local cars were banned from entry into the neighbouring Russian republic of North Ossetia. Pop-up recruitment posts were set up by the Russian army at border crossings into Georgia and Finland to catch fleeing reservists. And, just as in March, air tickets out of Russia changed hands for fortunes. 'Will swap a Toyota Corolla for a one-way ticket to Istanbul,' was one Russian social media post a friend sent me. By coincidence, I was once again in Moscow and had bought a ticket to Turkey in the small hours of the morning before Putin's mobilisation announcement. The young man sitting next to me was one of a whole class of recent graduates of a Moscow architecture school who had been called up on the basis that they had all received some military training as a compulsory part of their course. 'I am one of the frogs who jumped out of the boiling water,' he told me. 'I will fight to defend my own country. But I won't fight to take someone else's.' Draft offices were subjected to a renewed wave of arson attacks, with one recruitment office head shot on 26 September in the Siberian town of Ust-Ilimsk.[12]

Pranksters posing as draft officers called Kremlin spokesman Dmitry Peskov's son, 32-year-old Nikolai, ordering him to report for a medical examination the following day. 'Obviously not!' an indignant Nikolai replied to the pranksters, according to a video shared online. 'You must understand it is not right for me to be there. I have to resolve this on a different level.' The key word was 'obviously'. The idea that the children of Russia's elite would actually serve their country, rifle in hand, was to them an impertinent and self-evident absurdity. By contrast, many of Ukraine's most famous dancers, footballers, TV stars, bloggers and politicians made it a point of pride to join up.

The Kadyrovtsy

Dagestanis, Tuvans and Buryats were not the only colonial forces at the forefront of Russia's order of battle. Several units of Chechens, both irregulars deployed as assassination squads at the beginning of the war and regular troops, fought at all the war's major fronts, from Hostomel to Mariupol.

Chechens are terrifying soldiers. Despite Stalin's efforts to crush them, Chechens preserved a super-macho warrior culture that stood them in good stead after the fall of the Soviet Union, when Chechen gangs became some of the most successful and notorious mafia groupings in post-Soviet Russia. It was Russia's bloody victory over Chechnya that made then-Prime Minister Vladimir Putin's career. But to take and hold Chechnya Putin used local proxies – notably Ahmad-Haji Kadyrov, the former Mufti or religious leader of the independent Chechen Republic of Ichkeria, who turned coat and joined the Russian side. After his assassination in 2004, his son Ramzan took over as Moscow's satrap in the former rebel republic, maintaining his power with a combination of a deluge of funds from the Kremlin and a reign of terror that saw thousands kidnapped, tortured and murdered.

Ramzan Kadyrov often referred to Putin as his 'second father'. In return Putin made Kadyrov a Hero of Russia and allowed him free rein to establish de facto Sharia law in his republic, restricting the sale and consumption of alcohol and persecuting homosexuals. The invasion of Ukraine gave Kadyrov a perfect opportunity to show both his loyalty to Putin – and the operational independence of his fighters. The fighting elite of Kadyrov's forces number around 12,000 men, a significant number of whom were mobilised both to the first assault on Kyiv and the southern push-out of rebel Donbas towards Mariupol. The Chechen forces – known as 'Kadyrovtsy', or Kadyrov's People – were superbly equipped with the latest tactical gear, including helmet mikes, knee-pads, Kevlar helmets and wraparound shades. Unlike the regular Russian forces, they made liberal use of their mobile phones, regularly posting slickly filmed videos on TikTok of extravagantly bearded fighters firing whole belts of ammo from their PKM machine guns into civilian buildings in Mariupol and saving Ukrainian children from the rubble.

The leader of the Kadyrovtsy in southern Ukraine was 52-year-old Adam Delimkhanov, an impressive white-bearded former Chechen rebel commander who switched sides with Ahmad Kadyrov and became a member of the Russian Duma in 2007. At the end of April 2022 Delimkhanov – wearing distinctive black tactical gear designed to contrast with his long snowy beard and a black flak jacket festooned with Motorola radios – featured in a triumphal video filmed in the burning ruins of Mariupol's Azovstal plant surrounded by a company of his men. 'The special operation to destroy and clear Mariupol has been completed,' Delimkhanov told viewers. 'President Vladimir Putin's orders have been fulfilled.'[13] The following day Delimkhanov, like both Kadyrovs, was also awarded a Hero of Russia medal by Putin.[14]

Chechen fighters were among the Russian-led forces who briefly held Hostomel airport. Ramzan Kadyrov even published a video in which he claimed to be among his men at Hostomel where he could be seen poring over maps with commanders in an underground bunker. Western intelligence sources discounted the video as fake, based on mobile-phone tracking information for members of Kadyrov's security team. But active participation in Putin's war was, for Kadyrov, a vital part of his public image, showing how a great power's military depended on his band of

Chechen fighters. In April Kadyrov launched an Arabic-language channel on Telegram, apparently to capitalise on that prominence, an ambitious move for the leader of a small, non-Arabic speaking Russian region.[15] And Kadyrov launched a major recruiting campaign, using sports stars and martial arts coaches to encourage volunteers – who were offered a sign-on bonus of about $2,300 and pay of $1,000 a month, with extra for successful operations, one recruiter said in text messages to a prospective young fighter.

Chechen fighters were implicated in some of the worst war crimes of the conflict. In April Ukraine's ombudsman for human rights Lyudmila Denisova accused Kadyrovtsy of shooting their own wounded comrades and 'operating a torture chamber' in the glass factory on Yablonska Street in the Kyiv commuter village of Bucha. Artem Hurin, a member of the city council of the neighbouring town of Irpin who also served as a deputy commander in Ukraine's Territorial Defence Forces, was one of the first to visit after Putin's soldiers retreated when Ukrainian forces recaptured the town on 2 April. Hurin recounted a litany of horrifying stories from residents who were tortured and raped by lawless Russian troops and saw evidence of 'executed civilians' who lay dead on the street – many by a squad of Chechen fighters who had begun executing people as early as 5 March. One woman recalled how she endured four days of torture by one Chechen and one Belarusian soldier before they brutally shot her husband in the head. Anatoliy Fedoruk, Mayor of Bucha, told reporters that Chechen troops had tied white bands around the arms of captured civilians, apparently marking them for execution. Many of the bodies of executed civilians in the town bore such white armbands.

The Donbas Troops

One of the largest sources of new recruits for the invading army came not from Russia itself but from the mass conscription of young men from the Donbas republics. Even before the 2022 invasion the DNR and LNR had, by their own account, 44,000 troops under arms – some 1.5 per cent of the approximately 3 million population of the republics. By peacetime standards, that mobilisation ratio was already enormously high – applied to other countries the US military would be 4.9 million strong and the Chinese 21 million. In mid-February, as the Donbas republics reported a supposed intensification of Ukrainian attacks (which were denied by Kyiv), DNR President Denis Pushilin went on television to announce a general mobilisation. In addition to reservists with military experience, the mobilisation would include all able-bodied men aged between 18 and 65. A number of medical exemptions from the draft were also scrapped. By some estimates the mass mobilisation could have raised an additional 60,000 men – meaning that the Donbas separatist republics had over 100,000 men in the field – equal to 60 per cent of the entire original deployed regular Russian force.

By late April former DNR Defence Minister Igor Girkin reported on Telegram that the Donbas republics had been 'swept clean' of men. Alexander Khodakovsky, a former Minister of Security of the DNR who commanded the DNR's Vostok unit during the battle for Mariupol, complained that 'troops with no background in the military' were being mobilised. 'What can you expect from a musician from the conservatory, hastily mobilised with no motivation and no idea about military affairs?' Khodakovsky asked on Telegram, admitting that inexperienced DNR troops deployed to hold defensive lines around Kharkiv had suffered heavy casualties.

Girkin, despite his history of close cooperation with Russian military intelligence, emerged as a bitter critic of the way Putin's war has been fought. Even during the heaviest fighting of the First World War the Imperial Russian Army would give called-up peasant troops minimal basic military training, said Girkin – who before starting a real war was a prominent military re-enactor specialising in that period. The DNR and LNR's new conscripts, by contrast, were being called up and 'thrown into battle' in the hope that 'they will learn everything themselves in a couple of days – if they survive'.[16] Many Donbas units – who unlike their more disciplined Russian counterparts were allowed to keep their personal mobile phones – posted photographs of rag-tag groups of men dressed in motley uniforms. Many of them carried five-shot, bolt-action Mosin M1891 rifles designed two decades before the First World War and retired from Russian army service in the late 1930s.

And unlike their Russian counterparts, DNR conscripts were not shy about using social media to vent their vociferous anger at being deployed on front lines far beyond their Donbas homes. On 28 March a video filmed in the back of a military truck full of young separatist soldiers was posted to Reddit. 'We're conscripts from Donbas,' said the soldier making the film as he panned around his 20 comrades. 'Ordinary fucking workers!' chimed in another. 'Kids! We're just fucking kids. We're civilians. Ordinary students!' shouted a third as the rest begans to interject their own angry comments. 'We found ourselves in Russia with guns!' 'They took 18-year-olds!' 'We're all up shit creek! What the fuck are we doing here! We're in Sumy [province, northern Ukraine] for some fucking reason.' 'There's a video on YouTube where our guys were taken prisoner. We've been betrayed.' 'Tons of our guys were killed.' 'Right: the Russian Defence Ministry has no idea what we are doing here. We were taken illegally into Russia. Take us back to Donbas! We're being sent in with Kalashnikovs against Grad [multiple rocket launchers], artillery, mortars. We're from [separatist Donetsk towns] Shakhtar, Torez, Snezhnoe. Fifteenth Division, Fourth Battalion. All Donbas – listen to us!! We've been abandoned. I ask you to share this video!'[17]

Khodakovsky claimed that inexperienced conscripts would usually be kept in safer rear areas. But Girkin repeatedly complained that 'expendable' LDNR infantry were being routinely sent forward by Russian commanders in repeated frontal attacks. Several Ukrainian military bloggers reported LDNR conscripts being used to draw fire so that the Russians or professional separatist troops could identify the location of the Ukrainian fire positions. In any case, it was likely that high casualties among the separatist units accounted for the extreme discrepancy between official Russian army death tolls and Ukrainian reports of enemy casualties. The young men of the LNR and DNR were a major source of cannon fodder for the war. The other was a group of veterans, poor young men and criminals recruited as mercenaries by the Kremlin's own private army.

Wagner

The Wagner Group, a private military company group, was founded in 2014 by Dmitry Utkin, a former lieutenant colonel in the GRU special forces. He had been accorded the personal radio call sign 'Wagner' during his service in the Spetznaz's 2nd Independent Brigade because of his passion for the Third Reich. Photographs published in 2021 showed that he sported a *Waffen*-SS collar tab and *Reichsadler* Nazi eagle tattoos on his neck and chest. Utkin's original brief was to recruit military veterans as deniable mercenary forces to fight alongside Donbas separatists. They first appeared on the battlefield in Luhansk in the summer of 2014, and went on to fight in Syria, Libya, the Central African Republic and Mali, often on the side of forces aligned with the Russian government. And as we have seen, Wagner mercenaries were redeployed to Kyiv as covert assassination squads in the run-up to the 2022 Russian invasion.

The group's links to the Russian security forces were direct and well documented. A key Wagner training base in the Stavropol region of south Russia was owned by the GRU. Wagner troops were transported by Russian military aircraft and used Russia's military health care services – and passports were also issued to its members by the Russian state.[18] The initial funding was believed to have come from Yevgeny Prigozhin, a millionaire caterer from St Petersburg with close links to Putin. Though Prigozhin officially denied links with Wagner, by the summer of 2022 his face appeared on the company's recruiting posters all over the Russian provinces.

Wagner's mass-recruiting efforts proceeded in parallel – and in competition with – the official 'shadow mobilisation' conducted by the Russian army. But thanks to the background of its founder and many of its members, Wagner was able to reach out to groups of angry and violent potential soldiers that the Kremlin had been unable to reach. According to a May 2022 report by Germany's Federal Intelligence Service, leaked by *Der Spiegel*, Wagner extensively recruited Russian right-wing extremists and neo-Nazis. Among them was the Wagner 'sabotage and assault reconnaissance unit' Rusich, whose symbol was a pagan Slavic version of the Nazi Black Sun and whose co-founder Alexei Milchakov was infamous for YouTube videos of himself chopping the head off a puppy. 'I'm not going to go deep and say, I'm a nationalist, a patriot, an imperialist, and so forth,' Milchakov said in a December 2020 video. 'I'll say it outright: I'm a Nazi.' Another was the Russian Imperial Movement, a white supremacist group that was designated a 'global terrorist organization' by the United States two years ago.

In July 2022 the Wagner group was authorised to recruit prisoners from Russian jails. Yevgeny Prigozhin was filmed arriving at several Russian prison colonies in a helicopter and addressing groups of hundreds of black-uniformed convicts. Wagner's offer was unbeatable – a full reprieve for crimes up to and including murder in exchange for six months' service. 'I have 11 more years to spend in jail,' one prisoner who heard Prigozhin's pitch at penal colony No 8, in the Tambov region 300 miles south of Moscow, told the *Guardian*. 'Either I die in this shithole or I die there, it doesn't matter that much. At least I'll have a chance to fight for my freedom. We all compare it to Russian roulette.' Another Wagner recruit was Ivan Neparatov, who had served 13 years of a 25-year prison term for murdering three people who owed him money. Neparatov had also persuaded a neighbour to drive him into the house of a businesswoman in his hometown of Sergiev Posad, where he robbed and strangled the woman and stabbed the neighbour 88 times for good measure. Neparatov joined up with Wagner in early summer but was killed by a Ukrainian shell. Posthumously, he was awarded Russia's 'For Merit to the Fatherland' medal for his service. According to Olga Romanova, head of prisoners' rights NGO Jailed Russia, about 11,000 Russian prisoners had signed up to go to Ukraine by early September, a number that she said was growing rapidly.[19]

In one sense, Wagner's intensive prison recruitment campaign was undoubtedly a symptom of the Russian army's desperation. But it was also significant in another, less obvious way. By recruiting thieves and murderers, poor kids from distant provinces and troops from remote ethnic-minority republics, the Kremlin was also signalling that it wanted to keep the war on a low-key footing. Keeping casualties to an army of expendables reduced the chances of a popular backlash. And even when Putin announced in late September that he would be mobilising Russia's 300,000 military reservists, he was at pains to emphasise that 'we are not talking about people who know nothing of the military ... students will continue to study without disturbance.' In practice, that caveat was ignored and call-up papers rained down on men with no military experience at all. Nonetheless, for the opening six months of the war, Wagner fulfilled two important purposes: to provide fighting men for the front lines, but also to do so from parts of society where their deaths would be least politically inconvenient.

The Russian Steamroller

By the middle of May 2022 the war was concentrated into two desperate battles – for the Azovstal steel plant in Mariupol in the south and the twin towns of Severodonetsk and Lysychansk in the east. Putin had already declared victory in Mariupol on 20 April after the last civilians had been evacuated under the auspices of the UN from the complex of bunkers under the steel plant. Many of the Ukrainian regular army soldiers surrendered. Putin called off the full-frontal attack on the plant and ordered the remaining defenders be sealed off 'so tightly that even a fly cannot get through'.[20] But a few hundred dogged defenders, mostly members of the Azov Regiment that had become Russian propaganda's symbol of Ukrainian 'Nazism', held on. Extraordinary photographs taken by the last defenders showed the vast machine halls of the steelworks reduced to a post-apocalyptic cascade of twisted metal and blasted machinery. Underground, the remaining defenders inhabited a nightmarish labyrinth of underground passages, bunkers and storerooms as medicine and food dwindled. Finally on 17 May the remaining 211 able-bodied soldiers and 260 wounded walked out of the shattered factory and into brutal captivity in a prison in Olenivka in the DNR. Two months later 53 of the prisoners would be killed in an explosion that the DNR authorities claimed was a Ukrainian missile strike – but which Kyiv called a deliberate act of mass murder in order to eliminate evidence of torture.

As early as 10 May, US Defense Intelligence Agency Director Scott Berrier declared the war 'at a bit of a stalemate', with neither side making advancements in the south or east. Yet the Russian steamroller ground on, concentrating its forces on the last corner of Luhansk province still in Ukrainian hands. In an attempt to outflank Severodonetsk – the 'second capital' of Donbas – Russian National Guard and Army units repeatedly tried to cross the Siverskyi Donets River using pontoon bridges. Over three days between 6 and 8 May, successive columns of Russian armoured personnel carriers were systematically destroyed by Ukrainian artillery and helicopters.[21]

The operation to cross the Siverskyi Donets River was meant to be a joint operation between the regular military and the newer, paramilitary National Guard, whose primary role was not combat but quelling civil disobedience. But it was Russia's National Guard, or Rosgvardia, that bore the brunt of the casualties from the Siverskyi Donets disaster. The Rosgvardia's commander Viktor Zolotov, a former bodyguard to Vladimir Putin, was personally humiliated and furious that an operation supposed to showcase his men's ability in the field had ended in bloody defeat. According to a source who had close business ties to a senior *silovik*, what happened next became legendary in government circles. Zolotov stormed into a military planning meeting soon after the massacre and squared up to Defence Minister Sergei Shoigu, whom he apparently blamed for falsely giving the green light to repeated assaults though the Ukrainian threat had not yet been eliminated. 'Enough lying!' Zolotov shouted at Shoigu, according to the source – and then punched Shoigu in the face.[22] Though the story could not be independently confirmed, if true it showed both a level of frustration and a corrosive blame-game over the frustrating lack of progress on the battlefield.

Unable to outflank the Ukrainians, the Russian military reverted to type, bombarding Severodonetsk into rubble. By the end of May Luhansk's Ukrainian governor Serhiy Haidai reported that 90 per cent of the city's buildings had been destroyed. Zelensky also admitted that between 50 and 100 Ukrainian soldiers were being killed every day. But it was only a month later, on 29 June, that the Ukrainians finally pulled back from Severodonetsk and its twin town of Lysychansk, leaving the Russians to occupy empty, depopulated ruins.[23]

The grinding artillery duel over Severodonetsk was so intense that at the height of the battle Britain's Ministry of Defence estimated that Russian artillery was firing 20,000 shells a day. Ukraine's military said that it was using some 5,000–6,000 rounds daily, nearly exhausting its own supplies of Soviet-standard 152mm artillery ammunition, and making Kyiv reliant on the West for resupply. Drone footage of the area around the destroyed cities showed fields completely covered with shell craters in images reminiscent of the Western Front (though the rate of fire was still hardly comparable to the 1.5 million shells fired by the British on the first day of the Battle of the Somme). But Russia's choice of relentless artillery battery over a frontal mechanised assault with tanks and troops was itself highly telling. Taking an urban area by force required well-trained and, above all, highly motivated troops. The six-week-long siege of Severodonetsk was 'clear evidence', according to a senior Western military source who was following the war in detail in Kyiv, 'that the Russians are running out of men ... and don't trust the ones they have to do the job'.[24]

The First World War analogy was accurate not only in terms of the savage trench and artillery tactics of the battle for Donbas but in another vital aspect. The stalemate on the ground was about to be broken by an intervention by the United States not of men, but of game-changing military materiel.

Lend-Lease

On 9 May 2022 Joe Biden signed 'An Act ... to lend or lease defense articles to [the Ukrainian] Government to protect civilian populations in Ukraine from Russian military invasion, and for other purposes'. The bill had been passed days earlier with a massive 417–10 majority in the US Congress. The date was highly symbolic. 9 May was the day on which the USSR celebrated its victory over Nazi Germany – a victory that had been made possible by a massive programme of military assistance from America. Except this time Lend-Lease was being extended to Moscow's opponents, symbolically casting Russia in the role of the Third Reich.

In total, the 2022 US Lend-Lease assistance package to Ukraine would amount to a staggering $55 billion – almost as much as Russia's entire annual military budget. True, much of the money was earmarked to come directly back to US military contractors and to the US military itself. But hundreds of millions were to pay for direct and immediate supplies of deadly offensive arms to Ukraine's military.

But there was an important caveat from Washington's side. Putin's 27 February nuclear threat was not forgotten, nor was the Chinese warning that NATO should avoid direct involvement in the conflict. And though the early March deal between Washington and Beijing over the Polish MiGs was never formally renewed, the understanding that China would hold back on arming Russia as long as the US and NATO held back from full involvement in Ukraine was clearly understood by both new superpowers.

On 10 May – the day after the signature of Lend-Lease – the US and Russian Defence Ministers Lloyd Austin and Sergei Shoigu spoke by phone.[25] A key talking point of Austin's was, according to a UK source who was briefed on the conversation, to reassure Shoigu that the US was not about to enter the war and that aid should not be construed as a military attack on Russia.[26]

The US held back supplying Kyiv with arms that could strike inside Russia – such as MLRS systems that fired missiles with a 185-mile range. Russian propagandists denounced American aid as an act of naked aggression and Dmitry Peskov called sending weapons into a war zone 'pouring fuel on the fire'. But that was for public consumption. Inside the Kremlin, Washington's forbearance was noted. Former Russian President Dmitry Medvedev, despite reinventing himself as an arch-hawk, pronounced the US decision to hold back on long-range weapons 'reasonable'.[27]

The weapons that the US did send, though, would nonetheless be game-changing: highly accurate 155mm NATO-standard field artillery capable of firing GPS-guided, rocket-assisted shells and M142 High Mobility Artillery Rocket Systems (HIMARS). Over 100 M777 howitzers delivered by the US in early May had already helped make a vital difference to the battle for the Siverskyi Donets River. The key tactical difference was not so much the howitzers themselves but the variety of state-of-the-art rocket-propelled, satellite-guided artillery that they could fire. Costing up to $46,000 for a single round, some of the shells were accurate to 2.86 metres at a distance of 40 kilometres, according to Raytheon missile systems vice president James Riley.[28] In effect, the M777s turned every round into a miniature cruise missile, honing in with extraordinary precision on a specific target visible to the gunners in real time on a tablet screen.

HIMARS rockets were equally accurate, but with a longer range of 80 kilometres and carrying a much larger warhead. On 28 June Ukrainians used HIMARS to strike the Russian garrison on Snake Island – 20 kilometres off the Ukrainian coast by the Romanian border – that controlled the sea approaches to Odesa. It had been Snake Island's Ukrainian defenders who had sent the famous message of defiance to the cruiser *Moskva*. The Russian troops withdrew overnight in speedboats, allowing the Ukrainian army to claim a highly symbolic victory in the morning. Not only had the 'Russian warship' fucked off – to the bottom of the sea – but the Russian occupiers of Snake Island had as well.

CHAPTER 11

THE PRICE OF ILLUSION

There's lots of talk of off ramps. We want to close the off ramps and help Putin accelerate into the brick wall into which he is headed.

US Army Lieutenant General H. R. McMaster, 5 April 2022[1]

Economic Blitzkrieg

One of the main planks of the Kremlin's messaging, both to the Russian people and to the rest of the world, was that the Russian economy was shrugging off sanctions. 'The economic blitzkrieg against Russia never had any chances of success,' Putin told an audience at the St Petersburg Economic Forum in June that included no regional leaders apart from Belarus's Aleksandr Lukashenko – but did include a delegation from the Taliban. 'Like our ancestors, we will solve any problem; the entire thousand-year history of our country speaks of this ... Gloomy predictions about the Russian economy's future have not come true.'[2]

Russia's Ministry of Economics put out the superficially logical line that though exports of both oil and gas were down, rising prices more than compensated for the reduction. Many Western commentators bought it. As late as June 2022 Bloomberg reported that 'even with some countries halting or phasing out energy purchases, Russia's oil and gas revenue will be about $285 billion this year … That would exceed the 2021 figure by more than one fifth.'[3] Quoting those numbers, respected columnist Fareed Zakaria concluded in *The Washington Post* that 'it is now clear that the economic war against Russia is not working nearly as well as people thought it would … the Russian government will make considerably more revenue from oil and gas than it did before the war.'[4]

In fact the Russian government's statistics were a carefully concocted lie, falsely projecting relatively stable March figures on the future and, as key economic indices slid, cherry-picking numbers to conceal the true scale of the economic damage. The major study published in July by the Yale School of Management into the real impact of sanctions on the Russian economy looked past a wall of obfuscation by Russia's Ministry of Economics and used real-world data from retailers, energy traders and investors to reveal a picture very different from the rosy image presented by Putin.[5] The reality was that by May total monthly Russian oil and gas revenues had dropped to $14.9 billion, less than half earned in the first month after the invasion.[6]

Some Western commentators latched onto the apparent stability of the ruble (which after an early plunge soon returned to pre-war levels) and the relative health of the Russian stock market (the benchmark MOEX Russia Stock Index was down a mere 50 per cent) as evidence that Russia's economy was riding out sanctions relatively unscathed. In truth, both of those indicators have been deliberately manipulated. According to new rules introduced by the Central Bank in March, any company in Russia receiving income in foreign currency was forced to convert 80 per cent of it to rubles, skewing the market in the ruble's favour. Gazprom also forced its Western customers to pay for their gas in rubles – which in practice merely meant that they had to open ruble accounts at the few Russian banks that had escaped sanctions and formally convert their hard-currency payments into rubles before the contract was considered settled. In Moscow, only a fraction of pre-war volumes of rubles were actually traded, and then most were notional dollars, unbacked by actual hard-currency reserves.

As for the stock market, the reality is that foreign shareholders from 'unfriendly countries' (i.e. the West) were barred from closing out their positions – effectively keeping the market in a state of suspended animation. As Russian economist and Renaissance Capital founder Andrei Movchan pointed out, the suspension of normal stock trading effectively reduced the equity value of Russian stocks if not to zero, then 'to an unknowable value no longer determined by the market'. Functionally, shares were traded at a 30–40 per cent discount from their notional market value – which had already fallen by half. And since many companies relied on their own stock as collateral against loans, that meant that a large proportion of Russia's privately owned companies were, for all practical purposes, functionally bankrupt – along with all Russian banks that had lent against the value of Russian-listed stocks. That left 'the state as the lender of last resort', said Movchan – the only source of capital in a country cut off from international financial systems. And while the Kremlin could in theory print as much money as it wished, in practice the Russian economy remained far too reliant on imported equipment, technology, consumer goods and foreign expertise to prevent catastrophic inflation. 'When you create too much money you risk the Zimbabwe option [of hyper-inflation]', said Movchan. The value of the ruble, whether the Kremlin likes it or not, 'is still relative to [Russia's] imports'.[7]

In the first two months of the war well over 1,200 Western companies closed down their operations in Russia. The value of the Russian revenue represented by these companies and the value of their investments in Russia together exceeded $600 billion – and their departure 'almost single-handedly reversed three decades' worth of Russian economic integration' with the rest of the world, while 'undoing years of foreign investment into Russia', according to the Yale report. These foreign companies employed some 5 million Russians directly and up to 8 million indirectly.[8] Some of these workers found new jobs in clone businesses set up by new Russian owners. One was the *Vkusno i Tochka* ('Tasty and that's it') chain set up on the old premises of McDonald's, using the same equipment and offering a similar menu. Another was the Stars Coffee chain founded by the rapper Timati – best known for his hit song 'Putin Is My Best Friend' – which took over Starbucks' cafes and used a near-identical logo.[9] But millions found themselves out of a job – leaving the state little choice but to create new jobs in the public sector.

Ever since the Crimean annexation of 2014 and the Western sanctions that followed, the Kremlin had striven to make Russia's economy, and in particular its manufacturing sector, independent of imports and therefore immune to future sanctions. The first post-Crimea economic mantra was 'import substitution' – the concept that somehow Russia could survive and thrive without importing goods, services or talent from the West. The second was 'technological sovereignty' – the theory that Russia could create its own technologies, from mobile-phone transmitters to gas turbines, which would match Western ones.

Both initiatives failed. When the EU and US hit Russia with a full shutdown of the import of foreign parts, software and especially computer chips in 2022, the effect on Russia's economy was crippling. By the end of May, Russian car production had fallen by over 75 per cent. Russian gross domestic value added indicators fell by 62 per cent in the construction sector, 55 per cent in agriculture and 25 per cent in manufacturing. Russian manufacturers – including the arms industry – were forced to cannibalise and recycle parts.[10] By the end of March, Uralvagonzavod – Russia's largest tank factory, based in Nizhny Tagil – was forced to suspend production of T-72B3 tanks due to a lack of processors, according to Ukrainian intelligence.[11] 'We have reports from Ukrainians that when they find Russian military equipment on the ground, it's filled with semiconductors that they took out of dishwashers and refrigerators,' US Commerce Secretary Gina Raimondo said in May.[12] Aeroflot, Russia's flag carrier, was forced to ground some 40 per cent of its aircraft in order to use existing aircraft parts to continue servicing its remaining fleet – even though Boeing and Airbus had cut off all support and service and issued warnings that cannibalised aircraft were not safe for operation. 'All planes immediately stopped getting software updates,' one Kremlin-connected businessman complained to journalist Yevgenia Albats. '[So we] ask a young man with a black briefcase to come in and hack the software.'[13]

Officially, the Russia Consumer Price Index indicated a post-war inflation rate of around 20 per cent. But the real inflation figures in import-dependent sectors such as technology, hospitality and automobiles were, according to market research by major retailers, running between 48 and 61 per cent. Each day of the war cost Russian taxpayers about $500 million. In July Russian Finance Ministry statistics showed a federal budget deficit of 892 billion rubles, a year-on-year drop of 22.5 per cent in oil and gas revenues despite high energy prices, and a nearly 30 per cent drop in revenue from tax collection. The expected loss of GDP by the end of 2022 year was estimated at 8 per cent, with a further contraction of the economy over the course of a year and a half or two years.[14]

To cover the deficit, Russia's money supply doubled from February to June and Russian foreign-exchange reserves declined by $75 billion in the first six months of the war. Finance Minister Anton Siluanov admitted in July that by the end of the war the Russian government budget would likely be in deficit by an amount equivalent to 2 per cent of Russian GDP – a gap that he suggested closing by withdrawing fully a third of Russia's National Wealth Fund.[15]

So sanctions were undoubtedly hurting the Russian economy. But were they working? It depended on how you defined their purpose. In March Biden announced that sanctions were intended to 'inflict damage that rivals military might' to 'sap Russian strength' and to ensure that Russia 'would never be able to threaten its neighbours again'. By that measure, sanctions certainly seemed to have been effective in depleting the Kremlin's war machine. By the end of August Moscow was buying artillery shells from North Korea and drones from Iran, and had withdrawn aircraft, rockets and personnel from its military mission in Syria.

But were sanctions likely to erode Putin's power, or change his behaviour? Biden claimed that was never the point. 'I did not say that in fact the sanctions would deter him,' Biden told a NATO summit in March. 'Sanctions never deter.'[16] That was frankly disingenuous. According to a former White House official who was instrumental in drafting the first round of sanctions in 2014, a major part of the Biden team's strategy was 'to drive a wedge between the *siloviki* in the Kremlin and Russia's business class'. Admittedly, that strategy had not worked between 2014 and 2022 – but the principle that 'there is a contract between Putin and the [business] elite that they stay out of politics and he allows them to get rich' remains, the official stated.[17]

Some wealthy Russians did indeed flock to safe havens as sanctions bit. According to the Yale survey, some 15,000 – or 20 per cent – of Russia's high net worth individuals, defined as people worth more than $30 million, left the country. Despite restrictions, capital transfers out of Russia jumped from $22 billion in the first quarter of 2022 to over $70 billion in the second, by the Central Bank's own figures. Dubai real estate firms reported 100 per cent and even 200 per cent year-on-year increases in sales to buyers from Russia.[18] But these statistics can also be read the other way: 80 per cent of wealthy Russians remained. Most had no choice – their business interests were too closely tied to Russia, and to the Russian state, to make exile a rational choice.

The mood among the dozen or so wealthy Russian businesspeople I spoke to in Moscow in the months after the invasion was one of more or less stoical resignation – 'What can we do about it?' and 'It will all blow over' – combined with a deep and often furious anger directed not at the Kremlin but at the West. 'Those lickspittles [in Europe] were very happy to take my money and kiss my ass,' said the head of a major Russian technology importation firm who owned properties in Italy and London. He was not personally on any sanctions list but had nonetheless found his European bank accounts frozen simply because he was Russian. 'What happened to their rule of law and respect for private property?' Europe and the US 'has decided that we are all criminals, and must suffer for the crimes of one freak [Putin]', railed a St Petersburg-based telecoms magnate. 'They want us to sit here in Russia. Fine. We'll sit here, with our own.'

The Kremlin was accused of applying its own standards in its dealings with foreign countries – for instance its assumption that Zelensky and the Kyiv elite were venal and easily corrupted. But the West, too, seemed to assume that Russians would react like Europeans or Americans to the prospect of economic hardship – by blaming their leaders and demanding change. However, Russia's reality was very different. For one, economic crises – some worse than the 2022 sanctions-driven slump – had occurred within recent memory, from the hyperinflation of 1992–93 to the collapse of the ruble in 1997, 2008 and 2014. For most urban Russians, living something like a prosperous, European, middle-class life where Ikea, Starbucks and Zara were things to be taken for granted was something relatively recent. For the Russians who lived on or below the average wage of £802 a month – or the 14 per cent of the country who lived below the poverty line of £120 – the loss of luxury stores in Moscow or the price of imported electronics made little difference.[19]

More important, for the majority of Russians and for their government, was a clear sense that their sufferings were for a good cause. 'What do we live for, as Russians?' asked TV anchor Vladimir Solovyov in late August. 'Not for McDonald's or for Kentucky Fried Chicken. The purpose of our life is to stand up for truth, for what is right. To defend our brothers with our living bodies when they attacked by fascist scum.'[20] The constant message on Kremlin-controlled TV channels was that the West was facing economic devastation as a result of sanctions. 'People accustomed to false patriotic rhetoric can remain silent for decades. [The] limits of patience of ordinary citizens ... have not been really tested yet,' wrote economist Valery Kizilov of Moscow's Financial Research Institute in an influential essay part-titled 'Why Russians don't notice the economic crisis'. 'At the level of the highest Russian authorities, [this] cannot be called an outright crisis. The official view is that the economies of the opposing countries are suffering much more. In this sense, the regime has returned to the stagnant rhetorical models of the late 1970s and early 1980s.' Russia faced 'not collapse, but decay'.[21]

Perhaps the most telling sign that the Kremlin feared neither a backlash from the elite nor from the people over economic decline was Putin's decision to gamble Russia's main economic ace – Europe's dependence on Gazprom – in an attempt to gain political advantage.

Gas versus Guns

By early autumn 2022, it had become clear that the endgame of the Ukrainian war would be a battle between gas and guns. As Western-supplied weapons battered Russian positions on the ground, a gas cut-off by Russia battered European consumers with soaring energy prices and the worst cost-of-living crisis in a generation.

In 2021 Russian gas accounted for some 45 per cent of the EU's gas imports. Germany, Europe's biggest economy, was most dependent of all on Gazprom – and generations of its leaders had been instrumental in increasing that dependence. The logic had not been entirely irrational. Former German Chancellor Gerhard Schröder (who would join the board of the Nord Stream pipeline and of the Russian state oil giant Rosneft after stepping down in 2005) argued that German dependence on Russian gas equalled Russian dependence on German money. More economic integration would make for a more stable relationship between Europe and Moscow.

The moral hazard inherent in that equation became apparent after the Russian annexation of Crimea in 2014. As we have seen, instead of cancelling the planned Nord Stream 2 pipeline – and in defiance of strong US pressure – Schröder's successor Angela Merkel green-lit the €10 billion, Gazprom-financed project.

At a NATO summit in Brussels in July 2018, US President Donald Trump complained that 'we're supposed to be guarding against Russia and Germany goes out and pays billions and billions of dollars a year to Russia ... Germany is totally controlled by Russia, [because] they are getting 60 to 70 percent of their energy from Russia and a new pipeline ... I think that's very inappropriate.'[22] Trump's warnings were roundly ignored – and when he made a similar point at the UN General Assembly, German delegates openly laughed and scoffed.

Europe's gas Achilles heel was clearly apparent as Brussels prepared sanctions against Putin in the wake of his 2022 invasion of Ukraine. The sanctions included banking and export restrictions, and even an oil embargo to be enforced from December 2022. But they did not include gas – rendering the sanctions essentially toothless. In fact, Europe had become more dependent on Russian gas than it had been in 2014. Key EU energy-consuming nations had become politically fixated with green-energy agendas that meant the closure of coal-fired power stations, scrapping plans for hydraulic fracturing ('fracking') and, in Germany, closing nuclear power stations. Natural gas – which emits fewer pollutants and less carbon dioxide per unit of energy – was embraced as a semi-green stopgap until renewables such as wind and solar power could make up the gap left by coal and nuclear.

Gas was Russia's most powerful weapon in its diplomatic war to undermine Europe's political and military support for Ukraine. But instead of using escalating threats, over the summer of 2022 Putin simply cut supplies – not only effectively sanctioning himself but also giving Europe months of warning to prepare for winter gas shortages. From June onwards Gazprom cut off Poland, Latvia, Lithuania and Finland, and reduced the gas flow to Germany via the Nord Stream 1 pipeline by 40 per cent, ostensibly because a crucial set of gas turbines sent for repair by Siemens Energy in Canada had been sanctioned.

The immediate effect was, as Putin had hoped, panic. As Robert Habeck, Germany's Economy Minister, put it in July, a complete cut-off of Russian gas would be his country's 'nightmare scenario'. Under pressure from Berlin and the International Energy Agency, and ignoring Ukrainian objections, the Ottawa government lifted sanctions measures on the turbines. Canada's Minister of Natural Resources Jonathan Wilkinson justified the decision by claiming that 'our European friends and allies' needed to retain their 'access [to] reliable and affordable energy as they continue to transition away from Russian oil and gas'.[23]

In mid-July – the lowest gas-consumption month – German gas storage capacity stood at 63 per cent, far short of the goal of 90 per cent by 1 November. Contingency plans were put in place prioritising access to electricity and gas in case of serious cuts, with hospitals and emergency services top of the list, then households, then industrial concerns. Local authorities across Germany drew up plans to shut swimming pools, turn off street lamps and traffic lights, and repurpose industrial-scale dormitories designed for coronavirus patients as 'warm rooms' or 'warmth islands'.

Meanwhile demand for electric and oil heaters, infrared panels and camping stoves soared, and installers of wood-burning stoves and heat pumps reported long waiting lists and a chronic lack of parts and qualified personnel.[24] Klaus Müller, Germany's energy regulator, said gas prices for consumers might triple by 2023. And former German ambassador to London Thomas Matussek warned that 'if push comes to shove, we are probably entering the biggest economic crisis that Germany has experienced since the end of the Second World War.'[25]

In September the Kremlin announced that Nord Stream 1 would remain closed indefinitely for technical reasons – which would not be resolved until 'the collective West' lifted sanctions on Russia. Only Putin-friendly Hungary was still getting its full supply via older overland pipelines through Belarus.

Except the feared meltdown didn't happen. Europe – and Germany in particular – proved far more nimble in finding alternative sources of energy than Putin had expected. On the eve of the invasion Europe did indeed import some 46 per cent of its gas from Russia. But it also received 25 per cent from Norway via pipelines and 29 per cent in the form of liquid natural gas (LNG) from the US, Algeria and Qatar. Europe's imports of LNG ramped up with surprising rapidity. In January 2022 Europe was importing just over 4 billion cubic metres (bcm) of American LNG a month versus just under 8 bcm in piped gas from Russia (already a historically low figure, thanks to the introduction of renewables). But by the end of June imports of US LNG alone had increased by nearly 50 per cent to 5.5 bcm – compared with reduced Russian supplies of 4.5 bcm. German engineers rushed to build floating terminals that would double its LNG import capacity by November 2022. It was not enough to fully compensate for the near-complete cut-off of Russian supplies, but by 1 September German storage capacity was already 80 per cent full. More importantly, the country's politically powerful Green Party had acknowledged that political realities trumped climate goals and agreed to the reopening of coal-fired power stations and suspending the closure of the country's three remaining nuclear power stations.

Instead of bullying Berlin into submission, Putin's attempt at blackmail in fact alienated his most powerful one-time European ally. 'We must stop self-deception that we ever received cheap gas from Russia,' said German Foreign Minister Annalena Baerbock on 28 August. 'We might not have paid a lot of money for it but we paid for it with safety and independence. And Ukrainians already paid for it with thousands of lives.'[26]

For Russia, weaponising gas supplies was more than risky – it was the diplomatic equivalent of strapping on a suicide vest. On 1 September, when Gazprom announced its second 'temporary' shutdown of Nord Stream 1 since the invasion, the wholesale price of gas in Europe actually dropped by 21 per cent from 405p per therm to 320p, as the European Commission confirmed it was working on 'emergency measures' and the German government said it was 'prepared' for the winter.[27]

Russia 'is trying to attack with poverty and political chaos where it cannot yet attack with missiles', Zelensky said after news of the Nord Stream shutdown broke – as Germany announced a €65 billion (£56 billion) package of help for struggling consumers.[28] Weeks later, new British Prime Minister Liz Truss announced a state-funded energy price cap worth up to £100 billion to protect the economy from the price shock. But with wholesale gas prices up ten times on the previous year, energy bills soaring across the continent and inflation in the Baltic states topping 20 per cent, political unrest looked inevitable. In early September, over 70,000 protesters in Prague took to the streets to protest against their government's support for Ukraine. But the Europe-wide political crisis that the Kremlin had hoped for did not result in mass demands to capitulate to Moscow and resume business as usual. On the contrary, despite the economic pain, Europe's leaders resolved to move permanently away from reliance on Russian gas. On 5 September German Chancellor Scholz said Russia was 'no longer a reliable energy partner'. And EU Council President Charles Michel said that Russia's 'use of gas as a weapon will not change the resolve of the EU ... We will accelerate our path towards energy independence. Our duty is to protect our citizens and support the freedom of Ukraine.'[29]

The prospect of Europe breaking free from its dependence on Russian gas represented a strategic catastrophe for Russia. If the continent were to succeed in finding alternative sources of energy, Putin will have permanently blown up a source of income that accounted for over a third of Russia's overall energy exports, lost its largest gas export market and lost forever the political leverage over Europe built up over decades. On 26 September that destruction of Russia's energy relationship with Europe look literal form as four underwater explosions cracked both Nord Stream 1 and 2, causing the Baltic Sea to boil with kilometre-wide gas leaks as the estimated 300 million cubic meters of gas in each pipe bubbled to the surface. Putin claimed in a televised speech at a Kremlin ceremony to mark the annexation of four Russian-occupied areas of Ukraine that 'the West ... has switched to sabotage'. But according to Swedish, Danish and UN investigators, by far the most likely culprit was Russia itself. If true, the destruction of Russia's €23 billion Nord Stream pipelines was one of the most extraordinary acts of self-harm in the history of warfare, akin to Hernán Cortés demolishing (not, in fact, burning) his ships on landing in the New World in 1519. The blowing up of Nord Stream could have been meant as a threat to the West that Russia could do the same with a newly opened Norway–Denmark pipeline. Or it could, like the 1939 attack by German soldiers in Polish uniforms on the Gleiwitz radio station, have been intended as a false-flag operation to create a spurious justification for Russia's annexation of parts of Ukraine. Either way, the Nord Stream attack marked a point of no return for the war's endgame. Whatever deal would be eventually reached, a return to cheap Russian gas for Europe could now never happen.

But Putin was lining up – or so he imagined – a plan B: to export Russia's gas to China instead. In a video meeting with top energy and economy officials in April 2022, Putin admitted that 'Western countries' attempts to push out Russian suppliers and to replace our energy resources with alternative supplies will inevitably affect the global economy as a whole.' He claimed that 'the consequences of [sanctions] may be extremely painful, primarily for the initiators of the policy' and emphasised that it was essential for Russia 'to redirect our exports gradually to the rapidly growing markets of the south and the east. To achieve this, we must determine the key infrastructure facilities and start their construction in the near future.'[30]

But Putin's plans for a *povorot na vostok*, or pivot to the east, made little economic or practical sense. In February 2022 Russia exported 83 per cent of its gas, or 170 bcm, to Europe, 12 per cent to former Soviet states and just 2 per cent, or 12.5 bcm, to China. In autumn 2022 the westernmost Russian gas field with a pipeline connection to China was Chayanda, some 2,400 kilometres directly north of Beijing. Chayanda's maximum projected annual capacity was just 25 bcm – and then only by 2025. Connecting Chayanda to China was the Power of Siberia 1 pipeline, built between 2014 and 2019 at a cost of $45 billion and wholly financed by Russian banks. The massive cost, plus generous tax breaks offered to the Chinese, made the pipeline unprofitable – as Russian Deputy Minister of Energy Yuri Sentyurin admitted in April 2015 when he said that the Power of Siberia was 'not about investing in a project which has to pay off its costs'.[31] Other pipelines currently under construction will link Power of Siberia 1 westwards to the Kovytka field and eastwards to gas fields in Sakhalin and Khabarovsk via the Amur gas processing plant – which has a maximum capacity of 39 bcm annually, equating to about 9 per cent of China's annual gas consumption. That means that even at its maximum future capacity, Power of Siberia 1 can pump less than a single one of Russia's Europe-bound pipelines, the 55 bcm Nord Stream 1.[32] Furthermore, long-term gas contracts negotiated with the Chinese in 2019 were based on low, pre-crisis pricing.

The only way that Russia could come close to replacing its lost European customers would be through a projected 50 bcm-per-year Power of Siberia 2 pipeline that would link the Yamal peninsula in the Arctic to China via 2,800 kilometres of pipe running across the entirety of Siberia and Mongolia. But that so far remains a plan on paper. And who would finance it? Not the internationally sanctioned Gazprom, cut off from raising international finance and buying Western equipment. In anticipation of 'massive capital expenditures', Gazprom took the unprecedented step of suspending dividends for the first time in 30 years in April 2022. Essentially, 'if Russia cannot sell its gas to the West it cannot sell it to anyone,' said economist Andrei Movchan. 'That will mean capping off gas wells.'[33]

In other words, Putin's proposed 'pivot to the east' was entirely reliant on Beijing's goodwill and money. But despite ostensible diplomatic support from Beijing for Moscow, the threat of US sanctions on their global operations caused many leading Chinese banks such as ICBC, the New Development Bank and the Asian Infrastructure Investment Bank to withdraw all credit and financing from Russia. Chinese energy giants such as Sinochem also suspended all Russian investments and joint ventures. In August, UnionPay – the Chinese equivalent of Visa and Mastercard – also ceased its cooperation with Russian banks, citing sanctions.[34] Some Chinese companies remained active in Russia – but only those who had no operations outside Russia and China and nothing to lose from international sanctions.

Russia imagined itself a major political and economic partner of Beijing's, almost a fellow superpower. But the truth is that before the war Russia was only China's 11th-most important trade partner. In 2021 China's trade with the US was worth some $1.3 trillion, with the EU just over $1 trillion – and with Russia just under $70 billion. In the wake of the war Russian trade volumes with China soared to over $100 billion in the year to September, mostly thanks to increased Chinese imports of Russian crude oil. But Beijing's trade relationships with the EU and US were still more than 20 times greater. Furthermore, there was every reason to believe that Beijing was taking full advantage of Russia's sanctions-driven economic weakness.

Before the war, Russia accounted for some 12 per cent of global oil exports – 53 per cent of which went to Europe, 39 per cent to Asia. Unlike gas, Russian oil did not need expensive pipelines, so the oil no longer heading to Europe could be easily shipped to Asia instead. But both India and China ruthlessly insisted on a massive discount on buying Russian oil. Beijing had previously done exactly the same to Iran – one advantage of being the sanctions-busting buyer of last resort. Brent and Urals crude, which for decades had traded at near-parity, radically bifurcated by the end of March, with Urals retailing at a $35 a barrel discount – making the real price of Russian oil in late summer just over $60 a barrel. Moreover, shipping Russian oil had also become much more expensive because of sanctions that complicate maritime and load insurance as well as payments.

That meant that even a relatively small fall in world prices could be devastating for Russia. A 2019 study by Saudi Aramco found that Russia was one of the most expensive places in the world to produce oil, at around $42 a barrel for Russian onshore projects and $44 for offshore projects – compared with just $17 for Saudi crude. Factoring in the ongoing $35 discount on Urals crude and the $42 cost of production, a fall in world oil prices to less than $77 a barrel would push the profits from Russian oil below zero. And dropping world oil prices was precisely what Biden set out to accomplish.

World War Z

In July Biden headed to Riyadh for his first meeting with Crown Prince Mohammed bin Salman to negotiate an increase in Saudi oil production to 'stabilise' – i.e. lower – the price of crude. Using the Saudis to undermine Moscow was a tactic that worked for Ronald Reagan back in 1982. Congressman Charlie Wilson, among others, successfully persuaded the Saudis that the Soviets were annihilating their co-religionists in Afghanistan and needed to be taken down by a combination of Stinger missiles smuggled to the Mujahideen and low oil prices that would (and did) collapse the Soviet economy. Four decades later, though, the US had much less leverage over the Saudis – especially after Washington has blasted them for involvement in a brutal war in Yemen and over the kidnap and murder of dissident journalist Jamal Khashoggi in Istanbul in 2018.

Biden's effort did not bring any immediate results, and by September world oil prices had begun to creep upwards towards the psychologically important $100 a barrel. But it was Putin, ironically enough, who supplied the strongest potential argument for the Saudis to crank up production and drop prices. A week after Biden's visit to Riyadh, Putin showed up in Tehran to meet with Iran's President Ebrahim Raisi, as well as Turkey's Recep Tayyip Erdogan. The ostensible reason for the summit was to discuss the future of Syria – where Russia was instrumental in saving the regime of Iran's ally Bashar al-Assad against Saudi- and Western-backed resistance. The real reason was to showcase a newly emerging anti-Western, anti-democratic alliance between Moscow and Tehran.[35]

Post-Soviet Russia's relations with Iran had always been ambivalent. In the 1990s the Yeltsin regime constructed a civilian nuclear reactor at Bushehr and covertly helped Tehran develop its Shehab-3 medium-range ballistic missile. But under

Putin Russia joined the West in putting a halt to Iran's nuclear weapons programme – partly because Moscow was wary of a nuclear-armed Iran flexing its muscles in the region and partly because support for the ayatollahs had damaged Russia's economic relationship with the West. The Ukraine war changed all that, as Russia overtook Iran as the world's most-sanctioned pariah state.

With relations with the West irreparably broken down, an alliance with Iran came to look like an attractive strategic proposition for Moscow. In Tehran Putin's foreign policy adviser Yuri Ushakov told reporters that a 'trusting dialogue' had developed between Russia and Iran and that 'on most issues, our positions are close or identical.'[36] More immediately, Russia needed Iranian drones to counter the threat of Turkish-made Bayraktars that the Ukrainians had used to devastating effect.

Putin affected not to care about Russia's international isolation. On 8 July at the G20 summit in Bali, Indonesia, Russian Foreign Minister Sergei Lavrov had his first direct confrontation with Western leaders since Russia mounted its attack on Ukraine. '[Lavrov] spent a large part of the negotiations not in but outside the room,' Germany's Foreign Minister Baerbock told reporters. 'There is not a millimetre of willingness to talk on the Russia side.' Lavrov demonstratively walked out of the conference chamber when Baerbock began to speak – proof, she later said, that the mood in the room was '19 to 1 against Russia's invasion, even if disagreements existed on sanctions'. Western leaders then refused to be photographed alongside Lavrov.[37] In September Russia, Belarus, Afghanistan, Venezuela and Syria were pointedly not invited to even send their ambassadors to the funeral of Queen Elizabeth II – an event attended by representatives of North Korea and Iran.

China remained as Russia's last – and more or less only – major international ally. Chinese Foreign Minister Wang Yi denounced Western 'double standards' on sovereignty and territorial integrity, and accused unnamed countries of upholding Ukraine's sovereignty while they refused to recognise Beijing's claim to rule Taiwan – an impressive feat of logical contortion. 'The Chinese side rejects any attempt to draw parallels between the Ukraine crisis and the Taiwan question, and will firmly defend its core interests,' Wang declared. 'China opposes exploiting the situation to incite Cold War mentality, hype up bloc confrontation, and create a new Cold War.'[38] But that diplomatic support did not, as we have seen, translate into a willingness to break US sanctions, pay a market price for Moscow's oil, or supply Russia with desperately needed military materiel or financing.

But some other powers remained on the fence – notably India (which refused to participate in international sanctions, preferring to take as much cut-price Russian oil as it could) and Russia's on-again, off-again ally Turkey. Putin's relations with Erdogan had always been stormy, not least because Turkey remained an official US ally and stood on a different side of the fence to Russia and Iran on the conflict in Syria. At a meeting between Erdogan and Putin in Tehran in July, there was a clear shift in the balance of power between the two leaders who had once described each other as 'friends'. Erdogan kept Putin waiting awkwardly in front of reporters – a classic dictator's power play more usually employed by Putin himself, who famously kept Angela Merkel waiting for four hours and the Pope for nearly two.[39]

Turkey had hosted the first, abortive rounds of negotiations between Kyiv and Moscow in March and April. And in July, Russia, Turkey and Iran did find one thing to agree on: opposition to Syria's pro-American Kurds. Erdogan's transactional and occasionally confrontational relationship with Washington frequently aligned with the Russians' and Iranians' implacable hostility. In August Turkish Foreign Minister Mevlüt Çavuşoğlu also succeeded in persuading the Russians to open a maritime corridor for Ukrainian grain to be exported from Odesa – easing some of the criticism from African and Middle Eastern countries of Russia's shipping blockade that had caused world grain prices to soar.

Internationally, Russia stood almost alone. In a 5 March vote in the United Nations' General Assembly that 'deplored in the strongest terms the aggression by the Russian Federation against Ukraine', only Belarus, Syria, North Korea and Eritrea voted with Russia. Cuba spoke in Moscow's defence but ultimately abstained – along with 34 others, including all the members of Putin's Eurasian Economic Union and Russia's ambivalent allies China, India and Turkey.[40] North Korea, Russia's unexpected international supporter, offered to supply artillery to Moscow to help conquer Ukraine and manpower to rebuild it – an offer that DNR President Denis Pushilin welcomed warmly. But Putin's former allies in his own near abroad shunned not only Moscow but their association with Russia altogether. In August the leaders of Azerbaijan and Kazakhstan – both nominal Moscow allies – met in Baku but pointedly refused to speak Russian in public. Ukrainian flags were flown in cities across Kazakhstan.

Repression

As the war in Ukraine slowed to a bloody standoff over the summer of 2022, Putin stepped up his war against dissent in his own country – even though public opposition to his war had become almost invisible.

Apart from a scattering of small protests in the first days of the war and another, more serious flare-up of protest that followed Putin's partial mobilisation announcement in September, for most of the war's duration there was practically no discernible anti-war movement, no strikes, no civil disobedience, not even a graffiti campaign or mass internet protests or hacking attacks in Russia. On 14 March Channel One producer Marina Ovsyannikova interrupted a live broadcast of the evening *Vesti* news show by displaying a banner saying 'No to War!' She was on air for 15 seconds before the studio feed was cut away. Ovsyannikova was fined £200 – but a subsequent poll showed that only 9 per cent of *Vesti* viewers had even noticed her. In July she tried again to make an impact, staging a single-person protest at Moscow's Sofiisky Embankment holding a poster reading 'Putin is a murderer. His soldiers are fascists. 352 children died. How many more should die for you to stop?' This time she was put under house arrest for two months and later charged under fake news laws that could land her in jail for ten years.[41]

The depressing truth was that Putin's brand of highly targeted, high-tech repression worked. Ovsyannikova's was one of the 20,000 cases opened by Russian authorities under Article 20.2 of the Code of Administrative Offences that covered 'Violation of the established order of organising or holding meetings, rallies, demonstrations, marches or pickets'.[42] Over the first seven months of the war some 18,500 people were officially detained, according to the NGO OVD-Info. Many of these infractions were absurdly minor. The Russian internet was full of video clips of people being detained for surreally obscure acts of protest. One man held up a debit card from the state-owned Sberbank branded 'Mir', or 'Peace', and was hustled away by police. Another man brandished a copy of Lev Tolstoy's *War and Peace* by the Eternal Flame in Moscow, and was immediately arrested. One young woman who, in a brave display of Dadaist resistance, unfurled a piece of paper with the words 'Two Words' (implying *net voine*, or 'no to war') by Red Square was detained too – as was another girl who held up a completely blank sheet.

One thing that Putin's police state did very well was policing (another was local government, which was honed to a peak of customer-friendly efficiency unknown anywhere else in Europe). The machinery of repression worked with extreme effectiveness. Activists who had been spotted by Moscow's ubiquitous street cameras were traced to their homes by facial recognition software. Between March and July Russian courts handed down 3,003 convictions for misdemeanours under laws of military censorship – including for 'discrediting the army' – and 87 people were charged with the more serious crime of 'intentionally spreading deliberately false information', which was punishable by up to 15 years in jail. In September journalist Ivan Safronov was jailed for a staggering 22 years on charges of treason over a 2019 article in the *Kommersant* daily on Russian sales of fighter jets to Egypt. Hundreds of politicians, journalists and public figures were officially labelled as 'foreign agents' – in the case of *The New Times* editor Yevgenia Albats and Echo Moskvy editor Aleksei Venediktov because they earned money from a YouTube channel or from foreign advertisers.[43]

The online independent newspaper *The New Times* was fined four times for quoting international news-wire information about the bombing of Kharkiv, Odesa and Mykolaiv. But since the information the outlet published had not been published on the website of the Russian Ministry of Defence, the judge concluded that it hadn't happened. Besides, according to the prosecution, Putin had announced that the special military operation was being conducted 'in order to protect Russia from an invasion from the territory of Ukraine'.[44] When Albats – one of the bravest journalists still working in Russia – embarked on a tour of the Russian provinces to talk to ordinary people about the war in August, she found herself followed by heavy FSB surveillance, and everyone she met demonstratively photographed from black SUVs.

'When I asked people at a market in Tver, "What do you think of the special military operation?", only unequivocal supporters replied. Everyone else either declined to answer or slipped behind phrases like "We don't know everything" or "Who knows who started it?"' reported Albats. 'People who agree to speak in a pre-arranged place asked not to specify their profession or place of work since "the town is small and they'll figure it out."'

Several local journalists from the independent *Pskovskaya Guberniya* and activists from the opposition Yabloko party had been beaten by thugs apparently organised by the FSB. 'After that, many well-known people in the city left for the neighbouring Baltic states,' wrote Albats. 'The ones who stayed behind don't even post on social networks, let alone take part in any street actions.'[45]

Fear, then, and the efficiency of Putin's secret police were reasons why Russians did not protest against the war. Another was a lack of leadership. Prominent opposition bloggers like Ilya Yashin, Vladimir Kara-Murza and Evgeny Roizman had been tolerated before the war. But soon 'a certain unspoken rule [was] established for well-known people,' wrote Albats. 'First, the authorities [bring] three "administrative cases", followed by a window of 3–4 weeks for the person to leave, and if he/she does not leave, there is a search – just before 6 a.m. – and then arrest.'[46] Some activists were not so lucky. In May Alexei Gorinov, a municipal deputy in Moscow's Krasnoselsky District, spoke up to say that he would not discuss organising a proposed local children's art competition 'while children were being killed in Ukraine'. Gorinov was given no administrative conviction but instead was immediately sentenced to a criminal offence for 'military fakes' and sentenced to seven years in prison. But Gorinov was a known ally of the much more high-profile Ilya Yashin and his conviction was meant, by Yashin's account, as a signal for him to leave. 'But I refuse to leave,' Yashin told the Tel Aviv-based Fishman YouTube news channel. 'Why should I leave my own country? I have as much right to be here as anyone.'[47] Two months later Yashin was also detained and charged with the same crime as Gorinov – along with Vladimir Kara-Murza and Evgeny Roizman, a former governor of Nizhny Novgorod.

The fourth reason for Russians' silence was the effectiveness of the Kremlin's restrictions on access to information. Since the beginning of the war the General Prosecutor's Office and the courts blocked over 7,000 websites. By July, 25 million Russians were using virtual private networks (VPNs) to access alternative information on the internet. But the tech-savvy authorities caught on to that too, making the apps of state-owned banks and services shut down on phones that had VPNs installed.[48]

And finally there was the simple, depressing fact that after the mass exodus of the middle class in March and April, there were very few opposition activists left in Moscow and St Petersburg to protest. 'Why don't you stay in your own country and fight Putin there?' one Georgian cafe patron demanded of a table of Russian exiles from Moscow at a Tbilisi cafe in May. 'If you're not there to do it, who will?'[49]

It was a pointed question. At the height of the anti-Putin civil protests in Moscow in 2011–12, some 100,000 civic-minded citizens who were willing to risk arrest for their beliefs had taken to the streets. But in the wake of the 2022 invasion, at least 300,000 people – including much of the Moscow and St Petersburg intelligentsia, including journalists and activists – had left the country. Like the tsarist regime before the First World War, Putin's police state had succeeded in imprisoning or exiling almost every potentially dangerous revolutionary. In February 1917 a leaderless but hungry urban proletariat and a discontented urban middle class reluctantly rose against the regime. As long as the 'special military operation' remained largely invisible, out of sight and out of mind, between March and September, popular discontent seemed a remote possibility.

For ordinary Russians, any form of public protest had become not only unthinkably dangerous but also, more importantly, apparently pointless. What of the privileged Russians – whose children, as we have seen, felt sufficiently immune to the laws made for the little people to post defiant anti-war memes on Instagram? Albats's experience was much like my own. 'During the six months of the war, I did not meet a single person who was more or less well-known, or high-ranking, or rich, who openly supported the war,' she wrote in August. 'I was told, however, that one former deputy prime minister and now head of a state corporation came to the offices of the presidential administration wearing a black T-shirt with a defiant "Z" on his chest. Whether this person was trolling the administration or wearing the T-shirt as a sign of eternal loyalty remains unknown.' Like my own sources, Albats's were deeply paranoid about meeting in public or being overheard. One of the people she interviewed 'repeated several times that "society has completely failed to thoroughly consider the implications of using Novichok against opponents". Apparently the terror that the door handle of your luxury palace or car might be smeared with a military nerve agent never leaves many of the top Russian ruling elite for a moment.'

But if the Russian people had been successfully scared or brainwashed into silence, so, apparently, had much of the elite. They had reconciled themselves to the loss of their yachts and foreign holidays, property and assets, of prestige and the prospect of an overseas education or future for their children, as well as any future prosperity. 'Some give the regime until the spring of 2023, others predict a further intensification of repression in the coming months and are confident that the regime has enough strength to survive another ten years,' wrote Albats. 'They insist that the upcoming 2024 elections and the next round won't change a thing.' And yet, she asked, will Putin's ruling class, made up of dollar millionaires and billionaires and used to making money in Russia and spending it all over the world, 'agree to live and die in a cage? I'm not so sure.'[50]

The most reckless part of Putin's war was in destroying the delicate balance between the state and Russia's most effective wealth creators – the businesspeople and middle class who had been willing to tolerate the regime without protest as long as they had been left alone to make money. They had always been reflexive cheerleaders for the regime because their wealth had been built on the system and was guaranteed by it. They did not support the opposition – even if they privately agreed with its values – because political change represented a threat to their wellbeing and stability. But at the same time their support for the regime rested on the understanding that the state would allow them to become wealthy and more or less protect their property. As one prominent oligarch who was a business partner of a top *silovik* put it, 'Most Russian businessmen are patriots of their own property and nothing else.'[51]

The most senior members of the Putin-era *nomenklatura* – the bureaucrat-businessmen who controlled both the state and its major enterprises – had been reconciled to being cut off from the West and all its benefits after they were sanctioned following 2014. These men included the decision makers who led Russia to war again in 2022 – men who had nothing to lose from a total disengagement from the West.

The lesser members of the *nomenklatura* and business class were less sanguine and less reconciled to that loss. But they also had no formal or informal say in the Kremlin's decision-making process. Most such people could not leave because they had not made enough money to walk away from what they had in Russia. They definitely did not expect, need, nor actively support the war, which represented a serious blow to their interests, lifestyles and life prospects. But as the war unfolded, many remained self-described 'patriots' by inertia – not least because not being so was dangerous.

'Of course, the elites – at least part of the elite, including those who have lost everything or nearly everything – understand that all Putin's decisions, including the most important one of Feb. 24, are suicidal for the country and society, for the economy, human capital and the reputation of Russia,' wrote Andrei Kolesnikov of the Moscow Carnegie Center. 'But they do nothing to rectify the situation. They are afraid. Unable to join together. They do not have the instruments to change the autocrat. They destroyed those instruments themselves for lack of use during the past two decades, because they thought that democracy wasn't worth a damn, that the way to make money is by hooking up with the Kremlin and the FSB without any kind of competitive elections ... And so we continue our steady movement down the world's garbage chute.'[52]

But the war had created a large and powerful constituency of the quietly angry, a constituency who, after Putin's bombshell mobilisation announcement of 21 September, became more visible. Just as in the late USSR, Russia had a small minority of vocal dissidents but a much larger number of people who simply conformed because it was in their interests to do so. The war changed that. Now, new classes of latent opponents whose personal interests diverged from those of the Kremlin had emerged, including the relatives of young men who might be sent to fight who had not hitherto considered themselves opponents of the regime – large crowds who blocked roads in Makhachkala, Dagestan, for instance, or desperate young men who torched recruitment offices in Siberia. Cracks appeared even among prominent regime loyalists. Ramzan Kadyrov wondered out loud why a mass call-up was necessary when five million men serving in the FSB, Ministry of Emergency Situations and the OMON paramilitary police stayed at home. Colonel-General Sergei Melikov, former deputy director of Russia's National Guard and now head of the Republic of Dagestan, blasted over-enthusiastic recruiting officers for 'utter stupidity' and apologised to the people of Derbent, where loudspeaker cars had toured the streets ordering every man to report for recruitment. Putin's reserve of loyalty remained strong, not least because any Russian over 40 knew very well from personal experience that a change of regime spelled chaos, upheaval and prolonged economic crisis. But the millions frightened and angered by mobilisation might, under certain circumstances, be ready to go for an alternative to the current system as soon as a viable one appeared.

Westerners often argue that Russia could be better. Russians will habitually counter that it could be worse. Both would be right. But the basic reality of post-invasion Russia remained that things would have to get far, far worse – worse even than they had been in living memory, for instance in the early nineties – for that angry, silent middle class to be sufficiently desperate to contemplate regime change. 'There will be no political impact from sanctions,' predicted Movchan. 'They will prevent Russian economic development. They will cause a recession, inflation. But that will not be devastating. There will be no hunger rebellions. We will just regress by 20 years. And the road to recovery will be harder. And people will accept it as a result of Western hostility.'[53]

CHAPTER 12
TIL VALHALL

The Putin regime is all about stealing wealth that is buried under the earth. And one of the deepest buried resources in Russia is the profound conservatism of its people. Their lack of education, loyalty, resistance to change, ignorance and hostility to anything foreign or new is also a kind of oil, laid down in very deep and ancient layers. It is something valuable that can be mined and exploited like any other natural resource.

Russian poet and critic Dmitry Bykov, 2022[1]

Back to the Future

Nations start wars because they believe they can win them. Vladimir Putin expected a war that would be short and victorious. His plan of attack had been, first and foremost, for an aggravated military coup rather than a prolonged military campaign. Instead he got a war that became bloodier, longer and more destructive of his country than he or any of his inner circle could ever have imagined.

Every war ever fought has had three phases: the opening attack, the struggle for advantage and the endgame. That endgame inevitably has one of two outcomes: either the tide of war turns irreversibly in one side's favour, like the Allied victories in 1918 and 1945. Or the conflict ends in some kind of mutually agreed peace – at best a negotiated one, like that between Egypt and Israel in 1973, at worst an exhausted stalemate, like in Korea in 1953 or Cyprus in 1974.[2]

This book was written during the Ukraine conflict's struggle for advantage. By September 2022 a major Ukrainian breakthrough around Kharkiv saw an apparently change in the tide of the war as the Russians lost over 6,000 square kilometres of territory – some 6 per cent of the Ukrainian land they had taken since 2014. This phase – often a war's most bloody and protracted part – will remain unresolved as long as both sides still believe they might eventually prevail. 'Neither side is interested in negotiating because each side is trying to win outright, enhance their position on the battlefield, and thus have a stronger position from which to negotiate,' said Gideon Rose, author of *How Wars End*.[3] During early negotiations with the Kremlin in March and April, Kyiv had offered to give up its ambitions to join NATO, and consider recognising the annexation of Crimea and the independence of the Donbas republics in exchange for a Russian withdrawal to pre-24 February positions. By the autumn of 2022, such an outcome had become inconceivable. Zelensky vowed to retake not just the territory occupied by Russia in 2022 but Crimea too, and his army was making military inroads around Zaporizhzhia and Kharkiv. He also vowed not to talk to Putin, and formally applied for fast-track membership of NATO. The Kremlin, for its part, hurriedly announced local referendums to annex Donbas and the significant swathes of southern Ukraine it had occupied to Russia. That annexation would, Putin hoped, put an end to further Ukrainian advances by presenting them as attacks on Russia itself. And on 21 September Putin explicitly renewed his threat to use nuclear weapons if Russia – including, implicitly, Russia's new Ukrainian territories – were attacked. The sides were further apart than they had ever been.

From the moment that Lysychansk – the last city in Luhansk province still in Ukrainian hands – finally fell to Russian troops on 5 July, Putin could easily have declared victory and started to sue for peace. Instead, he doubled down. 'Today we hear that they want to defeat us on the battlefield. What can you say, let them try,' Putin told parliamentary leaders on 7 July. 'We have heard many times that the West wants to fight us to the last Ukrainian. This is a tragedy for the Ukrainian people, but it seems that everything is heading towards this. Everybody should know that largely speaking, we haven't even yet started anything in earnest.' Those were not the words of a leader who was serious about a negotiated peace.[4] And in his 21 September speech Putin not only threatened to use nukes and announced an initial mobilisation of 300,000 Russia's reservists, with a secret provision for a total of 1.3 million in the future, but also claimed that the West 'don't want us to be free, they want us to be a colony; they don't want equal partnership, they want to steal from us.' In a barely coherent 40-minute speech to the assembled Russian elites, Putin veered from denouncing the 'totalitarianism, despotism and apartheid' of today's West, to bringing up the historical pillaging of India, the bombing of Dresden towards the end of the Second World War and the 'many genders' in fashion in the West. In case there was any doubt that Putin saw the war in terms of the existential survival of the Russian people, he emphasised that Russia's mission was to 'defend our children from monstrous experiments designed to destroy their consciousness and their souls'.[5] As the Carnegie's Andrei Kolesnikov wrote on Twitter, Putin's speech was 'a set of unbelievably illiterate conspiracy cliches that 30 years ago could be read in marginal national-patriotic newspapers ... Now it has become the policy of the former superpower, which even in the days of the Soviet leaders could not afford such a discourse.'

In the early days and months of the war the Kremlin did what any institution would do in the face of a blown-up plan – mount a cover-up, and pretend that everything was meant to be that way. Putin's longer-term strategy appeared to be to wait for history to repeat itself. After Chechnya, Georgia, Crimea and Syria, Western indignation and resolve had eventually dissolved, eroded by domestic political concerns and hunger for cheap gas. In July CIA Director Williams Burns said that Putin expected the US to suffer from 'attention deficit disorder' and 'forget about Ukraine'.[6] When, by September, the West had not only not forgotten about Ukraine but was actively supporting a pushback in the field, Putin radically changed tack. After mobilisation, annexation, nuclear threats and the destruction of Nord Stream, the Kremlin was clearly signalling that they were willing to raise the stakes far higher than anything the West would tolerate. And so the conflict entered its final and most dangerous phase.

Expecting the future to be like the past was not an entirely unreasonable assumption. Especially when the former Marxists in the Kremlin also sincerely believed that inexorable historical forces were on their side. 'The sooner everyone realises that there are no alternatives to objective historical processes where a multipolar world is formed based on respect for the principle of sovereign equality of states ... the better,' Lavrov said in July.[7] In an echo – perhaps unconscious – of the rhetoric of the late Brezhnev period, Putin predicted the imminent economic and cultural collapse of the US, the EU, the dollar, the euro, Western economic liberalism and the West in general. The world is witnessing 'the beginning of the cardinal breakdown of the American-style world order', Putin told Duma leaders in July in the same St Catherine's Hall in the Kremlin where he had held his fateful Security Council meeting. 'This is the beginning of the transition from liberal-globalist American egocentrism to a truly multipolar world.' At the same time – and again apparently oblivious of the contradiction – Putin blamed this dying Western empire for causing the war. 'We are told, we hear today, that we started the war in Donbas, in Ukraine,' said Putin. 'No, it was started by the collective West.' For good measure he also blamed the West for deliberately 'holding Russia back' – without specifying exactly how or why the enemy had accomplished this.[8]

More importantly, what had turned out to be a disaster for Russia was not necessarily a disaster for the *siloviki*. They had, after all, got the Russia they wanted – one where their rule was to be unchallenged by a Westernised elite or middle class. 'Let those who want to do another Bolotnaya [Square protest of 2011] do it in Tel Aviv,' said one top Russian businessman and business partner of a top *silovik*, summarising his partner's thoughts. 'Are [the *siloviki*] sad? No. The programme has been fulfilled ... The vector has been reset.'[9] Russia's elite, thanks to sanctions, had been forcibly decoupled from their assets in the West – and, in the view of the *siloviki*, from their divided loyalties too.

Putin's July address to Duma leaders gave important clues to his vision of a post-war Russia. That vision rested on the Orwellian oxymoron of 'authoritarian liberalism' – the idea that Russia was actually more free than the West because it protected its citizens from the tyranny of minority liberal views that had undermined Western societies and destroyed their self-belief.

Putin was happy to ignore the fact that it had been a market economy, liberal trade and a rational monetary policy that had brought in the trillions of foreign dollars and euros that had enriched Russia – and his inner circle – for two decades. He also said nothing about how the economy would survive once Europe finally succeeded in weaning itself off Russian gas. He was silent on the looming budget deficit, falling disposable income and the fact that the economy was surviving principally by legalising illegal imports of technology and goods. Nor did he mention Russia's looming demographic disaster and the attrition of the working-age population, the flight abroad of the country's best specialists and managers, the huge war losses, or the impending primitivisation and nationalisation of the economy. Putin's vision was, in a nutshell, that Russia could stand alone in a globalised world – a plan that was 'both suicidal and archaic' wrote the Carnegie's Kolesnikov.[10]

The war had allowed Putin, Patrushev, Bortnikov and the rest to fulfil a dream that many old men may aspire to but very few achieve – to create a future that reflected an idealised version of their own pasts. The new Russia would be more typical of the mid-twentieth century than the twenty-first. While Europe erased borders and enshrined the free movement of people, capital and ideas, Putin made a fetish of defending a Russian national sovereignty that no one, in fact, had ever attempted to destroy. As the world moved away from empires and abandoned colonies, Putin built his power on an imperial vision of a Russia that had comprehensively collapsed in 1991. And like the great dictators of the previous century, Putin cultivated the obedience of the masses, fed them fantasies of militarism and heroic death, created a cult of the leader that conflated him with the state itself, banished any means for his own power to be challenged legitimately and sought to rule for ever. He used show trials to imprison his opponents or employed assassination squads to silence them, established total state control over the media and equated political opposition with treason. And with his September nuclear threats Putin made it clear that he equated his regime with Russia itself and was willing to go to the ultimate limits of destruction to ensure his own survival. Putin's Russia had become a kind of death cult.

'Millions Stand Behind Me'[11]

Did Russia truly stand behind Putin as he went to war against Ukraine? To begin to answer that question, it is important to remember that the secret of Putin's 22-year dominance of Russian politics has invariably been that his views and his policies always closely reflected those of the majority of his people. Putin was not a dictator who maintained his power solely by repression and propaganda. Rather he was, like his sometime ally Recep Tayyip Erdogan, one of the 21st century's most ruthlessly successful populists.

'I did not invent fascism,' Benito Mussolini told an early biographer in 1925. 'I extracted it from the subconscious of the Italian people.'[12] In the same way, Putin and his army of propagandists drew the mish-mash of Imperial Russian, Orthodox and Soviet values and symbolism that formed the ideology as Putinism from the deepest and darkest part of Russia's collective consciousness. The secret of Putin's success as a leader was that he both led and followed his people.

Most journalistic and political comparisons of Putin to Hitler are a lazy form of insult – just as misguided as Putin's own bizarre labelling of Ukraine's president Volodymyr Zelensky as a 'fascist'. But like the Führer and the Duce, Putin's rule had, up to the outbreak of war on 24 February 2022, been much more based on consent than coercion. He had been used to the active support of a critical mass of his people – with whom he shared a vision of Russia as a strong, powerful nation and his belief that the lesser peoples of the empire should bow down to Moscow with most of his countrymen.

But was the Ukraine invasion an extension of that shared belief, or a break from it? Pre-invasion polls showed that, in fact, the Russian people had a deeply ambivalent attitude to an actual war against Ukraine. In May 2014, when fighting in eastern Ukraine was at its peak, only 31 per cent of Russians supported, or more or less supported, 'sending direct military assistance, such as the introduction of troops'. By August 2015, that support fell to just 20 per cent.[13] In a July 2015 poll by the independent Levada-Center only 33 per cent responded positively or 'more or less positively' to whether they would support regular Russian army troops fighting with the Donbas rebels – down from 45 per cent in November 2014. In other words, despite blanket Kremlin TV propaganda support even for a limited operation inside

Ukraine fell after the first year of proxy war. By September 2017, just 41 per cent of Russians thought that Moscow should help the breakaway provinces of Donetsk and Luhansk in eastern Ukraine in any way. That helps to explain the Kremlin's reluctance to recognise the presence of Russian soldiers in eastern Ukraine between 2014 and 2022 – but makes the mystery of why Putin chose a full-scale invasion deeper.[14]

Polls in April 2021 showed Russians evenly split on a military intervention in Ukraine, with 43 per cent of respondents in a Levada survey saying that Russia should intervene in a conflict (18 per cent for 'definitely yes', 25 per cent 'somewhat supportive') versus 43 per cent who reported that Russia should not intervene (with 25 per cent 'not very supportive' and 18 per cent replying 'definitely not'). Significantly, 66 per cent of the under-25s reported having a 'positive' attitude towards Ukraine.[15]

The presidential administration had always been obsessed with opinion polls – so much so that in the early 2000s the Kremlin took over three nationwide independent polling institutions, backed up by federal and regional structures belonging to the Russian National Guard, the FSB and many others. All fed mostly confidential data on the public mood back to Moscow. The polling was generally accepted to be highly professional and anonymous.[16] So why did the Kremlin take the risk of invading Ukraine, when popular support was so deeply polarised?

Part of the answer was that, as with all opinion polling, the data depended what question you asked. According to an internet-based poll commissioned by CNN in Russia in February 2022, 50 per cent of respondents supported the use of force against Ukraine – if that meant stopping Ukraine from joining NATO. A further 64 per cent believed that Russians and Ukrainians were 'one people', and 71 per cent had a 'positive rather than negative' view of the old Soviet Union. Only 25 per cent of respondents opposed the use of force by Russia to reunite Russia and Ukraine.[17]

Then there was Putin's faith in the power of the Kremlin's media machine to shape the national narrative. The Kremlin's policies had always been invariably deeply calculated with public opinion in mind. But as we have seen, the Kremlin also formed that public opinion through the massive media empire on which the Russian state spent inordinate amounts of money. They were two sides of the same coin, a constantly self-reinforcing feedback loop.

So was the invasion Putin's war, or Russia's? In a radio broadcast to the Italian people on 23 December 1940, Winston Churchill said that 'one man and one man only was resolved to plunge Italy ... into the whirlpool of war.' Similar sentiments were expressed about Putin, both by Western politicians and media as well as by his Russian opponents. At the beginning of the war the writer Boris Akunin asked me to copy-edit a statement he had written with the dancer Mikhail Baryshnikov and economist Sergei Guriev. 'The real Russia is bigger, stronger and more durable than Putin,' wrote Akunin, Baryshnikov and Guriev. 'This Russia lives, and will outlive him. The dictator is fighting a war not only with Ukraine, but against the better part of his own country. He is smothering our Russia's future. Let us prove to the rest of the world that Putin does not speak for all Russians.'

I agree. Doubtless Russia's most educated part did oppose Putin. Unfortunately for both Russia and the world, that 'better' part was not the greater part. Once the invasion actually began, the numbers of Russians supporting it jumped to over 75 per cent. Polling in Russia, as we have discussed, may be distorted by self-delusion, a strong habit of public conformity when speaking to strangers and a personal phobia against being in opposition to the majority. Nonetheless, for the most part Putin was right. His propaganda machine did work – at least insofar as it produced a wide, publicly accepted consensus in favour of the war. The simple truth is that Putin did speak for most Russians. That might be depressing for me, my Russian wife and most of my

Russian friends. But the fact that we wished it were not true did not make it so. The invasion of Ukraine was the brainchild of Putin and a tiny group of highly paranoid men around him who became convinced that a pre-emptive blow against Western aggression was necessary for Russia's survival. But in an important sense it was not only the Kremlin's war. It was genuinely supported by a critical mass of the Russian people. How wholehearted or conditional that support might be would be put to severe test in the wake of the September mobilisation and as the war moved from a near-uninterrupted series of Russian victories to a series of tactical defeats.

'This Man Cannot Stay in Power'

Putin and his inner circle had been convinced for years that the US was set on achieving regime change in Moscow. Their paranoia was apparently confirmed by an off-the-cuff remark by Joe Biden as he made a speech to crowds in front of the Royal Castle in Warsaw in March. 'For God's sake, this man cannot remain in power,' Biden said.[18] White House press officers quickly clarified – Biden was not calling for Putin's removal, they insisted, but rather was saying that he must no longer have power to dominate his neighbours.

But the question remained. What would a post-Putin regime look like? Most of the epic military aggressions of the twentieth century had ended in defeat, military occupation and the creation of a new regime modelled on those of the victorious powers – most famously in Germany, Italy and Japan. Obviously with Putin's repeated threat to use nuclear weapons that option was not on the cards for Russia. There had been a few recent examples of an unsuccessful military adventure bringing down authoritarian governments and ushering in a new era of liberal democracy. The fall of the Argentinian junta after their humiliation by the British in the 1982 Falklands War was one; the transformation of Serbia into a more or less democratic European country after the fall of Slobodan Milošević in 2000 was another. Russia's defeat in the Crimean War in 1856 ushered in a period of relative liberalism that culminated in the liberation of the serfs and Russia's sale of Alaska to the United States.

Sadly for Russia, a liberal outcome following the fall of Putin was not likely for one simple reason – an addiction to imperial fantasies was not easy to flush out of the body politic. The poison ran too deep. As we have seen, most Russians wished for a restoration of their country to the status of superpower even in 1999 – before 20 years of Putin's relentless nationalist propaganda. Put simply, nationalism had been a far more powerful current in contemporary Russian popular opinion than pro-Western liberalism. And a military defeat at the hands of NATO weaponry would likely strengthen, not weaken, that tendency.

The Western press had tended to depict Russia's beleaguered liberals, such as the imprisoned Aleksei Navalny, as the main opposition to Putin's rule. But in truth Russia's ultra-nationalist right represented a much more formidable and dangerous potential opposition to Putin. People like Igor Girkin and Zakhar Prilepin (former officers of the FSB and OMON paramilitary police respectively) both bitterly criticised Putin for corruption and thievery before temporarily falling in line behind him when he began his military adventures in Ukraine. But as we have seen, even during the course of the 2022 war Girkin turned on the inefficiency and incompetence of the Russian military and its leadership, declaring in the wake of the Ukrainian breakthrough in Kharkiv in September that 'the war is lost ... it remains only to see how badly.'

In the wake of Germany's defeat in 1918 nationalist officers explained the disaster with the stab-in-the-back theory – the *Dolchstoßlegende* – that claimed that German armies were betrayed by weak civilian defeatists in Berlin. A post-defeat

Russian version of the *Dolchstoßlegende* would certainly involve laying blame on the corruption of the Putin inner circle that robbed the army of the material and political means to win. Avoiding such a nationalist backlash would be the first priority of Putin's inner circle if they wished to preserve their wealth, influence and lives.

'The West could be careful what it wishes for [in desiring the fall of Putin],' said one former senior Russian official who worked closely with Putin for over 15 years. 'Whoever comes after will be far worse ... If Patrushev and co have their way they will install someone more aggressive, more hard-line.'[19]

'History Will Absolve Me'

Despite a cost in blood and economic devastation that far exceeded the Kremlin's expectations, Putin did succeed in one thing. The Russian offensive had at least 'liberated' all of the Donbas province of Luhansk (though some of that territory was won back by the Ukrainians in September) and half of Donetsk. It had also succeeded in capturing some of Ukraine's richest farmland and controlled both banks of the mouth of the Dniepr, the country's greatest river. Russian troops had also seized nearly 600 kilometres of Ukraine's sea coast, leaving Kyiv in control of just 150 kilometres of Black Sea coastline. In all, between 2014 and 2022 Russia occupied some 21 per cent of Ukraine's territory.

But in every other important respect – and certainly in the terms which he set out at the beginning of the war – Putin had failed. In his 24 February broadcast Putin defined four objectives for Russia's 'special operation'. They were 'protecting the inhabitants of Donbas, demilitarising and denazifying Ukraine' and 'bringing to justice those who have committed innumerable bloody crimes'. Channelling Soviet leader Leonid Brezhnev before the invasions of Czechoslovakia in August 1968 and Afghanistan in December 1979, Putin claimed that he had decided to act in response to a request from the leaders of Donbas. He had also stressed that 'Russia has no plans to occupy Ukrainian territories' – which, it turned out, evidently meant that Putin's armies would occupy only supposedly 'Russian' parts of Ukraine.

Putin's idea of protecting ethnic Russians in Donbas, in the event amounted to killing tens of thousands of them. According to UK government analysis of drone footage, some 92 per cent of the buildings of Mariupol were destroyed or damaged during the Russian assault, and the city's economic capacity – centred on the Azovstal steel plant – entirely wiped out. In Severodonetsk and Lysychansk it was 90 per cent of the buildings. An estimated five million refugees fled the immediate war zone for safer parts of Ukraine and on to Europe, versus between 900,000 and 1.6 million who left or were deported to Russia. These numbers strongly suggest a powerful desire not to be 'liberated' by Moscow but to remain in Ukraine. Many refugees from Donbas with whom I spoke had previously been sympathetic to Russia and supportive of Yanukovych's Party of the Regions, but had changed their mind when confronted with the reality of Russian aggression and occupation.

'They say they came to save us – from what? We never asked to be saved from anyone,' said Larisa Boiko, the schoolteacher from Mariupol who spent three weeks in a cellar under bombardment before fleeing with her daughter Daria to Russia. 'We saw what this Russian "help" looks like. We buried our neighbours in the courtyard of our house. Our city was battered to pieces.'[20]

In the eight years after the much smaller Donbas rebellion of 2014, the cities and provinces of Luhansk and Donetsk had failed to restore more than a fraction of their pre-war prosperity – let alone rebuild the shattered airport at Donetsk or re-open many of the deep anthracite coal mines that collapsed or flooded in the course of the war. 'When I left [in 2014] parts of Donetsk looked like a war zone from a film,' said Dina Olevskaya, 39, a businesswoman who had fled to Kyiv during the fighting. 'Not so much because of the fighting but because everything had been looted and smashed up [by locals].' When Dina last went back to Donetsk in November 2021 to see her mother, 'they hadn't even replaced the glass in the liquor store that had been robbed back [in 2014],' she recalled. 'It was just boarded up. The only expensive cars I saw were being driven around by men in camouflage – local bandits. I asked my mother, "So, how are you enjoying being part of the Russian world?" She said, "They pay my pension in rubles, more than I got when we were under Ukraine."' Dina's mother refused to join her in Kyiv and was evacuated to Stavropol, Russia, in the first days of the war.[21]

The devastation and carnage wrought by Putin's 2022 war were by many degrees of magnitude greater than by the war of 2014 whose wrongs it was supposedly fought to reverse. In May an internal document produced by Russia's Ministry of Economics projecting the future prosperity of a Russian-occupied Donbas based on exploitation of the rich gas fields that lay under Izyum, Slovyansk and Kramatorsk circulated in the Kremlin. 'There were graphics, nicely produced, showing the projected revenues and how gas pipelines would feed into Blue Stream [Russian pipelines to Turkey],' said a Russian banking executive who was shown the document by a friend in government. 'The problem was that [most of] the towns were still in Ukrainian hands. And [the government friend] said that the study was being circulated by email only because the Ministry had run out of paper to print it on. *I smekh i grekh* ... it's funny, but a sin to laugh.'[22]

In late June the Kremlin announced a programme of economic recovery for the occupied territories that included twinning newly liberated towns and cities in Donbas with Russian ones, effectively tying dozens of local budgets to those of a destroyed and depopulated war zone. In October the occupied areas were formally annexed to the Russian Federation as four new federal provinces. But as we have seen, Russia's economy is already in catastrophic straits on its own terms. The chances of Moscow summoning the resources for the Marshall Plan scale of expenditure required to rebuild Donbas were close to zero – which explained the enthusiastic response of the DNR's President Denis Pushilin to offers of construction equipment and labour from North Korea.

The war not only failed to 'demilitarise' Ukraine, as Putin had demanded, but achieved the exact opposite. After six months of brutal conflict, the country's real military capabilities were, in the estimation of a senior UK military official based in Kyiv, 'bigger by a factor of ten than they were at the beginning of the war'. Ukraine had a million men and women under arms, with thousands being trained in Poland, the UK and US in the use of NATO's most sophisticated weaponry. Even in October there was still a waiting list at all Kyiv's recruiting offices of volunteers wanting to join up. 'To the Ukrainians this is a great patriotic war for survival,' said the UK official. 'There may be some problems with morale at the front lines. This is a nerve-shredding war. But when the troops come home they are treated as heroes. And you see people literally lining up to join up ... You compare that to the Russian [prisoners], the miserable state they're in, the things they say about how they've been commanded. You couldn't imagine a bigger difference. That's not propaganda, by the way. Go out to any shop and cafe, talk to young men. These are people who are ready to fight for their country.'[23]

As for Putin's goal of 'denazifying' Ukraine, it's hard to see how the Kremlin planned to demonstrate any kind of victory even in the event that the three-day blitzkrieg to decapitate the government had succeeded. Ukraine did, as already noted, indeed have its own small share of extreme right-wingers, including a single ultra-nationalist member of Kyiv's 450-strong parliament.

But 'Nazis' certainly did not dominate Ukrainian politics, and the prospect of finding enough to fill Nuremberg-style courtrooms after a Russian victory seemed absurd. 'Oh, don't underestimate my colleagues' resources,' joked a Russian TV news reporter whom I had first met in Donetsk in 2014 and who had reported from the Donbas front for Rossiya-1. 'I'm sure someone would have found some Nazi flags to show when we arrested some fascist paramilitaries in Kyiv. [Russian troops] probably brought a supply with them in their tanks.'[24]

In terms of 'bringing to justice those who have committed innumerable bloody crimes', Russian propagandists had to make do with prisoners from the Azov Regiment captured in the ruins of the Azovstal plant to parade for the cameras. On 9 May – Victory Day – a group of around 50 Ukrainian prisoners supposedly from the Azov Regiment were paraded, handcuffed, through the streets of Donetsk. Most looked as though they had been beaten. Some limped or nursed bandaged limbs. They were escorted by DNR soldiers in motley uniforms whose apparently scripted function was to protect the unfortunate prisoners from the wrath of the Donetsk locals, who obligingly shouted insults, aimed kicks and spat at the passing prisoners. In a deliberate echo of the parade of German prisoners through the streets of Moscow on 9 May 1945 (witnessed by my aunt Lenina), the Ukrainian prisoners of war were followed by a line of street-washing machines that sprayed the dusty roads clean of the fascist contagion. Special cages were built as part of the restoration of the destroyed theatre in Mariupol, which was evidently being prepared for a grand show trial of 'Nazi' war criminals. But in late September Russia released two dozen of its star defendants, commanders of the Azov Regiment captured at Azovstal, in exchange for jailed oligarch Viktor Medvedchuk and Russian prisoners of war.

And what of Putin's other war aims? Rather than stopping NATO expansion, Putin precipitated the alliance's biggest expansion since 2007. Before the conflict, Russia's direct borders with NATO ran along the semi-exclave of Kaliningrad, part of Latvia and Estonia, and a small piece of northern Norway. With Finland and Sweden in NATO, that border expanded by over 1,100 kilometres. Kremlin propagandist Dmitry Kisilev boasted that the Sea of Azov – a tiny, near-landlocked sea on the north coast of the near-landlocked Black Sea – had 'become a Russian sea' as a result of the Russian invasion. The flip side of that dubious victory was that the infinitely more strategically significant Baltic Sea had effectively became a NATO lake. Russia's border with NATO now ran within 60 kilometres of St Petersburg.

Putin 'set out to make Russia great again', said former CIA director David Petraeus. 'What he's really done is make NATO great again.'[25] In July Poland announced that it was acquiring 500 HIMARS rocket launchers from the US – as well as 48 fighter jets, 600 howitzers and 180 tanks from South Korea.[26] Germany agreed to boost its military spending by €100 billion – one and half times more than Russia's entire annual defence budget. In October Zelensky responded to Russia's formal annexation of the occupied territories by applying for fast-track NATO membership, which would make an attack on Ukraine an attack on the whole alliance. While that was probably an escalation too far for most NATO members, the war made it far more likely that Kyiv would at least enjoy NATO-like security guarantees from the world's most powerful nations and as close a functional military relationship with the alliance as any full member.

NATO's Endgame

Keeping an odious regime in power for fear of something even more unstable and dangerous has a long history in Western diplomacy. The US strongly desired to preserve the Soviet Union

– as evidenced by George H.W. Bush's notorious 'Chicken Kiev' speech in 1991 – for fear of a patchwork of failed nuclear-armed states that might replace it. By the same token, France's Emmanuel Macron 'had a 'strong fear of a Weimar [Republic]-like situation' if Putin were to fall as a result of the Ukraine war, according to a senior European statesman who spoke to Macron regularly during the crisis.[27] That fear was the root of Macron's controversial insistence that 'Putin must not be humiliated' in any future peace settlement – and that the EU must not follow the policy of 'the most warmongering types' in Europe since this would 'risk extending the conflict and closing off communications [with Putin] completely'.[28] Macron's position naturally infuriated the Ukrainians – and the Poles and Balts, whom he had implicitly accused of being *fauteurs de guerre*, or 'warmongers'.

The war had indeed united NATO as never before. But the cracks in that unity that the war's endgame would expose were already evident in September when Macron made his remarks on warmongering. They would grow further after Putin's extraordinarily hostile 21 September speech in which he promised the West that he was 'not bluffing' about the use of nuclear weapons, and the apparent demonstration of his capacity for self-destructive aggression a few days later with the destruction of Nord Stream. 'The Americans believe that Putin has run out of road, that there is no hope for improvement of dialogue, that any [other leader] would be better than Putin,' said the statesman. The view in the Élysée was that 'such logic is dangerous ... a weakened Putin is a better option for European security than a fallen Putin.'[29]

As Western countries pledged billions in military support in April and May, it became commonplace to argue that time was on Ukraine's side. Russia was isolated, unable to replenish its lost men and supplies. Ukraine had the active support of the most powerful and prosperous nations in the world, many of whom were actively sending military supplies. In fact, it became increasingly clear in the course of the summer that the reverse was true. The Ukrainians were in a race against time to gain as much territory before winter closed in and gave Putin's energy weapon real bite. As we have seen, Europe moved quicker to replace Russian gas than Putin had expected. And widespread Western resentment at Russian bullying and anger at the brutality of the war meant that NATO countries would never abandon their support for Ukraine and bend the knee to Putin. But given a choice between supporting Ukraine indefinitely in a forever war fought exclusively with NATO weapons and a negotiated peace, many European voters favoured the latter.

In June a report by the European Council on Foreign Relations (ECFR) on attitudes to the Ukraine war in ten European countries carried several fateful messages for the future. The good news for Kyiv was that there was near-universal support for Ukraine, with 73 per cent of respondents across the ten countries blaming Russia for the war and over 50 per cent – rising to 71 per cent in Poland – saying that governments should sever all economic and cultural relations with Moscow. And 58 per cent across the ten countries – rising to 77 per cent in Finland – wanted the EU to reduce its dependence on Russian energy, even at the expense of the bloc's climate goals.

But the bad news of the ECFR's polling was a clear divide between Europeans who wanted peace as soon as possible, even at the cost of territorial losses for Ukraine, and those who wanted justice, defined as restoring Ukraine's territorial integrity and holding Russia to account. Across the ten countries, 35 per cent backed 'peace' and 22 per cent 'justice' – with a third swing group, who shared the anti-Russian feelings of justice supporters but also the peace camp's fears of escalation, accounting for about 20 per cent of voters. Italian voters backed immediate peace most strongly at 52 per cent, while 41 per cent of Polish respondents favoured punishing Russia. But most worryingly for Ukraine, respondents in Germany, Italy and France said they were most concerned about the cost of living and energy prices, while the biggest fear for respondents in Sweden, the UK and Poland was the threat of nuclear war. Both positions favoured a negotiated peace.

'In the early stages of the war, countries in central and eastern Europe felt vindicated in their hawkishness towards Russia,' wrote the report's co-authors Mark Leonard and Ivan Krastev. 'But in the next phase countries such as Poland could find themselves marginalised if the "peace" camp broadens its appeal among the other member states'. As the conflict drags on and costs grow, governments will increasingly be forced to 'balance the pursuit of European unity with opinions that diverge both within and among member states', the authors wrote, pointing to a 'growing gap between the positions of many governments and the public mood in their respective countries'.[30]

'What is better – a frozen conflict, or continued war?' asked my statesman source, who had discussed the Ukraine crisis with Macron, Boris Johnson and other top European leaders. 'Nobody is saying that [frozen conflicts] are good or desirable situations. But there comes a point when a true friend to [Ukraine] will have to say – enough people have died. The time has come to rebuild your country, and we are ready and willing to help you to do that.' The source strongly rejected the idea that such a compromise would amount to a victory for Putin. 'The sanctions against Putin are of a scale that cuts Russia off from investment, technology, development. Moscow is totally politically isolated.' Ultimately, he said, 'real victory for Ukraine is not a matter of territory. The best victory is to be prosperous and free ... a country that Russians will envy.'[31]

The key question – and key stumbling block – for the peace talks would be moral hazard. The Catch-22 was stark. For all the setbacks and problems sanctions and military setbacks had imposed, Russia had manpower, vast supplies of old-fashioned ordnance and tactical nuclear weapons to defend most of the territory it had captured from Ukraine and formally annexed for a very long time. Russia's ruthless recruitment campaign of autumn 2022 – from Wagner's efforts in Russian prisons to Putin's partial mobilisation of reservists – ensured a steady supply of troops, albeit unmotivated and badly trained ones. Barring a complete collapse of morale and breakdown of the Russian military, it was hard to see how the war could end without some loss of Ukrainian territory. At the same time the West could not allow Putin to be rewarded for aggression.

In May the veteran former US Secretary of State Henry Kissinger drew an angry reaction from Zelensky for daring to suggest that retaking territory occupied by Russia in 2014 – including the LDNR and Crimea – would be a bad idea. 'Pursuing the war beyond [the pre-24 February line of control] would not be about the freedom of Ukraine, but a new war against Russia itself,' Kissinger told an audience at Davos. Zelensky countered by insisting that Ukraine would not agree to peace until Russia agreed to return Crimea and Donbas. In truth, that was a fantasy – as even friends of Ukraine admitted. 'I don't know any Ukrainians in the government who actually believe that they can remove Russia from Crimea or from the LDNR,' said Michael McFaul, former US ambassador to Moscow and adviser to Obama and, now, Zelensky. 'Though of course they won't be able to say that before negotiation.'[32]

Even the prospect of pushing Russia back to its pre-war positions in Donbas was remote – as one of Zelensky's allies privately admitted. Zelensky 'has to insist on Ukraine's [pre-2014] territorial integrity – it's an article of faith for any Ukrainian leader,' confided a member of Zelensky's Servant of the People parliamentary party. 'But will our troops really be able to push [the Russians] all the way back to where they started? Put it this way: I hope so. But frankly I don't believe so. Perhaps Kherson, parts of Zaporizhzhia, Kharkiv [provinces]. But retake Luhansk? Mariupol?' He winced and shook his head.[33]

Ukraine's Endgame

Putin was trapped in an illusion: if he simply fought on, then somehow a magical Crimean-style victory would appear and rescue Russia from the economic catastrophe into which his war had plunged it. But Zelensky, too, found himself trapped in an illusion: the idea that given sufficient Western arms, his soldiers could throw the Russians out of all the territory they had taken.

The conviction of an ultimate Ukrainian victory was shared not only by Zelensky and much of the Ukrainian political class but by its people too – as well as by many policymakers and commentators in Washington. The idea was born in the wake of the Russian withdrawal from Kyiv in late March and reinforced by Ukrainian successes in August and September, when HIMARS rockets enabled them to launch a counter-offensive in Kherson, and a much larger one in Kharkiv, as well as bold saboteur and drone operations that destroyed targets deep inside Crimea, sending Russian holidaymakers scuttling for home.

It was certainly true that it was unexpectedly fierce Ukrainian resistance that stopped the Russian advance on Kyiv in its tracks. But the defeats at Kyiv were also, in large part, of Russia's own making. False confidence, bad information about the lack of resistance, a lack of infantry, terrible armoured tactics – the Russians had made every mistake in the book, and paid dearly for it. Around Kyiv they were exposed on three sides in a long, vulnerable salient. Withdrawal was the Russian General Staff's first smart decision of the opening phase of the war. And, crucially, those mistakes would not be repeated a second time.

The situation in Russian-occupied eastern Ukraine was very different. For one, many of the soldiers fighting alongside Russian units were locals from Donbas. And whatever their shortcomings in morale and equipment, they were fighting to hold land they regarded as their home. Lines of supply from Russia into Luhansk and Donetsk were short and direct. Russia and its local proxies had eight years of experience of quickly 'Russifying' occupied territories with a mixture of terror, propaganda and money. Most importantly, the loyalties of the remaining locals were divided. Between 2014 and 2022 millions of people – predominantly those sympathetic to Kyiv – left the region and began new lives elsewhere in Ukraine. After the Russian invasion even more fled, leaving Severodonetsk and Lysychansk bombed-out ghost towns. That de facto ethnic cleansing was disastrous for the region's future – but politically and militarily it worked in Russia's favour.

Attack, as the Russians had found to their cost, turned out to be far harder and bloodier than defence. And though it was certainly true that Russia faced a crisis in replacing its most sophisticated armour and rockets and its trained troops, it suffered from no shortage of basic twentieth-century ordnance with which to pound the advancing Ukrainians and, after Putin's mobilisation, no shortage of cannon fodder.

The battle to retake lost Ukrainian territory would, therefore, be a numbers game. And it was by no means clear that the numbers, for Zelensky, added up. In most places along the front line, Russian heavy guns outnumbered Ukrainian ones by a ratio of up to eight to one. Yet the numbers of heavy weapons provided by the West remained in double figures. By early September, just 24 US HIMARS rocket systems were operational (compared, for instance, to the 500 ordered by the Polish military for their own national defence). In June, Netherlands Prime Minister Mark Rutte was one of a stream of Western leaders who visited Kyiv bearing promises of self-propelled howitzers and modern armoured vehicles – but in practice that promise meant five tanks and 12 guns.

'It's a question of quantity versus quality,' said one senior NATO military diplomat in Kyiv, himself a former British infantry officer. 'Artillery accuracy is important. It can be devastating and [the Ukrainians] are counting on it being a game changer.

But quantity counts too ... let's say one triple-7 [US 155-mm howitzer] is worth five Russian heavy guns. Ten, even. But that doesn't really get you very far if you're facing 20 or a hundred [Russian guns].'[34]

Hope of a full victory was what sustained Ukrainian resistance in the first months of the war and helped keep both general morale and support for Zelensky sky-high. Early in the war, Washington had assured Zelensky and the world in categorical terms that Putin could not be allowed to win. 'We stand with you. Period,' Biden said in Warsaw in March. 'We must remain unified today and tomorrow and the day after ... There will be cost, but it's a price we have to pay because the darkness that drives autocracy is no match for the flame of liberty that lights the souls of free people everywhere. In the perennial struggle for democracy and freedom, Ukraine and its people are on the front lines, fighting to save their nation and their brave resistance is part of a larger fight for essential democratic principles that unite all free people.'[35]

By September the US was strongly encouraging Zelensky to believe that he could win. To David Petraeus the September Kharkiv breakthrough was a sign that 'the tide clearly has turned ... Ukraine has been incomparably better than Russia in recruiting, training, equipping, organising and employing additional forces.'[36] Like many observers in Washington, Petraeus believed that 'the implications are stark. They're very, very clear. Ukraine will over time experience tough fighting, more casualties, more punishing Russian strikes on civilian infrastructure. But Ukraine will over time, I think, retake the territory that Russia has seized since 24 February.'

Washington promised that it was up to the Ukrainians to decide their own future and that NATO would not negotiate over their heads. There was also a strong conviction within the Ukrainian government that any territorial concessions would simply whet Putin's appetite for land – a hypothesis with strong support inside the Washington Beltway. Nothing short of a Russian defeat – preferably followed by the implosion of the Putin regime – would secure Ukraine from future Russian aggression. 'He can't seize his neighbour's territory and get away with it, simple as that,' Biden said after Putin announced his annexations in September. 'America and its allies are not going to be intimidated by Putin and his reckless words and threats ... We're going to stay the course, continue to provide military equipment so that Ukraine can defend itself and its territory and its freedom.'

But that 'no surrender' attitude – doubtless unavoidable in wartime – came with its own dangers for Zelensky and for the future of Ukraine. Zelensky was on the record admitting that the war would only end 'through diplomacy'. In March and April, as we have seen, he had stated his readiness to relinquish Ukraine's NATO ambitions (in exchange for Western security guarantees) in exchange for a Russian withdrawal to the pre-invasion line of control. But with the successful Ukrainian offensives of September, such compromises were off the table.

Yet, objectively, with the Ukrainian government facing an astounding $600 billion in infrastructure damage (and counting), a devastating 45 per cent drop in GDP and a quarter of its population displaced inside or outside the country, a forever war was economically unsustainable. By August Kyiv's budget deficit ran at $5 billion a month and, by the end of 2022, foreign donors will have spent at least $27 billion paying the salaries of Ukrainian public sector workers and soldiers.[37] By the end of July the Ukrainian military was already warning that they had run out of shells. The war was being fought by Ukrainian blood and grit, but was sustained solely by Western money and arms.

The illusion of a total victory sustained Ukrainian morale. But it also made compromise with Putin impossible. It was a paradox so fundamental it was little wonder that Ukraine's political class resolutely refused to discuss or contemplate its resolution. The massive exodus of internally displaced persons from Donbas presented a massive political and economic problem for Zelensky. The new refugees, quite justifiably, hated Russia. They looked to Zelensky to liberate their homes. If that did not happen, their anger would be redirected at 'anyone and everyone that they believe betrayed Ukraine', warned one Zelensky ally, a member of parliament. 'That could be NATO – as in, you promised to help us but you didn't give us enough guns. Or it could be Europe, if Macron and Scholz and the rest start to press us to make peace with Putin. People will say, thanks so much for your nice words, but we see you were too addicted to your Russian gas to really help us, you bastards.'[38]

In the worst-case scenario, the pro-Zelensky MP feared that compromise with Putin could lead to 'a new Maidan – but a nationalist one, of people who will never accept any kind of deal with Putin' that would topple any Kyiv government who tried to propose peace on any terms other than total victory. It would make the 'No Compromise' mini-Maidan of October 2019 – when Zelensky attempted to agree on a referendum in the rebel Donbas republics – 'look like nothing', he said. 'War united us ... but [a negotiated] peace could tear us apart.'

Yet the alternative to a negotiated settlement would be an unending war in Ukraine, which would further devastate that country and its people – as well as continue disruptions to energy and food supplies, with all the resulting pain for the world's economy and the political turmoil that would follow. And there was of course another even more terrifying scenario if Putin were to use tactical nuclear weapons, which would place the West in an impossible dilemma. NATO could make good on its threats to deliver a devastating conventional response on territory that Russian now regarded as part of the Motherland, and risk further Russian attack – or do nothing, and effectively legitimise the battlefield use of nuclear weapons, opening a new and dangerous chapter in the history of warfare.

Peace without Honour

In September, after a four-month hiatus, Kremlin spokesman Dmitry Peskov signalled that Putin was 'ready to negotiate with President of Ukraine Volodymyr Zelensky on how the special operation will be terminated and the observance not of conditions, but of Russia's interests'.[39] It was hardly a hopeful start. And Putin's angry speeches in late September, escalating the conflict from a regional 'special military operation' to something close to a new great patriotic war, showed that he had no intention of backing down.

Putin had to win or die. Therefore, whatever the final outcome of the war on the ground or at the negotiating table, Putin would have to claim it as a victory. In conversations with senior Kremlin officials in August, a well-connected source was told some occupied territory 'could be negotiable' – though it was also made clear that Putin wanted to negotiate only with Washington, not with Zelensky, which was directly contrary to Biden's own stated position that Kyiv would be doing any talking necessary.[40]

Clearly, with Zelensky still insisting on the return of Crimea to Ukraine and with his armies on the advance in Kharkiv and Luhansk, the expectation gap between the two sides remained vast. But after the euphoria of war, the realisation was dawning among many members of the Russian elite that the time had come to begin consolidating their gains and cutting their losses. More importantly, internal polling circulating in the Kremlin in August showed that public support for the war was flagging, according to a source who spoke to several senior officials who had seen the numbers. Though the source was not shown the detailed polling, he was told about its basic conclusions: 15 per cent of the public was actively in favour of the war, with a similar percentage actively against. A further 35 per cent were passively in favour, and 35 per cent passively against. In other words, a population roughly split in half – with diehard minorities for and against divided along almost exactly the same lines as the April 2021 Levada polling over a military intervention in Ukraine. Putin could have cashed out or doubled down. He chose to double down in the most dramatic way possible.

Putin had hoped and expected that his lightning invasion would not only decapitate the hydra of Western meddling once and for all, but also that his quick victory would propel him back to Crimea-levels popularity. He has been proved very wrong.

Putin had also intended the invasion of Ukraine as his apotheosis, a great act of gathering together the three Slavic nations of Russia, Belarus and Ukraine that would secure his status as one of the state-building heroes of Russia. During celebrations of the 300th anniversary of Peter the Great's death in St Petersburg in June, Putin openly compared himself to Russia's first emperor. 'Peter was faced with the task of taking back what was his,' Putin said. 'And now we are required to do the same.'

If Putin's blitzkrieg had succeeded, he could have stepped down from the presidency with a triumph that cemented his legacy. But just like the immediate aftermath of the impulsive Crimean annexation, Putin found himself once again trapped by the events that he had set in train. He could not step down from power because the opportunists around him might make him the scapegoat for the failure of the war in Ukraine. His political future and even his life had become hostage to the avoidance of a major battlefield defeat. And unlike the great dictators of the mid-twentieth century, Putin's regime was unsupported by any kind of coherent ideology. Putin had exploited a deep vein of Russian nationalism that existed before he came to power. But there was no such thing as Putinism – only a chimerical mixture of religious ethno-nationalism, a paranoiac, millenarian fear of foreign interference, and kleptocracy. Not only would Putin would leave no lasting ideological legacy, but any legacy of prosperity and stability that he may have created had been destroyed by his own decision to make war on Ukraine. He had gained a fifth of Ukraine and increased the size of Russia by half a per cent. The price of his illusions was not only thousands of lost lives, but also a lost future for Russia. Most ominously of all, the misbegotten war had opened a Pandora's box of alternative futures for Russia that were much more scary than Putin's regime had ever been.

REFERENCES

INTRODUCTION

1. 'Vremya Pokazhet', NTV, 14 April 2014.

PROLOGUE: THE BRINK

1. Transcript of Security Council Meeting, Kremlin.ru, 21 February 2022.
2. Interview with the author, Moscow, April 2022.
3. Kremlin.ru, 21 April 2022.
4. Kremlin.ru, 23 April 2022.
5. Kremlin.ru, 23 April 2022.
6. Interview with the author, Istanbul, March 2022.
7. Yuri Butusov, 'Отвода войск РФ от границ Украины нет, а замечена новая активность врага, – Бутусов' ['No retreat of Russian forces from the Ukrainian border, new enemy activity sighted'], Censor.net, 18 February 2022.
8. Interview with the author, Kyiv, July 2022.
9. Ukrainian MP Lesia Vasylenko, @lesiavasylenko, Twitter, 14 February 2022.
10. Interview with the author, Kyiv, July 2022.
11. Interview by Vladimir Sevrinovsky, *Meduza*, 19 May 2022.
12. Svyatoslav Khomenko and Nina Nazarova, '"Things just turned out that way": the journey of Russian soldier Vadim Shishimarin from the Ukrainian border to a Life Sentence', BBC Russian Service, 28 May 2022.

13. Interview with the author, Moscow, March 2022. Some details have been changed to protect her identity.
14. Interview with the author, Moscow, March 2022. Some details have been changed to protect her identity.
15. Interview with the author, Kyiv, July 2022. Some details have been changed to protect her identity.
16. Interview with the author, Kyiv, July 2022. Some details have been changed to protect his identity.
17. Irina Filkina memorial page, Epitsentr K website, 6 March 2022.
18. Epitsentr K website, 6 March 2022.

CHAPTER 1: POISONED ROOTS

1. Mykola Riabchuk, 'Ukrainians as Russia's negative "other"', *Communist and Post-Communist Studies*, vol. 49, no. 1, *Special Issue: Between Nationalism, Authoritarianism, and Fascism in Russia: Exploring Vladimir Putin's Regime*, pp. 75–85, March 2016.
2. Vladimir Putin, 'On the historical unity of Russians and Ukrainians', Kremlin.ru, 12 July 2021.
3. Interview with the author, Rome, March 2022.
4. Serhii Plokhy, Chapter 1 'The edge of the world', *The Gates of Europe: A History of Ukraine*, Penguin, 2016.
5. Janet Martin, 'Introduction', *Medieval Russia, 980–1584*, Cambridge University Press, 2007.
6. Plokhy, Chapter 4 'Byzantium North', *The Gates of Europe*.
7. Plokhy, Chapter 8 'The Cossacks', *The Gates of Europe*.
8. Norman Davies, 'The forgotten history of Poland and Ukraine', *The Spectator*, 3 July 2022.
9. Alexander Mikaberidze, *The Russian Officer Corps of the Revolutionary and Napoleonic Wars*, The History Press, 2005, p. 38.
10. Plokhy, Chapter 13 'The new frontiers', *The Gates of Europe*.
11. Plokhy, Chapter 14 'The Books of the Genesis', *The Gates of Europe*.
12. Plokhy, Chapter 16 'On the move', *The Gates of Europe*.

13. Anne Applebaum, Chapter 1 'The Ukrainian Revolution, 1917', *Red Famine: Stalin's War on Ukraine*, Penguin, 2017.
14. Serhii Plokhy, 'Casus belli: did Lenin create modern Ukraine?', The Ukrainian Research Institute at Harvard University, 27 February 2022.
15. Plokhy, 'Casus belli'.
16. Applebaum, Chapter 6 'Rebellion, 1930', *Red Famine*.
17. Applebaum, Chapter 7 'Collectivization fails, 1931–2', *Red Famine*.
18. Applebaum, Chapter 11 'Starvation: spring and summer, 1933', *Red Famine*.
19. Applebaum, Chapter 13 'Aftermath', *Red Famine*.
20. Applebaum, Chapter 11 'Starvation: spring and summer, 1933', *Red Famine*.
21. Applebaum, 'Introduction', *Red Famine*.
22. Applebaum, Chapter 15 'The Holodomor in history and memory', *Red Famine*.
23. 'On June 22, at 4 o'clock sharp', Spasstower.ru, 22 June 2020.
24. Plokhy, Chapter 22 'Hitler's Lebensraum', *The Gates of Europe*.
25. Plokhy, Chapter 22 'Hitler's Lebensraum', *The Gates of Europe*.
26. Putin, 'On the historical unity of Russians and Ukrainians'.
27. Plokhy, Chapter 24 'The second Soviet Republic', *The Gates of Europe*.
28. M. E. Sarotte, *Not One Inch: America, Russia and the Making of Post-Cold War Stalemate*, Yale University Press, 2022.

CHAPTER 2: 'AND MOSCOW IS SILENT'

1. Simon Saradzhyan, 'Does Russia really need Ukraine?', *The National Interest*, 25 February 2014.
2. Ray Furlong, 'Showdown in Dresden: the Stasi occupation and the Putin myth', Radio Free Europe/Radio Liberty, 2 December 2019.
3. Chris Bowlby, 'Vladimir Putin's formative German years', BBC News, 27 March 2015.
4. Bowlby, 'Vladimir Putin's formative German years'.
5. Serhii Plokhy, Chapter 25 'Good bye, Lenin!', *The Gates of Europe*.

6. Vladimir Putin, 'On the historical unity of Russians and Ukrainians', Kremlin.ru, 12 July 2021.
7. Plokhy, Chapter 25 'Good bye, Lenin!', *The Gates of Europe*.
8. Plokhy, Chapter 25 'Good bye, Lenin!', *The Gates of Europe*.
9. Owen Matthews, 'Epilogue', *Stalin's Children*, Bloomsbury, 2008.
10. Putin, 'On the historical unity of Russians and Ukrainians'.
11. 'Putin: Soviet collapse a "genuine tragedy"', Associated Press, 25 April 2005.
12. Putin, 'On the historical unity of Russians and Ukrainians'.
13. Oleg Shchedrov, 'Putin honours Stalin victims 70 years after terror', Reuters, 30 October 2007.
14. Andrew Roth, 'Vladimir Putin says he resorted to driving a taxi after fall of Soviet Union', *Guardian*, 13 December 2021.
15. Interview with the author, Kyiv, July 2014.
16. 'Trust in public institutions', Levada.ru, 6 October 2021.
17. Interview with the author, Moscow, 2008.
18. Interview with the author, London, November 2006.
19. Lana Estemirova, 'Putin's terror playbook: if you want a picture of Ukraine's future, look to my home', *Guardian*, 13 April 2022.
20. Interview with the author, Moscow, April 2022.
21. Plokhy, Chapter 26 'The Independence Square', *The Gates of Europe*.
22. 'Memorandum on security assurances in connection with Ukraine's accession to the Treaty on the Non-Proliferation of Nuclear Weapons', Treaties.un.org, 5 December 1994.
23. 'NATO expansion: What Yeltsin heard', National Security Archive, Washington, DC, 16 March 2018.
24. Jamie Dettmer, 'Russia's Putin says Western leaders broke promises, but did they?', VOA News, 11 January 2022.
25. James Goldgeier, 'Not Whether But When', American University, 1999.
26. M. E. Sarotte, *Not One Inch: America, Russia and the Making of Post-Cold War Stalemate*, Yale University Press, 2022.
27. Interview with the author, Moscow, July 2019.
28. 'Fishman' with Mikhail Fishman, YouTube, 4 April 2022.

29. DonPress, 31 October 2018.
30. Malcolm Haslett, 'Yushchenko's Auschwitz connection', BBC News, 28 January 2005.
31. 'Fishman', 17 April 2022.
32. Jonathan Wheatley, *Georgia from National Awakening to Rose Revolution*, Burlington, 2005.
33. Charles Fairbanks, 'Georgia's Rose Revolution', *Journal of Democracy*, vol. 15, no. 2, p. 113, 2004.
34. Igor Lopatonok, *Revealing Ukraine – A Film*, executive producer Oliver Stone, 2019.
35. 'Yushchenko to Russia: Hand over witnesses', *Kyiv Post*, 28 September 2009.
36. Plokhy, Chapter 26 'The Independence Square', *The Gates of Europe*.
37. tsenzor.net, 'Viktor Medvedchuk questioned by SBU', 25 September 2008.
38. Nathaniel Copsey, 'Ukraine', in Donnacha Ó Beacháin and Abel Polese (eds), *The Colour Revolutions in the Former Soviet Republics*, Routledge, 2012, pp. 30–44.
39. Interview with the author, Moscow, April 2022.
40. William J. Burns, *The Back Channel – A Memoir of American Diplomacy*, Penguin Random House, 2020.
41. Owen Matthews and Anna Nemtsova, 'The Kremlin has a new weapon in its war on real or imagined enemies, from opponents at home to foreign revolutionaries', *Newsweek International*, 28 May 2007.
42. Boris Reitschuster, 'Putin's Prügeltrupp' ['Putin's beat down squad'], *Focus Magazine*, Munich, 2 April 2007.
42. Viktor Yushchenko, 'I've dealt with Putin before: I know what it will take to defeat this brutal despot', *Guardian*, 24 April 2022.
44. Anne Applebaum, 'Epilogue: the Ukrainian question reconsidered', *Red Famine*.
45. Intelligence Squared debate with Radosław Sikorski and Owen Matthews, 9 March 2022.
46. 'Disturbing role of American consultants in Yanukovych's Ukraine', Freedom House, 28 February 2014.

47. Christopher Miller and Mike Eckel, 'On the eve of his trial, a deeper look into how Paul Manafort elected Ukraine's president', Radio Free Europe/Radio Liberty, 27 July 2018.
48. TASS, 4 October 2011.
49. Interview with the author, Moscow, December 2021.
50. Ekaterina Gordeeva interview with Aleksei Venediktov, Tell Gordeeva, YouTube, 10 March 2022.
51. Steven Pifer, 'Does the Kremlin understand Ukraine? Apparently not', *The Moscow Times*, 21 December 2021.
52. 'Fishman', 17 April 2022.
53. Plokhy, Chapter 26 'The Independence Square', *The Gates of Europe*.
54. *Argumenty i Fakty*, 17 August 2013.
55. Sonia Koshkina, *Maidan: The Untold Story*, Bright Star, 2015.
56. Mikhail Zygar, Chapter 16 *All the Kremlin's Men: Inside the Court of Vladimir Putin*, PublicAffairs, 2016.
57. 'The whole truth about the terrible secret Yanukovych told Angela Merkel', YouTube, 1 December 2013.
58. 'John McCain tells Ukraine protesters: "We are here to support your just cause"', *Guardian*, 15 December 2013.
59. Zygar, Chapter 16 *All the Kremlin's Men*.
60. Zygar, Chapter 16 *All the Kremlin's Men*.
61. 'Answers to journalists' questions', Kremlin.ru, 17 February 2014.
62. 'Fishman', 17 April 2022.
63. Plokhy, Chapter 26 'The Independence Square', *The Gates of Europe*.
64. Zygar, Chapter 16 *All the Kremlin's Men*.
65. Zygar, Chapter 16 *All the Kremlin's Men*.
66. Zygar, Chapter 16 *All the Kremlin's Men*.
67. '1.5 thousand paratroopers and 400 Marines are being deployed to Kyiv', LV.ua, 20 February 2014.
68. Interview with the author, Kyiv, July 2022.
69. Sonia Koshkina, *Maidan*.

CHAPTER 3: THE BLEEDING IDOLS

1. Vladimir Putin, 'On the historical unity of Russians and Ukrainians', Kremlin.ru, 12 July 2021.
2. Owen Matthews, 'Thinking with the blood', *Newsweek* eBook, 2015.
3. Mikhail Zygar, Chapter 16 *All the Kremlin's Men: Inside the Court of Vladimir Putin*, PublicAffairs, 2016.
4. Sonia Koshkina, *Maidan: The Untold Story*, Bright Star, 2015.
5. Interview with the author, Moscow, April 2022.
6. Zygar, Chapter 17 *All the Kremlin's Men.*
7. Zygar, Chapter 17 *All the Kremlin's Men.*
8. Andrey Lipsky, 'Представляется правильным инициировать присоединение восточных областей Украины к России', *Novaya Gazeta*, no. 19, 24 February 2015.
9. Daniel Treisman, 'Why Putin took Crimea: the gambler in the Kremlin', *Foreign Affairs*, vol. 95, no. 3, May–June 2016.
10. Treisman, 'Why Putin took Crimea'.
11. Treisman, 'Why Putin took Crimea'.
12. Zygar, Chapter 16 *All the Kremlin's Men.*
13. Interview with the author, Istanbul, March 2022.
14. 'Putin Q&A: Full Transcript', Person of the Year special issue, *Time*, 19 December 2007.
15. Ekaterina Gordeeva interview with Aleksei Venediktov, Tell Gordeeva, YouTube, 10 March 2022.
16. Zygar, *All the Kremlin's Men.*
17. Roman Anin, Oleysa Shmagun and Jelena Vasic, 'Ex-spy turned humanitarian helps himself', Organized Crime and Corruption Reporting Project, 4 November 2015.
18. Zygar, Chapter 17 *All the Kremlin's Men.*
19. White House, Office of the Press Secretary, 'Remarks by President Obama and Prime Minister Netanyahu before bilateral meeting', 3 March 2014.
20. Zygar, Chapter 17 *All the Kremlin's Men.*
21. 'Fishman' with Mikhail Fishman, YouTube, 1 May 2022.
22. Interview with the author, Donetsk, August 2014.
23. Interview with the author, Kyiv, July 2022.

24. 'Участник "прослушки" Глазьева: "Это компиляция и подтасовка"' [One of the people in Glazyev's wiretapped conversations: "This is a compilation and a set up"'], Business FM (bfm.ru), 23 August 2016.
25. 'English translation of audio evidence of Putin's adviser Glazyev and other Russian politicians' involvement in war in Ukraine', *UaPosition: Focus on Ukraine*, 29 August 2016.
26. 'English translation of audio evidence of Putin's adviser Glazyev and other Russian politicians' involvement in war in Ukraine'.
27. 'Беседы "Сергея Глазьева" о Крыме и беспорядках на востоке Украины. Расшифровка', *Meduza*, 22 August 2016.
28. Interview with the author, Kyiv, August 2014.
29. Interview with the author, Donetsk, August 2014.
30. Interview with the author, Donetsk, August 2014.

CHAPTER 4: TOMORROW BELONGS TO ME

1. @visegrad24, Twitter, 21 August 2022.
2. Charles Clover, 'The unlikely origins of Russia's manifest destiny', *Foreign Policy*, 27 July 2016.
3. Anton Shekhovtsov, 'Aleksandr Dugin's Neo-Eurasianism: The New Right à la Russe', *Religion Compass: Political Religions*, vol. 3, no. 4, pp. 697–716, 2009.
4. Aleksandr Dugin, 'Мы должны забрать у либералов как минимум половину медийного поля!' ['We must take at least half of the media field from the liberals!'], Nakanune.ru, 28 September 2012.
5. Vyacheslav Golyanov, 'Владимир Путин как спаситель от "сатанинского" Запада', ['Vladimir Putin as a saviour from the "satanic" West'], Baltinfo.ru, 13 June 2012.
6. Interview with the author, Moscow, 2007.
7. Masha Gessen, *The Future Is History: How Totalitarianism Reclaimed Russia*, Riverhead Books, 2017, pp. 388–9.
8. 'Политолог, философ Александр Дугин: Это великая война континентов' ['Politologist and philosopher Aleksandr Dugin: This is a great war of continents'], *Komsomolskaya Pravda*, 20 February 2014.

9. Aleksandr Dugin, 'Шестая колонна' ['The Sixth Column'], *Vzglyad*, 29 April 2014.
10. 'Daughter of Russian nationalist hailed as martyr', Reuters, 23 August 2022.
11. Courtney Weaver, 'Malofeev: The Russian billionaire linking Moscow to the rebels', *Financial Times*, 24 July 2014.
12. Owen Matthews, 'Vladimir Putin's new plan for world domination: After Sochi and Crimea, the world', *The Spectator*, 22 February 2014.
13. Weaver, 'Malofeev'.
14. Weaver, 'Malofeev'.
15. 'Oshybka Prezidenta', *Forbes Russia*, issue 1, January 2015.
16. Charles Clover, 'Putin and the monk', *Financial Times*, 25 January 2013.
17. Timothy Snyder, 'Putin's rationale for Ukraine invasion gets the history wrong', *The Washington Post*, 25 February 2022.
18. Alec Luhn, 'Russian Orthodox Church suggests tsar's death was a Jewish "ritual murder"', *Daily Telegraph*, 28 November 2017.
19. Cécile Chambraud, 'The Russian Orthodox Church closes ranks behind Putin over Ukraine war', *Le Monde*, 20 April 2022.
20. Boris Kagarlitsky, 'Glazyev opts for hara-kiri', *The Moscow Times*, 2 September 2003.
21. Interview with the author, Moscow, 2018.
22. 'English translation of audio evidence of Putin's adviser Glazyev and other Russian politicians' involvement in war in Ukraine', *UaPosition: Focus on Ukraine*, 29 August 2016.
23. Vladislav Surkov, *Almost Zero*, Inpatient Press, 2017.
24. 'Assessing Russian activities and intentions in recent US elections', Office of the Director of National Intelligence, 6 January 2017.
25. Interview with the author, Moscow, 2017.
26. US Department of Justice Office of Public Affairs Press Release, 3 March 2022.
27. Interview with the author, Moscow, November 2016.
28. Interview with the author, Moscow, 2015.
29. 'Saakashvili resigning from post of Odesa Regional State Administration head', Interfax-Ukraine, 7 November 2016.
30. Interview with the author, Moscow, 2015

31. Iuliia Mendel, *The Fight of Our Lives: My Time with Zelenskyy*, Signal Books, 2022.
32. Interview with the author, Moscow, August 2021.
33. Melinda Haring, 'Why Zelenskyy needs a new Chief of Staff right now', Atlantic Council, 27 September 2019.
34. 'Eight Ukrainians make Forbes magazine's list of world billionaires', *Kyiv Post*, 8 March 2012.
35. Interview with the author, Kyiv, July 2022.
36. 'President v oligarch', *The Economist*, 28 March 2015.
37. Interview with the author, Kyiv, July 2022.
38. Serhii Rudenko, *Zelensky: A Biography*, Polity Books, 2022.
39. Rudenko, *Zelensky*.
40. Mendel, *The Fight of Our Lives*.
41. *Revealing Ukraine*, directed by Igor Lopatonok, executive producer Oliver Stone, 2019.
42. Mendel, *The Fight of Our Lives*.
43. Rudenko, *Zelensky*.
44. Interview with the author, Moscow, 2019.
45. Interview with the author, Moscow, August 2019.
46. Zelensky interview with *Time*, 2 December 2019.
47. Rudenko, *Zelensky*.
48. Rudenko, *Zelensky*.
49. Andrei Soldatov and Irina Borogan, 'Prison swaps, Putin style', *The Moscow Times*, 16 August 2022.
50. Interview with the author, Kyiv, June 2022.
51. 'Ukraine conflict: anger as Zelensky agrees vote deal in east', BBC News, 2 October 2019.
52. '"Серйозний успіх Москви": у Росії радіють через підписання Україною "формули Штайнмаєра"' ['"A serious success for Moscow": Russia rejoices at Ukraine's agreement to the "Steinmeier Formula"'], TSN.ua, 1 October 2019.
53. 'Thousands protest Ukraine leader's peace plan', France 24, 6 October 2019.
54. 'Far-right groups protest Ukrainian president's peace plan', Associated Press, 14 October 2019.
55. Interview with the author, Kyiv, June 2022.
56. Rudenko, *Zelensky*.

57. Mendel, *The Fight of Our Lives.*
58. Mendel, *The Fight of Our Lives.*

CHAPTER 5: WARPATH

1. Stephen Kotkin, 'Uncommon Knowledge with Peter Robinson, Hoover Institution', YouTube, 4 March 2022.
2. Interview with the author, Moscow, August 2019.
3. Interview with Dmitry Bykov, 'Vkhod-Vykhod' with Stanislav Kryuchkov, Khodorkovsky Live, 9 May 2022.
4. Interview with Dmitry Bykov, 'Vkhod-Vykhod'.
5. Interview with the author, Moscow, June 2022.
6. 'First Person: An Astonishingly Frank Self-Portrait by Russia's President Vladimir Putin', Public Affairs, 2000.
7. Interview with the author, London, 2001.
8. 'First Person'.
9. Michael Khodarkovsky, *Russia's 20th Century: A Journey in 100 Histories*, Bloomsbury 2019.
10. 'Директор Федеральной службы безопасности России Николай Патрушев: Если мы «сломаемся» и уйдем с Кавказа – начнется развал страны' ['FSB Director Nikolai Patrushev: If we break and abandon the Caucasus the country will begin to fall apart'], *Komsomolskaya Pravda*, 19 December 2000.
11. Oleg Kashin, 'How hallucinations of eccentric KGB psychic influence Russian policy', *Guardian*, 15 July 2015.
12. 'Interview with Nikolai Patrushev', *Rossiskaya Gazeta*, 26 April 2022.
13. Vitaliy Tseplyaev, 'Puppet mastery in action: Nikolai Patrushev on the methodology of coloured revolutions', *Argumenty i Fakty*, 10 June 2020.
14. 'Who and why was Litvinenko killed?', *The New Times*, no. 1, 5 February 2007.
15. Interview with the author, Moscow, July 2018.
16. Interview with the author, Moscow, July 2022.
17. Interview with the author, Moscow, January 2017.
18. Mark Galeotti, 'Surkov's end and the kleptocrats' triumph', *The Moscow Times*, 21 February 2020.

19. Mark Galeotti, 'Surkov hints Putin himself no longer essential for the system to persevere', *The Moscow Times*, 12 February 2020.
20. Mark Galeotti, 'Surkov's end and the kleptocrats' triumph'.
21. 'I created the system': Kremlin's ousted "Grey Cardinal" Surkov, in quotes', *The Moscow Times*, 27 February 2020.
22. Interview with the author, Moscow, June 2022.
23. BBC Russian Service, 2 October 2021.
24. 'Thanks to Covid-19, Vladimir Putin has become almost invisible', *The Economist*, 2 October 2021.
25. Michel Rose, 'Macron refused Russian COVID test in Putin trip over DNA theft fears', Reuters, 11 February 2022.
26. Mikhail Rubin, Dmitry Sukharev, Mikhail Maglov, Roman Badanin, with the participation of Svetlana Reuter (*Meduza*), 'Investigation for Vladimir Putin's 70th birthday', Proyet.media, 1 April 2022.
27. Sam Tabahriti, 'Oliver Stone claims Vladimir Putin has "had this cancer"', *The Insider*, 22 May 2022.
28. Interview with the author, Moscow, December 2021.
29. Nahal Toosi, 'CIA director: Putin "too healthy"', *Politico*, 20 July 2022.
30. Mikhail Zygar, 'How Vladimir Putin lost interest in the present', *The New York Times*, 10 March 2022.
31. William Burns, speech at Georgia Tech University, 14 April 2022.
32. Interview with the author, Moscow, June 2022.
33. Roman Badanin, Mikhail Rubin and the Projekt Media team, 'A portrait of Yury Kovalchuk, the second man in Russia', Projekt.media, 9 December 2020.
34. Nataliya Gevorkyan, Natalya Timakova and Andrei Kolesnikov, Chapter 4: 'The Young Specialist', in *First Person: Conversations with Vladimir Putin*, Public Affairs, 2020.
35. Badanin et al., 'A Portrait of Yury Kovalchuk'.
36. Badanin et al., 'A Portrait of Yury Kovalchuk'.
37. Anastasia Kirilenko, 'Putin and the mafia. Why Alexander Litvinenko was killed', *The Insider*, 21 January 2016.
38. Gabriel Ronay, 'A tale of Russian mafia, a Bulgarian businesswoman and 1bn', *The Sunday Herald*, 22 February 2009.

39. 'Investigative authorities in Bulgaria suspect the Estonian company AS "Tavid" of large-scale money laundering', SKY Radio, 5 January 2009.
40. Badanin et al., 'A Portrait of Yury Kovalchuk'.
41. Badanin et al., 'A Portrait of Yury Kovalchuk'.
42. Badanin et al., 'A Portrait of Yury Kovalchuk'.
43. Badanin et al., 'A Portrait of Yury Kovalchuk'.
44. Luke Harding, 'Revealed: the $2bn offshore trail that leads to Vladimir Putin', *Guardian*, 3 April 2016.
45. Harding, 'Revealed'.
46. Zygar, 'How Vladimir Putin lost interest in the present'.
47. Zygar, 'How Vladimir Putin lost interest in the present'.

CHAPTER 6: TRUTH OR BLUFF?

1. Interview with the author, Moscow, June 2022.
2. 'Zelenskiy: Russian passports in Donbas are a step towards "annexation"', Reuters, 20 May 2021.
3. 'Havrysh: Ukraine–NATO cooperation not excluding strategic partnership between Moscow', *Kyiv Post*, 26 May 2010.
4. 'Ukraine drops NATO membership bid', *EU Observer*, 6 June 2010.
5. Sir Winston Churchill, *Reader's Digest*, December 1954.
6. 'Deschytsia states new government of Ukraine has no intention to join NATO', Interfax-Ukraine, 29 March 2014.
7. 'Ukraine crisis: PM Yatsenyuk to seek Nato membership', BBC News, 29 August 2014.
8. 'Ukraine's parliament backs changes to Constitution confirming Ukraine's path toward EU, NATO', Ukrainian Independent Information Agency, 7 February 2019.
9. 'Russia as aggressor, NATO as objective: Ukraine's new National Security Strategy', Atlantic Council, 30 September 2020.
10. 'Zelensky said in Britain that Ukraine needs a MAP in NATO', UNN Agency, 8 October 2020.
11. Interview with the author, London, December 2021.
12. Interview with the author, London, December 2021.
13. Ekaterina Gordeeva interview with Aleksei Venediktov, Tell Gordeeva, 10 March 2022.

14. Iuliia Mendel, *The Fight of Our Lives: My Time with Zelenskyy*, Signal Books, 2022.
15. Interview with the author, Kyiv, July 2022.
16. Mendel, *The Fight of Our Lives*.
17. Kira Latukhina, 'Putin spoke about the genocide in the Donbas', *Rossiyskaya Gazeta*, 9 December 2021
18. Mendel, *The Fight of Our Lives*.
19. Interview with the author, Kyiv, July 2022.
20. Interview with the author, Moscow, December 2021.
21. Anton Stepura, 'DNR militants declare permission to conduct "preemptive fire for destruction"', Suspilne, 3 March 2021.
22. 'Ukraine: Purpose of upcoming Defender Europe 2021 exercise is to practice for war with Russia', *UAWire*, 4 April 2021.
23. Evgeny Kizilov, 'Russia draws troops to the border with Ukraine – Khomchak', *Ukrainska Pravda*, 30 March 2021.
24. 'Russia transfers ships from the Caspian Sea to the Black Sea', mil.in.ua, 19 January 2021.
25. 'Russia is not a threat to Ukraine, the movement of Russia's army should not be a concern', Radio Free Europe/Radio Liberty, 5 April 2021.
26. 'NATO Secretary General: It is not up to Russia to decide whether Ukraine will be a member of the Alliance', *Evropeiskaya Pravda*, 14 June 2021.
27. Shane Harris, Karen DeYoung, Isabelle Khurshudyan, Ashley Parker and Liz Sly, 'Road to war: U.S. struggled to convince allies, and Zelensky, of risk of invasion', *The Washington Post*, 16 August 2022.
28. Interview with the author, Moscow, June 2022.
29. Interview with the author, Moscow, February 2022.
30. Interview with the author, Moscow, June 2022.
31. Interview with the author, London, February 2022.
32. Harris et al., 'Road to war'.
33. Harris et al., 'Road to war'.
34. Harris et al., 'Road to war'.
35. Interview with the author, Moscow, 2008.
36. Harris et al., 'Road to war'.

37. Interview with the author, London, February 2022.
38. Harris et al., 'Road to war'.
39. Harris et al., 'Road to war'.
40. Interview with the author, Kyiv, June 2022.
41. Harris et al., 'Road to war'.
42. Vladimir Solovyov and Marina Kovalenko, 'For our neighbouring country', *Kommersant*, 3 December 2021.
43. Interview with the author, London, February 2021.
44. Interview with the author, Moscow, June 2022.
45. David Batashvili, 'Geostrategic activities', *Rondeli Russian Military Digest*, no. 118, 30 January 2022.
46. Ekaterina Gordeeva interview with Aleksei Venediktov.
47. Interview with the author, Istanbul, March 2022.
48. Greg Miller and Catherine Belton, 'Russia's spies misread Ukraine and misled Kremlin as war loomed', *The Washington Post*, 19 August 2022.
49. *Ukrainskaya Pravda* interview with Oleksandr Vikul, 10 May 2022.
50. 'Fishman' with Mikhail Fishman, YouTube, 4 April 2022.
51. Miller and Belton, 'Russia's spies misread Ukraine and misled Kremlin as war loomed'.
52. Interview with the author, Moscow, January 2021.
53. Interview with the author, Moscow, May 2022.
54. Interview with the author, London, May 2022.
55. Interview with the author, London, May 2022.
56. Interview with the author, Istanbul, March 2022.
57. Interview with the author, Istanbul, March 2022.
58. Harris et al., 'Road to war'.
59. Harris et al., 'Road to war'.
60. Harris et al., 'Road to war'.
61. Interview with the author, London, February 2022.
62. Interview with the author, London, February 2022.
63. Harris et al., 'Road to war'.
64. Mia Jankowicz, 'Rare video shows France's Macron trying to talk Putin down from invading Ukraine'. 4 days later, he attacked', *The Insider*, 4 July 2022.
65. Interview with the author, Istanbul, March 2022.

66. Mark Galeotti, 'The personal politics of Putin's Security Council meeting', *The Moscow Times*, 22 February 2022.

CHAPTER 7: CRY HAVOC

1. 'Putin decided to conduct an operation to de-Nazify and demilitarise Ukraine', TASS, 24 February 2022.
2. Interview with the author, Kyiv, June 2022.
3. David M. Herszenhorn and Paul McLeary, 'Ukraine's "iron general" is a hero, but he's no star', *Politico*, 8 April 2022.
4. Interview with the author, Kyiv, June 2022.
5. Serhiy Nuzhnenko, 'Unlocking Kyiv's Soviet-era bomb shelters', RFE/RL, 21 December 2021.
6. Glenn Kessler, 'Zelensky's famous quote of "need ammo, not a ride" not easily confirmed', *The Washington Post*, 6 March 2022.
7. Livia Gerster, 'Sie wollen seine Worte nicht hören', *Frankfurter Allgemeine Zeitung*, 28 March 2022.
8. Interview with the author, Kyiv, June 2022.
9. 'Zelensky signs decree declaring general mobilization', Interfax-Ukraine, 25 February 2022.
10. Luke Mogelson, 'How Ukrainians saved their capital', *The New Yorker*, 9 May 2022.
11. 'Kyiv residents take up arms as Russia advances', BBC News, 25 February 2022.
12. Interview with the author, Kyiv, June 2022.
13. Interview with the author, Kyiv, June 2022.
14. Interview with the author, Kyiv, June 2022.
15. Sam Denby and Tristan Purdy, 'The failed logistics of Russia's invasion of Ukraine', Wendover Productions, YouTube, 5 March 2022.
16. 'Zelensky hastily fled Kiev, Russian State Duma Speaker claims', TASS, 26 February 2022.
17. Iuliia Mendel, *The Fight of Our Lives: My Time with Zelenskyy*, Signal Books, 2022.
18. Manveen Rana, 'Volodymyr Zelensky: Russian mercenaries ordered to kill Ukraine's president', *The Times*, 28 February 2022.

19. Mogelson, 'How Ukrainians saved their capital'.
20. James Beardsworth and Irina Shcherbakova, '"Are there even any left?" 100 days of war in Ukraine for an elite Russian unit', *The Moscow Times*, 4 June 2022.
21. Beardsworth and Shcherbakova, '"Are there even any left?"'.
22. Tim Robinson, 'Air war over Ukraine – the first days', www.aerosociety.com, 2 March 2022.
23. Craig Hoyle, 'Ukraine claims Russian aircraft losses as invasion begins', *Defence News*, 24 February 2022.
24. Beardsworth and Shcherbakova, '"Are there even any left?"'.
25. Beardsworth and Shcherbakova, '"Are there even any left?"'.
26. CaucasusWarReport @caucasuswar, video posted to Twitter, 1 June 2022.
27. Interview with the author, Kyiv, June 2022.
28. Interview with the author, Kyiv, June 2022.
29. Interview with the author, Kyiv, June 2022.
30. Interview with the author, Kyiv, June 2022.
31. Interview with the author, Kyiv, June 2022.
32. Interview with the author, Kyiv, June 2022.
33. Svyatoslav Khomenko and Nina Nazarova, '"Things just turned out that way": the journey of Russian soldier Vadim Shishimarin from the Ukrainian border to a life sentence', BBC Russian Service, 28 May 2022.
34. Khomenko and Nazarova, '"Things just turned out that way"'.
35. Mykhailo Tkach, 'It is important that they look at themselves in the mirror more often', *Meduza*, 18 May 2022.
36. Tkach, 'It is important that they look at themselves in the mirror more often'.
37. Tkach, 'It is important that they look at themselves in the mirror more often'.
38. Khomenko and Nazarova, '"Things just turned out that way"'.
39. Khomenko and Nazarova, '"Things just turned out that way"'.
40. Khomenko and Nazarova, '"Things just turned out that way"'.
41. Khomenko and Nazarova, '"Things just turned out that way"'.
42. Khomenko and Nazarova, '"Things just turned out that way"'.
43. Khomenko and Nazarova, '"Things just turned out that way"'.
44. Khomenko and Nazarova, '"Things just turned out that way"'.

45. Khomenko and Nazarova, '"Things just turned out that way"'.
46. Khomenko and Nazarova, '"Things just turned out that way"'.
47. Khomenko and Nazarova, '"Things just turned out that way"'.
48. Interview with the author, Przemysl, June 2022.
49. Interview with the author, Przemysl, June 2022.
50. Greg Miller and Catherine Belton, 'Russia's spies misread Ukraine and misled Kremlin as war loomed', *The Washington Post*, 19 August 2022.
51. Interview with the author, Przemysl, June 2022.
52. Yaroslav Trofimov, 'A Ukrainian town deals Russia one of the war's most decisive routs', *The Wall Street Journal*, 16 March 2022.
53. Trofimov, 'A Ukrainian town deals Russia one of the war's most decisive routs'.
54. Trofimov, 'A Ukrainian town deals Russia one of the war's most decisive routs'.
55. Trofimov, 'A Ukrainian town deals Russia one of the war's most decisive routs'.

CHAPTER 8: THINGS FALL APART

1. Interview with the author, Moscow, March 2022.
2. Interview with the author, Moscow, March 2022.
3. Interview with the author, Moscow, March 2022.
4. Interview with the author, Moscow, March 2022.
5. Interview with the author, Moscow, March 2022.
6. 'Exile, fines or jail: censorship laws take heavy toll on anti-war Russians', *The Moscow Times*, 26 August 2022.
7. @vkaramurza, Twitter, 26 August 2022.
8. Interview with the author, Moscow, February 2022.
9. 'Poll shows 81% of Russians trust Putin', TASS, 26 August 2022.
10. Interview with the author, Moscow, February 2022.
11. Giulia Carbonaro, 'Russian TV viewing figures falling amid coverage of Ukraine invasion', *Newsweek*, 24 August 2022.
12. 'Exile, fines or jail', *The Moscow Times*, 6 March 2022.
13. 'Exile, fines or jail', *The Moscow Times*.
14. Michael Warren Davis, 'Why are Putin's propagandists so bad at their jobs?', *Spectator US*, 13 May 2022.

15. Peter Beaumont, 'British pro-Kremlin video blogger added to UK government Russia sanctions list', *Guardian*, 26 July 2022.
16. Sonia Smith, 'War of Words: Meet the Texan Trolling for Putin', *Texas Monthly*, April 2018.
17. Gonzalo Lira @GonzaloLira1968, Twitter.com.
18. Davis, 'Why are Putin's propagandists so bad at their jobs?'
19. Interview with the author, Moscow, March 2022.
20. Interview with the author, Moscow, March 2022.
21. Interview with the author, Moscow, March 2022.
22. 'Vkhod-Vykhod' with Stanislav Kryuchkov, Khodorkovsky Live, YouTube, 9 May 2022.
23. Ekaterina Gordeeva interview with Aleksei Venediktov, Tell Gordeeva, YouTube, 10 March 2022.
24. Interview with the author, Moscow, March 2022.
25. Jeffrey Sonnenfeld et al., 'Business retreats and sanctions are crippling the Russian economy', Yale Chief Executive Leadership Institute, August 2022.
26. Martin Farrer, Andrew Roth and Julian Borger, 'Ukraine war: sanctions-hit Russian rouble crashes as Zelenskiy speaks of "crucial" 24 hours', *Guardian*, 28 February 2022.
27. Ekaterina Gordeeva interview with Aleksei Venediktov, Tell Gordeeva.
28. Interview with the author, Moscow, March 2022.
29. Interview with the author, Moscow, March 2022.
30. Interview with the author, Moscow, March 2022.
31. Interview with the author, Moscow, March 2022.
32. Interview with the author, Moscow, March 2022.
33. Interview with the author, Moscow, March 2022.
34. Interview with the author, Moscow, March 2022.
35. Interview with the author, Moscow, March 2022.
36. Interview with the author, Moscow, March 2022.
37. Interview with the author, Moscow, March 2022.
38. Report on Frontex border crossing data, DPA, 25 August 2022.
39. 'TASS: more than 1M Ukrainians taken to Russia', Associated Press, 3 May 2022.
40. Interview with the author by phone, March 2022.
41. Interview with the author, Rome, April 2022.

CHAPTER 9: OVERREACH

1. Paul Sonne, Isabelle Khurshudyan, Serhiy Morgunov and Kostiantyn Khudov, 'Battle for Kyiv: Ukrainian valor, Russian blunders combined to save the capital', *The Washington Post*, 24 August 2022.
2. Iuliia Mendel, *The Fight of Our Lives: My Time with Zelenskyy*, Signal Books, 2022.
3. Sonne et al., 'Battle for Kyiv: Ukrainian valor, Russian blunders combined to save the capital'.
4. 'Germany to ship anti-aircraft missiles to Ukraine – reports', Deutsche Welle, 3 March 2022.
5. James Marson, 'Zelensky says Russia is striking military and civilian targets', *The Wall Street Journal*, 26 February 2022.
6. 'Putin tells Xi that Russia willing to hold high-level talks with Ukraine – China's CCTV', *Financial Post*, 25 February 2022.
7. 'Putin says Ukrainian neutrality key to any settlement', Reuters, 28 February 2022.
8. '"No progress" as top Russia, Ukraine diplomats talk in Turkey', Al Jazeera, 10 March 2022.
9. 'Volodymyr Zelensky says he accepts there is "not an open door" to Ukraine joining Nato', *Independent*, 15 March 2022.
10. Max Seddon, Roman Olearchyk and Arash Massoudi, 'Ukraine and Russia draw up neutrality plan to end war', *Financial Times*, 16 March 2022.
11. Interview with the author, Kyiv, June 2022.
12. Interview with the author, London, March 2022.
13. Interview with the author, London, March 2022.
14. Lingling Wei, 'China declared its Russia friendship had "no limits." It's having second thoughts', *The Wall Street Journal*, 3 March 2022.
15. Interview with the author, London, March 2022.
16. Blake Herzinger, 'Sending old fighter jets to Ukraine is a terrible idea', *Foreign Policy*, 14 March 2022.
17. Christopher Nehring, 'Debate about Polish fighter jets for Ukraine was divisive – and distracting', Deutsche Welle, 11 March 2022.

18. Interview with the author, London, March 2022.
19. 'Defence Secretary says UK buys Soviet, Russian weapons across globe to send to Ukraine', Fans News Agency, 13 May 2022.
20. Masha Gessen, 'The prosecution of Russian war crimes in Ukraine', *The New Yorker*, 1 August 2022.
21. Irina Filkina memorial page, Epitsentr K website, 6 March 2022.
22. Interview with the author, Bucha, June 2022.
23. Gessen, 'The prosecution of Russian war crimes in Ukraine'.
24. Tara John, Oleksandra Ochman, Eoin McSweeney and Gianluca Mezzofiore, 'A Ukrainian mother had plans to change her life this year. Russian forces shot her as she cycled home', CNN, 7 April 2022.
25. Gessen, 'The prosecution of Russian war crimes in Ukraine'.
26. John et al., 'A Ukrainian mother had plans to change her life this year'.
27. John et al., 'A Ukrainian mother had plans to change her life this year'.
28. 'Pentagon: Russian troop movement near Kyiv area likely "a repositioning, not a real withdrawal"', CNN, 29 March 2022.
29. John et al., 'A Ukrainian mother had plans to change her life this year'.
30. 'Ukraine: apparent war crimes in Russia-controlled areas', Human Rights Watch, 3 April 2022.
31. 'Biden says Putin should face war-crimes trial for alleged Bucha atrocities', Bloomberg, 4 April 2022.
32. Interview with the author, Kyiv, June 2022.
33. Andrei Soldatov and Irina Borogan, 'From bad intel to worse. Putin reportedly turns on FSB agency that botched Russia's Ukraine prep', *Meduza*, 11 March 2022.
34. Interview with the author, Moscow, May 2022.
35. '12 National Guards Appeal Dismissal For Refusing To Invade Ukraine. They will later decide to resign from the National Guards or stay', *The Moscow Times*, 25 March 2022.
36. 'How is the Special Operation progressing?', OSN.ru, 26 March 2022.
37. Interview with the author, Moscow, May 2022.
38. Interview with the author, Moscow, May 2022.

39. Interview with the author, Moscow, May 2022.
40. Interview with the author, Kyiv, June 2022.
41. 'Mayor of Kharkiv says nowhere in Ukraine's second city "safe"', France 24, 28 July 2022.
42. 'Even before they took the bag off his head I said straight away – it's him', *Meduza*, 16 June 2022.
43. 'Even before they took the bag off his head I said straight away – it's him'.
44. 'Опубликовано видео, где, предположительно, украинские солдаты стреляют по ногам пленным россиянам. Бастрыкин велел начать проверку', ['Video published showing alleged Ukrainian soldiers shooting prisoners in the legs. Bastrykhin orders investigation'], *Meduza*, 27 March 2022.
45. 'Even before they took the bag off his head I said straight away – it's him'.
46. Isabel van Brugen, 'Russia-installed Kherson leader has fled to Russia, video analysis suggests', *Newsweek*, 30 August 2022.
47. Interview with the author, Przemysl, June 2022.

CHAPTER 10: STANDOFF

1. Yevgeny Tarle, *Krymskaia voina*, Moscow and Leningrad, 1950.
2. Ian Traynor, 'Putin claims Russian forces "could conquer Ukraine capital in two weeks"', *Guardian*, 2 September 2014.
3. Interview with the author, London, April 2022.
4. 'Fishman' with Mikhail Fishman, YouTube, 17 April 2022.
5. 'Fegin Live' with Alexei Arestovich, YouTube, 18 February 2022.
6. Pjotr Sauer, '"I could not be part of this crime": the Russians fighting for Ukraine', *The Moscow Times*, 14 June 2022.
7. 'Putin addresses mothers of Russian soldiers', YouTube, 8 March 2022.
8. 'Russian Defense Ministry confirms presence of conscripts in Ukraine war for first time', RFE/RL's Russian Service, 9 March 2022.
9. Interview with the author, London, March 2022.
10. Paul Wood, 'Cornered: could Putin go nuclear?', *The Spectator*, 24 September 2022.

11. 'Russian casualties in Ukraine', Mediazona count, updated 16 June 2022.
12. 'Commander shot at military enlistment office in Ust-Ilimsk, Russia', News.az, 26 September 2022.
13. 'Chechen lawmaker says Mariupol "destroyed" on Putin's orders', *The Moscow Times*, 22 April 2022.
14. 'Chechen commander awarded "Hero of Russia" for Mariupol siege', *The Moscow Times*, 26 April 2022.
15. Emma Graham-Harrison and Vera Mironova, 'Chechnya's losses in Ukraine may be leader Ramzan Kadyrov's undoing', *Guardian*, 22 March 2022.
16. Igor Girkin, Telegram, 16 July 2022.
17. 'Conscripts from Donbas launch a video declare [sic] that they won't fight for Russia in Ukraine near Sumy', YouTube, 28 March 2022.
18. Owen Matthews, 'Putin's secret armies waged war in Syria – where will they fight next?', *Newsweek*, 17 January 2018.
19. Pjotr Sauer, '"We thieves and killers are now fighting Russia's war": how Moscow recruits from its prisons', *Guardian*, 20 September 2022.
20. Anton Troianovski, Ivan Nechepurenko and Richard Pérez-Peña, 'Calling off steel plant assault, Putin prematurely claims victory in Mariupol', *The New York Times*, 21 April 2022.
21. 'Bloody river battle was third in three days – Ukraine official', BBC, 13 May 2022.
22. Interview with the author, Moscow, June 2022.
23. 'Severodonetsk: Ukrainian forces told to retreat from key eastern city', BBC, 24 June 2022.
24. Interview with the author, Kyiv, June 2022.
25. Idrees Ali, 'In first since Ukraine invasion, Pentagon chief speaks with Russian counterpart', Reuters, 13 May 2022.
26. Interview with the author, London, June 2022.
27. Ali, 'In first since Ukraine invasion, Pentagon chief speaks with Russian counterpart'.
28. 'Task and purpose – Can US artillery stop the Russian war?', YouTube, 7 June 2022.

CHAPTER 11: THE PRICE OF ILLUSION

1. 'GoodFellows: Conversations from the Hoover Institution', YouTube, 5 April 2022.
2. St Petersburg International Economic Forum Plenary session, Kremlin.ru, 17 June 2022.
3. 'How the world is paying for Putin's war in Ukraine', Bloomberg News, 1 June 2022.
4. Fareed Zakaria, 'The West's Ukraine strategy is in danger of failing', *The Washington Post*, 5 July 2022.
5. Jeffrey Sonnenfeld, Steven Tian, Franek Sokolowski, Michal Wyrebkowski and Mateusz Kasprowicz, 'Business retreats and sanctions are crippling the Russian economy', Yale Chief Executive Leadership Institute, July 2022.
6. 'Russia hides budget spending but shows how ruble hit oil revenue', Bloomberg News, 14 June 2022.
7. Interview with the author, Rome, May 2022.
8. Sonnenfeld et al., 'Business retreats and sanctions are crippling the Russian economy'.
9. 'Russia's version of Starbucks reopens with a new name and logo', Reuters, 19 August 2022.
10. Sonnenfeld et al., 'Business retreats and sanctions are crippling the Russian economy'.
11. Christiaan Hetzner, 'Russia's largest tank manufacturer may have run out of parts', *Fortune*, 22 March 2022.
12. Jeanne Whalen, 'Sanctions forcing Russia to use appliance parts in military', *The Washington Post*, 11 May 2022.
13. Yevgenia Albats, 'Six months of war: what Putin wanted; what Putin got', *The Moscow Times*, 1 September 2022.
14. Sonnenfeld et al., 'Business retreats and sanctions are crippling the Russian economy'.
15. 'Russia needs huge financial resources for military operation – finance minister', Reuters, 27 May 2022.
16. Alexander Ward and Joseph Gedeon, 'What Biden means by "sanctions never deter"', *Politico*, 25 March 2022.
17. Interview with the author by phone, May 2022.

18. Sonnenfeld et al., 'Business retreats and sanctions are crippling the Russian economy'.
19. 'Average monthly nominal wage in Russia from 1998 to 2021', Statista, 1 September 2022.
20. James Beardsworth, 'Russian schoolchildren return to classrooms changed by war', *The Moscow Times*, 2 September 2022.
21. Valery Kizilov, 'Not collapse, but decay. Why Russians don't notice the economic crisis and how it will develop', *The Insider*, 19 July 2022.
22. Jeff Mason, 'Trump lashes Germany over gas pipeline deal, calls it Russia's "captive"', Reuters, 11 July 2018.
23. 'Canada exempts Russian gas turbine from sanctions amid Europe energy crisis', *Guardian*, 10 July 2022.
24. Kate Connolly, 'Germany braces for "nightmare" of Russia turning off gas for good', *Guardian*, 10 July 2022.
25. Patrick Wintour, 'Costs of Ukraine war pose tests for European leaders – and things may get worse', *Guardian*, 18 July 2022.
26. German Foreign Affairs Minister @ABaerbock, Twitter, 28 August 2022.
27. Alex Lawson, 'Wholesale gas prices fall as Europe's plan to avert winter energy crisis takes shape', *Guardian*, 1 September 2022.
28. 'Russia prepares for energy attack on Europeans in winter; answer should be our unity and increased pressure – address of President of Ukraine', president.gov.ua, 3 September 2022.
29. 'Russia wants to destroy Europeans' normal life, Zelensky warns', BBC News, 4 September 2022.
30. 'Meeting on current situation in oil and gas sector', Novo-Ogaryovo, Kremlin.ru, 14 April 2022.
31. Mikhail Krutikhin, 'Power of Siberia or power of China?', Al Jazeera, 19 December 2019.
32. Sonnenfeld et al., 'Business retreats and sanctions are crippling the Russian economy'.
33. Interview with the author, Rome, September 2022.
34. 'UnionPay ограничила прием в России своих карт, выпущенных за рубежом' ['UnionPay restricts use of their cards issued abroad in Russia'], RBK, 2 September 2022.

35. Mark Almond, 'Vladimir Putin is forging a new alliance of pariah states that'll be a graver threat to the West than the old Soviet bloc', *Daily Mail*, 19 July 2022.
36. 'Putin visits Iran for first trip outside former USSR since Ukraine war', Reuters, 19 July 2022.
37. Patrick Wintour, 'Lavrov walks out of G20 talks after denying Russia is causing food crisis', *Guardian*, 8 July 2022.
38. Shannon Tiezzi, 'Wang's G20 meetings highlight China's Ukraine messaging', *The Diplomat*, 8 July 2022.
39. 'Putin holds meetings in Tehran with Iranian, Turkish Leaders', RFE/RL, 19 July 2022.
40. 'UN resolution against Ukraine invasion: full text', Al Jazeera, 5 March 2022.
41. 'Russia journalist who made TV Ukraine war protest arrested and has home raided', Euronews, 11 August 2022.
42. Yevgenia Albats, 'Six months of war: what Putin wanted; what Putin got', *The New Times*, 22 August 2022.
43. Albats, 'Six months of war'.
44. Albats, 'Six months of war'.
45. Albats, 'Six months of war'.
46. Albats, 'Six months of war'.
47. 'Mikhail Fishman on why Ilya Yashin refused to leave and went to prison', TV Rain, YouTube, 22 July 2022.
48. Albats, 'Six months of war'.
49. Interview with the author, Moscow, March 2022.
50. Albats, 'Six months of war'.
51. Interview with the author, Moscow, June 2022.
52. Andrei Kolesnikov, 'The unique banality of Vladimir Putin', *The Moscow Times*, 13 July 2022.
53. Interview with the author, Rome, May 2022.

CHAPTER 12: TIL VALHALL

1. 'Vkhod-Vykhod' with Stanislav Kryuchkov, Khodorkovsky Live, YouTube, 9 May 2022.
2. Fareed Zakaria, 'It's time to start thinking about the endgame in Ukraine', *The Washington Post*, 16 June 2022.

3. Peter Arnett, 'Report on Battle of Ben Tre', Associated Press, 8 February 1968.
4. 'Putin says if West wants to defeat Russia on battlefield, "Let them try"', AFP, 7 July 2022.
5. Shaun Walker, 'Putin's annexation speech: more angry taxi driver than head of state', *Guardian*, 30 September 2022.
6. Jason Lemon, 'Putin thinks U.S. "attention deficit disorder" will help him win war: CIA', *Newsweek*, 21 July 2022.
7. @mfa_russia, Twitter, 18 July 2022.
8. 'Meeting with State Duma leaders and party faction heads', Kremlin.ru, 7 July 2022.
9. Interview with the author, Moscow, June 2022.
10. Andrei Kolesnikov, 'The unique banality of Vladimir Putin', *The Moscow Times*, 13 July 2022.
11. Adolf Hitler: 'At the age of 25, I joined the war, at the age of 31, I returned, and today, at the age of 42, millions stand behind me.' 'Mit 25 Jahren bin ich ins Feld, mit 31 kam ich zurück, und heute, mit 42 Jahren stehen Millionen hinter mir.' Speech at Darmstadt, 13 November 1931.
12. Nicholas Farrell, 'Do Russians support Putin's war?', *The Spectator*, 5 March 2022.
13. Frye, *Weak Strongman: The Limits of Power in Putin's Russia*.
14. Timothy Frye, *Weak Strongman*, Princeton University Press, 2021.
15. Mary Chesnut, '5 Polls that contextualize the Russia-Ukraine crisis', Russiamatters.org (Belfer Center for International Affairs, Harvard Kennedy School), 17 February 2022.
16. Owen Matthews, 'Vladimir Putin's Secret Weapon', *Newsweek*, 15 June 2016.
17. Farrell, 'Do Russians support Putin's war?'
18. Erin Doherty, 'Biden says Putin "cannot remain in power"', *Axios*, 26 March 2022.
19. Interview with the author, Moscow, May 2022.
20. Interview with the author, Rome, May 2022.
21. Interview with the author. Kyiv, June 2022.
22. Interview with the author, Moscow, June 2022.
23. Interview with the author, Kyiv, July 2022.

24. 'Ukraine will win the war', David Petraeus's interview with CNN's Jim Sciutto, 18 September 2022.
25. Interview with the author, Moscow, March 2022.
26. NextaTV, 27 July 2022.
27. Interview with the author, London, August 2022.
28. 'Macron vows to prevent Russia from winning war in Ukraine', Associated Press, 1 September 2022.
29. Interview with the author, London, August 2022.
30. Jon Henley, '"Justice" for Ukraine overshadowed by cost of living concerns, polling shows', *Guardian*, 15 June 2022.
31. Interview with the author, London, August 2022.
32. Michael McFaul, 'GoodFellows: Conversations from the Hoover Institution', YouTube, 5 April 2022.
33. Interview with the author, Kyiv, May 2022.
34. Interview with the author, Kyiv, May 2022.
35. 'Remarks by President Biden on the united efforts of the Free World to support the people of Ukraine', Whitehouse.gov, 26 March 2022.
36. 'Ukraine will win the war', Petraeus's CNN interview.
37. *Financial Times* correspondent Shashank Joshi, @shashj, Twitter.com, 26 August 2022.
38. Interview with the author, Kyiv, May 2022.
39. @nexta_tv, Twitter.com, 4 September 2022.
40. Interview with the author, Rome, August 2022.

ACKNOWLEDGEMENTS

1. Svyatoslav Khomenko and Nina Nazarova, '"Things just turned out that way": the journey of Russian soldier Vadim Shishimarin from the Ukrainian border to a life sentence', BBC Russian Service, 28 May 2022.
2. Yaroslav Trofimov, 'A Ukrainian town deals Russia one of the war's most decisive routs', *The Wall Street Journal*, 16 March 2022.

ACKNOWLEDGEMENTS

I would like to thank my old friends and colleagues Andrew Kramer of *The New York Times*, Anna Nemtsova of the *Daily Beast*, and Yaroslav Trofimov and Allan Cullison of *The Wall Street Journal* for their invaluable help and advice in Kyiv – a city they know far better than I do. Also Andrew Meier and Mark Franchetti, who were enormously helpful in editing the manuscript. Andrew Jeffreys and Orlando Mostyn-Owen provided much-needed refuge in Umbria while I was writing. Imogen Gordon Clark at HarperCollins was infinitely patient with endlessly shifting deadlines and breaking news, and Martin Redfern and Diane Banks at Northbank and Joel Simons at HarperCollins made this book happen.

Many of the sources quoted in this book either asked for anonymity or made their comments in social, off-the-record conversations. It is probably most tactful, therefore, to mention all the people who have helped me understand Russia both before and after the invasion without identifying those who spoke to me about the war. Years of official interviews, on and off the record, as well as private conversations with the following people have taught me everything I know about Russia. The mistakes and ignorance that remain are all mine.

From the Kremlin, I would like to thank Dmitry Peskov (Putin's spokesman since 2012) for chats in his Kremlin office and over dinner that have been tours de force of adamantine defiance of reality as I understand it. I am also grateful to Sergei Kiriyenko (Prime Minister March–August 2008 and First Deputy Chief of Staff of the presidential administration since 2016); Sergei Stepashin (Director of the Federal Security Service 1994–95, Prime Minister May–August 1999); Igor Shuvalov (First Deputy Prime Minister 2008–18); the late Sergei Prikhodko (Deputy Prime Minister 2013–18, First Deputy Head of the Russian Government Office 2018–21); Oleg Sysuyev (Deputy Prime Minister 1997–98); and Aleksandr Voloshin (chief of Boris Yeltsin's presidential administration who hired Vladimir Putin and later helped install him as president) for their official and especially their unofficial remarks. Usually the most significant things in any interview are said after the notebook is closed. Thanks also to the veteran Kremlin spin doctors Gleb Pavlovsky and Stanislav Belkovsky, who helped me understand the foundations of the Putin project.

From the Duma and Federation Council, thanks for insights and advice to Senator Oleg Morozov (Member of the Federation Council for Tatarstan 2015–20 and head of the presidential office for domestic policy 2012–15); Aleksandr Khinshtein (Duma Deputy for United Russia 2003–present and adviser to Rosgvardia head Viktor Zolotov); Leonid Slutsky (Chairman of the State Duma Committee on International Affairs, head of the Liberal Democratic Party of Russia 2022–present); Sergei Zheleznyak (United Russia Duma Deputy 2016–21); and Gennady Zyuganov (General Secretary of the Communist Party of Russia since 1993). The late Vladimir Zhirinovsky – leader of the Liberal Democratic Party of Russia 1992–2022 – threatened on live TV to have me 'sent to the gulag' – but during a gruelling two-hour one-on-one debate in front of his entire parliamentary party at their Duma offices I learned almost as much about the mindset of Russian politicians as I had during two decades of reporting. The late Boris Nemtsov – whom I first met when he was Deputy Prime Minister under Boris Yeltsin – always gave fearlessly clear and intelligent insights into the workings of power, which he had seen from both inside and out before being shot down in front of the Kremlin by Chechen gunmen in 2015.

From the Russian security services and military I would like to thank the bravely outspoken Colonel Mikhail Khodaryonok (Chief of the 1st Group of the 1st Directorate of the Main Operational Directorate of the General Staff 1998–2000); Major General Yury Kobaladze (spokesman of the Foreign Intelligence Service, 1992–99); Major Valery Velichko of the KGB Veterans club; Colonels Aleksandr Lebedev, Mikhail Lyubimov and Oleg Gordievsky, all former officers of the KGB's First General Directorate in London; Major General Oleg Kalugin; Colonel Aleksandr Klubnikov of the Foreign Intelligence Service, who saved my backside in Afghanistan; Major Aleksandr Koshelev of the Russian Interior Ministry Forces, who hosted me in Chechnya; and retired Lieutenant-General Evgeny Buzhinsky, whose analysis of Russian military failures showed an admirably robust dedication to facts over spin.

Various Russian businessmen have been generous with their hospitality and time. Among them are Aleksei Miller, Deputy Chairman of Gazprom; Pyotr Aven and Mikhail Fridman of Alfa Group; Rustem Tariko of Russky Standart; Yandex founder Arkady Volosh; and Stuart Lawson, the former CEO of five Russian banks.

Many Russian journalists, on both sides of the ideological divide, have given me invaluable help – as well as insights into the inner workings of the Kremlin's highly sophisticated propaganda machine. Olga Skabeeva and Evgeny Popov invited me to appear as a guest on *60 Minut*, Rossiya-1's top-rated politics talk show, over 40 times. Andrei Norkin of NTV's *Mesto Vstrechi* and Vladimir Solovyov – who went on to become one of the vilest and most hysterical of the Kremlin propaganda machine's attack dogs – also hosted me on their shows. The experience was unpleasant, but educational both on the methods of the Kremlin propaganda machine and on the assumptions and obsessions of Russia's political class. Konstantin Ernst, CEO of Channel One Russia since 1999, is one of the most intelligent and talented people in the Kremlin's media machine. Conversations with him have never been anything but revealing – both of how propaganda is created and of the mindset of former liberals like Ernst who have found a new ideological home at the heart of the new regime. Veteran broadcaster Vladimir Pozner has been gracious and invariably fascinating on how the Putin elite thinks. Ekaterina Shevchenko, news editor at Rossiya-24, and Maria Baronova, formerly of RT, have also given important glimpses into the belly of the propaganda beast.

Some other passionate supporters of the Kremlin deserve my thanks – though in the opinion of most liberal Russians they have become, in the pungent Soviet-era phrase, *nerukopozhatniye*, or people whose hand one can no longer shake. Oscar-winning filmmaker Nikita Mikhalkov is a dacha neighbour and old friend of my wife's family; his daughter is my son's godmother. I find his Orthodox-fundamentalist, ultra-nationalist, openly imperialist views obnoxious. But I am grateful to Mikhalkov for his hospitality and his straight-talking frankness. He minces no words. Some things – the worst things – need to be heard straight. Ultranationalist ideologist Aleksandr Dugin – one of the few people I have ever interviewed who uses the term 'fascist' with approval – also falls into this category, as does the late Eduard Limonov. And of course the writer Zakhar Prilepin, who gave me a glimpse into one of Russia's possible futures.

On the liberal side, I would like to thank Ksenia Sobchak, TV personality and Vladimir Putin's goddaughter. Aleksei Venediktov, founding editor-in-chief of the Echo Moskvy radio station, is by far the best-connected political journalist in Russia. Natalia Sindeyeva, founder of the independent Dozhd TV, former editor-in-chief Mikhail Zygar, anchor Anna Mongayt and former Dozhd Kremlin pool reporter Anton Zhelnov have also been incredibly helpful. Mikhail Fishman, my former colleague at *Newsweek*, has done an extraordinary job of reporting the war from exile in Tel Aviv. Yevgenia Albats and Andrei Soldatov's knowledge of the Russian security services has been a touchstone for years. Andrei Vasiliyev and Konstantin Remchukov, former editors-in-chief of *Kommersant Daily* and *Nezavisimaya Gazeta* respectively, have always been impressively well informed and generous with gossip.

In Ukraine, I would like to thank Iuliia Mendel, Volodymyr Zelensky's press secretary until December 2021, and Presidential Chief of Staff Andriy Yermak's adviser Serhiy Leshchenko for their frankness. Also Evgeny Kisilev, once Moscow's most famous TV news anchor and now Kyiv's; my old friend and political analyst Olesya Yakhno; Yulia Mostovaya, editor-in-chief of the *Zerkalo Nedeli* magazine. The incomparably talented Vlad Troitsky, the members of the Dakh Daughters group, artists Ilya Yusupov, Ilya Chichkan and his wife Masha Shubina, in different ways showed me the amazing spirit and, later, cheerful resilience of Kyiv.

Boroslav Bereza, who despite being proudly Jewish was the deputy head of the Ukrainian ultra-nationalist Right Sector political movement and militia, broke many stereotypes. So did Anatoly Ivanov, a softly spoken judge from Omul and volunteer Right Sector officer, who was very far from the 'fascist' caricature of Russian propaganda.

Across the front lines in the Donetsk People's Republic (DNR), Fyodor Berezin – a fantasy novelist turned deputy defence minister – offered the best insight into the mentality of the romantic-nationalist wing of the DNR leadership. Boris Litvinov, Chairman of the Supreme Soviet of the Donetsk People's Republic, and Aleksandr Kalyusskiy, Deputy Prime Minister of the DNR, demonstrated respectively the Soviet-bureaucratic and (to put it politely) business sides of the rebel republic's leadership.

I have tried to base this book as closely as possible on Russian and Ukrainian sources and voices. Nonetheless, many Western experts – including academics, politicians, diplomats and journalists – have been enormously helpful in various ways and at various times. I would like to thank former Polish Foreign and Defence Minister Radosław Sikorski, former US ambassadors to Moscow Prof. Michael McFaul and Senator John Huntsman, and former British ambassadors Sir Rodric Braithwaite and Sir Andrew Wood.

I could not have told such a complex story without also drawing heavily on the work of many brilliant colleagues, whose hard work tracking down sources in both Russia and Ukraine underpins many of the personal narratives used in this book. The BBC Russian Service's Svyatoslav Khomenko and Nina Nazarova's two-month-long investigation into the story of Sergeant Vadim Shishimarin,[1] *The New York Times*'s Yousur Al-Hiou, Masha Froliak, Evan Hill, Malachy Browne and David Botti's careful reconstruction of the events at Bucha in the first month of the war and *The Wall Street Journal*'s Yaroslav Trofimov's reconstruction of the battle for Voznesensk in the early days of the war,[2] and Manveen Rana of *The Times* of London's contacts inside the Wagner Group are just a few examples of stellar reporting on which I have drawn.